THE BROADWAY TRAVELLERS
EDITED BY SIR E. DENISON ROSS
AND EILEEN POWER

# DON JUAN OF PERSIA
## A SHI'AH CATHOLIC
### 1560–1604

*Translated and Edited with an
Introduction by G. Le Strange*

PUBLISHERS
HARPER & BROTHERS
NEW YORK AND LONDON

*First published in* 1926

PRINTED IN GREAT BRITAIN BY
BILLING AND SONS, LTD., GUILDFORD AND ESHER

# PREFACE

In 1604, one year before the first edition of the First Part of *Don Quixote* was in print, the book of the *Relaciones* of Don Juan of Persia was published at Valladolid in a small 4to of 396 pages. It has never been reprinted, nor has it ever been translated from the Castilian into any other language. The author was a Persian Moslem who had become a Spanish Roman Catholic. He had kept a careful diary during his long journey from Isfahán to Valladolid, and it appeared to him now that this was worthy of presentation to those whose faith he had adopted. Further he would tell them of Persia and its history. Don Juan, of course, is no authority for ancient or mediæval history, but his description of Persia and his account of the wars waged by the Persians during the 16th century against the Ottoman Turks contain much that is of interest, for the author gives many details of recent events that notably add to our knowledge of the history of this somewhat obscure period. Further, he succinctly describes the Safavi rule as first established, and the system of government set up in the golden prime of Sháh 'Abbás. Lastly, the journal of his journey through Russia, Germany and Italy to Spain is quaintly entertaining.

As in the case of most of the books printed in Spain at the beginning of the 17th century, the proof-correcting of the *Relaciones* was not attended to with care. Proper names of persons and places are inexactly and confusedly printed, even when avowedly, or tacitly, a quotation is made from the work of some contemporary author. The book mentions a very great number of foreign places and persons, and it is

# PREFACE

often difficult to determine whether the extraordinary spellings found in the Spanish are due to the ignorance of Don Juan, or to the carelessness of his printer. Something more on this subject will be said in my Introduction. Here all that need be noted is that names of persons and places when recognizable are given in the translation under the usual English form, but in the Index Don Juan's spelling of the same is generally added in brackets. When I cannot identify a place or personal name, I give it in my translation as it stands in the Spanish text, but then it appears in the Index by itself and not in brackets.

For the identification of the Russian place-names I have had the help of Dr. E. H. Minns, and for the German Mr. W. F. Reddaway, who has an intimate knowledge of the Thirty Years War period, has come to my aid. Also Mr. S. Gaselee, who has the Library of the Foreign Office to refer to, has solved some questions that were puzzling. To Professor F. C. Burkitt I am indebted for help in regard to the authorities used by Don Juan for the early history of Persia; and for assistance with the Byzantine historians the Rev. W. H. Kent, O.S.C., has very kindly sent me notes which proved useful. Further, I am much indebted to Señor A. G. Palencia, the author of the well-known *Historia de la Literatura Española*, who through the kind offices of a friend sent me a reference to the works of Salas Barbadillo edited by E. Cotarelo, which supplies details regarding the death of Don Juan at Valladolid and some other matters of interest. Again, a Castilian proverb referred to by Don Juan, the first half alone quoted, has been identified and completed by a Spanish correspondent to whom my friend Mr. Lawrence Lockhart kindly wrote on my behalf, thus filling in the gap. To all these good friends my thanks are due; and in sadness I here add the name of my friend the late Professor E. G. Browne,

# PREFACE

whose recent death has left Oriental learning the poorer in a fashion that cannot easily be recovered. It was he, the year before last, who first drew my attention to the *Relaciones*, which he had made use of, quoting from it, in the latest volume of his *Persian Literature in Modern Times*. From time to time he also gave me much help in the identification of the Oriental names; and I have to thank his son Mr. Patrick Browne for calling my attention to the translation recently published of the *Fugger News-Letters*, 1568–1605, which report the doings of the Persian Ambassador in Prague and Rome. Lastly, for the bibliographical matter to be found in the notes, very gratefully do I acknowledge a debt for continuous help from Mr. E. J. Thomas of the Cambridge University Library. The title of a book referred to is generally only given, with the author's name, in the first case where it is mentioned; and for later references to the work the author's name must be sought in the Index.

# CONTENTS

## INTRODUCTION

PAGES

*Uruch Beg, otherwise Don Juan of Persia—The Sherley brothers—The Persian embassy to the courts of Europe—The ambassador and his secretaries—The Embassy sets out from Isfahán, and reaches Moscow—They travel on to Archangel—Thence by sea to the mouth of the Elbe—Journey by land to Prague through Saxony—The Imperial Court at Prague, journey on to Mantua, Florence and Rome—Rome to Valladolid—The reception of the Embassy by Philip III—The ambassador proceeds to Lisbon and returns by sea, round the Cape of Good Hope to Persia—The conversion of Don Juan, and two other Persians who remain in Spain—The death of Don Juan—How his book was written—Book I of the "Relaciones"—Description of Persia—The early history of Persia—The history of Moslem times—The rise of Uzun Hasan—Shi'ah and Sunni: the claims of the House of 'Ali—The words Súfi, Safavi and Sophi—The reign of Sháh Isma'íl—Sultan Selim the Grim: his victory at Chaldirán—Sultan Selim invades Syria and Egypt—Sultan Sulaymán and Sháh Tahmásp—Isma'íl II and the Princess Pari-Khán-Khánum—The blind king Muhammad Khudá Bandah—Sultan Murád III invades Georgia—The mutiny of the Turkomán tribesmen—The Turks take Tabríz—Uruch Beg (later Don Juan) present when his father is killed under the walls of Tabríz—The murder of Prince Hamzah—Sháh 'Abbás becomes king—His treaty with the Turks—The arrival of the Sherleys—The Embassy to the European powers sets out—Description of the Valladolid 1604 edition of the "Relaciones"* . . . . . . 1–32

## THE TRANSLATION

### BOOK I

#### CHAPTER ONE

*Don Juan gives thanks that he, together with two of his fellow Persian secretaries, has become a Christian—The reason for the composition of the following book—The works of Minadoi and Botero—The journey from Persia to Spain, and its unique character* . . . . . . 33–37

# CONTENTS

## CHAPTER TWO

PAGES

*Ancient Persia or Fárs, Shiráz—Luristan and Susiana—Persian 'Iráq—Isfahán the capital of Persia—The province of Qazvín—The Hamadán, Gílán and Shirván provinces—The Astarábád and Mázandarán provinces—Khurásán, Qandahár and Sistán—The city and district of Ganjah—Azerbayján and Tabriz city—Khoy and Salmás in Kurdistán—The Maràghah and Khurramábád Districts—Arabian 'Iráq* . . . . 38-44

## CHAPTER THREE

*The mode of government in Persia—The thirty-two noble families in Persia—Matters of war are directed by the Kháns—The attendants of the King—The King's Palace, and the Palace of the Queens* . . . 45-48

## CHAPTER FOUR

*Plurality of wives and divorce—The dress of the nobles—The turban or Cap with Twelve Points—No carriages, ships or galleys—The Persian horses—The army: weapons and armour—The Sháh when on campaign: his State Umbrella—The Bodyguard of Georgian Renegades—Magic: the Alcoran—Medicine and physicians—The tombs of the Sophi Kings and Saints—Customs at funerals—Marriage customs—The Gypsies, and public women in Persia* . 49-57

## CHAPTER FIVE

*The early history of Babylonia and Assyria, from Nimrod to Sardanapalus—The ancient glory of Persia and its rulers* 58-62

## CHAPTER SIX

*The history of Sardanapalus, and his fall—The rebellion of Arbaces and Belesys—Arbaces King of Persia* . . 63-65

## CHAPTER SEVEN

*Cyrus the Great—Kings from Darius to Alexander the Great—The Roman Empire—Two of the three Magi, Persian Kings—Cæsar and Christ Jesus—Satraps in Persia till Sassanian times* . . . . . 66-69

# CONTENTS

## CHAPTER EIGHT

PAGES

*Saint Jude and Saint Simon preach the Gospel in Persia—The Christian martyrs—The story of Babek and Sasan—Ardashir Babegán, the first Sassanian—Sapor I and the Emperor Valerian—Sapor II, born a King—The bishop Saint James and the siege of Nisibis—Yazdagird, and the Emperor Arcadius* 70–77

## CHAPTER NINE

*Chosroes Anushirván, and the Emperor Justinian—Defeat of Chosroes and loss of the Sacred Brazier—Varahrán or Bahrám Chúbín—Chosroes Parvíz defeats Bahrám Chúbín—Maurice succeeded by Phocas, and then by Heraclius* 78–82

## CHAPTER TEN

*War between Chosroes Parvíz and Heraclius—The Persians invade Palestine and carry off the True Cross—Victory of Heraclius over the Persians—The return of the True Cross to Jerusalem—The death of Chosroes—Siroes the parricide—Shahr-Bárz and the last Chosroes—The Caliph Omar invades Persia—His death at Jerusalem—Othman becomes Caliph* 83–86

## CHAPTER ELEVEN

*The destruction of the Colossus of Rhodes—'Alí and Mu'áwiyah—The Coran—The Caliph Yazíd—The death of Husayn—'Abd-al-Malik, Caliph, and Walíd, in whose time Spain was conquered—Later Omayyad Caliphs—The rise of the Abbasids—The Caliph Mansúr—The Caliphs Mahdi and Hárún-ar-Rashíd—The latter's two sons Amín and Mámún—The foundation of Baghdad* . . . 87–92

## CHAPTER TWELVE

*The later Abbasid Caliphs: the rise of the Turks—Basasiri and Tughril Beg—The later Turkish or Tartar overlords—The seven Turkish Amirs in Asia Minor—The rise of the Ottoman power—Othman establishes himself at Brusa—Bayazid and Tamerlane—The Embassy of Clavijo* 93–96

## CHAPTER THIRTEEN

*Sultan Muhammad the Conqueror and Uzun Hasan—Josaphat Barbaro—His Book of Travels—The battle of Terján—Death of Sultan Muhammad the Conqueror and of Uzun Hasan* 97–100

# CONTENTS

## BOOK II

### CHAPTER ONE

PAGES

Sultan Bayazid II—The year 1500, birth of the Emperor Charles V—Birth of Sháh Ismaʻíl in 1472—Shaykh Haydar of Ardebíl, his father—The rights of ʻAli, son-in-law of the Prophet Mahomed, to the Caliphate—Death of Husayn, son of ʻAli—The doctrines of the Shiʻahs and of the Sunnis, as held by the Persians and Turks respectively—Shaykh Haydar of Ardebíl marries the daughter of Uzun Hasan—Sháh Ismaʻíl begins to preach the doctrine of the Shiʻah Faith—He gains possession of Tabríz—The Qizil Básh Cap of Twelve Points—As to the title of Grand Sophi       103–111

### CHAPTER TWO

Sháh Ismaʻíl defeats Alvand and Murád Khán—Sultan Bayazid II and the Shiʻahs—The canpaign of Tekelli in Asia Minor—Sultan Bayazid is put to death by his son Sultan Selim—Sultan Selim invades Persian Armenia—The battle of Chaldirán    .    .    .    .    112–119

### CHAPTER THREE

Sultan Selim I again invades Armenia—Sháh Ismaʻíl makes a treaty with Qánsúh the Mamlúk Sultan of Egypt—Qánsúh marches from Cairo to Aleppo—Victory of the Turks before Aleppo, and death of Qánsúh—Túmán Bey becomes Sultan of Egypt, but is defeated and put to death—Egypt becomes a province of Turkey—Deaths of Sultan Selim and of Sháh Ismaʻíl—Sháh Tahmásp succeeds in Persia, and Sultan Sulaymán the Magnificent in Turkey—Sultan Sulaymán appears before Tabríz—The Sultan goes to be crowned emperor at Baghdad—The lamentable state of Tabríz—Death of Sultan Sulaymán, who is succeeded by Sultan Selim II    120–127

### CHAPTER FOUR

Peace between Persians and Turks—The death of Sultan Selim II, and of Sháh Tahmásp—His son Muhammad Khudá-Bandah being blind, Ismaʻíl, a younger son of Tahmásp, succeeds—Pari-Khán-Khánum persuades the nobles to proclaim Haydar, another son of Sháh Tahmásp—Haydar is killed—Sháh Ismaʻíl II and his cruelties—He is put to death by the nobles—Sultan Murád III prepares to invade Georgia—Accession of King Muhammad Khudá-Bandah—Prince Hamzah his deputy    .    .    .    .    128–135

# CONTENTS

## CHAPTER FIVE

PAGES

The Turks, under Muṣṭafá Pasha, invade Armenia and Georgia—The Persians are defeated at Childir—Description of Georgia—Intrigues of the Turks and of the Persians with the princes of Georgia—Muṣṭafá Pasha captures Tiflis—Prince Iskandar joins Muṣṭafá Pasha, who marches into Shirván   136–146

## CHAPTER SIX

The city of Eres occupied by the Turks and fortified—Muṣṭafá Pasha marches back to Tiflis and to Erzerúm—'Ádil Ghiray, Prince of the Crim Tartars, marches into Shirván—Prince Hamzah surprises 'Ádil Ghiray and takes him prisoner—The reported intrigue of 'Ádil Ghiray and the Begum: both are put to death—Othman Pasha puts Shamkhál the Georgian Prince to death   .   .   .   .   147–155

## CHAPTER SEVEN

Qars rebuilt and fortified by the Turks—Hasan Pasha victorious over the Persians and Georgians—Tiflis is regarrisoned—Hasan Pasha's disastrous retreat to Erzerúm—Sinán Pasha in Tiflis: on his homeward march is defeated—The Sháh offers peace terms: the Persian ambassador goes to Constantinople—The insult offered him—Georgia again invaded—Muhammad Pasha returns to Erzerúm: the court-martial on Manuchihr—Manuchihr escapes the toils laid for him   156–165

## CHAPTER EIGHT

The Sháh marches on Herát—'Ali Quli Khán and Prince 'Abbás—The siege of Herát abandoned—The conspiracy against the Vizier Mirzá Salmán: his death—Farhád Pasha sent against Eriván—This city taken and fortified—Manuchihr and Simon, the Georgian princes, steal the Turkish treasure—David, brother of Simon, joins the Turks, but Simon remains on the Persian side—Amir Khán, the chief of the Turkomans, rebels in Tabríz, but is taken and put to death—Farhád replaced by Othman Pasha, whom the Grand Vizier seeks to kill—How the plot failed: the disgrace of the Grand Vizier—Hasan Pasha governor of Egypt—The revolt of the Druses in Palestine suppressed by Ibrahim Pasha—Othman Pasha leaves Erzerúm, marching on Tabríz—The Turkish army plunders Tabríz—Tabríz described—Othman Pasha falling sick, dies—The Persians attack the Turkish rearguard at Shenb-Ghazán   .   .   .   166–186

# CONTENTS

## CHAPTER NINE

PAGES

*The Persians reoccupy the town quarters of Tabríz and lay siege to the Turkish fortress—Ineffectual attempt of the Persians to carry the fortress by storm—Don Juan's father, Sultán 'Alí Beg Bayát, tries to surprise the fortress, but is repulsed and slain—His memorial portrait in the Mosque of Haydar at Tabríz* . . . . . 187–193

## CHAPTER TEN

*The Turkoman tribesmen of Tabríz—Their treacherous conduct to the Sháh—They kidnap Prince Tahmásp—The tribesmen occupy and plunder Qazvín—They set up Prince Tahmásp to be Sháh, governing in his name—Prince Hamzah marches on Qazvín—The battle and the victory of the royal army—Prince Hamzah returns to Tabríz—A Turkish army reinforces the fortress at Tabríz: in consequence the Persians abandon the siege—The Persians leave Tabríz in possession of the Turks—The Persian headquarters removed to Ganjah—The Persian army begins its march back to Qazvín* 194–202

## CHAPTER ELEVEN

*Esmi Khán: his conspiracy to kill Prince Hamzah—Khudá-Verdí the Barber—Prince Hamzah murdered in his tent—The barber is put to death and the traitors go unpunished—Prince Hamzah buried at Ardebíl—'Alí Khán, the Turkoman, rebels in Káshán, and Farhád Beg, the Georgian, in Isfahán—Prince 'Abbás governor in Khurásán—The rivalry between 'Alí Qulí Khán and Murshíd Qulí Khán—Murshíd overcomes his rival—The nobles in Qazvín call upon Prince 'Abbás to come to Qazvín and re-establish order: his father, the blind king Muhammad Khudá-Bandah, abdicates—Sháh 'Abbás is proclaimed King of Persia* . . . 203–211

## CHAPTER TWELVE

*Rebellion in the provinces: Sháh 'Abbás makes peace with Sultan Murád—Khán Ahmad rebels in Gílán—Gílán subdued—The revolt in Luristán next suppressed: followed by the revolt in the Mázandarán province—'Alí Beg the prince of Astarábád rebels—The Uzbek Tartars, and their Prince 'Abd-Allah Khán—They invade Khurásán, take Herát and plunder Meshed—The Tartar war continues for eight years until the death of 'Abd-Allah Khán, when the Uzbeks are finally vanquished—Death of Sultan Murád III, suc-*

# CONTENTS

*ceeded by Sultan Muhammad III—The capital of Persia transferred from Qazvín to Isfahán—Tálim Khán the Uzbek overruns Khurásán—Shah 'Abbás marches to Khurásán and defeats him—His death—The Sháh returns to Qazvín—Arrival of the Sherley brothers* . . 212–228

## BOOK III
### CHAPTER ONE

*The embassy from the Sultan of Turkey—Sir Anthony Sherley: he, with a Persian ambassador, is accredited to eight Christian sovereigns of Europe—The coming of two Portuguese Friars from India—The departure from Isfahán of Sir Anthony Sherley with the Persian ambassador and the two Portuguese Friars—Their journey to the Caspian—The Tartars of Manquishlágh—The Idol—The Volga mouth is reached—Astrakhan—The special Persian ambassador to Muscovy—Description of Astrakhan* . . . 231–240

### CHAPTER TWO

*The journey up the Volga in galleys—The Nogay Tartars—Journey from Kazan towards Moscow: the freezing of the Volga: the journey in sledges—Nizhni-Novgorod: the custom of their bath-houses—The Perekop Tartars—Vladimir: arrival at Moscow* . . . . 241–250

### CHAPTER THREE

*Grand Duke Boris Godunof—The extent and power of Muscovy—The Duke receives the ambassadors in audience at the Kremlin—The Great Bell of Moscow—The Treasury of the Grand Duke—Departure from Moscow—The disappearance of the Dominican Friar—The journey down to the Arctic Sea—Arrival at Archangel—They embark for Embden* 251–262

### CHAPTER FOUR

*The Laplanders, and their reindeer—Voyage past the North Cape—Arrival at Embden, and reception by the Duke of Oldenburg—Passage through Thuringia—Reception by the Landgrave at Kassel—Leipsig and the Palace of the Duke of Saxony* 263–271

### CHAPTER FIVE

*The journey to Prague—The reception in Prague of the Embassy by the Emperor Rudolf II—That winter is passed in Prague—The road to Munich* . . . . 272–278

# CONTENTS

## CHAPTER SIX

*The journey to Nuremberg and on to Augsburg—Munich : the Duke of Bavaria—The journey down into Italy : Mantua—The ambassador proceeds to Florence—They visit the Grand Duke at Pisa—Siena : on the way a quarrel breaks out with Sir Anthony Sherley—The Embassy reaches Rome and is received in audience by the Pope—The disappearance of Sir Anthony Sherley, and the conversion to the Christian Faith of three of the Persian servants—From Rome to Genoa—By Savona the Embassy comes to Perpignan—Crossing the Pyrenees, Barcelona is reached—The Persians come on to Tudela*  279–288

## CHAPTER SEVEN

*Don Juan proceeds to Valladolid and arrangements are made for the reception of the Embassy—The entrance of the Persians into Valladolid—The reception of the Persian ambassador by Philip III—The nephew of the Persian ambassador is converted to the Christian Faith—The ambassador takes leave of the Spanish Court—The journey to Segovia—Madrid to Aranjuez and Mérida—The Persian "Alfaqui" is killed by a fanatic—Badajos to Lisbon—Don Juan travels back to Valladolid—Going to the Jesuit House he talks with the ambassador's nephew, and is himself converted to Christianity* . . . . . 289–301

## CHAPTER EIGHT

*Don Juan returns to the ambassador at Lisbon—Boniyat Beg, the third secretary, declares himself to be a Christian—Boniyat Beg is baptized under the name of Don Diego de Persia—Don Juan, pensioned by the King, takes up his residence in Spain* . . . . . 302–308

NOTES . . . . . . 309–338
INDEX . . . . . 339

---

# MAPS

*Journey of Don Juan of Persia, 1599 to 1602* . . 1
*Map of Persia in the year 1600* . . . . 39
*Map to illustrate the Georgian Campaigns, 1500 to 1600* . 103

xvi

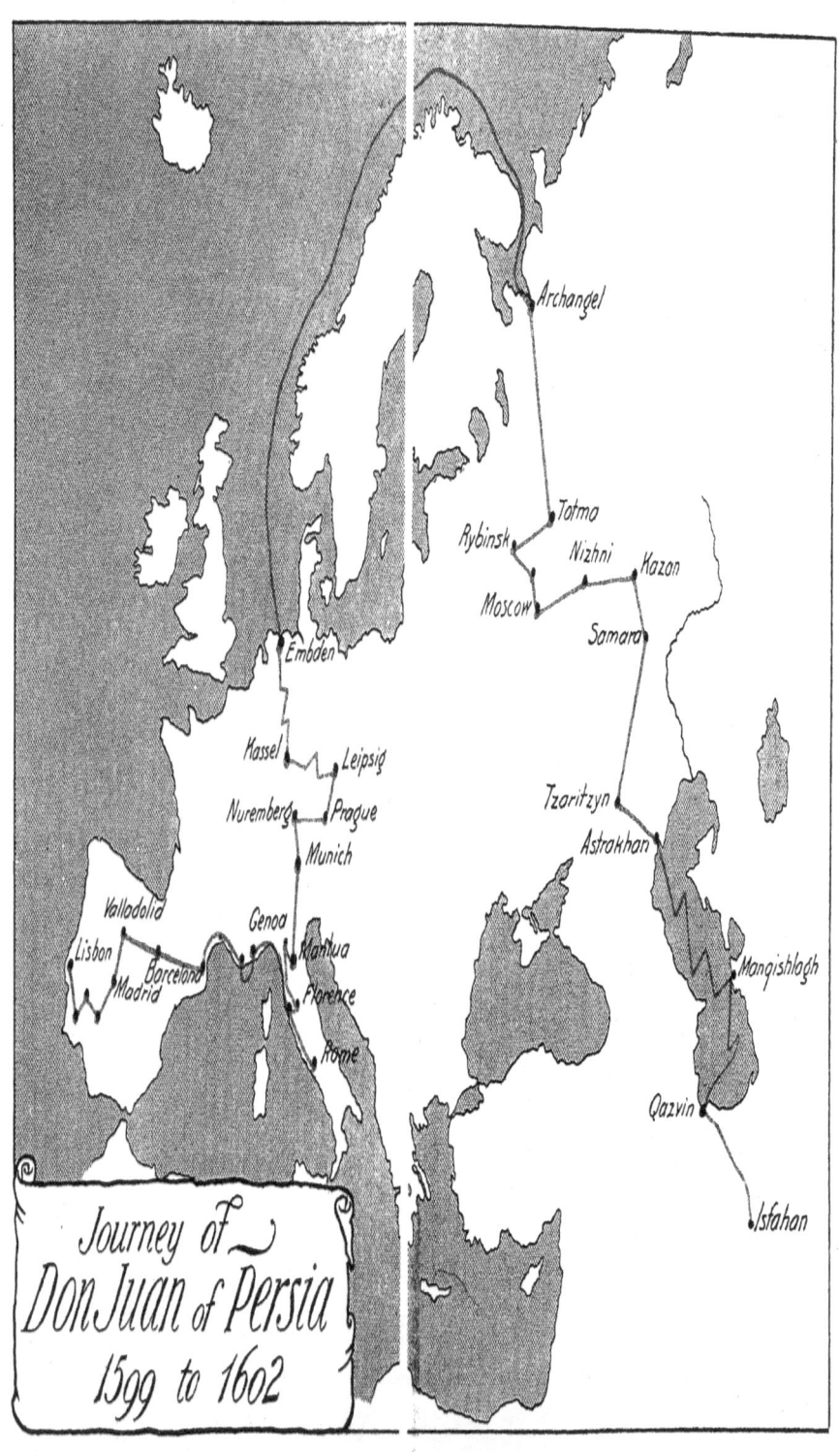

# Don Juan of Persia

## INTRODUCTION

DURING the years 1602 and 1603, in Spain, and after he had become an ardent Roman Catholic, Don Juan of Persia, as he was now proud to be called, compiled his *Relaciones*. The work is divided into three parts: the First Book describing his native country and its government, followed by an epitome of ancient and mediæval Persian history; the Second Book treating of the late wars between the Persians and the Turks, and the Third Book dealing with his journey from Isfahán into the countries of the West. He had left Persia in the year 1599, being one of the four secretaries to the Persian ambassador whom Sháh 'Abbás was sending to the princes of Europe under the guidance and personal conduct of Sir Anthony Sherley, and Don Juan of Persia at this period was a Shi'ah moslem, and bore the name of Uruch Beg.[1]

As regards the Englishman who was to conduct this Persian embassy, Sir Anthony Sherley was already of European fame for his services in the Low Countries under the Earl of Essex, and in France, where King Henry IV had knighted him, a rank, however, never officially confirmed by Queen Elizabeth. Also he had led a celebrated expedition to the West Indies and the Spanish Main, and then had left England late in 1598 on what proved a fruitless political mission to bring help and intervene in the affairs of the Duke of Ferrara. His services in North Italy, however, not being accepted or required, he and his brother Robert, with twenty-five other Englishmen, took ship at Venice in May 1599, proceeding to the East, where, landing at the mouth of the river Orontes, the party went up to Antioch. Thence they passed on to Aleppo, and then crossing the desert to the Euphrates, floated down in boats, reaching the neighbourhood of the ruins of Babylon, which lay at no great distance from Baghdad, at that time in the occupation of the Turks. From here they made their way into Persia to Qazvín, and thence on to Isfahán, where the Englishmen found favour with Sháh 'Abbás the Great." In the first decade of the 17th century Persia, then a great power, was enjoying a state of prosperity that had been unknown since the Arab conquest in the 7th century. Its frontiers were once more very nearly those that had been held under the Sassanian kings. A century before this, the founder of the Safavi monarchy, Sháh Isma'íl, great grandfather of Sháh 'Abbás, had made the Persians a nation by the vigour of his rule, further by proclaiming that the Shi'ah faith, with the peculiar doctrine of the Imáms (from whom he traced his descent), was to be the one and only orthodox belief; thus branding the Turks of the Sunni sect as heretical and infidel. For a hundred years he and his successors down to Sháh 'Abbás had continually waged war against the Turkish Sultans, but with such varying success that Sháh 'Abbás had now made up his mind to seek alliances with the Christian powers of Europe, who, he trusted, would be willing to combine with him against the Sultan and by making a flank attack on Constantinople mortally harass the Turk.

Sherley therefore had come at a propitious hour; he had no credentials to show from Queen Elizabeth, but he represented himself as a noble in her confidence, and offered to introduce the Sháh's ambassador to her Majesty and to the sovereigns of the various courts of Europe. The Persians of that age were well accustomed to embassies from Christian potentates, and of Englishmen in particular in the reign of Sháh Tahmásp,

# INTRODUCTION

the grandfather of Sháh 'Abbás, Anthony Jenkinson, coming from Queen Elizabeth, had been received very honourably at Qazvín in the year 1562. The embassy therefore was forthwith organized and set out, Sherley and one Persian ambassador being jointly accredited to eight of the European courts, and a second special ambassador was sent forward to await their coming at Astrakhan who would accompany them as far as Moscow, where this envoy was to remain and represent Persia at the court of Tzar Boris Godunof. The ambassador to the western powers, as we learn from the *Fugger Letters*,[3] was an imposing personage of a respectable age with grey hair, Husayn 'Ali Beg by name, and he had with him, as already said, four secretaries. One of these was his nephew 'Ali Quli Beg, but he who held the position of First Secretary of Embassy was Uruch Beg, subsequently Don Juan of Persia, the writer of the *Relaciones*. Uruch Beg was at this time probably just under 40 years of age, and he was the son of the late Sultán 'Ali Beg, who had been killed in 1585 at the siege of Tabríz, which city the Persians were then trying ineffectually to recover from the Turks. This was in the reign of Sháh Muhammad Khudá Bandah (father of Sháh 'Abbás), and Sultán 'Ali Beg, of the Bayát family, had been a prominent noble of his court. With a regiment of 300 horse, raised entirely at his own expense, and accompanied by his son (the future Don Juan) Sultán 'Ali Beg had held command in the royal armies; and after his death his son had been given the command of his father's regiment by the Sháh. We may suppose Don Juan to have been at that time about 25 years old, hence he would have been born about the year 1560.

Setting out from Isfahán in July 1599, Sherley and his Persian colleague travelled by slow stages to a port in Gílán (probably at or near Resht), where they embarked on the Caspian for Astrakhan. All August and September they were buffeted by contrary winds, and narrowly escaped shipwreck, but by the beginning of October the ship made the mouth of the Volga. Here they disembarked, were transhipped into galleys and were rowed up the broad estuary to Astrakhan. From this city to Kazan Don Juan states that it took them in boats a two months' voyage, but the distance being but little more than 1000 miles in a direct line along the river, one month at most probably was the time actually spent in travelling. At one stage above Kazan the Volga became frozen; they then transferred themselves to sleighs and finally entered Moscow early in November. In Moscow as the guests of the Tzar the embassy spent the first winter of the outward journey, and here on a question of precedence Sherley quarrelled with his two Persian colleagues, at first declining to pay his respects to Tzar Boris Godunof; but matters were arranged finally, and after Eastertide of the year 1600 he and his colleague—the Special Envoy remaining behind in Moscow—set forward on their journey. They went first by land to Yaroslav on the upper Volga, where again they embarked on galleys, travelling up the stream to Rybinsk. In this stage Don Juan calls the river Volga by the name of *Batem* or *Barem*, a curious mistake or misnomer the origin of which I have been unable to trace. From Rybinsk their next objective was Prague in Bohemia, but instead of taking the direct land route westward, they were advised, keeping at first to the galleys, to go by water viâ Archangel, probably on account of their heavy boxes of presents and goods (referred to later by Don Juan), and they therefore voyaged on slowly northward. This meant crossing from Rybinsk on the Volga by canal to Totma, on the upper waters of the Northern Dvina, down which Archangel on the White Sea was ultimately reached. Between Rybinsk and Totma the exact waterway is difficult to follow in

# INTRODUCTION

Don Juan's narrative, but affluents to one and the other river have their sources in common ground, and the watershed here is very low. As already said, Don Juan calls the upper reach of the Volga at Rybinsk the *Batem* or *Barem*, and he gives this name also to the waterway across to Totma and again to the river down which their galleys rowed to Archangel, this laſt river in faƈt being the Northern Dvina.

At Archangel they took ship, and in due course, but after a very ſtormy voyage round the North Cape and down the coaſt of Norway, reached Stode[4] at the mouth of the Elbe, where Parry, who aƈted as Secretary to Sir Anthony, disembarked, going ſtraight to England with despatches, while Sherley and the Persian ambassador went on to Embden, at the mouth of the Weser. Here they left their ship, and on landing were received and hospitably entertained by the Duke of Oldenburg, who showed them the wonders of his palace, after which Sherley and the Persians set out by land for Kassel. At Kassel the Landgrave of Hesse paid them every attention, and Don Juan hereupon takes occasion to insert a brief account (borrowed, without acknowledgment, from Botero) of the chief cities of Central Germany. From Hesse-Kassel the embassy passed into Saxony, where they ſtopped at the Duke's residence, but did not see him, as he was out hunting, being, as Don Juan notes, a young man much addiƈted to sport. From Kassel to Prague it is difficult to follow ſtage by ſtage the route on the map, by reason of the aſtonishing Caſtilian spellings of the German place-names. The capital city of Saxony is called Syplilit, a name which it is hard to identify with Dresden, and which more probably is Leipzig, where the youthful Duke Chriſtian II is ſtated to have had his palace. To this point the route followed appears to have been: Kassel, Weimar, Halle and Syplilit, which is Leipzig. From here to Prague, going doubtless up the Elbe through

5

the Saxon Switzerland, most of the places named, till we reach Bohemia, are unrecognizable on any modern or 17th century map. Passing the Saxon frontier the embassy entered the territories of the Empire, proceeding on to Prague in Bohemia, where they found the Emperor Rudolf II in residence. This was in the autumn of the year 1600, the same in which at Eastertide they had left Moscow, and at Prague they wintered, being sumptuously entertained at the Imperial Court.[5]

The following spring, with an Imperial Chamberlain to see them on their way, they set out from Prague for Munich (viâ Nüremberg and Augsburg), where the Duke of Bavaria, who had recently abdicated, William II, surnamed the Pious, showed them the contents of his treasury and his gardens. Our author has hitherto given every stage of the journey, from Embden to Munich (though in many stages, as already remarked, the place-names are unrecognizable), but from this capital onwards only the places where the embassy was entertained in state are noticed. From Munich, therefore, doubtless passing through Inspruck and over the Brenner to Botzen and by Trent, they entered Italy and went direct to Mantua, where the Duke Vincenzo Gonzaga gave them a noble entertainment. The ambassador had been commissioned by Sháh 'Abbás to present his Letters to the Doge of Venice, but the Signory, when duly warned, declined to receive the Persian envoy, sending for excuse that at this moment they were busy with the reception of a Turkish ambassador, and the Persians, therefore, from Mantua went on to Florence. Here they learnt that the Duke Ferdinand de' Medici was at Pisa, on a hunting expedition, but his servants welcomed the embassy and showed the foreigners the sights of the city. At a later date the Duke and Duchess received them at Pisa, when further they were taken down to Leghorn to see the new great port in the making, and Don Juan

# INTRODUCTION

writes that 5,000 slaves were kept busy here on the works of the fortress and harbour. From Pisa to Rome they travelled by Siena, where the ambassador and Sir Anthony had a violent quarrel, the former accusing the latter of having stolen and sold to his private profit the gifts destined by Sháh 'Abbás for presentation to the Pope. This made it impossible for the mission to proceed further together. Sherley and the ambassador were received in separate audience by Pope Clement VIII, after which Sir Anthony gave up his ambassadorial commission, in shame or disgust, and set out for Venice. While the Persians were staying in Rome incontinently the ambassador's cook and two others of his suite announced their conversion to the Catholic faith, much to the embarrassment of their master.[6]

From Rome the embassy then set out for Spain, travelling by land to Genoa, and thence by sea to Savona, from which place they came up to Avignon. Here the Papal Legate entertained them, forwarding them in due course on to Perpignan, where crossing the Pyrenees they reached Barcelona, and thence through Zaragoza they finally reached Valladolid, where the Spanish Court was then in residence. For two months they sojourned at the Court of Philip III, who received them graciously when presented to him by the all-powerful Duke of Lerma. The Persian ambassador now decided to go home, having accomplished his mission to the three potentates of Germany, Rome and Spain, deeming that a visit to the five remaining sovereigns on his list—namely those of England, Scotland, France and Poland, with the Doge of Venice who had declined to receive him—might be left over for some more auspicious occasion. To avoid the long land journey homeward across Europe, he made up his mind to take his passage back to his native land by sea, round the Cape of Good Hope, thus to Ormuz on the Persian Gulf, whence Isfahán might conveniently be reached. The settlement of Ormuz at the date in question was still in the occupation of the Portuguese, but as such was a port in the Spanish dominions, for it will be borne in mind that from 1583 to 1640 Philip II, III and IV of Spain were in succession kings also of Portugal. On their departure from his court Philip III generously provided for the expenses of the embassy by land to Lisbon, and thence on by sea with a free passage to the Persian Gulf: for besides many magnificent presents, the Persians were given 11,000 ducats in cash for journey money. Indeed all along their route, on taking leave in audience of the various sovereign princes to whom the embassy was accredited, the ambassador and his secretaries had invariably received a variety of gold cups, often some gold chains, and much silver plate. This in addition to cash, namely from the Pope 2,000 ducats, from the Emperor 4,800, from the Tzar 3,800, a grand total of 21,600 ducats, equivalent to £7,200 sterling of those days, and to perhaps ten times as much in the value of money at the present time. Such were the emoluments of an embassy in the year 1600, with free board and lodging everywhere during sojourn.

From Valladolid therefore the Persians now set out and travelled in a leisurely manner, passing by Segovia and the Escoreal to Madrid and Toledo, whence across Estremadura Truxillo was reached, and thence by Mérida and Badajos on to Lisbon. At each town they were sumptuously entertained in accordance with orders sent on by Lerma, but when passing through Mérida two stages before reaching Lisbon a regrettable incident occurred. Among the retinue of the Persian ambassador was a Shi'ah doctor of theology, a Mulla, or, as the Spaniards called him, an *Alfaqui*, whose business it was to see to it that the members of the Mission walked in the path of Moslem orthodoxy. This man, standing at the gate of their lodging in

# INTRODUCTION

Mérida, was by some mischance stabbed to death by a fanatic Spaniard, and the ambassador was much put about as to what course to pursue. On consideration he decided to go on to Lisbon, where he laid his case before Philip III's Viceroy in Portugal, and Uruch Beg (soon to become Don Juan) was then sent back to Valladolid to claim redress of the Spanish government. This matter was in due course seen to after delay, and then from Lisbon the ambassador finally, early in the year 1602, set sail on his long sea voyages. He must have reached Ormuz during the course of the summer: but we do not know the date, nor has any record come down to us of his reception, at his homecoming, by Sháh 'Abbás, to whom he doubtless reported the rather meagre results of his embassy, and what had happened to those of his suite who had not returned with him.[7] For before the ambassador had left Spain three principal members of his suite had acted in a way causing him much embarrassment. Moslems, whether Sunnis or Shi'ahs, rarely change their religion. Indeed, in their own country to do so is equivalent to suicide, for a renegade by the law of Islam suffers death. As we have seen, three followers of the Persian Embassy already had remained truant in Rome, having abjured the faith of the Prophet, and now, when the ambassador was about to leave Spain, three of his secretaries proceeded to join the Roman communion.

One, 'Ali Quli Beg, was the ambassador's own nephew, and this change of faith, which his uncle regarded as perversion, was no light matter; nothing, however, could be done to prevent the catastrophe. Philip III was to be this nephew's godfather, giving him his royal name; and he duly became Don Philip of Persia; though what was his subsequent history is totally unknown. At the same time and along with him was baptized the author of the *Relaciones*, and to the new Don Juan of Persia Margaret of Austria the Queen of Spain stood sponsor. The third convert was Buniyad Beg, who took the name of Don Diego of Persia, and concerning his subsequent history we learn something from the details of a lawsuit he had with Salas Barbadillo, a well-known playwright and poet of those days. Señor Emilio Cotarelo y Mori, who has recently edited the works of Salas Barbadillo, further takes occasion in his Introduction to recount briefly the sad fate that overtook our author, Don Juan, in the year following the publication of his *Relaciones*. On the 15th of May of 1605, when still resident in Valladolid, he was involved in a scuffle with the men attending a law officer, an Alcalde de Corte, and in the brawl he came to be stabbed, cut down and killed. To spare embarrassing questions his body was then and there flung into a desolate gulley near the capital, where, as reported, it was eaten by the town dogs.[8]

Of the book of the *Relaciones* and how it got itself written, something must now be said. The work, as judged by competent critics, is composed in excellent Castilian, and Uruch Beg, as he then was called, had come to Spain at the close of 1601 knowing no Spanish to speak of. The *Aprovación* to print is dated February 1604, and Señor Cotarelo is of opinion that during the previous two years Uruch Beg, now become Don Juan, was unlikely to have learnt Spanish enough to have composed it. How the book was produced is explained in a letter prefixed to the text of the *Relaciones*, in which the Licentiate Alfonso Remón, who states that he is an intimate friend of Don Juan's, introduces the book to the special notice of the Royal Chaplain and Almoner, Don Álvaro de Caravajal. This ecclesiastic had superintended the conversion of Don Juan in 1602, and had baptized him by royal command in the Palace Chapel at Valladolid. Remón, after praising his new friend, as a man well educated in

# INTRODUCTION

accordance with eastern standards, stating further that his knowledge of the history and geography of Persia was astonishingly profound, continues that he, Remón, had recently been helping Don Juan to compose in Castilian the work following, translating it page by page from the original draft which Don Juan had written out in Persian. Now in the penultimate chapter of his *Relaciones* Don Juan has taken occasion to tell us that from the moment when he left Isfahán he had carefully kept his Diary, and daily had noted down during the long journey all incidents that had seemed to him of interest; in order, as he adds, that when he should return home to Persia this Diary might be presented to Sháh 'Abbás and copied out for the instruction of his countrymen.

This Diary, of course, had been kept in Persian, as indeed Remón mentions incidentally, adding that for many months after coming to Spain Don Juan was quite incapable of writing Spanish. Don Juan indeed confesses that while he was a catechumen and learning the dogmas of Christianity he was perforce obliged to write out all the prayers he had to get by heart, as best he could in the Persian script. His colloquial knowledge of Castilian possibly began to be acquired soon after the embassy had left Rome, for we are told the Pope had sent with the Persians, to act as guide and interpreter, a Spanish priest named Don Francisco Guasque, Canon of Barcelona, who stayed with the embassy all the time they were in Spain. From his companionship and constantly having to talk Spanish, Don Juan doubtless in the year before his conversion must have acquired a practical colloquial knowledge of the tongue. Having regard to the original Diary, however, Persian being written in the Arabic character, is as ill-adapted as may be for registering Russian and German place-names, hence the astonishing spellings that we meet with in the itinerary. Further, these names during the composition of the *Relaciones* had to be read out aloud by Don Juan from his draft Diary to Remón, who, listening to Don Juan's utterances, proceeded to dictate what he heard to an amanuensis, who wrote it all down in accordance with Castilian orthography. For it is evident from many mistakes that are of the ear, not of the eye, that the book before us was transcribed by one who set down what was dictated. This is clear both from his version of the strange names pronounced by Don Juan, and from what Remón was reading aloud from the authorities (Italian and Spanish) he was consulting in the compilation of the historical parts of his work.[9] Then followed the lack of proof correcting, to which reference has been made in my Preface. Remón indeed had no easy task, and to fill in historical blanks and to guide him in the account of the journey through Russia and Germany, two countries with whose geography he must have been but imperfectly acquainted, he now kept open before him the excellent contemporary geographical compendium written in Italian by Giovanni Botero,[10] already referred to. Botero, however, is not by any means the only author quoted in the *Relaciones*, as will be seen from the list given in the note.[11]

Leaving now the Diary of the long journey through Europe (forming the contents of the Third Book), some account is due of the first two Books of the *Relaciones*. The initial chapter of the work, it is clear, must have been entirely the composition of the Licentiate Remón, and sets forth very piously the satisfaction felt by Don Juan at having embraced Christianity. He is also very proud of that long journey of his, which he says may take a third place after Marco Polo and Magellan; and he promises to correct the geography of Botero and the history of the wars between Turks and Persians which Minadoi had recently published.[12] The second chapter gives a description of the various

# INTRODUCTION

provinces of Persia, but for the most part this is merely a re-arrangement of what Remón found in Botero: Don Juan, however, has here and there added a few details of interest from personal recollections of his native land. The next two chapters, which are entirely the composition of Don Juan, Remón only holding the pen, are interesting. The first deals with the mode of government of Sháh 'Abbás. The names are given of the 32 noble families whose ranks supplied all the officers or government officials, and the various departments of the state are enumerated. In more than one case, as might be supposed, it is evident that Persia is much changed from what obtained in the early 17th century. The palace which the Sháh's many wives inhabited was then called the *Haram*, a term now only applied to the sanctuary of a Mosque. This was, of course, in the main guarded by eunuchs: but as well as these people Don Juan states that there were in attendance a number of "escuderos" or squires, aged 70 and upwards, who looked after and diverted the ladies. These Duennas of the male sex are a novelty not mentioned apparently elsewhere, and at the present day the king of Persia would certainly not tolerate gentlemen even of 70 to attend and wait upon his wives. The succeeding chapter is on manners and customs, and is in every way noteworthy. How burials and marriages were conducted, how the soldiers were armed and of their armour (which was then manufactured in such abundance in Persia as to be a commodity of export to Muscovy), the cost of living and the loose morals of the gypsies, all these and other matters are touched on, and what we learn proves that Persia at the present day is no longer what it was in the spacious days of Sháh 'Abbás.

The *Relaciones* now takes up the history of Persia beginning with the times of Nimrod, the following five chapters (5 to 9 of Book I), which are doubtless the work of Remón, in a jejune epitome, bringing us down to the fall of the Sassanian monarchy and the subsequent rise of Islam. The moſt part is a mere liſt of kings from Berosus or Ctesias, with a display of classical erudition on the part of Remón, who is always remiss in correcting his proofs. Being a very patriotic Persian, Don Juan was anxious to get his friend and editor Remón to show clearly how the Persian monarchy of the Safavi kings was in fact the heir-general of the Assyrian and Babylonian dynaſties which had ruled these countries since hiſtory began. All notice of the Parthians is omitted, and the Sassanians are dealt with by Remón from the classical standpoint, his chief authority being Agathias, whose *Hiſtory* had recently been published, the Greek text with a convenient Latin translation by Scaliger and Dousa. The laſt four chapters of the Firſt Book take up the annals of the Moslem Empire, and here it muſt be remembered that Don Juan is unlikely to have brought with him from Persia any manuscript providing a compendium of Islamic hiſtory, such, for inſtance, as would have been Hamd Allah's *Guzídah*. For lack of some such work (and the libraries of Valladolid certainly would not have supplied any Persian texts) he had to rely on what Remón could glean from Botero's *Relationi Universali*, and from such of the Byzantine hiſtorians as had been published (the Greek texts with Latin translations) before 1600. This meagre course was supplemented, and commented on, by what Don Juan himself could remember, from the teaching of his school days in matters of hiſtory. In 1600 no Arabic text of any Moslem hiſtorian had yet been printed, for the firſt to see the light was the *Hiſtoria Saracenica* of Elmacin, published by Erpenius at Leyden in the year 1625. In this case, of the Byzantines, Remón appears to have made use of Cedrenus (Bâle, 1566), Scylitzes (Venice, 1570), and Zonaras (Paris, 1567, or

# INTRODUCTION

Frankfort, 1587), where in each case, beside the Greek text a Latin version, in aid, is supplied. The *History* of Theophanes, which would have been a more reliable guide, was unfortunately not available, as the earliest edition is that of Paris, 1655. Don Juan, aided by Remón, from these very jejune authorities has, on the whole, given a very fair summary of the history of the Caliphate. He discreetly says little about the Prophet Mahomed, and in the pride of his new faith only gives passing allusions to the abominable doctrines of the Coran.

Coming to the first three Caliphs, he explains how the three wicked men Abu Bakr, Omar and Othman kept 'Ali out of his rights, and the history of the Omayyads and Abbasids is told as leading up to the victory of the House of 'Ali and the Shi'ah faith in the person of Sháh Isma'íl, the founder of the Safavi monarchy. His hero in Omayyad times is Mukhtár, who avenged the death of 'Ali's son Husayn, and with the coming of the Abbasids it is Abu Muslim, their missioner in Khurasán, who is his hero: and Don Juan claims that both these men were among the ancestors of Sháh Isma'íl. Following on the story of the Baghdad Caliphate the Seljuq Turks and the Tartars are briefly referred to, which leads to an account of the rise of the Ottoman Sultans in Asia Minor, in later days to become the chief adversaries of the Safavi kings of Persia. As already explained, it is evident that when composing the text of the *Relaciones* Remón had open before him various volumes of the Byzantine historians, and this method of composition must account for the curious spelling of many proper names. Some mistakes, however, are doubtless due to lack of proof correcting, which may explain why Omar appears as Hosmaz or Oromaz, and Othman as Odman or Ozmin. It is generally quite easy to identify the person who is meant from the date and the incidents recorded, but while, for instance, the names of Hárún-ar-Rashíd and Mámún are plain, Amín, the elder brother of the latter Caliph, appears as Imbrael, and Tughríl Beg the Seljuq, son of Mikhail, figures under the Byzantine disguise of Trangolypico Moncaleto (following Zonaras and others). This name became well known in Europe, for Richard Knolles, a contemporary of Don Juan, has much to tell of Tangrolipix in his *Generall Historie of the Turkes*,[13] where he relates how he, the "chief of the Salzuccians, slays Pisasiris, Calyph of Babylon."

With the rise of Shaykh Haydar to power the history of Persia as a nation begins. He was the father of Sháh Isma'íl, and we are given an account of the ancestors of the Safavis, with an exposition of the rights of the House of 'Ali, also how and why the Shi'ahs differ in all points from the Sunnis; why, in short, Persians and Turks never can agree. This leads in the first instance to the biography of Uzun Hasan (1466 to 1478), "Tall Hasan," the great chief of the White Sheep Turkomans, who just before Safavi times ruled Persia very gloriously, and contended on no unequal terms with Sultan Muhammad II, the Conqueror of Constantinople. Uzun Hasan is a figure of some note in the pages of the various works translated in the volume of *Travels of Venetians in Persia*,[14] where Zeno refers to him as Ussun Cassano and the Anonymous Merchant as Assambei, describing the magnificent palace which Uzun Hasan built at Tabríz and which Sháh Isma'íl occupied in later days. Don Juan states (but giving no authority) that Uzun Hasan was descended from a certain Hasan Beg who was one of the many Turkish chiefs ruling in Asia Minor during the latter part of the 14th century, when this country was divided under the Ten Turkish Amirs; of whom one family survived to become the House of Ottoman. The sister of Uzun

# INTRODUCTION

Hasan was the mother of Shaykh Haydar, and to him, his nephew, Uzun Hasan subsequently gave his daughter in marriage, who became the mother of Sháh Isma'íl. Uzun Hasan's wife was Despina, daughter of Kalo Joannes, the last Greek Emperor of Trebizond. Thus through his mother and maternal grandmother Sháh Isma'íl claimed descent from the Comneni Emperors of Constantinople, while on the father's side he was, in the direct male line, the representative of the Seventh Imám Musa Kázim, fourth in descent from Husayn, the grandson of the Prophet Mahomed. Of how Sháh Isma'íl, the son of Shaykh Haydar, established the dynasty of the Safavis and became the first king of all Persia more will appear later. It is of importance clearly to point out that for Persia this coming of the Safavis was more than a mere change of rulers, for it produced a change of religious belief. The outstanding fact that came to be established by the new government of Sháh Isma'íl was that the Persians had become a nation. And this he had effected by imposing on all Persia the Shi'ah creed, which once for all differentiated them from their neighbours on the west, the Sunni Turks. The Shi'ah doctrine, the right divine of the Imáms to supreme kingship, and therefore for their descendants the right to govern the land of Persia, was already before this period an ideal of the majority of Persians; and two centuries before the date of Sháh Isma'íl, according to Hamd Allah Mustawfi, in many towns throughout Persia those of the Shi'ah faith equalled those of the Sunni population. He, Sháh Isma'íl, came to rule, being the direct descendant of the Prophet through the Imáms; and the blood of Sassanian kings also was in his veins, for his ancestor Husayn (grandson of Mahomed) had married Shahr-Banu, the daughter of Yazdagird, the last of the Sassanian kings, and her son was Zayn-al-'Ábidín the Fourth Imám.

# DON JUAN OF PERSIA

Toleration in religious matters was disregarded in the East as in the West in the 17th century, and Isma'íl insisted that all Persians should at prayer time curse the first three Caliphs in Islam, Abu Bakr, Omar and Othman, who had robbed 'Ali, "the Friend of God," and his lawful descendants of their birthright during the last thousand years. Further, to distinguish the orthodox from the heterodox, Sháh Isma'íl's followers all now wore the Red Cap, with twelve points, so fashioned to typify very clearly the number of the orthodox Imáms. From that date *Qizil Bash* ("Red Head") therefore became the Turkish name for the Persian Shi'ahs, and the Red Cap with twelve gussets in many colours is carefully described, this, according to Don Juan, being a form of bonnet that had been invented originally by 'Ali, the Prophet's son-in-law: he, however, gives no authority for this fantastic statement. The missioners of the Shi'ah doctrines were the Súfís, and their name has been often wrongly connected with Safaví, the name of the new dynasty. In Persian the word *Súfí* (a dervish, otherwise a mystic) is said to be derived from *Súf*, "wool," the material from which the garments of these religious mendicants was commonly made; while the dynasty of which Sháh Isma'íl was the founder took its name of Safaví (the adjective form of Safí) from Shaykh Safí-ad-Dín of Ardebíl, the illustrious and saintly ancestor of the royal house. Etymologically, therefore, *Súfí* and *Safaví* have nothing to do with each other, but the names being much alike, and both in common use, led European travellers and writers of the 16th and 17th centuries to call the Safaví king of Persia the Grand Sophi. The origin of this name being thus in dispute, Don Juan on more than one occasion states very emphatically that the Grand Sophi was indeed the great Súfí or Dervish, but that this name was not derived either from the Greek word σοφὸς, "wisdom,"

# INTRODUCTION

as falsely asserted by some, or as might follow by implication from Safaví, the family name of the monarch of Persia. Don Juan indeed makes the distinction between the proper name Safí and Súfí quite clear, for when mentioning Shāh Ismaʻíl I. in speaking of his tomb, it is as *Xiek-Sofi* or *Xiche Sophi* that he appears in his transliteration.[15]

The Second Book of the *Relaciones* takes up the history of Persia during the 16th century, the period of the long duel between the Turks and the Persians. Ready at hand for relating the events of this 16th century, Don Juan, or rather his editor the Licentiate Remón, had open before him the well-known work on these famous wars, composed in Italian by Giovanni Thomaso Minadoi, and the errors of this book, as already mentioned in the first chapter of Book I of the *Relaciones*, Don Juan has been at much pains to correct.[16] Further, Remón appears to have used the *History of the Ottoman Sultans* written in Latin by Boissard; this work also being the chief authority on which Richard Knolles depended for composing his great *Historie of the Turkes* mentioned on a previous page.[17] The whole of Book II of the *Relaciones* may indeed be regarded as a condensed and rearranged translation of Minadoi, corrected and amplified by what Don Juan knew, from his father, and from oral tradition about the events of the century just elapsed, covered by the reigns of father, uncle and grandfather of Shāh ʻAbbás. In many ways it is an ample and graphic picture of mediæval Persia during the early days of that country's greatest prosperity.[18]

After describing in some detail the rise of the Safavi power under Ismaʻíl the first Sophi, an account is given of Ismaʻíl's war against Sultan Bayazid II. At this time Tekelli, in command of the Persian irregular forces, was carrying fire and sword throughout

## DON JUAN OF PERSIA

Anatolia (Asia Minor), where a recent massacre, by the Sultan's orders, of his Shi'ah subjects had provoked the ardent sympathy of their Persian co-religionists; and Don Juan speaks of a great victory gained by Tekelli over the Turks, who were under the command of Prince Qurqud, Sultan Bayazid's son. Tekelli's victorious career across Asia Minor, according to our author, at one time brought him up to the shores of the Bosporus, so that he came near to raiding the suburbs of Constantinople, but on this incident the Turkish historians are entirely silent. With the accession of Sultan Selim the Grim to the throne, the tables were quickly turned. Western Persia was invaded, and in 1514 the great victory of Chaldirán enabled Selim temporarily to occupy Tabríz (at that time Sháh Isma'íl's capital) and the king had to retire with his beaten army eastward. For the Turks, however, it proved an almost barren victory. Don Juan is proud to tell of the immense number of the combatants engaged on either side in this celebrated battle, and he says that in his youth he had known old men, living at Isfahán, who told him stories of their deeds of valour in that war. The Turks soon afterwards evacuated Tabríz, and Sháh Isma'íl, back in his capital, now seeking an ally against the Sultan, despatched an embassy to Cairo to the Burji Mamlúk, Sultan Qansuh. This move Sultan Selim countered by ordering the immediate invasion of Syria. The Egyptians were defeated in a battle fought outside the walls of Aleppo, where the Turkish artillery made havoc of the famous cavalry of the Mamlúks, and Sultan Qansuh was left dead on the field, from which his army fled. Thus Syria was lost, and Selim marched on to Cairo. All Egypt, after another battle lost, submitted, which thenceforward became a province of the Turkish Empire.

In 1520 Sultan Sulaymán the Magnificent succeeded

# INTRODUCTION

his father Selim the Grim, and four years later Sháh Tahmásp was king in the room of his father Isma'íl, governing Persia for the next fifty-two years, during the course of which on five different occasions the north-western provinces (Azerbayján and Georgia) suffered invasion by Turkish armies, Baghdad also, with most of Mesopotamia, passing into the power of the Turkish Sultan. Sulaymán the Magnificent died in 1566, being succeeded on the throne by his son Selim II, known as the Sot, and ten years later the long reign of Sháh Tahmásp reached its close. His eldest son Muhammad Khudá Bandah, being partially blind, was easily ousted by his brother Isma'íl, who for two years with much shedding of blood ruled as Sháh, first with and then without the support of his remarkable sister, the Princess Parí-Khán-Khánum. His death in 1578 brought his elder brother, the blind Prince Muhammad, back to the throne; the princess was decapitated, and her head stuck on a lance point was exposed at the gates of Qazvín, now become the Persian capital—a shocking sight to the people, which Don Juan much deplores; and he may indeed have seen it, for he must have been a youth of eighteen at this date. The government then came into the hands of Prince Hamzah, the blind king's eldest son, who loyally and to the best of his capacity carried out his father's behests; the Persians doing their best to resist the renewed Ottoman invasion of Georgia. Here the troops of Sultan Murád III (the son of Selim the Sot, who died in 1574) had appeared in 1577, under the command of Mustafá Pasha, already famous as the conqueror of Cyprus. The semi-independent kingdom of Georgia, for the most part inhabited by Christians, had suffered much in the earlier years of the 15th century by the ravaging conquest of Tamerlane. It was now in the last quarter of the 16th century ruled by six independent princes who had hitherto chiefly looked for support to Persia, but they were already being constrained to bow before the invading Turkish power. The Georgian princes, from this period onward, perforce became renegades, Sunni or Shi'ah, as best suited the exigencies of the moment. The Turkish armies, coming up through the Armenian mountains, took and garrisoned Tiflis on the river Kur (or Cyrus), and next sought to dominate the Shirván province which lies to the eastward, extending down to the Caspian and as far as Derbend, a celebrated fortress, which the Turks called Demír Qapú (the Iron Gate), and the Arabs Báb-al-Abwáb (the Gate of Gates).

To the events which resulted in the subjugation of Georgia by the armies of Sultan Murád III, Don Juan devotes several chapters of his work, explaining how in a few years Georgia, with all the lands lying to the south of the Caucasus range, namely Mingrelia and much of Armenia, became a province of the Turkish Empire. The invasion began in 1578, and for the most part Minadoi is the source used by Remón, whose knowledge of the Italian frequently fails him, with the result of not a few mistranslations. He might with advantage have used Herrera's excellent Spanish version of Minadoi, but this apparently was not then available in the Valladolid library. At the time of the Turkish invasion of Georgia Don Juan must have been almost grown up, and he may in the later days of the conquest have heard of, and when writing his *Relaciones* have remembered many of the events related in the pages of Minadoi's *History*. Leaving aside for the moment the affairs of Georgia on the western frontier, Don Juan next devotes a long chapter to Herát in the north-east, where Prince 'Abbás (afterwards Sháh), then a boy of twelve, was governor of Khurasán in the name of the Sháh, his father; and here the many mistakes of Minadoi as to what was actually happening in Herát are corrected by the accounts that Don Juan heard from

## INTRODUCTION

the lips of his father Sultan 'Alí Beg Bayát, who was at Herát in attendance on the young prince. Our author next reverts to Georgia, where the Turks were settling their conquest in preparation for a southward move on Eriván, whence they might threaten and ultimately get possession of the rich Persian province of Azerbayján, with the great city of Tabríz, its capital. Pasha succeeded Pasha as Ottoman commander-in-chief in Georgia, while Sultan Murád III personally directed the campaigns by orders sent from Constantinople. Slowly but surely the conquest was effected. Qars, which was the Turkish frontier fortress, was now connected by strongly garrisoned posts back with Erzerúm and thence north to the Black Sea at Trebizond, to which port supplies were constantly shipped from Constantinople.

As against the Persian lack in this arm, the great advantage of the Turks lay with their artillery, with which all their armies were well provided. Tiflis they garrisoned and successfully held against all attempts of the Georgians to retake it, and the passes of the mountains were safeguarded by many forts commanding the long road by which convoys passed from Trebizond to Erzerúm and Qars and the Tomanis pass up into Georgia. To reach Eriván a well-guarded road direct from Qars was established, and Eriván was then quickly taken from the Persians; becoming a great Turkish stronghold, and base, by the building of a new fortress on the heights above the town, of which the remains may still be admired. All these works required large sums of money, which the Turkish government had to convoy safely in cash to their commanders in the outpost garrisons; but at Tiflis and elsewhere it is evident that the troops found no difficulty in supplies, and they were able to buy their provisions from the friendly renegade Georgians, round and about, whose country they were slowly but surely engaged in absorbing. Up to this moment the Turks had been engaged in overrunning the tributary provinces lying beyond Persia proper, but Sultan Murád's next move was against Tabríz, then the most important commercial city of Persia, where the caravan routes from the west and from the east met. Tabríz was peopled by unwarlike merchants, and its fighting strength had to come from the Turkoman tribesmen settled as nomads at some distance from the city in the fertile plains of the Azerbayján province. Unfortunately the Turkomans were at the time in a state of feud against the Persian government, for their chief had recently been put to death by Prince Hamzah under suspicion (wrongfully, it was said) of an intention to rebel against the Sháh. Thus Tabríz, almost undefended, quickly fell to Othman Pasha, who proceeded to build a great fortress here, to be held by a strong garrison. The Persians strove for many months to retake what had been so ingloriously lost; and our author, then known under the name of Uruch Beg, makes his first appearance on the scene, as a young man fighting at his father's side in the Persian army laying siege to the Turks in their new stronghold, and present when his father was killed in a gallant attempt to storm the main bastion of the fortress.

During the next fifteen years all that happened in Persia is described from the observations, or recollections, of an eye-witness, for our author succeeded to his father's place in the Sháh's favour, and fought under the command of Prince Hamzah the regent. Do what they would Tabríz fort could not be retaken from the Turks, and the next move of the rebellious Turkoman tribesmen was boldly to kidnap one of the Sháh's younger sons, Tahmásp Mirza, a boy of twelve, and the rebels marching away from the neighbourhood of Tabríz captured and occupied Qazvín, at that time the capital city of Persia. The season was winter; the

# INTRODUCTION

Sháh and Prince Hamzah were detained besieging the Tabríz fortress, and they had to endure the affront of the Turkomans taking possession of the capital, where they set up the boy Tahmásp as nominal king. During that winter Tabríz suffered many things. The spring, however (of 1586), saw the turning of the tables. Prince Hamzah, leaving his father in camp before Tabríz fort, marched with all available forces on Qazvín. The Turkomans evacuated the capital to meet the prince in the open field, and were completely routed; young Tahmásp Mirza, being taken prisoner, was despatched, blinded, to end his days at Alamút, the famous castle in the hills north of Qazvín, where five centuries before the Chief of the Assassins, the " Old Man of the Mountain " of Marco Polo, had established the centre of his power. During this short campaign against the rebel tribesmen our author was in command of a squadron of horse under Prince Hamzah, and the details of the struggle are narrated at first hand. With the prince he now returned to the camp at Tabríz, and learnt that the Turks had sent an army of 200,000 men from Constantinople under Cigala Pasha, in part to reinforce the garrison of the Tabríz fort, and in part to strengthen their outposts on the frontiers of Persia at Eriván and Tiflis. It now became evident to Prince Hamzah that the blockade of Tabríz fort would not lead to its capture, and under his orders the Persians evacuated their camp, dismantling the town fortifications. Then the civil population, urged and aided to carry off with them all their goods and chattels, were escorted out and sent to people neighbouring towns further in the interior of the country. The king and Prince Hamzah at the head of the army now marched north to Ganjah, the capital of the mountainous district of Qarabagh lying to the south-east of Tiflis: this with the view of effecting a demonstration in force that should safeguard the Persian frontier in that quarter.

## DON JUAN OF PERSIA

This done, the army, after resting awhile, set out from Ganjah on its return to Qazvín, the capital, and it was on the march thither that an event occurred—namely, the unexpected murder of Prince Hamzah by his barber—which entirely changed the political situation. Don Juan (as Uruch Beg) was present in the camp when the deed was done, and the details are carefully chronicled. The cause of the crime has been variously given, but according to Don Juan it was a political plot of several great nobles of the Shámlú Clan, who wished by removing Prince Hamzah to bring in his son, a boy under age, as nominal regent, whom they should govern while continuing to rule the state in the name of the blind king, the boy's grandfather. The event turned out otherwise, and served to bring Prince 'Abbás (at that time a youth in his seventeenth year) on the scene from Herát, where he was acting governor. Forthwith begins his reign of over forty years, for his blind father abdicated the kingship and in 1588 (the year with us of the Spanish Armada) Sháh 'Abbás the Great assumed the crown. The beginning of the reign found Persia beset on the west by the Ottoman armies, and threatened on the north-east by the Tartar hordes otherwise known as the Uzbeks. Also most of the home provinces of Persia were seething with revolt against the newly established government at Qazvín. Young Sháh 'Abbás showed his grasp of statesmanship by making terms without delay, though at heavy cost, with the Turk. A formal treaty with Sultan Murád III left Tabríz with most of the province of Azerbayján, and all Georgia, in peaceable possession of the Ottoman power; and Sháh 'Abbás was thereby enabled to concentrate his forces against the petty potentates who were rebelling in Gílán, Luristán and Mázandarán. Next the Uzbeks, who unchecked had been overrunning and plundering all Khurasán, were defeated in a great battle near Herát, and Persia was

## INTRODUCTION

then, for the first time for many a long year, at peace.

Seven years later, when the reign of the feeble Sultan Muhammad III, who had succeeded in 1595 his father Murád III, was drawing to its close, Sháh 'Abbás deemed that the time had come to denounce the peace treaty and turn the Turks out of Tabríz, re-establishing Persian dominion over Azerbayján and Georgia. But this only began to get accomplished in 1602, which is after the date when Uruch Beg had left Persia on the embassy to the western powers, and hence does not come within the scope of the present narrative. In nearly all the campaigns, during the first eight years of his reign, which Sháh 'Abbás waged in order to settle his government, our author took his part as a fighter, and the history of the time is told by him with much detail. The incidents are characteristic of the age. In Luristán the rebel prince takes shelter in a fort garrisoned by Turks: the Sháh is nominally at peace with the Ottoman power, but the Persians arriving in force burn the gates of the fort and capture the fugitive, the Turks further unmolested making no opposition or protest. In Gílán the local prince is defeated and takes ship to cross the Caspian with his treasures and his beautiful Georgian slave girl (she had cost him 10,000 crowns): landing on the west coast (probably at Bákú) they cross Georgia to the eastern shore of the Black Sea (probably to near Poti), and then embark for Constantinople, where both are well received by the Sultan and take up their abode unmolested in his capital. To the east of Gílán in the Asterábád province the rebel prince plays a trick on the Persian commander, keeping him the whole winter besieging a castle built of boards, but covered with white plaster so as outwardly to simulate stone work. After the great battle near Herát when the Uzbek power was annihilated, the army marched home, bearing with them, according to Persian custom, 24,000 Tartar heads. Indeed, as late as forty years ago in Persia (and possibly it may still there be the custom) the only proof that a rebel was duly disposed of and dead was the production in public of his head, generally accompanied by the heads of as many of his followers as could conveniently be collected. Book II of the *Relaciones* closes with an account of the transference of the capital from Qazvín to Isfahán, and then our author relates the coming of the two Sherley brothers in 1599. This immediately brings Don Juan to his account of how the Persian Embassy to the powers of Europe was resolved on, followed by the description of the journey which forms the subject of Book III, the summary of which has been set in the forefront of the present Introduction.

In conclusion, it may prove interesting to describe the volume belonging to the Cambridge University Library, of which the following pages give a translation of the Castilian text. The pages of this little 4to measure 20 cm. by 16 cm., and, beginning with the title, there are twelve unnumbered folios (which it has seemed needless to translate) before coming to the numbered (*recto* and *verso*) folios of the three Books of the *Relaciones*. The title-page bears date of *Año* 1604 and continues: *con privilegio, Valladolid, por Juan de Bostillo en la calle de Samano*. On the next folio are the corrigenda, which, however, leave most of the misprints unnoticed. Its *verso* has the *Aprovación* of the Jesuit Francisco de Galarza, and the *Tasa* of three and a half Maravedis for each sheet. The next folio contains the licence to print of King Philip III addressed to Don Juan de Persia, and the following folio sets forth Don Juan's Dedication to his Catholic Majesty. The fifth folio contains a short address from Don Juan to his Reader, but this mentions nothing of any interest. The next folio (*recto*) prints a Sonnet in honour of Don Juan, written by Doctor Maximiliano

# INTRODUCTION

de Céspedes, and (*verso*) is followed by another Sonnet from the pen of Doña Ana de Espinosa y Ledesma, a native of Segovia; neither seems worthy of translation. The next two folios contain the interesting letter, already spoken of above, p. 10, written by the Licentiate Remón to Don Álvaro de Caravajal, Court Chaplain to the King and Queen, in which he, Remón, explains how he came to help Don Juan, in his ignorance of Spanish, to compose the work that follows. The last three unnumbered folios give us seven more Sonnets, written by various friends of Don Juan in his honour; but these, like the other verses, may reasonably be left to be read in their native Castilian tongue.

Then come the three Books which go to form the *Relaciones*, starting on folio 1 *recto*, and ending on folio 173 *recto* with *Laus Deo* to conclude the 345 pages of text. From folio 173 *verso* to folio 175 *verso* we have ten groups of *Exemplos* (Sayings), which Don Juan gives us as the cream of Persian wit and wisdom. The *Exemplos* are turned out in quatrain form, and should best be appreciated in the original Spanish, being, in the form printed, without doubt the work of the Licentiate Remón. The next twelve folios provide a Table of Contents of the three Books of the *Relaciones*, the pages duly cited of the text, and this table, it may be noted, gives more details than are to be found in the summaries prefixed to each of the chapters. The penultimate folio *verso* and the last folio of the book (*recto* and *verso*) contain a short vocabulary of the Persian and Turkish words occurring in the Spanish text, and this shows the method, or lack of method, of transliteration by Don Juan under the guidance of the Licentiate Remón.

FIRST Book of the Account of Don Juan of Persia, in which the Provinces subject to the Great Sophi of Persia are described, with the several peculiarities of these lands. Whereto also is added an account of the chronology of the Persian kings and rulers since the days of Nimrod.

## CHAPTER I

[*The Author, having become a Christian, proceeds to write a summary account of the History of Persia, and, later, to narrate the events of his voyage into Spain.—Of the errors in the works of Giovanni Botero and Thomas Minadoi.—The Author's travels may well rank with those of Marco Polo and Magellan.*]

WELL may I begin quoting what the Apostle Paul sayth: *Gratias ago Ei, qui me confortavit in Christo Jesu Domino nostro, qui fidelem me existimavit ponens in ministerio, qui prius blasphemus fui, et persecutor, et contumeliosus, sed misericordiam Dei consecutus sum, quia ignorans feci in incredulitate, et cetera.* Blessed be the mercy of God, for that He can, from the by-ways, bring souls into His Church. And of a truth the Apostle also continues with these words following in the Epistle which he wrote to Timothy, saying: " I give thanks to Him who hath strengthened me, even to Christ Jesus our Lord, for that He hath counted me faithful: and He hath brought me out of the darkness of the false sects of idolatry and Judaism, and taught me the true evangelical doctrine, arming me with the buckler of the faith, and giving me the inexpugnable fortress of the Catholic Doctrine."—For this indeed is what is meant by the words of the Epistle: *me confortavit in Christo Jesu.* " For indeed aforetime I was a blasphemer and a persecutor of the Church, an evil-speaker, an unbeliever, and in fine an infidel. But God took me. Not because I was worthy, but because it so pleased Him, that in His most merciful intent, and by His divine providence, I might be accounted afterwards among the faithful, to make me a participator in the ineffable mystery of His most holy Passion. Thus I am now become His faithful servant, for I hold that the Divine Majesty in so deigning to grant me this supreme mercy, saw and pitied the crass ignorance in the which I had been hitherto overwhelmed, being born one of a false and faithless creed. So was it done, for all was by His divine mercy."[1]

Thus far we have been following Saint Paul, though of a certainty these are words many of which I must not take to myself, being so great a sinner, though some indeed of them after a fashion may be applicable to the Divine mercy shown in my case, I too having been called. For my parents and fore-bears were all misbelievers, and I myself grew up in this same state of misbelief, being of the false sect of Mahomed, and living in the country and under the rule of an infidel Prince, a country situate far distant, more than three thousand leagues from Spain, where I now write this Book in the city of Valladolid. But God indeed showed very singular mercy towards me, using me with all favour, in that I was chosen to be one of the Secretaries of the Embassy sent by the King of Persia to this kingdom of Spain; thus to make manifest in me the truth of the Gospel, even as in Divine Wisdom it is said: *Quasi myrrha dedi suavitatem odoris, vel odorem suavitatis*: the which is a sweet savour to my soul.

And this same allegorical interpretation we may apply in a practical sense, for verily this is indeed the understanding of things which experience gives to a prudent man, and forsooth it is the sign which David sayeth is stamped upon all our foreheads. Thus to me was granted this sweet savour of the mode of life of Christian folk: and the effulgence of the Gospel Doctrine entering into me by this gate caused me, from the moment that I understood, to desire to strive faithfully to believe those dogmas which, though yet they may not be fully understood by me, are indeed necessary to orthodox belief: namely, the Mysteries of the

## HIS CONVERSION

Faith. So at last I came to desire, even as did Saint Peter, that I should be bathed in the water and dew of the Doctrine of Christ Jesus: *non tantum manus et caput*, but indeed my very soul in the waters of baptism. Of my conversion, however, and the manner thereof, I shall now not speak more fully, leaving this matter for later, where in its proper place I shall describe the same in detail.

Now the voyage we took from Persia into Spain was of a very great length, and was through most remote lands and by diverse seas, and the same was by a very different route from that which the Portuguese now take when they go to India, or to Ormuz, which same is on the borders of the Persian kingdom; and we saw many strange matters during our long voyage. Further, it is borne in on me that I be not slow in manifesting gratitude to God for the merciful kindness which He vouchsafed to me and to my two companions—an incomparable grace, and, by human effort, one never to be repaid—in that He caused us to become Christians. Thankfulness also is due for the great liberality shown to us at the august hands of his Most Catholic Majesty, who indeed has treated us, and daily does treat us, after a most noble and Christian fashion.

Therefore now I, who have studied somewhat in the Arabic and Turkish tongues, learning the principles too of the Alcoran, shall proceed to give to the Kingdoms of the West a description of all that our eyes have seen on this same journey, in order that here in Spain the Faithful, seeing what diversity of provinces and peoples the Demon still holds under his sway, in the first place may give due thanks to God for His singular and ever present mercy in having brought those of the Orthodox Faith, as we may say, into port, where they are subject to the law of His divine grace; and in the second place, that they may in their prayers give due thanks, beseeching that it may please God to ordain the prompt conversion to Christianity of these infidel folk.

Further, it will not be found contrary to the general desire of our readers that we here describe carefully all the many provinces and diverse races of men whom we visited, carefully noting their various rites and ceremonies. At the same time, I do protest, and call on God to witness—who, as I well know, shall never be invoked for any untrue statement, *quia Deus in cælo fidelis est*—that we only now describe what we have actually ourselves seen in the course of our travels, without adding thereto for the sake of pleasing, or diminishing therefrom for the sake of displeasing, wherefore we say, *quod vidimus testamur*. Further, to conform to the canon of good custom in our writings, we shall begin this Book by the description of the kingdom of Persia, where we were born and from whence we set forth, and we shall do this making no special reference to the cosmographies of ancient days, on which same already so many authors have written. We shall give a succinct but exact description of our country as it is at the present time, setting down the native Persian names, which may thus be compared and adjusted to those given by ancient and modern authorities who have written or shall in the future write from hearsay. For indeed in this matter I speak as an eye-witness, and therefore, if in the works of Thomas Minadoi or Giovanni Botero any diversity of names be found from what I shall here set down, the reader must know that mine are the real Persian names, as spoken in the native tongue of my country, while theirs are but mistaken versions, being, in fact, misunderstood or wrongly pronounced words.

And to finish, I do not think there has been any voyage comparable to ours from Persia to Spain, since the travels published and described by Marco Polo

# THE LONG JOURNEY

the Venetian, and the recent record of discoveries attributed to the Infant of Portugal, [Prince Henry the Navigator,] and the circumnavigation of the globe made by the ship named *Victoria*;[2] and so I trust that my account which follows may be found acceptable.

## CHAPTER II

*The description of Persia, and of the provinces subject thereunto.*

ACCORDING to Strabo, Persia is the country lying south of Parthia and Carmania, between the provinces of Media on the west and Hircania on the east, having—if we are to believe Peter Apianus[1]—Arabia to the south of the same. But Giovanni Botero, in his book, justly remarks[2] that Ancient Persia is in fact solely the province which is now known as Fárs, or Fársistán, whose frontiers lie at the rivers Sirto and Iesdri, and the same extends from the borders of Carmania, now called Kirmán, to the borders of Media, now known as Hamadán,[3] these frontiers standing at a distance of more than 400 leagues one from the other.

The principal metropolitan city and the capital of Fárs is Shíráz, which stands on the banks of the river Band-i-Amir.[4] This city was in ancient days called Persepolis, the same that was burnt down by Alexander the Great, and its population is to-day little less than it was then, seeing that within its present walls the inhabitants number 70,000 householders[5] [31,500 souls]. Now Josaphat Barbaro gives Shíráz a circuit of 20 miles; but I, who frequently have walked about this city and so to speak measured it, am of opinion that in its extreme length and breadth—including the orchards and gardens, for there is no house here but has its own garden—the circumference of Shíráz may be set down at four Castilian leagues. The city has much commerce by reason that all the merchandise from Zagatay [or Tartary] to India has to pass through this town, it being the custom-house or land-port for those parts. To Fárs or Fársistán also belong the

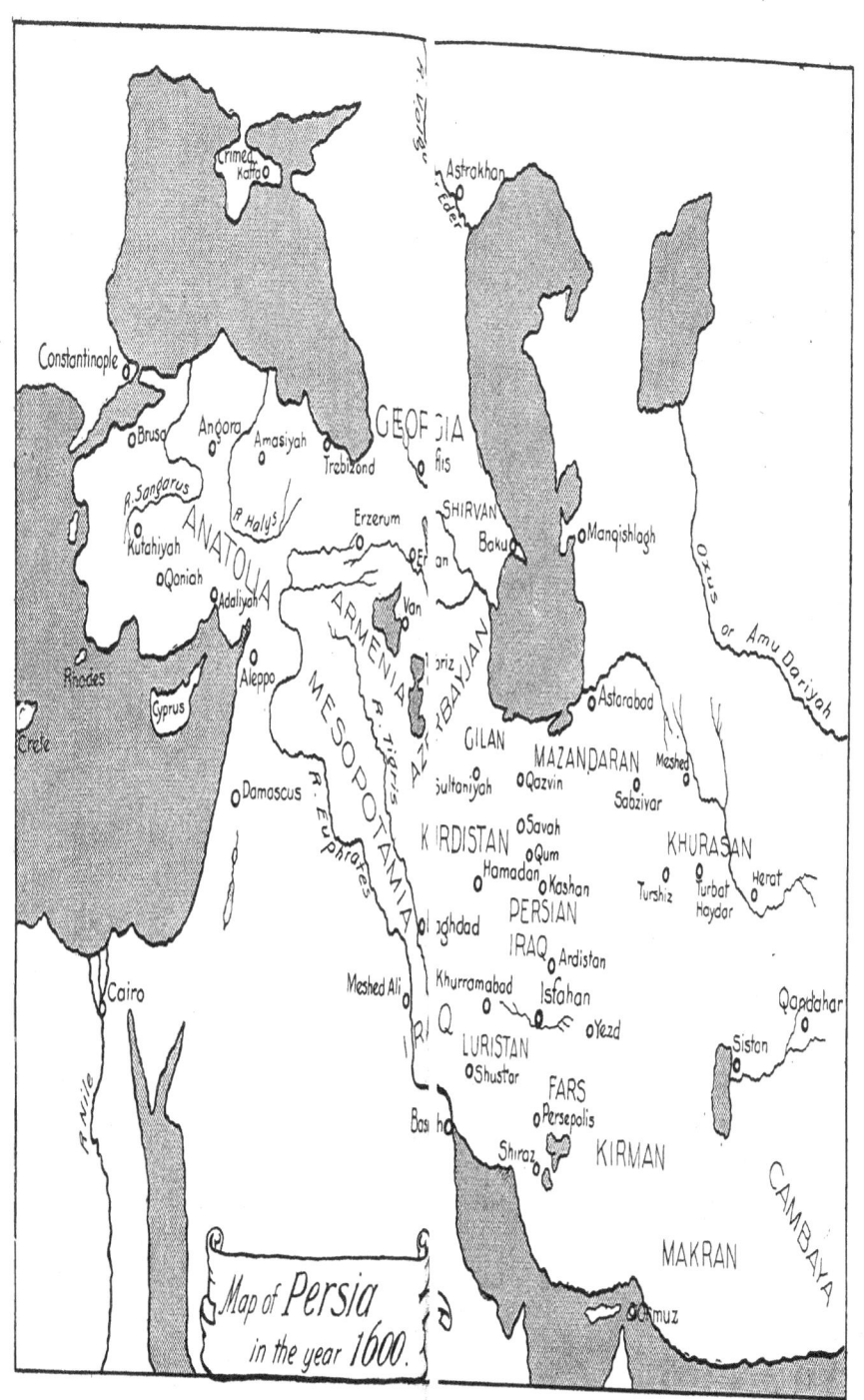

districts of Lur [otherwise Luristán]; and included in Lur is the province of Susiana, whose chief town is Shustar, lying on the river Saymarah; and the climate here is so hot that the people, in the height of the dog-days, put themselves in water up to their necks, in order the more comfortably to pass the heat of the day.

To the north of the province of Fárs, as already said, lies Parthia, which at the present time is the province of Persian 'Iráq, the capital of which is the city of Isfahán, where the kings of Persia now hold their court, and from the which city we set forth on our journey to Spain. Isfahán is at present so populous that they call it the city of *Nisf-i-Jahán*, which in the Persian tongue signifies Half-the-World; but reduced to actual count its population may number 80,000 householders [or 360,000 souls], more rather than less. The concourse of men here is notable, and may be realized by the number of hostels that stand at the entrance gates of the city, upwards of 600 in number, and called here caravanserais. There are also 300 bath-houses which they call Hammáms. The country round and about Isfahán lies low, being somewhat swampy, and from the exceeding dampness not very healthy. The city lies on the banks of a river, which is known as the Zandarud. Within its walls 10,000 shops of merchants are to be found, shops both of clothes-stuffs and of supplies for victuals, these shops being called the Bazaar. And from its very origin its star had made Isfahán to be the King's Court, for, as we learn from Strabo, this is the ancient Hecatompylos—which means the City of a Hundred Gates. At the present day Isfahán still counts a hundred very notable buildings, namely, at least that number of towers rising up above the private houses of the city. These are watch-towers, and they are so lofty that, besides beautifying the appearance of the town by their structure, you may overlook the country round from their windows to a distance of more than six leagues. The greatest of all these towers is the one that stands in the Royal Stables; and its summit is built up of an extraordinary material, for it is formed of 30,000 skulls of deer and harts which were all killed in the battue of a day's sport by King Tahmásp,[6] when, it is related, that of the retinue he took with him, the beaters alone numbered over 20,000 men. In the district round Isfahán silk-worms are reared, and many silk-stuffs are very skilfully woven here, as likewise elsewhere in the outlying districts of the towns of Ardistán, Káshán, and Yezd, Qum and Sávah.

Towards the Caspian Sea lies the province of Qazvín, and Qazvín city is where, until very lately, the kings of Persia have been wont to hold their court, this having been subsequent to the time of the ruin of the famous city of Tabríz, which was formerly the capital. The city of Qazvín lies to the north-west of Fárs; the country round is most fertile: it has great orchards and extensive gardens. Its population numbers above 100,000 householders [or 450,000 souls], and, that one may know its greatness, I have, for curiosity, counted many times over its mosques, and of these there are more than 500. The royal quarter and the palace both are most sumptuous, and so extensive that you may go in a straight line through the purlieus for over a quarter of a league. In the province of Qazvín there are 20 walled towns, and 1,000 open villages. Between Qazvín and Kurdistán lies the province of Hamadán, which may measure 50 leagues across in extent. There are here 15 cities, and all its people are merchants. Lying nearer to the Caspian Sea comes the province of Gílán, the chief town of which is the city of Láhiján,[7] holding a population of 70,000 householders [or 31,500 souls]. The land is mountainous and rugged, also very unhealthy by reason of its great heat and dampness, which two principles,

## PROVINCES OF PERSIA

wheresoever they predominate, do breed corruption. The women of this province are very fat, and the men very feeble. There are some 30 townships, but none populous. The houses are built of wood, but from their situation on the mountain slopes may be well defended. Further north and lying along the western coast of the Caspian towards Bákú is the province of Eriván [or Shírván],[8] which extends for a distance of 100 Spanish leagues, and its people occupy 15 towns. The city of Eriván is its capital, holding a population of 50,000 householders [225,000 souls]. The country is very healthy, having a fine climate. Much silk is produced, and there is abundance of game, more especially deer, in its woods.

With the Caspian Sea lying on its northern and western quarters, and with Grand Tartary to the eastward, comes the province of Astarábád, which adjoins the province of Khurásán. The Astarábád province measures a bare 60 leagues in extent, and contains only 12 towns. The city of Astarábád has a population of more than 50,000 householders [or 225,000 souls], and boats come up to it from the Caspian Sea through a river estuary. Adjoining Astarábád comes the province of Mázandarán, which extends in length for 50 leagues, and has 25 towns. Its capital is Mázandarán,[9] with a population of 50,000 householders [or 225,000 souls]. The country is cold and very mountainous, so that no fruit here ripens. The province of Khurásán[10] is the largest of those which are subject to the king of Persia, for it extends in breadth for above 200 leagues. It includes more than 35 towns, each of great populousness, and its capital is the city of Herát, the population of which is so great that it exceeds 100,000 householders [4,500,000 souls]. With its gardens and pleasure-houses which lie adjacent beyond the city walls Herát measures a circuit of more than six leagues. The country round is a great plain, and is well populated. The townsmen are merchants who trade with India, Muscovy and the two dominions of Tartary. To the eastward again lies the province called Qandahár, and its people are vassals of Prester John. This country is very rich, and extends for some 60 leagues across. The chief city, which gives its name to the province, is Qandahár, with 70,000 householders [or 315,000 souls]. It is a hot country and the people here are merchants. On the south of Qandahár and somewhat to the eastward lies the province called Sístán, which measures 50 leagues across, and its chief city and capital is, like the province, called Sístán. It possesses 15 towns, and the population of its capital city numbers 50,000 householders [225,000 souls]. The country round is very damp and unhealthy, though mountainous, and the people are very warlike.

[In the north-west of Persia and] some distance to the south [of the Shírván province] lies the city of Ganjah, the chief town of the district bearing the same name.[11] This district in extent is barely 40 leagues across, it comprises seven or eight towns, and as regards Ganjah city the number of its householders may be some 50,000 [or 225,000 souls]; the town stands in a cold country, and the people are very warlike. Ganjah possesses a notable building, which I may here mention. This is a tower built up, from foundation to summit, with the skulls of Turks, and the number must exceed 50,000 heads. These are set in mortar among the stones of the tower, a monstrous sight. It was erected here by a certain Persian general named Khán Sayyid Oghlú[12] after he had conquered the Turks in a pitched battle at this place.

On the western border of Persia lies the province of Azerbayján, whose chief town is the famous city of Tabríz. This province and its capital are still in the power of the House of Ottoman, for the Turks here

## AZERBAYJÁN

have succeeded in getting the better of the Safavi monarchs of Persia. The province contains more than 30 cities, the largest being Tabríz, which, before the Turks had conquered and devastated it—as will be narrated fully later on—contained a population of over 80,000 householders [or 360,000 souls]. It is a pleasant land, with abundance of fruits, and with flocks of sheep like those seen in Spain, though here the beasts run to greater bulk: for the Persian sheep are as big as the calves with us in Spain, being a full quarter heavier in weight. The people of Azerbayján are very warlike and ever given to fighting, the nobles more especially. The province has an extent of 150 leagues across.

Further to the south-westward come the three provinces of Kurdistán, lying in the direction of Arabian 'Iráq or Babylonia. The nearer of the three provinces of Kurdistan, the one of which we now speak, marches with the province of Azerbayján, and its capital towns are the cities of Khoy and Salmás, whose combined population may amount to 30,000 householders [or 135,000 souls]. In the outlying parts of this province there are 15 other towns. The people here are not very civilized, and being warlike are given to constant fighting. They live half the year in their tents camped in the open country, after the fashion of the Moors [of Morocco], though otherwise they are quite unlike these latter folk. Further to the south-west lies the district of Malaga or Marághah, which is the second portion of the three Kurdistán provinces, and its chief town is Marághah. And again, this province marches with another which is likewise called Kurdistán, and of which the chief town is Khurramábád, but this town is more generally considered as of Luristán. The province of Babylonia or Arabian 'Iráq, known from its capital as the Baghdád province, lies westward beyond this again. The three provinces aforesaid of the

Kurdistáns measure some 300 leagues across at their extreme width; they are all very populous and their people are warlike, for never do they lack occasion for fighting against the Turks, their neighbours in Arabian 'Iráq. And from this point going south the Persian Gulf is the boundary of the province of Luristán, dividing it from the province of Ormuz.

Thus we have now brought to an end our description of the districts and lordships subject to the king of Persia. His state is confined on the northern side by the Caspian, on the south side by the Persian Gulf. In its greatest breadth the kingdom of Persia has for its western frontier Chaldea, Syria and Upper Mesopotamia—now known as Diyár-Bakr, and lying between the upper reaches of the Euphrates and the Tigris. From here the frontier goes north up to the limits of Gurjistán or Lesser Georgia, with Northern Tartary and that part of Muscovy which borders on the river Eder, more commonly known as the Volga. To the south of Persia extend the two countries called Desert Arabia and Happy Arabia. Wherefore if we should trace an imaginary frontier circle beginning from the Caspian Sea and going westward, this would pass down by the Lake of Gokchah[13] and thence along the Tigris bank to the Persian Gulf. From the eastern end of that gulf we shall pass up on the eastern quarter of Persia, northwards by the kingdom of Cambaya, which is near Makrán, and so meet the northern frontier which marches along the river Oxus, otherwise called Abiano.[14] Then we have made a complete circuit, including all the provinces subject at the present time to the crown of Persia, and this circuit would include a space so great as to measure more than 21 degrees of longitude from east to west, and more than 18 of latitude from north to south.

## CHAPTER III

*The way of government in Persia.*

THE method of government of the Persian kings being peculiar, we shall treat of the affairs of this kingdom in some detail in order to make the matter perfectly clear. The king of Persia for his support and guidance always has recourse to his nobles, this both for the service of his person, and for the government of the state in all affairs, both those pertaining to the administration of justice and to the conduct of war, and these two are the matters which in Persia take precedence over all others.

Now there are with us thirty-two clans or noble families recognized as having in Persia pre-eminence and the first place in the country. Their names are as follows: and the termination *lú*, which it will be noted concludes many of their names, shows that the clan in question is of, or belonging to, a chief of that name. To begin with, the Ustájlú are the clan in chief, and of them for the most part are the favourite servants of the king, and they always hold the great and honourable posts about his person. The Shámlú are as the grand chamberlains in Spain, and men of this family with us Persians always hold that office. Next come the Afshár: those of this name are mostly the presidents and ministers of justice. Next Turkomans: from these come the commanders, princes and generals, for they are great soldiers, and the kings of Persia have ever sought alliance in marriage with their families. Thus Sháh Tahmásp married a Turkoman princess. The family of Bayát: a most noble house and lineage, and all are, as we might say in Spain, dukes; so also are the family known as the Takkeh-lú clan. The Harmandalú are, as we might say, marquesses. The Dhúl-Qadarlú are as dukes, being a clan of warlike virtue and all very valiant men. The families of Qájar[1] and Qarámánlú are as dukes, and as counts those of Bayburtlú, Ispihrlú and Oriath. The Cháushlú are as dukes, the Assayshlú as counts, and likewise as counts are the following, namely, the Chamish-Qazaqlú, the Sarozolachlú, the Qárábachiqlú, the Barachlú, the Cuiniorilú, the Griclú, the Boschalú, the Hájí-Faqíhlú, the Hamzah-lú, the Solachlú, the Mahmúdlú, the Qárá-Chumaqlú and the Qárá Quyunlú.[2] As dukes are the Cossi-Boyezlú, the Peyclú, the Inazlú, and lastly the Kuh-Giluyahlú.

The government, as we have said, as a general rule is given into the hands of men of these families, and every governor appointed to any of the various cities, who is known with us in the Persian tongue as its *Hákim*, is invariably a nobleman, and is chosen from among the men of these clans. The *Darogahs*, or mayors of the towns, are of the same class, but these the king, when dissatisfied or angry with them, will change at pleasure. Criminals are judged and punished by being brought before the Grand Vazir, who is, as we should say in Spain, the Secretary of State, being of the Council; he gives injunction to his Deputy or *Vakíl*, who is, as we say here, the President, and, after the Grand Vizier, the chief minister. The matter is then brought before the king, but the king has deputed all minor details of justice to the governors and mayors of the various cities. In matters of policy and in affairs of state, and in all that pertains to war, the nobles and viceroys of provinces have jurisdiction, and they are called Kháns. The Kháns, though their offices are considered hereditary, for they hold them as though of their own property, are liable to be dismissed by the king at his pleasure, should

## GOVERNMENT OF PERSIA

they anywise be found in fault, for they are but his servants; and indeed all the Kháns and governors who serve the state holding positions of importance are liable to be arbitrarily dismissed at any moment. The Grand Chamberlain is known as the *Ishik-aqási-báshí*, and those next below him, his deputies, are known as the *Ishik-aqási*, for the word *Báshí* means "chief," and these last mentioned deputies are like the four Chamberlains in Ordinary to the king of Spain.³ The office of the Chief Porter is known as that of the *Qápúchí-báshí*; and between these officials that we have mentioned matters of criminal justice are judged, cases as they occur being summarily despatched.

As to how the king of Persia is attended, this is always on a scale of pomp and majesty, especially when the Court is in residence in the capital. For the most part, when the king goes out it is riding on horseback, and he will set forth to play the sport of tilting with the reed-spear, or to shoot with the bow at game. It is his wont to do this frequently, and at that time will have speech freely with the poorest of his subjects, and listen to any who may have need of him. But on no occasion does he ever go forth for sport or hunting accompanied by less than 12,000 mounted men, and of foot-soldiers he will always have about him more than 4,000 who are arquebusiers. At the king's table all the chief nobles who happen to be present, or are in attendance, take their meal with him.

The king's palace is known as the *Dawlat Khánah* or Government House, and the queen's palace is called the Harám; or rather we should have said the palace of the Queens is so called, for in the Harám there are more than four hundred ladies, which same is like the establishment known in Turkey as the Saray, and which we in Spain speak of as the *Ceralle*. This palace is guarded and served by above one hundred eunuchs, with two hundred squires, who are all old men of seventy years and upwards. The eunuchs they call in Turkish *Akhtah*, and the squires *Harám-Ishik-aqási*, or Masters of the Harám Threshold. If any other man besides these just mentioned should dare enter the palace of the Harám, he would be cut down, killed and cast forth to be burnt. The inner walls of the rooms of the palaces are adorned with paintings, and the like is found in the houses of the nobles. There is no tapestry on these walls, but there are very costly carpets on the floors, and such are known in Persian as *Qálí*. The dishes at meal-times are lain not on tables but on the floor, as notably it is the custom with all the nations of the Moors; and it is for this reason of the floor being so used, rather than as a custom of respect—and all must do so within the palace precincts—that on entering a room the shoes are always taken off.

## CHAPTER IV

*Of manners and customs peculiar to the kingdom of Persia.*

THE way of life of the common folk in Persia is much the same as that which obtains among other Mahomedan and Arabian nations, more particularly as to domestic rites and ceremonies, though in matters of religion—as we shall see later—the Persians hold peculiar views, for they opine that they alone are orthodox disciples of the Prophet Mahomed. The Persians among the nobility enjoy a plurality of wives, in fact these take as many wives as they please, but among the common people only seven are proper and allowed; divorce, on the other hand, is the everyday custom. The difference in dress which distinguishes the nobles from the common folk, is that the nobles alone are allowed to wear as their headgear the Turban ornamented with Twelve Points, which the first Sophi king Isma'íl instituted—as will more particularly be described later—and which in Persian is known as the *Táj* or "Crown." In Persia the clothes of all folk, to speak generally, are made of coloured stuffs, and there are few who do not wear silk, for this is quite cheap. Thus velvet of double and a half pile will hardly cost ten *reals* [less than six shillings] the yard, and eight yards of coloured taffeta, which may be of pearl-colour, can be had for five *reals*, or a *pesa* [namely, three shillings]. The price of muslin and linen goods, which same are imported in great abundance from India, is so moderate that 20 yards of either may be bought for a sum not exceeding four *reals* [half a crown], and this though the material be as fine as our holland of Cambray.

# DON JUAN OF PERSIA

The crops grown on most of the cultivated lands in the provinces of Persia are so abundant, namely and in particular wheat, barley and rice, that 100 pecks[1] of wheat may be bought for twelve *reals* [seven shillings], and the same quantity of barley for half a ducat [three and sixpence]. There are great numbers of water-mills all along the banks of the rivers and lagoons, these being made after the fashion of the water-wheels and mills that we see on the Tagus. Butcher's meat is mostly veal and mutton, the latter from the great sheep which, as already described, are a quarter heavier in weight than the Spanish sheep. We have in Persia rabbits,[2] partridges and other wild fowl in infinite quantity, but they do not eat the rabbit; there are also found deer in abundance, whose flesh is much esteemed. The wild beasts of the forest are seen in great numbers, and besides those met with in the hill country, may be come upon in the plains and sandy deserts, where many districts in the past have become depopulated. Such here are lions, tigers and bears, and in those parts none can journey but in company many together and riding on their camels, which are in Persia the usual beasts of burden.

The Persians make use of no waggons, coaches nor litters of any kind or sort; nor indeed are there any ships, or galleys for the more special purposes of navigation, and only a kind of light boat is in common use. Horses there are in abundance, and their coats are very fine, and indeed they resemble most the Andulacian horses of Spain. In staying powers they can go thirty hours without a feed of corn, and in skirmishing raids they will travel for a whole day and a night. The army for the greater part consists in cavalry, and they ride with the short stirrup,[3] but yet not so short as they are wont to use now in Spain. Their arms are lance and buckler, and they wear coats of mail and light breastplates with helmets[4] of thin

## THE ARMY IN WAR

steel plate, cunningly forged, and this armour is now produced throughout Persia in such quantity that much of it is exported into Muscovy, just as in Spain we import the like from the Milanese. The manner of mustering troops for war is for the chief of each of the noble families [whose names have been given on a former page] to call out eight, ten or twelve thousand horsemen of his clan and a like number of foot-soldiers armed with their arquebuses. Our wars are generally waged either against the Tartars or against the Turks, and sometimes against the two kings of the Georgians who are neighbours of Persia, though these last, for the most part, remain the humble vassals of the Persian king. They are indeed Christians of the Greek Church, but they hold to standing in friendship with the Persians, who show them tolerance in the matter of their Christian religion, for the king of Persia does not ever molest them in this respect, though the Turkish Sultan will continually be pressing them to become renegades. When the king of Persia personally goes out on campaign, the fact is advertised to all by his standard, which is then carried before him. Further, the umbrella of state is seen held over the king and his horse as he rides, and the same umbrella is adorned with precious stones, so that it glitters in splendour like the very sun. The number of troops present in the army is exactly known by the number of standards that are seen, for with every thousand men present a separate standard is unfurled, this being after the manner of the Roman Centuries, and thus there are as many thousand men present as there are standards to be seen. And such is the power of the king of Persia, as proved by what I myself have witnessed, that very easily he can call out 200,000 cavalry. On many of the campaigns, in the past that I have taken part in, I have counted two hundred standards displayed, and though the same number of flags may often be counted in any poor regiment of Spanish infantry, the fact with us here is of different import, for in Persia, unless there be one thousand horse or one thousand foot-soldiers present under arms, no standard is shown.

The Persian method of fighting is by challenging to single combat, with a trumpet sounded or a king-at-arms sent forward, and no ambush is allowed—though indeed, as to this matter, such is human guile, that in times past, but in remote and unknown or barbarous lands, much treachery of this sort, so contrary to all good custom, has not been unknown. Yet it may be affirmed in clear terms that the Persian way of fighting is now in open combat, in hand-to-hand battle; and as to their artillery, they mask it or hold it in reserve—as we shall see later when speaking of the wars between the Persians and the Ottoman Turks. The royal bodyguard is of infantry, and for the most part the men are Georgian renegades who are known as the *Tufangchis* or match-lock men, and these are like the Janissaries of the Turkish Sultan. The nobles are much addicted to the study of magic, and to what they call the Sacred Science, which is the Alcoran, in the Arabic language, and there are the Alfaquis [priests] and professors in most of the cities to instruct publicly in the same, who receive a suitable stipend. The houses throughout Persia are for the most part built of stone, though there are many that are built of wood, but all have terraced roofs and most have gardens after the fashion of Italy and Flanders. In the matter of curing disease they do as with other nations of the barbarians, using herbs and ordering a strict diet. In acute illnesses, such as in cases of quinsy, pleurisy and the like, they bleed. The people are very superstitious, being given to regarding auguries, and imagine that by praying in the mosque they can favourably affect, or at least prognosticate, the issue of all their maladies. Prayers more especially should be offered up in those

## FUNERAL CUSTOMS

mosques where the kings, the Grand Sophis are all buried, or some one of the great Kháns, or other person who in life was held to have been a saint; and so more particularly in the mausoleum of him whom they regard with much veneration, and whom they call Shaykh Sophi.[5]

The customs at funerals are very extraordinary, and they differ in many particulars from those of all other Mahomedan nations. If it be a person of some position who is dead, all his servants will march, naked to the waist, preceding the bier, each having made wounds in his right arm by scarifying the flesh all down the side; and the sons of the dead man have to do the same. Some two hundred men are harnessed by ropes that pull the bier; and thus they transport the body, and all these go reciting in a loud voice prayers and versicles and petitions that are addressed to the Prophet Mahomed. In front of these men march twenty boys, who, two by two, in turn bear on their shoulders a chair richly adorned, and as they go they recite the Alcoran of Mahomed. In front of these again march a number of men carrying small trees and green boughs from which hang down painted papers[6] and coloured ribbons, and such fruits as are in season. Coming after the procession follow the horses, all that the dead man possessed, each one led by the bridle in the hand of a groom, and these horses are fully caparisoned, and they carry the arms that the dead man used in war, and the trophies which he won in battle; and their grooms go naked to the waist and self-wounded with the blood streaming down from their shoulders. With all this company in attendance the procession marches on till they come to one of those stone troughs, which are in Persia like those we have in Spain for watering beasts. Then in such a trough they proceed to wash the corpse publicly, and next to wrap it in a piece of fine holland cloth. Afterwards the procession moves on as before, and to all the poor they may meet they distribute food, which same has been brought for this purpose laden on five or six camels. All this time with kettle-drums and trumpets they are making doleful music, the instruments being played held low and reversed. In this fashion they come finally to the graveyard out in the countryside, where the tombs are, in one of which they now proceed to lay the body, and next the procession returns to the city in the same order as the mourners set forth. For a whole year after his death the relations of the dead man are bound daily to go out to the grave and recite the Alcoran there and say many prayers.

The Persians pride themselves much on their poets, and these, though without art, compose an infinity of verses. They also have many books written in the Arabic language full of poesy and choice prose. All such verse-making, as is well known, and contrariwise, in the government of the Ottoman Sultan, is a strictly forbidden pastime, and is one universally contemned.[7] In Persia, however, as we have said, all write verses and illuminate them, and these the young men send to ladies with whom they are in love and are proposing to marry. Further, a Persian youth who wishes to pose as a faithful lover must behave in a very extraordinary way; indeed, so strangely that it were impossible for its very extravagance to pass the matter over in silence. The lover who would prove that his love is sincere must painfully burn himself in various parts of his person with a slow match made of linen stuff, that in effect acts exactly like the caustic which, with us in Spain, the surgeons apply for opening issues such as may be needful in the legs and arms. Then the lover displays himself in the sight of his lady, he being a very Lazarus for the number of his sores: whereupon she will send him cloths, napkins and bandages of silk or holland, with which to bind his wounds, and these he wears until they are cured. Later, he who can show

## MARRIAGE CUSTOMS

most signs of these cauteries is the one most beloved of the fair dames, and he most promptly will come to matrimony. Marriage and burial being two very notable incidents in every man's life, it seemed important not to pass over either in silence, but to note what in each case may be peculiar to the manners and customs of the Persians. In truth, both are events which in all countries, whether civilized or barbarous, characterize and pertain to the propagation and conclusion of existence. For are not these, as we might say, the one the prelude and means for bringing about the continuance of our race; while the other is as a fee and tribute that all must pay at the end, being a charge incumbent on whomsoever he be, who shall have lived through this mortal life ? Further, as to customs of both events, the manner in Persia is indeed most strange, they differing from those in use among all other peoples, whether of civilized states or of barbaric nations.

Now as regards marriage, when a Persian of good position in the state is about to wed, the day being fixed, all his relations and friends assemble at the house of the bridegroom. Nearly all are on this occasion dressed in clothes that seem to match in livery those of the bridegroom, but more particularly his groomsmen; the other guests likewise, if they can afford it, but otherwise any may appear in what is their common dress. The bride at the proper time comes forth from her home riding a horse after the Persian fashion, and her attendants, if they can compass it, are apparelled in clothes to match her livery; and the bride wears over her face a piece of taffeta on which is painted in gold the semblance of the sun or the moon. In front of her march many musicians playing on various kinds of instruments. The two processions now join company, and the bridegroom attending the bride, the whole concourse turns about and re-enters the bride's house.

Here there is a chamber set apart for the menfolk, and richly adorned, in which they begin a ball, somewhat after the fashion of the Italians or the French. The mode of the festival is that of different dances; and over the heads of each of the young men who may step forth to dance their friends throw in handfuls many small coins, which same none but the musicians who are playing may pick up. Thus, therefore, the musicians, as the young men step forth and dance, gather for themselves a rich harvest. The ladies dance in a separate room, and they are wont to have coins which are crown pieces stuck upon their foreheads—with a certain mucilage like the paste which we in Spain make of elm and almond gum—and these coins as the ladies move in dancing fall off, whereby this money too stands to the benefit of the musicians. On this account in Persia the musicians all become very rich by attendance at such balls and festivities.

When the dancing is done for the day, they all sit down to supper in the house of the bride; while on the following day they dine in the bridegroom's house, and on each occasion a very splendid assembly of guests is invited. On the first night, that of the supper, when the hour for retiring has come, two old women appear and with a show of violence catch hold of the bridegroom and bring him into the chamber of the bride. The bride then comes in by another door; and meanwhile the dancing of both the male and the female relatives at the ball continues till it is midnight. Then the two old women reappear, bringing with them a cloth stained with blood and show this to the relations of the bridegroom; and upon this all take their leave very contentedly. If, however, as to this cloth the contrary be the case, and no mark of blood can be shown, the two old women bring out the bride, and the bridegroom coming forth, scornfully and publicly repudiates her. But he then pays her a certain sum of

## THE GYPSIES

money, which for being but a trifle need not be specified, and they send her back to her parents, while the bridegroom marches home again with his friends and relations. In Persia, unlike other countries among the Mahomedan nations, there is never seen any great number of public women. The gypsies, or Egyptians, however, who live in the provinces of the frontier that neighbours Persia, enter our country in bands and troops—as did the Arabs into Spain aforetime—and they bring in their families with them; and among these their women make a livelihood by proſtitution. It is the cuſtom on these occasions for their husbands to take them to the house of any Persian with whom the woman has engaged to pass the night; and on the morrow the husband will duly appear to carry away his wife, with her looking-glass and paints and headgear and pins and belts, and he then receives the price ſtipulated for. But indeed this is a hideous and beſtial cuſtom to be thus tolerated among men who muſt be held to be beings possessed of a conscience. I myself at one time took occàsion to enquire of the Egyptian folk who inhabit the country where these public women come from, and they told me that no man there would marry a girl unless she would promise and undertake to feed and clothe her future husband with gains made in this abominable commerce. But now this is enough, forsooth, of the manners and cuſtoms of the kingdom of Persia.

## CHAPTER V

*As to the antiquity of the Persian kingdom and the origin of the Monarchy.*

ONE of the regions of the world which, after the Universal Deluge, was first to receive its population, was the territory which now the Turks call Baghdad, which same is Babylonia. As some authorities would have it, this land owed its settlement to Nimrod, son of Cush and grandson of Ham, in the year 150 after the Flood; which, however, is not an account that seems credible. We therefore, to avoid an erroneous conclusion, should prefer for our information to rely on the excellent authority of the Susianian Library, further on the Oriental Annals of Belochus,[1] and other such eminent ancient authorities. Therefore we now say that Babylon being founded in the year 1700 of the Creation, Belus, son of Nimrod, was the first king of Babylonia; and coming to the Plains of Shinar, he peopled the country there about, together with that country which lies more to the eastward. Procopius, however, states —though the matter appears to rest on no reliable foundation—that the father of Belus was Saturn, and that Saturn is identical with Noah. In the eighth year of the reign of Nimrod, his brother Sheba, the son of Cush and grandson of Ham, was sent by Noah (his great-grandfather) to people Arabia—and with him went Gag with his sons Ganges and Indus, who subsequently gave their names to those two famous rivers of India; and Sheba named those same provinces of Arabia after himself, Sabæa.

In the Babylonian monarchy Belus was succeeded by Balæus,[2] or Beleus the Less, in the year 1753 after the creation of the world: according to the historian

# BABYLONIA

Megasthenes. He conquered all the Eastern Indies, and most of the nations that had settled in the south and in the two Arabias: whereby, from this time onwards, the nations that had there grouped themselves together are styled monarchies by those authors who treat of their affairs. Thus the years went on, but much is related in the histories that is not here to our purpose, till it came to the year 2000 after the Creation, when the Babylonian monarchy was ruled by Ascatades, and next Mamuthos, whom we may count as the 13th king of Babylonia according to the reckoning of Berosus. From this point onwards we get more light as to the succession of these princes, for matters come clearer and there are more authorities to consult, and so we reach the year 2325 after the creation of the world with Machchalatheus, who was king, occupying the throne of Assyria during a reign of thirty years. To him succeeded Sphærus, 15th king of Babylonia, in the year 2350 after the Creation, and at this time, according to the authority of the Susianian Library, they began to give the name of Assyria or Syria to this upper region and monarchy, the name coming from Syris, the son of Abraham.[3] In the foregoing account we have followed the authors above mentioned, on whom we mostly rely for our information, but if we are to give credit to the historian Belochus, Syria, until the time when Cyrus established the seat of his government in Persia, was the name given to all the region of the south that was subject to Babylonia. Next, according to Lucian of Samosata, it was in the third year after the birth of Moses, corresponding with the year 2375 after the Creation, that Mamuthos became monarch of Babylonia, reigning for thirty years, and to him succeeded Aschalius, who was the 18th king of Babylon; and it was, they say, in the tenth year of his reign that Moses brought forth the Hebrew people out of their captivity. Lucian of Samosata continues the history of these kings with the name of Belochus the Second, in the year 2530 after the Creation, who, he says, reigned for twenty-five years, making Sosares his contemporary, though other authorities state that he succeeded Belochus. In the seventh year of the period, when Deborah judged Israel, Lampraes began to reign in Babylon and governed, they say, for thirty years. To him followed Pannas in the year 2677 after the Creation, who occupied the throne during forty-five years. Then came Sosarmus, who was succeeded by Teutamus, otherwise Tautanes, who was contemporary with Jephtha of Holy Writ, celebrated as the Captain of the Hebrew People. To Teutamus followed Teutaus, but his reign was in truth shorter than some authorities have stated. Next was Timeus, who reigned for thirty years, and he was succeeded by Dercylus, who was the 31st king of Babylon, and approximately a contemporary of King David; to him following Eupacmes, shortly after the time when Solomon had begun to build the Temple. Then came Laosthenes, then Pertiades, next Ophrataeus, and then Acraganes, whose reign lasted forty-two years.

The Persian historian Megasthenes—and it is he whom we have chiefly followed in the above list of kings—closes his chronological survey with King Sardanapalus, to whom he assigns a reign of fifteen years and calls him by the name of Thonus-Concolerus. Now the Greek historians state that he was the son of Anacyndaraxis, and according to Suidas he was the direct descendant of Ninus and Semiramis. If, however, we follow the account given by Suidas there had been 38 kings between Nimrod and Sardanapalus, and their names are to be found in the writings of Ctesias, an author on whom we may confidently rely. The end and ruin of Sardanapalus we shall describe presently, but first we would explain why this ancient history of the Babylonian kings has been here given by us in

## PERSIAN MONARCHY

such detail. This was in order that the antiquity of the Persian monarchy might be clearly established, as also the ancient status of its people. For we find that when King Teuthanes arrived with aid for King Priam of Troy, being in fact his vassal, coming at the head of an army of 10,000 Ethiopians from Arabia, he brought with him also a like number of men from Susiana with 200 war chariots, and these all came under the command of Menon, son of Titon their captain, who was governor of Persia.[4] Then again in the year 2690 after the Creation we observe two notable facts. The first is that, already at this date, the province bears the distinctive name of Persia, and is a province of itself, being one of the chief districts of the kingdom of Babylonia and of the Assyrian monarchy. And the second fact is that there were then already Princes governing opulent districts in Persia, for Menon was a Persian prince, and Titon, his father, was the Governor of Persia, they being by descent, or by affinity of blood-relationship, in the right line of the Babylonian kings. All this I should not venture to state were it not set down clearly in the writings of Berosus and Megasthenes, being a tradition found in the Eastern Annals of Belochus and in the Books of the Susianian Library. Thus the antiquity of Persia as a kingdom is proved to be only a little less than the antiquity of the kingdom of Assyria, and the Persian kings in descent are even as the kings of Babylon; and therefore, if the Babylonian monarchs may take pride in being descended from Nimrod, the monarchs of Persia may pride themselves on the same fact. In truth it must be admitted, however, that we find no earlier mention than this of the kingdom of Persia, or the name of any Persian prince before the days of Lampraes and Pannas, who flourished in the year 2670 after the Creation. Still, there are those authors aforesaid who indirectly refer to Persia, before this date, as being already a separate province, with its Princes who were Governors of the same, namely, Titon and Menon, given as nephews and cousins of the kings of Assyria and Babylonia. Our authorities, we may add, completely fail to tell us how the province of Persia came to be so named, and our readers must lay the fault for the omission in this particular at the charge of the Chaldean and Greek historians, whom we have named above.

## CHAPTER VI

*In which is continued the genealogy of the Persian kings.*

IN the foregoing chapter we have mentioned that Sardanapalus was the laſt king of the Babylonians, and his ruin came about in the following manner, if we are to credit the ſtory as given by Megaſthenes. King Sardanapalus held his court in the well-known city of Nineveh, so famous for its immense population, and among his captains there were two who governed in his name, superintending the affairs of war. These were Arbaces, a very valiant soldier, and Belesys, the captain commanding in Babylonia. Now Belesys was a great aſtrologer, and he had knowledge by that science that the end was imminent of the monarchy of the kings of Assyria of the family of Sardanapalus. We may indeed believe that God, to serve His divine purpose, did thus ordain that this man should be able to trace out and get to know what was to come to pass; and though I myself do place very little credence in aſtrology as a science, yet I in no wise should venture to discredit its general principles. In this case, however, I deem the faɕts are manifeſtly certain, and that those two valiant captains, further coming to know that Sardanapalus was sunk in disgraceful vice—living the life of a woman rather than that of a man, in fact behaving as a brute beaſt and not as should behave a great prince—it became clear to them that it were necessary to bring about some change in the State. For it is patent that the firſt sign of the ruin of any dynaſty is when the monarch takes to viciousness and behaves like a silly woman. Indeed, let those who govern note well how great a curb on evil-doers is in effeɕt the sight of a prince who, being virtuous and severe, has ever about him a majesty of presence.

To continue, therefore, we learn that Belesys having taken counsel with Arbaces—or Arbates, as some give the name—the two conspired, and it was agreed that Belesys should come and see with his own eyes what Sardanapalus did and how he lived. According to one account it is affirmed that these officers found him seated among the two thousand women whom he kept in company about him, and that he was spinning at a wheel, his beard shaved off, a woman's golden coif on his head, bracelets on his arms and earrings in his ears. On seeing this state of things the two captains broke out cursing the king, whom, up to then, they had held in all reverence; and in disgust at the sight of the effeminate wretch whom they had hitherto faithfully served, they both now threw off their allegiance. Declaring war on him, and at the head of a mighty army of Babylonians and Medes—the Persians not joining in, but remaining neutral—the two captains forthwith began the campaign and appeared in rebellion. Sardanapalus now at length, but all too late, set himself at the head of his army, urged thereto by his brother-in-law Salamenus, but Sardanapalus being more at home in matters of pleasure than in the conduct of war, no sooner had the trumpets sounded the charge than he turned his back on the foe, and retired to shut himself up in Nineveh. Of the army, he gave over the command to his brother-in-law Salamenus, deputing him to lead the troops in the battle on which his life and fortune must depend; and here that valiant man Salamenus lost his life, but not his honour, for that indeed he died to keep.

Encouraged by their victory in the field, the conspirators now proceeded to lay siege to Nineveh, where the cowardly king had shut himself up; who, finding he was at last being abandoned by those in whom he

## SARDANAPALUS

had trusted aforetime, and seeing the number of his enemies daily increase, determined to die by his own hand rather than fall alive into the power of Arbaces and Belesys. Thus, to end his days as he had lived, he caused all his rich raiment and jewels to be brought together—and it is said these were of an infinite number—and setting all on fire, thus burnt himself and them on a pyre in the middle of the great square of Nineveh. Shortly after this the capital capitulated to the arms of the conspirators, and all the neighbouring cities then were conquered, but Belesys, now seeking under cloak of pious intention to appropriate to himself the major part of the booty in Nineveh that had not been already burnt in the fire, fell out with his fellow conspirator, and the friends were on the point of becoming declared enemies. Almost it came to be that the power which they had thus gained in the affairs of state was lost; but not so: and of all this we need say no more to avoid prolixity in telling the story of the fall of Sardanapalus. Finally Arbaces pardoned his friend, and on partitioning the provinces Belesys became Satrap of Babylonia, Arbaces taking for himself Media and Persia, of which last he proclaimed himself the king. Throughout all his reign, however, troubles were never lacking to him in regard to his lieutenant who governed the peoples of Syria and Palestine.

Thus from Nimrod to Sardanapalus the line of kings had continued unbroken, and during 1,370 years they had held empire over Syria, Babylonia, Persia and Media. But from the time when Arbaces came to the throne, and for some time afterwards, the government of Media and Persia was in the hands of tyrants, the land being ruled by satraps during the next 340 years: even until the date when Cyrus and Darius, transferring the seat of their empire to Persia, made that province the headpiece in the State, as we shall set forth in the following chapter.

## CHAPTER VII

*In which is continued the line of succession of the kings of Persia.*

IN the year 528 before Christ there was born Cyrus the Great, who proclaimed himself the world autocrat and emperor of Persia. He was succeeded by Cambyses, after whom followed the two Magi brothers [Smerdis and Pausoutes]. Next in succession came Darius I, Xerxes I, Artaxerxes I, Xerxes II, called Sogdianus, Darius II, surnamed Nothus, Artaxerxes II, Mnemon, who is said to be that Ahasuerus who is named in the Scriptures, though it appears that of this attribution there is not much foundation in fact. After him came Ochus, or Occus, and next Artaxerxes III, although many deny the existence of this Artaxerxes, which indeed we think the more reasonable view. According to some we should place a certain Arses before the last Artaxerxes, and after him, they say, came Darius III, who was succeeded by Alexander the Great. The Persian monarchy next passed into the hands of the two Ptolemies—namely, Ptolemy Philadelphus and Ptolemy Euergetes—and then the line became extinct. Now the empire of Cyrus the Great and his successors, which lasted during 309 years, in the blindness of the faith of the Gentiles had by its extension, and greatly to its honour, spread over the eastern quarters, also to the south and to the north, conquering all the famous kings and princes thereof during the Fifth Age. After this Age followed the Roman Empire with the grandeur of its superb armies and their many great captains, by whose victories and labours the greater part of Europe and Asia, and even a portion of Africa, came under the sway of Rome, thus inaugurating the Sixth

## CÆSAR AUGUSTUS

Age, in which appeared on earth the Prince of Peace, Jesus Christ.

At that time the second lord universal of the world as then discovered, who was the great Octavianus Augustus Cæsar, ordered the opening of the gates of the Temple of the Two-faced Janus, as a sign of universal peace; though some authorities do assert that it was shutting, not opening, those gates that was the sign thereto. In this question, however, we may best follow the account of Virgil, in his panegyric of the Emperor, though indeed he is rather a poet than a reliable chronicler. There is one more matter which is not the least indeed of the honours pertaining to the Persian kingdom, with the mention of which we shall end our account of those of her kings who reigned before the time when Christ Jesus was born into the world. If we may rely on the assertion made by the poet Juvencus in the first book of his *Evangelical History*,[1] it is there by him clearly stated that those three Saints, the Kings of the Magi, who came to adore Christ the Eternal King of kings, all three were kings, and that two of them were from Persia, while the third, who was dark skinned, was from Arabia. Now this account does not alone rest on the authority of Juvencus, but is confirmed by the writings of Saint Basil and by the works of that great Doctor of the Greeks, Athanasius, also by Chrysostom, Theodoretus and Nicephorus. Saint Antoninus on the other hand, it must be said, makes all three Kings of the Magi to come from Media and from the city of Vixaria; while Peter Apianus asserts that they all were from that Arabia called Felix. In any case it is the more reasonable that this matter should be understood in the anagogic, mystical and moral sense, as it may well be: for were the Magi not indeed happily the first men to merit the privilege of recognizing and paying their adoration to the Word made flesh, Jesus, God incarnate, thus clothed in our human nature? A fact so great and so divine, that His omnipotence alone could have compassed it, while it was the love He bore for men that, so to speak, forced on Him the accomplishment of the same. And thus was born into the world Christ Jesus, the Saviour, the King of kings, while outwardly the earthly monarchy was in the hands of Octavianus Augustus.

In Persia and Media there ruled at this period governors, and princes under the name of satraps, all subject in point of fact to Rome; we may therefore consider Augustus to have been at that period the actual king of Persia, even if we allow the opinion of those who assert that the three Magi were not indeed Persian kings. For the Emperor Octavianus Augustus was supreme in the government, appointing his exarchs and viceroys throughout those eastern provinces, even as in after times the Greek Emperors of Constantinople appointed the like governors in the west throughout Italy, where these held their courts in Rome and Ravenna, being acknowledged there and obeyed just as though they had been truly the native lords of those districts. We conclude, therefore, averring that Octavianus Augustus was the last king of Persia before the date of the coming of Christ into the world, and the first of those to reign there after His birth. Not, indeed, that Augustus Cæsar was the native king of Persia, but that he, so to speak, continued the line of succession of their kings until the rise of the new monarchy under Artaxerxes [or Ardashir Babegán the first Sassanian]: or, as others would have it, and as we shall explain shortly, till the time when the first Sapor became king of Persia. This statement we freely make, but at the same time hold to our opinion that the three Kings of the Magi—so called—were in fact and deed the princes who themselves and in their family carried on the succession of the Persian royal

## THE THREE MAGI

line during the age when no kings are chronicled—
namely, from Ptolemy Euergetes down to Sapor;
and during this interregnum we consider that they were
in truth Persian monarchs, and though subjects for
the time being to the Emperors Octavianus Augustus
and Tiberius Cæsar, this in no wise militates against
their right to be accounted kings in Persia.

## CHAPTER VIII

*In which the genealogy of the Persian kings is continued, and it is shown who first preached the Gospel in Persia.*

WE are told in the Sacred Scriptures how the Apostles were sent forth through all the provinces of the world to preach, and from Perionus and Abdias[1] we learn that to Saint Judas Thaddæus, and to Saint Simon the brother of Saint James, the lot fell to carry the Gospel into Persia and Media. The fruit of their preaching was such that 70,000 persons received baptism. Now at that time Xerxes was reigning in Persia,[2] who was also king of Babylonia, and he was then waging war against the Jewish people. So the two glorious Apostles coming thither, forthwith were brought before Barardach, the general of Xerxes—who, according to the account given by Berosus, was the last Xerxes who reigned in Persia—and thereupon the Apostles had great disputations with Zaroes and Arfaxat, two of the Magian priests, who were also magicians. The diabolic obstinacy of these men was in the end overcome, and Abdias afterwards was consecrated Bishop of Babylon, where subsequently again more than 20,000 persons were baptized.

Next through the power of the Cross the whole of that country mercifully came to be delivered from a plague of small but very poisonous serpents, which same the winds had brought, even as in Egypt it is a plague of flies and locusts that may appear. But the Demon could not suffer in peace the conversion of so many souls to the Christian faith, and he forthwith raised up against those two glorious Princes of the

# CHRISTIAN MARTYRS

Church a persecution which did not rest, and in the end they both were delivered up to death, their martyrdom taking place, as the Church office has duly recorded, in the city of Suanyr. Persia none the less was sanctified by the first-fruits celestial bestowed on her by those Captains of the Gospel army, and their teaching scattered the seed of the faith throughout the whole of that land, as we see clearly by the many persecutions which afterwards took place there. Then in later times also the Church suffered—namely, from the days of Nero to those of Valerian and Gallienus, in which period more than a million Persians accepted martyrdom, willingly dying rather than that they should be apostates from the baptism that they had received. Wherefore, placing my hope in God, may it soon come to pass that through the intercession of all these sainted martyrs, all natives of Persia, that the miserable blind Persians of to-day, who in such numbers must be on the way to Hell, may find salvation. Thus let it be, even though Persia haply should have no other glorious example to her credit than that which Nicephorus Callistus mentions in Book VIII, chapter xxxvii, of his great *History*,[3] where he relates how one hundred Persian bishops suffered martyrdom together rather than deny the name of Christ. By this same example God Almighty will, we hope, bring about the ultimate salvation of our dear country and native land. But so many indeed are the martyrdoms suffered throughout Persia in the days of that barbarous and warlike King Sapor II—as recorded in Book III of the *Tripartite History*—that I must needs pass most of them by in silence, for their number is beyond count. He, however, who would care to know of the more notable facts concerning the Christian martyrs of Persia, let him turn to the account written by Esaias, son of Adabus,[4] a gentleman of the court of King Sapor II, who narrates the martyrdom of Barasichius and Jonas[5] with thirteen others, during the thirteenth persecution of the Church [in A.D. 327]. Here the reader will find notable and wondrous facts narrated. Surius[6] also has touched on this matter in his works, but only very succinctly.

Patriotic sentiment for my native land and its affairs has thus far led me somewhat astray from the principal subject of this chapter, which is to continue to expound the chronology of the kings of Persia. In this matter our various authorities often recount events very differently; but we may turn to Agathias, who in Book II of his *History* relates an anecdote which, though it may in sooth be merely an unauthentic legend, yet, coming from so respectable an authority, we shall here transcribe, as being, we think, founded on an historical incident currently known at that time among the Persian people. It is related that in the days of the Roman Emperor Alexander Severus, the son of Mammæa, and in the fourth year of his reign [Ardashír I whom the Greeks call] Artaxerxes founded the dynasty of the Sassanian monarchs of Persia, and the origin of this man Ardashír was after this wise. There lived in those days near the shores of the Caspian Sea in Hyrcania a certain man, and he was of such lowly condition, according to Agathias,[7] that I shall not mention his trade here, but he was at the same time a great astrologer and magician, his name being Bábek. To the house of this man there came for lodging a soldier, whose name was Sásán, and Bábek by means of his astrology and magic learnt of a certainty that from the son of this man Sásán would descend a line of great kings and princes. Thereupon Bábek, wishing to have this honour for his own, and that his descendants should be those of the son of the man Sásán, and having no daughter of his own to give Sásán in marriage, yet sought to compass it that the other should become as it were his son-in-law: for he was most ambitious that the honour foretold by the horoscope should be his. Bábek thereupon resolved on an act more vile and base than ever man before had done —namely, to give his own wife to Sásán in wedlock. To this extremity his wicked and bestial ambition having driven him, next innocently, and not knowing that it was in adultery, Sásán lived for several months with the wife of Bábek as her husband. She was in due time delivered of a boy, to whom the name of Ardashír was given, though that he should bear this name became the cause of a lawsuit, for the real husband of his mother, namely Bábek, wished that the boy, though a bastard, should be called Bábek after himself.

We know that God Almighty is wont to chastise the arrogance of the proud, making them to suffer an affront through the very honours which they have sought to gain by evil acts; and through what they hope the more therein to prosper, do they the less profit in the end. After this fashion the brutish Bábek was indeed thus abased by that same honour which he had sought to gain for himself. While the lawsuit about the name was being carried on before the judges of those barbarous times, the boy grew up, coming to years of discretion, and then learning the truth, held in abomination the vile act of his mother's husband. He therefore determined to call himself Ardashír, not Bábek; and afterwards, by effort of his genius in a short while he came to what had been predicted. As history relates, Artabanus [the last king of the Parthian Dynasty] was slain by this same Ardashír, who, assuming the style and title of king of all the land, became the first of the Sassanian monarchs of Persia, and reigned for fifteen years. This therefore was the origin and beginning of the third epoch and restoration of the Persian State. We, however, must confess that we scarce know whether to give credit to the foregoing story, which we shall now leave to our readers without further comment. Ardashír was succeeded by King Sapor I, and he it was who took the Emperor Valerian a prisoner of war, afterwards carrying him about with him everywhere in chains, and mounting his steed standing on the Emperor's shoulders [as on a horse-block]: a very ignominious and not small affront to put upon him who was imperial lord of the Greeks and Romans. This Sapor, it is said, also overran all Mesopotamia, Cilicia, Syria and Cappadocia, for he had at his bidding an army more powerful than ever barbarian prince commanded before his days. It is on record that in order to pass through any mountainous country he was wont to fill up the valleys and plains and gorges, bringing the lowlands up to the level of the heights by throwing into the hollows the dead bodies of his enemies—namely, of those whom he had killed in battle. At the end of a reign of thirty years, however, he was murdered at the hands of Odenathus, the celebrated prince of Palmyra, who, it is reported, in his early days had been but a common soldier. Sapor left a son who succeeded him as Hormisdas I, but his reign only lasted one year and ten days. Then his son, again, named Varahrán I, followed, who reigned three years; and after him came his son Varahrán II, who reigned ten years; Varahrán III following next, who bore the surname of Segestáni,[8] from the country [of Segestán or Sístán] which had been conquered by the second Varahrán, his father. To him followed Narses, who reigned seven years and seven months, when his son Hormisdas II[9] succeeded, who reigned another period of the same length. He it is who was the father of that famous barbarian king Sapor II whose reign lasted seventy years, and whose birth, with the horoscope of his reign, were together so astonishing; for he was king before he was born, the circumstances being as follows.

## SAPOR II

When Hormisdas died, it was found that his wife was with child, and the Persian nobles, wishing to know whether the infant to be born would be a boy, took counsel of the Magi and astrologers. These gave answer that it was a male child whom the queen carried in her womb. The nobles, however, not being persuaded that the truth could be known thus for certain, brought a mare who was with foal before those same Magi, saying that if they could foretell truthfully the sex of the foal of which the mare was pregnant, credit would then be given to what they and the astrologers had prognosticated to be the case in regard to the queen—such being the superstitious incredulity of those blind Persians. The Magi on this affirmed that the foal that the mare carried in her belly was a horse-colt; upon which, having killed her and opened her body, they found the case in fact to be as the Magi had foretold. Thus satisfied, the nobles brought in the royal crown, and holding it over the body of the recumbent queen, swore allegiance to the son whom she should bear, and in due time after this ceremony Sapor II was born. He was indeed a second Attila, for it was he who besieged the city of Nisibis in Mesopotamia, being the contemporary of the Emperor Julian the Apostate, and of Jovian, who reigned after him. It was this same Sapor whose army, when that king was besieging the above-named city, God Almighty destroyed with a plague of innumerable flies, sent against them at the prayer of Saint James, at the time bishop of Nisibis. Sapor II was succeeded by his brother Ardashír II, and some authorities state that by force he took the sceptre from Sapor in the latter's lifetime; but be that as it may, this Ardashír only occupied the throne during a reign of four years. He was succeeded by his son Sapor III, who was king of Persia for fifteen years, and who was followed by his son Varahrán IV, whose reign lasted eleven. To him succeeded his son Yazdagird I, the Persian king who was so great a friend to the Emperor Arcadius that he appointed him at his death to be guardian of his son the Emperor Theodosius II.

Yazdagird reigned for twenty-one years, and was succeeded by his son Varahrán V, who reigned twenty years. The writer Juan de Tornamira, in his *Chronologia*, it is true gives this Varahrán a reign of only seventeen years, and some authorities insert here the name of another king of Persia [namely, Yazdagird II] following Varahrán V. Then after him ruled Perozes,[10] the rash and vainglorious monarch who came to his death in the concealed trench which, as a trap, the Ephthalites had dug for his destruction. The authorities give him twenty years of reign, but it cannot indeed have been as long as this. He was followed on the throne of Persia by Vahán,[11] and then by Qobád, the latter being the son of Perozes. We shall conveniently end this chapter with the account of why King Qobád subsequently fled for shelter to these same Ephthalites. The Persians were always jealous for their wives, that being a very ancient characteristic of the men of this nation. Qobád, however, to satisfy his lust, and to serve him in a certain particular case, caused a law to be promulgated ordaining that all women whatsoever and wheresoever should be held in common, and any woman might belong to any man who should desire her. The men of Persia, however, felt the outrage in the matter of this ordinance so strongly, that they would have put the king to death had he not forthwith fled the country. But this having happened, in the event they were satisfied with banishing and deposing him, and giving the crown to Balas or Palash,[12] who some say was the uncle of Qobád, while according to others he was his brother. Qobád, however, shortly afterwards returned from his banishment, having married the daughter of the king

## QOBÁD

of the Ephthalites, and he was supported by a mighty army. Balas in consequence had to vacate the throne, and Qobád restored, then governed in peace for thirty years, dying in the fifth year of the reign of the Emperor Justinian. He was succeeded by Chosroes, the first king of Persia of that name.

## CHAPTER IX

*In which the genealogy of the Persian kings is continued, with curious details that are apposite to the case.*

THE first Chosroes [known as Anushirván] was one of the greatest kings that ever ruled Persia. No day of quiet did he let the Emperor Justinian, who was at that time ruling in Constantinople, enjoy. Among the rest it were enough to recall that memorable invasion of the Greek Empire which Chosroes brought about in the year 577 after Christ. On this occasion the number of the Persian troops was so great that the cavalry alone were counted at over 15,000, and it was then that Daras, a very famous city on the frontiers of the Greek Empire, was taken. But matters on the return home of Chosroes after this incursion were not so favourable to him, for Justin, who was Justinian's nephew[1] and Captain-General of the Greeks, encouraged by the valour of Kurs, the commander of the Scythian right wing of the Imperial army, now attacked Chosroes, when his men fell back in much disorder with a slaughter of so many among the Persians that it was never possible exactly to discover the number of those slain. In that battle, too, Chosroes lost what was of much more importance even than the men who fell, for the Imperialists in defeating him took possession of the Sacred Brazier of the Fire God, a piece of jewelwork greatly valued by the Persians, who worship the Fire as their Divinity. When therefore it was known that this Brazier had been lost, such Persian troops as still remained under arms mutinied and would have put Chosroes to death, intending to desert his standard. Chosroes, however, succeeded fortunately at last in quelling this mutiny, and withdrawing his army under

# CHOSROES I

cover of night, sought refuge in the city of Melitene. He afterwards crossed back over the Euphrates, which river he forded riding an elephant, and thus finally found himself in safety from the attack of his enemy.

Then peace was made, and Chosroes promulgated a law which he decreed was to be observed by all his successors, and the nobles of the kingdom were by its terms bound on oath in future to prevent any Persian troops being sent to fight against the Greek Emperor or his generals outside the limits of the Persian Empire. The Greeks, however, were not to be restrained by the proclamation of any such ordinance, being made arrogant by reason of the victory they had gained. The Emperor Justinian in the lapse of time was succeeded on the throne by Tiberius II, and he depriving Justin of the post of Captain-General of the armies, conferred this charge on Maurice, who forthwith proceeded to overrun and devastate the Persian lands, where he slew Tamchosro, a brave Persian commander, and would have done the like to his fellow captain Adarman had he not made his escape by flight. Then Maurice, following on his retreating foes, victoriously entered the kingdom of Persia, burning and ravaging the countryside till he had crossed the river Zirma, coming to the Argian Fields [on the banks of the river Araxes]. Here he found himself within sight of Chosroes, who by reason of the great heat of that summertide had retired to the territories of the Carduchians [in Kurdistán]. From this, his place of retreat, the Persian king could see the flames and the smoke of the burning hamlets which continued to be set on fire by soldiers of the Greek army, where they had crossed into the Persian territories.[2] This sight so affected Chosroes that, causing himself in haste to be carried back to Seleucia on the Tigris, he died there shortly afterwards of his chagrin.

# DON JUAN OF PERSIA

Chosroes was succeeded on the throne by his son Hormisdas IV, to whom the Emperor Tiberius, being at this time fully occupied with his wars in Italy, now sent to make overtures for peace. The Byzantine historian Zonaras, an author to be relied on, states that the Persian monarch in his barbarian pride refused at first to treat, although the Emperor Tiberius had sent him as ambassador Justinian [son of Germanus], who was Captain-General of his armies. But finally an armistice was agreed upon to last three years, though the faithless Hormisdas very shortly afterwards broke the peace by invading Armenia and ravaging all this countryside, which was then under the protection of the Greek Emperor. In the year 584 after Christ, however, when Maurice had succeeded to the Empire, to whom Tiberius aforetime had given his daughter Maria in marriage, and who now was reigning in the room of his father-in-law—Maurice (I say) three times over gave check to the audacious Persians, causing them to retire, and next he ejected them in headlong rout from the city of Martyropolis, which they had recently taken from the Greeks by a double treachery on the part of the traitor Sittas. The Persian captains were much humiliated by the very disgraceful loss of this town, and fearing to appear before their cruel master King Hormisdas, retired with their beaten army to the city of Nisibis, where they took counsel what to do. It was thereupon agreed that they should raise the standard of revolt against Hormisdas, and they chose for their leader Varahrán [better known as Bahrám Chúbín], a valiant soldier, who many times already had fought against the Turks, at that date a new unknown nation who were now invading Persia on the eastern frontier. This Bahrám Chúbín promptly undertook the charge laid on him, and acting for the public good put Hormisdas to death, together with his wife and certain of his sons.

## BAHRÁM CHÚBÍN

The Emperor Maurice, however, showed favour to Chosroes, the eldest of the sons of Hormisdas, who had escaped death at the hands of the conspirators, and the Emperor aided him with troops. Whereupon Chosroes made his attack on Bahrám Chúbín and his companions the Persian traitors, whom certain of those Turks had joined in the conspiracy, and in the result the Persian royal troops, supported by the Greek army, defeated and slew Bahrám Chúbín with all those traitors in a great battle. A curious matter is mentioned by Fray Juan de Pineda,[3] who may, I think, have taken it from the historian Zonaras, which is that these Turks aforesaid, who were at that time crass idolaters—for naturally this was long before they had become Mahomedans—none the less bore on their foreheads the mark of a cross. On it being asked of them why, as Gentiles and unbelievers, they should bear this Christian sign on their heads, it was answered by some that when in past time there had been a terrible pestilence in their country, the people had been cured by the Sign of the Cross, which a certain Christian missionary had brought and laid on them. Again, Saint Antoninus, the Archbishop of Florence, relates what it would be hard to credit were it not set down in Part III, chapter iv, of his well-known work the *Chronicorum Opus*, being to the effect that King Chosroes was so much the friend of the Emperor Maurice that the latter gave him one of his daughters in marriage, who after becoming his wife brought it about that Chosroes let himself be baptized as a Christian. Now this possibly may be true, but withal I know not how if this Chosroes were really a Christian he could be the same monarch who later devastated Syria, Palestine and Phœnicia, with Armenia, Cappadocia and Paphlagonia, even coming up to Chalcedon, which stands over against Constantinople.

But be this as it may, what alone needs to be related

in the present case is that the Emperor Maurice having come to be murdered by Phocas, who then for a time occupied the purple, Heraclius in due course compassed the death of Phocas, and thus becoming Emperor, was publicly crowned in Constantinople together with his wife Eudocia, otherwise known as Fabia: all this in the year 612 of our Redemption. The reign of Heraclius lasted for thirty years, and in the following chapter we shall tell of the events which took place during this period, as between Chosroes and the Emperor Heraclius. We shall conclude our account in the present chapter by mentioning a fact which Matthæus Palmerius has recorded in his book called the *Chronicon*—namely, that when this Heraclius became Emperor of Constantinople, in Spain the famous Visigothic king Sisebut was his contemporary.

## CHAPTER X

*Which continues and concludes the genealogy of the ancient kings of Persia.*

CHOSROES [II, surnamed Parvíz] was the great rival of Heraclius, and Chriſtianus Massæus,[1] in Book XIII of his *Chronicles*, relates that the Persian king feeling himself now to be more powerful than his neighbour, three times over rejeċted the offers of peace which Heraclius made him, refusing also to accept the rich gifts which, if we are to credit the annals of the time, the Emperor sent to him. Indeed, the Persian king proclaimed that he would only grant peace under conditions so disgraceful to the honour of the Chriſtians that the contemporary chronicles keep silence as to the terms, so insulting were they. That famous and valiant Emperor Heraclius, however, now firſt made a peace with Dagan, king of the Arabs,[2] and then returned to wage war againſt Persia for the glory of Chriſtendom and the Greek Empire. On this Chosroes [sent his general Shahr-Bárz] to invade Paleſtine, he ravaging the land so mercilessly that in Jerusalem alone he slew 20,000 men. Further, and what was the more pitiful, and a matter of dire confusion for all the Chriſtian peoples of that age, the Persians carried off from Jerusalem the Relic of the Moſt Precious Cross, on which our Lord Jesus Chriſt had suffered death.

All this promptly coming to the knowledge of the Chriſtian Emperor Heraclius, he suffered moſt intense grief therefrom, and was filled with an anxiety to recover possession of that Holy Relic, also to regain possession of the lands that had been loſt to the Empire. He therefore marched out from Conſtantinople at

Easter-tide, and in spite of unequal numbers determined to come to an issue with the Persian king. At the passage of the Taurus mountains he furiously attacked the satrap Shahr-Bárz, who was second in command under orders of Chosroes his master. Heraclius, according to the account of a reliable authority, on this occasion cried aloud, shedding many tears, and prayed saying, "*Deus judica causam tuam.*" He then furiously charged the enemy, and putting them to rout, took possession of the city of Agazago,[3] from whence Chosroes had just fled. Here he entered the Temple of the Sun, and taking possession, carried off all the rich treasures that Chosroes had amassed, and above all with every reverence he removed and brought back to Jerusalem that most Precious Cross. Some authorities, on the other hand, state that after Heraclius had put the Persian armies to flight, he marched on, and entering the Temple of the Sun there found Chosroes seated in all majesty on his throne. Then through magic arts the thunder rolled and rain fell, while the Sun and the Moon and the Stars were at the feet of Chosroes, and at his right hand stood the most Holy Cross, and at his left was a Cock. But Heraclius coming in upon Chosroes slew him. The more authentic account, however, is different from the above, and is to the effect that the Persian king did not die by the hand of Heraclius; but in fact otherwise, as we shall now explain. For Chosroes lived on, and after a time was succeeded by his son Siroes,[4] he after a most tyrannical fashion coming to be king of Persia. And this he accomplished contrary to all law and reason, for Siroes, disregarding both duty and filial affection—which, indeed, by natural instinct the very brute beasts display and pay, though rudely, to their parents who have begotten them and brought them into the world —Siroes (we learn) slew his father with his own hand, further his mother and his brothers. Then by the help of certain of the satraps he gained possession of the whole kingdom of Persia; but his reign lasted only for a single year, and that with many terrible accidents, the same brought about by his evil course of life.

Now there are some historians who state that there was more than one king who reigned between Siroes and his successor, the satrap Shahr-Bárz, but I can find no confirmation of this. Most authorities indeed agree that Shahr-Bárz ruled Persia only for half a year or less, in succession to Siroes, and that to him followed Barnares or Harnares,[5] one of the sons of Chosroes Parvíz who had escaped the murderous hands of his cruel brother Siroes. He during seven months occupied the throne of Persia, but ever in constant fear and dread, and without liberty of action. On his death he was succeeded by Hormisdas,[6] the last of the Chosroes, and he reigned for ten years. Joseph Scaliger states that in the tenth year of the reign of this same Hormisdas, the king being weary of life and harassed on the one side by the attacks of the Greek Emperor, and on the other side by the incursions of the Arabs, as also much disturbed at home by divers rebellions of the satraps, called in Omar the Caliph of the Moslems to his succour. Whereupon Omar entering Persia enabled the king, it is said, forthwith to pacify or subjugate his rebellious people. Other authorities, however, relate the matter differently, stating that it was the Turks, who were at that time idolaters, who were called in by King Hormisdas. Be the matter, either that they called in both Moslems and Turks together, or that it was only the one party who came, it is stated that the Persian king did not sufficiently reward his two allies—or whichever party it was who alone had come to his aid. Nay, on the contrary, in place of thanks he gave them only evil words, calling them dogs. Hence those who had powerfully helped him were distressed and next became indignant. Then the Arabs, who were much disappointed in the expectation of rich gifts in money from Hormisdas, joined forces with the Turks who were encamped in the foot-hills of the Taurus range, and together they attacked the Persians, becoming in a short time masters of the richest provinces of both Persia and Media.

The Caliph Omar now coming to know his own power vigorously pushed on the war against the Persian kingdom. At the end of ten years of fighting he had brought to naught all opposition of the Persian nobility, and had subjugated all those princes that were left of the descendants of the royal house of the Arsacids—namely, of the progeny of Arbaces, Chosroes, Hormisdas, Xerxes, Artaxerxes, Darius and Cyrus. Omar thus made himself absolute master of their empire and state, introducing and spreading among their people the new poison of the bestial sect of Mahomed; and it is on this account that Joseph Scaliger very exactly describes Omar as he who did waste and spill the blood of the Persian kings. Then Omar at last tired of all this slaughter, and betook himself to Jerusalem, where he established his sect of the Moslems. By the advice of certain wretches he next undertook to rebuild the Temple of Solomon; but a Persian whom he had carried with him thither in his train, and whose name was Margancia,[7] calling to mind the lamentable tragedy of his native country, on a certain night slew Omar, in honourable but barbarous revenge. Omar, however, did not die on the spot, and in the hours that he still lived he named as his successor in the Caliphate Othman, he being one of his chief captains.

## CHAPTER XI

*In which is told the beginning of the history of the Moslem Arabs who were masters of the Persian kingdom, with other matters of import to be known.*

WHEN Othman in the year 640 after Christ had succeeded Omar in the Caliphate, and he had been the captain of the Moslem armies before this time, he forthwith turned to matters of policy and government, being intent also on introducing some innovations in religion, whereunto he made a new and foolish decree in the matter of the Moslem faith, which is since known as the *Shari'ah*. Further, being prone to destroying from jealousy all those objects which are most worthy of preservation in the remembrance of the world, and from avarice selling their relics, among many other remarkable monuments that he brought to ruin was the Colossus of Rhodes. This always had been held as one of the Seven Wonders of the World, and with reason; for as reliable authorities relate, it was a figure in bronze of such monstrous size that it measured 120 feet in height, being most curiously wrought exactly to reproduce the semblance of a living man. That celebrated artificer in metal-work, Chares of Lindus, spent twelve years of labour in moulding, adjusting and burnishing the statue, and it had stood intact for 1,370 years when Othman caused it to be destroyed. To carry away the bronze was the burden of 900 camels, each bearing a charge of thirty *arrobas* [or about 7 cwt.] of the metal.

Othman did many other extravagant acts, and finally died, murdered, it is said, by the hand of a slave whom 'Alí ordered to do this deed. He had been Caliph of Babylonia, Persia and Media during twelve years, and of such murders as this, among the great of the various Moslem sects, I shall frequently mention examples. And now it is not my intention to do more here than name briefly in succession those Caliphs who held rule over Persia. I say therefore that Othman was succeeded by 'Alí, who also came to a violent death, being murdered in the city of Kúfah by order of Mu'áwiyah.[1] As Caliph of Baghdad in Babylonia,[2] and ruling also over Persia, Mu'áwiyah followed 'Alí, but until the twelfth year of his reign he had not a moment of peace, being continually at war with the Emperors of Constantinople; at length, however, a treaty for an armistice was concluded between them to last, it was agreed, for thirty years. Then Mu'áwiyah, finding himself free from the business of war, went back to the city of Damascus, and calling a parliament strove to set the affairs of his false religion in better order. At that time, as he rightly perceived, the Moslems were rapidly becoming divided up into many opposing sects, and he proceeded to appoint a commission of six wise men, whose names were Mulciano, Báario, Buora, Sidi-Noccio, Sidi-Tanuin and Sidi-Daud.[3] Next giving over into their hands the various scrolls and papers which the Prophet Mahomed had left at his death, those six Alfaquís, or Masters in Religion, set to work and composed a book of precepts, articles and commandments, which those who followed the law of the Prophet were forthwith bound to obey. To this book they gave the name of Alcoran, decreeing penalties for all those who should follow any other sect but theirs.

In the year 703 after Christ there ruled at Baghdad[4] over the kingdom of Persia, the Caliph Yazíd, the son of Mu'áwiyah, who in place of warlike business, which in those unquiet lands was the more important task to see to, played the part of a lover, and wrote poetry to such purpose as to become as it were a very Virgil

# YAZÍD I

of Mantua, but indeed after a barbarous fashion; though as his enemies have burnt all his poetic works we lack any exact knowledge of their value. Then 'Abd-Allah, the brother of Yazíd, wearying of all this verse-making and neglect of the affairs of government and of the army, according to one account with his own hand put Yazíd to death, though the more probable story is that this 'Abd-Allah was [not his brother] but an accomplice with other partisans [of the House of 'Alí] who contrived and carried out the plot to get rid of the Caliph. Be this as it may, these men then proclaimed Husayn,[5] son of 'Alí, as Caliph, but he too was shortly afterwards slain by these same conspirators.

Then in these days when there were many chiefs, who time and again arose, making themselves leaders of faction in the diverse provinces, there appeared in Persia—which is the country we now are chiefly dealing with, and shall deal with in the following pages—a man who was an Arab of the name of Mukhtar,[6] who caused himself to be proclaimed Grand Caliph of Persia, but he found so many opponents to his claims that scarcely for a day did he live in peace, the reigning Caliph of Baghdad being ever against him. His chief adversary, however, was Mus'ab [brother of Ibn Zubayr the Anti-Caliph of Mecca], who finally slew him in battle. But after this 'Abd-al-Malik— he whom the Arabs settled in Persia, where they had been much persecuted and who now were in open revolt, had recently acclaimed as their Caliph—this 'Abd-al-Malik, avenging the death of Mukhtar, slew Mus'ab, thus finally coming into undisputed possession of the Caliphate over Persia, Mesopotamia and Arabia. 'Abd-al-Malik was succeeded by his son Walíd, who was so famous throughout the western lands of Europe and Africa, for the most reliable authors agree that this was the Caliph who, to our undoing in Spain, commanded that Moslem aid should be given to the traitor Count

Julian in the year 708 after Chriſt. And indeed it muſt be this Caliph Walíd who helped Don Julian, for Chriſtian Spain was not loſt in the year 714, as some have reported (but in 708), and it was this same Caliph who was generally called "the Sword of God." When Walíd died he was succeeded by Sulaymán, and he in turn by Omar II, but these three Caliphs had enjoyed during their reigns so little peace and quiet that scarcely could it be said that for an entire day any one of them was really and fully recognized as sovereign over all Persian lands.

To these three, after continuous wars, succeeded Yazíd II as thirteenth Caliph, and when he died his son Hishám came to the throne in the year 748, who called himself Grand Caliph of Syria and Persia. But at about this date another Grand Caliph was elected in Egypt to oppose him, who was named Marwán [and he was to be the laſt Omayyad Caliph], and he made a treaty with the Emperor Conſtantine, the fifth of that name, becoming tributary to him, whereby he thought to oppose Hishám the more successfully. And this indeed was so, for coming againſt his enemy and making open war in the field, with the aid of the Emperor he overcame Hishám, slaying him, and thus Marwán became the undisputed ruler of Babylonia and Persia, the fifteenth Caliph in the line of the Omayyad House. Now about this same time Persia came to be divided up between two great parties in the ſtate, one the Keisite Arabs of Modar, and the other the Háshimites [of the House of 'Abbás], who, these laſt, were known as followers of the law of the Imám Ja'far [great grandson of Husayn]. Taking advantage of this division of opinion, a certain Persian, a man of great valour called Sulaymán[7] Abu-Muslim, arose, and he preached the doctrine of Mukhtar [spoken of above, namely, that of the Sect of the Shi'ah], asserting that the Caliph 'Alí truly had been a greater prophet

## ABU-MUSLIM

than even the Prophet Mahomed. Next Abu-Muslim proclaimed himself Amir-al-Muslimin (Commander of the Moslems), and proceeding to attack the Keisite faction overcame [Nasr] Ibn Sayyár, who was their chief, and slew him. On this, Abu-Muslim, having at command an army of 100,000 men, quietly awaited the attack of the Caliph Marwán, who was marching against him with 300,000 men. There now took place one of the most bloody and fiercely contested battles that the nations of the East had ever seen, for it was fought between Medes and Persians; and the number of men in the army of Marwán with their followers at last had reached a total of 400,000. At the close, Marwán, completely defeated, fled with his wife and his sons, followed by all those of his household. Marwán sought refuge in Egypt, but Zelma,[8] the son of Abu-Muslim, following after, finally brought him to his death in the year 754 after Christ. From Abu-Muslim, otherwise called Amir Sulaymán, was descended[9] Músá Kázim (the Seventh Imám), who at a later date strove in the interest of the Family of the Prophet Mahomed to regain the Caliphate; and from Músá Kázim again were descended the Sophi kings of Persia through the line of Mukhtar (already mentioned) and of Muhammad or Ahmad[10] [namely, the Imám Al Mahdi, the twelfth in descent], from 'Alí and Fátimah, the daughter of the Prophet Mahomed, as will be more fully explained later. The Persians, after their victory described above, elected [Abu Muslim, otherwise] the Amir Sulaymán as their Caliph,[11] but after this 'Abd-Allah Ibn Muhammad [who came to be known as the second Abbasid Caliph Mansúr], the brother of Abu Ja'far[12] [namely, Saffáh the founder of the dynasty], was before long acknowledged as supreme Caliph throughout Syria. This Caliph Mansúr, a man of great astuteness, forthwith brought all his adversaries to their deaths, naming them as traitors, and remaining then the sole and absolute Caliph, he with evil machinations next compassed the murder of the Amir Sulaymán Abu-Muslim, his all too powerful general.

The Caliph Mansúr at his death was succeeded by his son Muhammad, called Mahdi, who reigned for nine years, and after him came his eldest son Hárún-ar-Rashíd, who reigned for twenty-three years, being the nineteenth in succession of the Moslem Caliphs. Then on his death, when it had come to the year 792, his two sons Muhammad [Amín] and 'Abd-Allah [Mámún] both together succeeded to the throne, and the strife between the two brothers was such that there was no peace from war and insurrections till such time as when the party of Muhammad [Amín] had finally gained the ascendant. Then the Caliph Amín, now in possession of supreme power, founded among the ruins of Babylonia a famous city, to which he gave the name of Baghdad,[13] which, untouched by time, flourished until it was destroyed by the Tartars [under Húlágú Khán] in the year 1258 after Christ.

## CHAPTER XII

*Continuation and conclusion of the succession of Saracen Caliphs, who reigned over Persia, down to the time when the Ottoman Turks began to govern there.*

THE Caliphs of Baghdad ever continued to gain glory and honour in governing Persia, and Imbrael [otherwise the Caliph Amín], who succeeded [his father[1]] in the year 846, reigned fifteen years, and till the day of his death greatly fostered the affairs of the Persian people. He was succeeded by his brother Mámún, who was killed in battle, he and his sons, after but a short reign: some say this was when fighting against the armies of the Emperor Michael, others that it was the troops of the Emperor Theophilus.

After him came Mu'tasim, who was inimical to the Persians, for he is of all men the one they hate most; further, he it was who in truth inaugurated the ruin of Persia, for in his days the Persians called in the Turks to their aid and succour against the Arab tyranny. The Turks indeed then must have found the land of Persia much to their liking, and even to the present day it has been impossible to get them gone therefrom. This Mu'tasim was Caliph for twenty-three years, and at his death was succeeded by Qáim, who died after reigning forty-four years. Then in the year 980 after Christ, Persia, Egypt and Baghdad were divided up among three Caliphs, and in Persia Muhammad, son of Ignaro,[2] had rule, whom the Caliph of Baghdad, Pysasyri, so greatly harassed that he (Ignaro) was forced to call in his neighbours the Turks to help him; but a time came later when Pysasyri himself was paid back justly for his evil deeds and tyrannies to both Persians and Turks. For he having robbed and put to death very many of the Turks who inhabited the Caucasus mountains, these latter sent for aid to Trangolipix[3] [as the Byzantines call Tughril Beg the Seljuq]. He then with a great army invaded the country of Islam, and though the Caliphs of Baghdad and Persia opposed him and successfully defended the ford known by the name of Hamete—where the river Araxes of Armenia is crossed—the enemy took possession of all the mountain region of Armenia, and thence descending into Persia, and the kingdoms adjacent, put an innumerable multitude of folk to death by the sword; finally also killing both the Caliphs [namely of Baghdad and Persia].

It was on this occasion that the Turks finally became overlords of Persia, and with other provinces that he subsequently conquered Tughril Beg became Grand Sultan, being succeeded in due time by his nephews: and hence after this the Caliphs of Baghdad entirely ceased to have rule over Persia, and the Turks dominated the country; in time abandoning their idolatrous religion—for originally they had been pagans—and becoming Mahomedans. After this wise therefore the rule and sway of the Turks continued until the government came to Belcepho, who, ruling as autocrat, took occasion to be called the Emperor of Persia. He it was who made his nephew Alphagalo governor of Lesser Armenia. Alphagalo becoming ambitious of glory, being intent to rival the deeds of Alexander the Great, conquered Cilicia, Pamphylia, Lycia, Lycaonia, Cappadocia, Great Armenia, Galatia, Paphlagonia, Pontus and Bithynia, assuming the title of Grand Sultan, and commanding that he should be called Salamansa (which is Sulaymán) or, as we say, Solyman.[4] From the year 1000 after Christ to the year 1200 the affairs of Persia remained as we might say in abeyance, for the country was governed either by civil or military chiefs sent to rule the land by some one of the various overlords of Mesopotamia, whether of the Turk or of the Tartar nation. For these two peoples, alternately supreme, were fighting against each other during this period, and they were ever and anon committing all kinds of massacre and robbery throughout the lands of the East. Finally the Tartars got the better of their rivals after the year 1244, and remained in power till the year 1280, when the Turks again came to their own.[5] But afterwards the seven provinces [of Asia Minor] which the Turks had now gained were reduced in number, and their seven Amirs came to be no more than four principal governors in the Amirates, under four chiefs of families whose names were Caraman, Candelor, Othman and Hasan Beg, from the last of whom was descended Uzun Hasan the valorous king of Persia, as will be told later. To the Amir Othman here mentioned succeeded his youngest son Orkhán, and these two Amirs laid the foundation of the sovereignty of the Ottoman House, as is stated by Genebrardus in Book IV of his works.[6] The father, Othman, is reported to have been of very humble origin, for he was the son of a common soldier named Ertoghrul, and was born at a village called Sugut [Thebasion]. He having gained possession of many lands, set up his court in the city of Brusa in Bithynia—that same city which King Prusias built who gave aid to Hannibal. But he who would more particularly have details of the history of the Ottoman House must read Cuspinianus and Georgievits, and these authorities have treated of the matter very copiously.[7] For our present purpose, here, it will be enough to say that the successor of Othman was Orkhán, followed by Sultan Murád I[8] and Bayazid I, who was the rival of Timur Beg or Tamerlane. These Ottoman Sultans had now established their dominion over most parts of Asia Minor, and further as their own subjects and in their dependence they now held all the native princes of

# DON JUAN OF PERSIA

Persia and Media, until the time when, as above mentioned, the Great Tamerlane having conquered most of Asia, overcame Bayazid I [at the battle of Angora], and then put him in a cage, afterwards using him as a block from which to mount his horse.

It appears to us further that we may count the Great Tamerlane among the number of the kings of Persia, and we call the attention of our readers to the fact that at his death there were present the ambassadors of Spain, who had been sent by Henry III, king of Castile, to treat with Tamerlane, Ruy Gonzalez de Clavijo being one of these ambassadors, the same who wrote the account of that embassy.[9] Then during the period of troubles arising when there was war between the claimants to the inheritance of the Great Tamerlane—whom the Turks call Ilderim,[10] which is as much as to say the Whirlwind or the Lightning—his grandson the tyrant Omar Mirza obtained the supreme power and invoked the aid of our ambassadors, who (on their return journey) were at Van, a city lying to the west of Tabríz. All this country was part of the ancient kingdom of Persia, and at that time was under the dominion of those tyrants who had in the first instance, by craft, succeeded to the heritage of Tamerlane—namely, his grandsons Sugurghatmish and Baysunqur. But both these tyrants and others soon lost their hold on the states that Tamerlane had in the short time of his life conquered, and all this country afterwards came back under the government of Sultan Muhammad I, the youngest son of Sultan Bayazid I, who had succeeded (in 1402) to his father's throne by deeds of violence, and by the murder of all his elder brothers. After him came Murád II (in 1421), when the great king of the Tartars of Cathay (Sháh Rukh) took over rule in all those eastern countries, until the date (as will be shown later) when the Sophi kings of Persia finally restored that monarchy to its pristine power and glory.

# CHAPTER XIII

*In which the affairs of the Ottomans and of the Persians are continued to their final stage.*

SULTAN MUHAMMAD II (who succeeded in 1451), son of Murád II,[1] was surnamed the Great [and was the conqueror of Constantinople]. As Johannes Cuspinianus relates, he prospered greatly in his policy, both in Europe and in Asia, though not without a rival on the side of Persia, for here Uzun Hasan was now king,[2] who has already been mentioned as a descendant of Hasan Beg, one of the early Turkish Amirs of Asia Minor. He ever opposed Sultan Muhammad valiantly, being the chief enemy whom the latter had now to compass among the many potentates who were his neighbours. This Uzun Hasan was indeed as much a Turk, by blood, as the Sultan himself, but he prided himself greatly in being of true Persian nationality, and not an Asiatic Turk (as was the Ottoman Sultan).

This in fact is what we may deduce from the happenings when the Venetians took up arms against Sultan Muhammad II, and when Venice made that valiant soldier Pietro Mocenigo captain-general of her sea forces.[3] It was then that Uzun Hasan, king of Persia, sent his first embassy to the Venetians, and while Pietro Mocenigo was still at the island of Rhodes.[4] When the Persian ambassadors from Uzun Hasan came to him, it became quite clear to the Venetians what was this enmity which has ever existed between the Persian and the Turk; for the Persian ambassador had been told to promise that Uzun Hasan would attack the Sultan on the side of Armenia at the very same time that the Venetians made their attack, for they were then on the point of laying siege to the city of Adaliyah in Pamphylia. Thus he who was the enemy of both parties might peradventure be totally overcome. Fray Juan de Pineda in his *Monarchia Ecclesiastica* mistakenly calls Uzun Hasan the Sophi of Persia, and I know not how such a grave author can have so forgotten himself, for indeed the title of Sophi was never known in Persia till the beginning of the 16th century, as we shall explain more exactly in the opening pages of our Second Book. The reply which the Venetians on this occasion gave to the embassy of Uzun Hasan did not satisfy him, but next coming to know that Pietro Mocenigo was gone to Napoli di Romania [Nauplia in Greece], he forthwith sent a second ambassador who should explain the matter more clearly, and at the same time urgently demand potent succour against the Turk. This ambassador afterwards came on to Venice, and the Signory now began to perceive that the quarrel which they had on hand with Sultan Muhammad made it of great importance for them to be in close alliance of friendship with Persia. The treaty therefore was concluded, and the Venetians despatched three small vessels, under sail, but reinforced by rowers, to their captain-general Pietro Mocenigo[5] in Greek waters. From thence these ships took on board 100 artillery-men of experience and capacity, who were immediately sent on to Persia, for in the matter of their artillery the Persian armies suffered greatly from a paucity of cannon, while on the other hand the Turkish armies in Asia were very well equipped in this arm, and they could effect much damage in their attack. On this occasion the ambassador whom the Venetians sent was that Josaphat Barbaro, already mentioned, who was well acquainted with the Persian tongue, and he was the bearer of many rich jewels as gifts to the Persian king.[6] Josaphat Barbaro set sail therefore from Venice, and though his embassy to Persia produced little effect, he none the less made report to the Signory of many things that he saw there with his own eyes, speaking of the great power of Persia, and this was of much importance coming later to the knowledge of the kingdoms of the West, through being faithfully set down in the book which he subsequently wrote.[7] The reason indeed that his embassy to the Persian king effected so little was that the Persians having no ships at sea, never could make their power felt against the Ottoman Sultans, hence at no time could they bring any force in aid to Pietro Mocenigo, who was now effectively harassing the Turks [with the Venetian galleys] off the coast regions of Cilicia and Syria. Pietro Mocenigo at this same season was busied with restoring to their own, in the kingdom of Cilicia, the two Qaramán brothers whom Sultan Muhammad had dispossessed. These princes were Pír Ahmad, who had taken refuge at the court of Uzun Hasan, and Hasan Beg, his younger brother.[8]

Sultan Muhammad, feeling much vexed by the opposition which the Persians had put up against him in Asia Minor, was now making preparations to march and invade Western Persia with an immense army, including both horse and foot, and numbering 320,000 men. But the army which the Persian king had assembled was yet greater, for the writer Bernard of Breydenbach[9] states that the squadrons of the cavalry alone of the Persians exceeded in number 350,000 horse. There followed one of the most celebrated battles that ever came to be fought in Asia between rival Moslem potentates,[10] for the two mighty armies having been drawn up in battle array, set to, and the struggle lasted for two whole days before the victory was declared. And again, although with some truth it may be affirmed that the Turk was here the victor, yet the victory cost him so dear that Sultan Muhammad never again dared to attack Persia, and in the future turned all his attention to the wars in Europe. Here more particularly he intervened in the affairs of Italy; where in the terrible destruction which the Turks wrought at Otranto in [July, 1480] the Roman Pontiff (Sixtus IV) himself was put in no small peril. Then by the mercy of God Sultan Muhammad II died suddenly [May, 1481], whereby Christendom was delivered from its most arrogant enemy. Uzun Hasan, too, on his part was overwhelmed by his defeat [at this battle of Terján], and was so cast down by the death of his eldest son and heir, who was killed in the engagement, that he immediately retired, marching back to Persia, there very shortly afterwards dying of melancholy.

With him the line of Hasan Beg the Turk Amir came to an end, and no other Turkish prince afterwards governed in Persia, though during the next score of years this country was ruled by the two successors[11] of Uzun Hasan [namely, Sultan Ya'qúb and this prince's nephew Rustam, but at least on the mother's side] these princes were rather to be accounted Arabs than Turks. These successors of Uzun Hasan therefore came to power and for a while held rule over Persia, but with a further interval Isma'íl, the first Sophi monarch, arose to kingship, with whose strange adventures we shall begin our Second Book. We have therefore now finally done with all these foreign kings, or Caliphs, whether Arabs or Turkomans or Ottomans, who in long past times and seasons have held rule over the lands of Persia.

SECOND Book of the Account of Don Juan of Persia, in which the origin of the Sophi Kings of Persia is explained, and an account given of their wars against the Turks; in some part of which same wars Don Juan of Persia and his father, Sultan 'Ali Beg Bayát, took their share.

# CHAPTER I

*In which is described the history of the first Sophi King of Persia, with divers curious events thereto happening.*

AND now came the year 1500, so celebrated and worthy of remembrance for many events that profited Christendom; and not the least of these the wars that had burst out and flamed up among the various infidel states of Asia. This was after the death of Sultan Muhammad II, who, as we have seen, was succeeded by his son Bayazid II in the year 1481. Sultan Bayazid, following in the ambitions and the tyrannical footsteps of his father, forthwith prosecuted the war against Ibrahím the prince of Qaramán,[1] and also, on the other hand, allowed no moment of peace to the Burjí Mamluk Sultan of Grand Cairo. We might, too, say much about the insurrections and plots stirred up by his elder brother Prince Jem [Jamshíd], as also of the rebellion in Constantinople of his son the young Qurqud, but all these matters are indeed beyond the scope of this book, and so we shall leave the telling of them to those who have more particularly dealt with the same. For our purpose, all that need here be said, is that Sultan Bayazid finding himself at last in peaceful and unquestioned possession of the supreme power, now gave over warring and vilely betook himself to a vicious life of ease, though this was quite foreign to what his former masterful character seemed likely to have disposed him.

The year 1500, however, is further most memorable for having seen the birth of the Great Cæsar Charles V, that mighty column of Christendom, the glory of the House of Austria, and the supreme honour of Spain, who indeed was ever an inexpugnable wall of defence for the True Faith, and to the close of his life the terror of all her enemies. This therefore will ever suffice to make that age, which indeed runs continuous with our own, most famous, but further detail concerning it is beyond our present purpose, and we may now forthwith return to those matters that we have promised more especially to treat of.

I say, therefore—and in spite of the fact that opinions differ on this subject between such authorities as Amandus of Zieriksee[2] and Bernard of Breydenbach as against Paulo Giovio[3]—I say that at a date that was more or less some twenty-four years previous to the first year of the 16th century—and in this we follow the common report which was current among us Persians—namely, at a date which, if our reckoning be exact, may be set down at the year 1472, Isma'íl the son of Shaykh Haydar of Ardebíl was born, who afterwards was known as the Sophi, Ardebíl being the city of which his father was lord. Now Shaykh Haydar was a learned astrologer, being also held as a Saint in the opinion of the Moslems of Persia, and when his son was born he foretold by his art that the boy would grow up to be a great prince, and a most zealous defender of the True Faith, which is the Law of 'Ali the son-in-law of Mahomed the Prophet, and further that Isma'íl would live to be one of the most famous sovereigns of Asia. This prophecy, as we shall see later, was amply fulfilled; and in order that we may show this the more clearly, it will be well here to explain fully two matters of importance—namely, what was this Law of 'Ali, and who was Isma'íl and from whom was he descended?

To explain the first point we must now go back many centuries of history and write concerning the times of the Prophet Mahomed, when matters fell out as follows. At the period when the Prophet had attained his greatest reputation among the Arabs, and had founded his false religion—the tenets of which are more in accordance with the bestial appetite of man than in conformity with divine truth or reason—he being then at the age of seventy-three years and feeling himself near to death, proceeded to make his will and testament. In this he devolved the succession to the governance of the state, giving the supreme authority in all matters of religion to 'Ali, his son-in-law, the husband of Fátimah, his daughter by his first wife, and naming him to be Grand Caliph. But further he added this incongruity to others of his making, for he established 'Ali, as a person might say, to be at one and the same time emperor and pontiff, otherwise king and archbishop. Now for his second wife Mahomed had married Ayishah, daughter of Abu Bakr, a man of great importance in the state, and this Abu Bakr was much vexed that his son-in-law—the Prophet Mahomed—had not named him, Abu Bakr, to be his successor as Caliph, but that he should have preferred to him a youth like 'Ali, a person, said he, of little importance and less experience. This Abu Bakr being therefore a man of great wealth, and of authority in matters of war, and always able to accomplish all that which he thought the right, and further having the support of Omar and Othman, he, Abu Bakr, aided by these two men, put himself at the head of a great concourse of Arabs, and forthwith dispossessed 'Ali of the government. Thus Abu Bakr, after the death of the Prophet, without a battle, became supreme Caliph, but he died shortly after this, whereupon Omar succeeded to the Caliphate, and next Othman. The two last named in truth paid dearly for their usurpation, for Omar (as has been said above) was murdered by a Persian slave, a miller, and Othman was killed very traitorously by a soldier, who it was said, but untruthfully, was urged to do the deed by 'Ali. Then next in turn, and to avenge, as he said, the death of Othman his kinsman,

# DON JUAN OF PERSIA

Muʻáwiyah had ʻAli put to death, according to the common account given. The more true version, however, is that ʻAli, having come at length to be Caliph after the deaths of the three Caliphs his predecessors and enemies [namely, Abu Bakr, Omar and Othman], was one day prompted charitably to adopt a foundling whom he had by chance come upon lying outside the door of a certain Mosque, and to whom he gave subsequently the name of ʻAbd-ar-Rahman Ibn Marjan.[4] On growing to manhood this wretch, in the very Mosque outside which he had been found as an infant by ʻAli, stabbed his benefactor to death, using a dagger poisoned with the fat of a venomous serpent which in Persia is known as the *Zahr-Már* [or Poison-snake]. This event took place in the city of Kúfah, which stands on the Euphrates some distance to the westward of Baghdad. The place has since been named by the Moslems Meshed ʻAli, which is as much as to say "the Place of Martyrdom of ʻAli," for ʻAli was buried there, and his shrine is now one of the most notable Mosques in all Asia, to which all Persians flock in pilgrimage to make their devotions. It is a place of great richness, for before ʻAli's tomb more than 2,000 gold or silver lamps burn continually, and the Mosque is served by some 400 *Sayyids* [descendants of the Prophet], whom the Turks speak of as *Faqíhs*, who are, as we should put it, the Chaplains of the Shrine.

But to return to our history. The men of Kúfah after this raised Husayn, the son of ʻAli, to be Caliph; but shortly afterwards he too was murdered, with all his family and household, by order of the Caliph Yazíd, the son of Muʻáwiyah. Now whether Omar and Othman were indeed the lawful Caliphs, or whether ʻAli had of right the succession thereto, was matter that did beget much difference of opinion and was the cause of many great wars; for the Persians say

## SHAYKH HAYDAR

that, in conformity with the will and testament of Mahomed, 'Ali was the true Caliph and the Law he promulgated the true law; but the Turks, who follow in this the doctrine taught by the Arabs, assert that the rightful Caliph was indeed Abu Bakr and the doctrine he taught the only orthodox faith.

And now it will be well for us to give an account of Shaykh Haydar [the father of Sháh Isma'íl, the first Safavi monarch of Persia, otherwise the Grand Sophi]. This Haydar was of the House of 'Ali, of whose affairs we have been speaking, being a descendant of Músá Kázim [the Seventh Imám], who was [great-great-grandson[5]] of Husayn, the son of 'Ali, by his wife Fátimah, the daughter of the Prophet Mahomed. Shaykh Haydar was on terms of intimacy with that king of Persian Armenia of whom we have already written so much, and who was called Uzun Hasan, and the intimacy became such that Uzun Hasan gave Haydar his daughter (Martha) in marriage. Haydar thus became his son-in-law, and by this marriage Isma'íl, his son, could claim descent (through his mother) from the former kings of Persia, while on his father's side he was descended from the noble House of 'Ali [through the Imáms]. Then again the mother of Shaykh Haydar's wife, Martha, was indeed a Christian, being the daughter of the Christian Princess Despina, who was the wife of Uzun Hasan, aforesaid, and she was herself a daughter of Kalo Joannes [the last Christian] Emperor of Trebizond.[6] Whereby it follows that it is no idle boast for the Safavi king of Persia to claim to be a friend of the Christian potentates of Europe, for the half of his house and blood comes, in direct descent, from that most noble Christian House of the Greek Emperors of Constantinople.

Having thus explained the descent of Sháh Isma'íl I proceed, and say that when Uzun Hasan, king of Persia, died, his son, Sultan Ya'qúb succeeded to his estate. But he, as it is said, had now become ashamed of having for his brother-in-law a common man like Haydar, whom he in no wise considered as the equal in rank to a powerful king like himself. In consequence, Yaʻqúb took counsel and compassed the death of Haydar, whom he slew, and would have compassed that of Haydar's son Ismaʻíl, though he indeed was his very own nephew, being at that time a boy ten years old. Ismaʻíl, however, managed to escape, and betook himself to the frontiers of Tartary, seeking a safe refuge in the city of Zezian, not far from the Caspian Sea, where he was charitably entertained by the king of that country, Pír ʻAli, who caused him to be well educated, and later brought him up at his court. Here in time Ismaʻíl, by a hypocritical pretence of piety, gained the reputation of being a Saint, and so it came about that the people began to reverence and follow after him.

Giovanni Botero, however, relates these events somewhat differently in his *Relationi Universali*.[7] He calls the Persian prince Uzun Hasan by the title of Hasan Beg,[8] and his son who succeeded to him he names Yaʻqúb Beg, and goes on to explain that the true reason why Yaʻqúb had caused his brother-in-law Haydar to be put to death was not because (as we have stated above) he, Yaʻqúb, was ashamed of his connection by marriage with one of such low degree. And in this Botero appears to me to be in the right, for Haydar (as we have explained) through his father was descended from the noblest blood in all Arabia, and through his mother (the sister of Uzun Hasan) was connected with the kings of Armenia and the Christian Emperors of Trebizond. Further, Haydar was already in possession of the lordship of the famous city of Ardebíl, all of which is quite enough, in quality as in quantity, to have warranted King Uzun Hasan in giving him a third or even a fourth daughter in marriage. But the fact of the matter seems to have been that Haydar was all too famous as an astrologer, seeing that many of his prognostications had already come true, so that all Persia believed in his prophecies: hence the edge of the sword that took off his head was not whetted by a sense of shame, but rather by a sense of envy of the future greatness of his descendants.

Botero further relates that Haydar, having two sons, Isma'íl and Sulaymán, Sultan Ya'qúb, as soon as his father, Uzun Hasan, was dead, sent a message to one of his captains, named Mansúr, to carry off both the boys to Zalga, a very strong fortress in the mountains, and this was equivalent to ordering him to put them to death in cold blood. But Mansúr disobeyed the order, and, revealing the whole matter to Isma'íl, afterwards brought him up in his house as one of his family. Now I know not which of these two accounts most to credit, for though the first that we have mentioned is the story now everywhere current in Persia, the second account, as Botero has it, appears to me the one that has the more likelihood in it.[9]

Whichever be the true version, it is a fact beyond doubt that Ismá'íl, when he came to be nineteen years of age, began to preach the doctrine of the Shi'ah faith—as against the tenets of the other seventy-eight sects into which the Moslems are divided—and being a very great hypocrite he boldly condemned all other beliefs as heresy. Then having begun with a following of only twelve or fourteen disciples, he soon afterwards found himself at the head of 300 well-armed partisans. At their head he made a descent into Persian territory, being joined there by a multitude of vagabonds and bandits, with whose help forthwith he stormed and took possession of the city of Shamákhí. All the districts of Armenia round and about now fell under his power, and he became the king of that country. Next, Sultan Ya'qúb having come out against him,

# DON JUAN OF PERSIA

Isma'íl found means by poison forthwith to compass the death of Ya'qúb, and sending for his body, had it publicly burnt, thus seeking to avenge the murder of Shaykh Haydar his father. After this became known the chief men in Persia began to come in to Isma'íl, and the princes of all the neighbouring states fell to regarding him much more favourably. Isma'íl thereupon holding that his power was now sufficient, set out to obtain possession of the city of Tabríz, which was then considered the seat of empire of him who would be the king of Persia. For this city was already so populous that it is stated to have contained 200,000 houses, and it was in truth the capital of Armenia and, as it were, the metropolis of the East. Isma'íl marching against Tabriz, laid siege to and took it, but as he entered its gates his two cousins [the sons of the late Sultan Ya'qúb, the princes] Alvand and Murád at that moment managed to effect their escape.

When Isma'íl found himself thus master of Tabríz, he elected to proclaim himself the Grand Sophi of Persia; and he took as his title to be styled Isma'íl Shaykh Ardebílí Qizil Básh Ithná-'ashariy,[10] and what these names signified was as who should say, " Great Isma'íl, Restorer of the cotton or woollen Cap or Turban of Twelve colours." For as we have seen, the sect that the Persians belonged to was the Sect of 'Ali, and it was 'Ali who instituted this form of headgear, which was a bonnet or high hat made of cotton-stuff or wool, of a red colour. This is what the words *Qizil Básh* signify, namely " Red Head," and it is for this, as we shall find later, that the Turks call the Persians the Qizil Básh. On the top of this red bonnet the Persians were wont to set twelve knots,[11] or points, each of a different colour, which same is what is indicated by the word *Ithná-'ashariy*, which in Arabic means " twelve." The revival of the ancient custom of wearing such a form of headgear, which Isma'íl had thus inculcated among his followers, a people ever ardent to have novelty, made them now ready to shed their very heart's blood in his service. Hence, before long, Isma'íl became prince and master of one of the greatest states, indeed one of the most potent kingdoms of all Asia, for he became Grand Sophi of Persia. Of this title the word *Sophi* does not mean " wise," as some erroneously instructed have said, imagining that it came from the Greek word *Sophos*, " wisdom," for it is a Persian word, and *Sof* (or *Súf*) in that tongue means " wool " or " cotton." Thus Isma'íl Sophi, descended from 'Ali, son-in-law of the Prophet Mahomed, proclaimed himself to be a very zealous missioner of that sect, abhorring the creed of the Caliphs Omar and Othman; but after becoming a most powerful monarch, he did not live in peace, for it was he who inaugurated the wars which have continued down to our present day between the Persians and the Turks. After this fashion it was that the first Sophi king of Persia began his reign.

## CHAPTER II

*Of the many wars that Isma'íl Sophi had to wage.*

HARDLY had the great Isma'íl Sophi grasped with his hand the sceptre of government in the new Persian Empire when it became necessary to lay that sceptre of peace aside, and taking up the lance and the sword, fight valiantly against his many enemies. Those who at first gave him the greatest trouble were his two cousins Alvand and Murád Khán, who, holding many strong places in the Nissat mountains, lying between Armenia and Upper Mesopotamia, and relying on the inaccessibility of their country, and the great number of their clansmen, were constantly making raids that resulted in inflicting great damage on the neighbouring Persian lands. These two princes were indeed at this time hoping to get back the power that they had possessed formerly in these districts, also intending if possible to extend their sway over the country lying beyond. Therefore, as soon as he came to hear of their doings Sháh Isma'íl forthwith assembled a mighty force, and marching against them with his people, gained a complete victory over them, putting their army to the rout and killing Prince Alvand. Murád Khán with his remaining tribesmen passed down into 'Iráq, whither Isma'íl immediately followed him, and again Murád suffered defeat, but again escaped. Isma'íl now entered into possession of 'Iráq, thus becoming undisputed master of the whole of Mesopotamia, as also of most of Azerbayján.

The news of these matters was in due time brought to the ears of the careless and peace-loving Sultan Bayazid II, who now began to feel the prick of envy at the rising fortunes of Isma'íl Sophi, fearing him also as a rival in empire. Many of the subject princes of the Turkish dominions were at this period refusing to pay the Sultan their proper dues, and some whom he had dispossessed of their governments were in open revolt. Further, Bayazid was troubled by the great power that was coming into the hands of Tekelli.[1] This man [the son of Hasan Khalífah], one of the original disciples of Shaykh Haydar, Isma'íl's father, was a very skilful soldier and a great hypocrite in his religion, and he had been given the post of captain-general in the Persian army that was fighting for the Sophi cause. At the head of an immense multitude of various tribesmen he recently had crossed the Turkish border and overrun all Cilicia,[2] where he defeated an army commanded by the two princes, the grandsons of Sultan Bayazid, who had been sent to oppose him. For lack of artillery Tekelli had been unable to take Qoniah, but coming suddenly upon Bayazid's son, Prince Qurqud, he might easily have taken him prisoner or even killed him, but again contented himself with putting Qurqud to an ignominious flight. Tekelli Qizil Básh—thus the Turks called him—now passed forward into Bithynia, and on the banks of the river Sangarius encountered Qarakúsh, Beglerbeg of Anatolia, who was encamped there, being in touch with Prince Ahmad, Bayazíd's eldest son. This Prince Ahmad had under his command another great body of troops, and it was hoped that these two Turkish armies would be able to surround Tekelli and overpower him. He, however, getting warning of the plan, avoided the grip of these two armies, though not without some loss, for 7,000 men of his rear-guard were captured and put to the sword. Tekelli, however, avenged his defeat before long, for storming the town of Kutahiyah, the chief city of Galatia, to which Qarakúsh had retired for a season of repose, Tekelli took him prisoner, sacked the town, and then marched off without meeting with any hindrance from the other forces of the enemy.

It was Tekelli's intention next to capture Brusa, the chief town of Bithynia, but having news that [the Grand Vizier Khádim] 'Ali Pasha from European Turkey, with Qurqud the Sanjaq in command of Qaſtamuniyah and Prince Ahmad were on his heels with a very great army, well appointed and disciplined, such indeed as Sultan Bayazid had not before had at command, Tekelli prudently turned aside and escaped into the open country. By craft disguising his line of march, he carried off his troops swiftly by devious ways, and always as much as might be avoided any engagement with the enemy. In this, however, he was not entirely successful, for 'Ali Pasha closely following him, at laſt came up and slew a number of his men. Tekelli was much enraged at being thus caught, and unable by craft to escape him, proceeded to vent his wrath on the unfortunate Beglerbeg of Anatolia, Qarakúsh, his prisoner, whom he caused to be impaled publicly, and in full sight of the Turkish camp and army. 'Ali Pasha, however, undeterred, pressed on, harassing and closely following after him; and leaving Prince Ahmad behind with the infantry, he pursued rapidly with his cavalry. Advancing at the head of a body of 8,000 horse, he finally came up with Tekelli in mount Oliga close to Angora, which of old was called Ancyra. Tekelli, however, managed to repulse the Turkish attack, making great use of his mounted arquebusiers, for the Persian cavalry are armed with this weapon, and 'Ali Pasha, who was exposing himself in the battle front, fell mortally wounded. The Persians were of course greatly elated by this success, but Prince Ahmad coming up suddenly with the remainder of the Turkish force, compelled them once more to retreat. Passing over mount Oliga, the Persian army crossed the river Halys, retiring on Tassia, where

# SULTAN SELIM

Yúnus Pasha, general of the troops from European Turkey, caught them up, forcing Tekelli to take refuge finally in Little Armenia, where he found Sháh Isma'íl encamped at the head of the main body of his army.

Here Tekelli took some rest for a while, content with the glory that he had gained, for indeed he had put all the Asiatic provinces of the Turkish Empire in great straits, so that there was hardly a city of Anatolia that he had not captured, or at least plundered, his men appearing in force at their gates with his kettle-drums. Indeed it is said that at one time, having crossed over the Straits he, Tekelli, came to be so near to Constantinople that one morning, riding up to the outermost wall he broke the locks on the city gate. After this Sháh Isma'íl marched out from Lesser Armenia to oppose Prince 'Álem, Bayazid's second son, who had advanced to threaten the Persian frontier, but though the two armies on more than one occasion came face to face and in battle array, no engagement of importance ensued.

It was at this time that Selim, the son of Bayazid, in Constantinople took possession of the throne by means most foul and by a most tyrannical conduct. For he had compassed the death of his father, Bayazid, by effect of a poison draught. This is their inhuman custom in the House of Ottoman, where he who succeeds to the throne must put to death all his brothers, nay, even his own father, lest any of the blood-royal should live and attempt to oppose his succession. Among the brothers of Sultan Selim, however, there was one who had escaped arrest and the death sentence. This was Prince Amurath or Murád, who fled, seeking shelter with the Sophi, the great enemy of his family and people; for it is the proud boast of the monarchs of the royal house of Persia to show charity to all princes who may seek their amity and friendship. Isma'íl Sophi therefore not only gave Prince Murád a kindly reception, but far from treating him as an enemy showed himself to be his sincere friend, nay, indeed a relation, granting him one of his daughters in marriage. Afterwards giving him 30,000 horsemen, he despatched him to take possession of the province of Qaramán, which Prince Murád asserted was his appanage, left him by his father, Bayazid, in his will. When Sultan Selim heard of these happenings he was much vexed in mind, and every day chafed the more at the doings of those whom the Sophi was befriending. He promulgated an ordinance that none of his people should have commerce with the subjects of Sháh Isma'íl, threatening most heavy punishment to any who disobeyed, and anathematizing the Shi'ah religion and the Sect of 'Ali, which he declared to be rankly heretical. Next he began to collect his troops, both those from Europe and from Asia Minor, forming a great army which came to number 200,000 men, Khayr-ad-Dín Pasha being appointed to the chief command.

Sultan Selim himself next declared it to be his intention personally to take part in the campaign, and though many of his Pashas tried to dissuade him, as the season was then in the depth of winter, such was the impatience of his anger that nothing could restrain him. The Sultan therefore set out at the head of the army, marching into Great Armenia, and attempted to pass across the Taurus mountains, where, to his annoyance, the snows now greatly delayed his advance. Here he found that the Persians had already burnt, or destroyed, all the crops of this countryside, so that the Turkish army could gain no booty or profit. Selim now approached the lands of 'Alá-ad-Dawlah[3] in that part of Cappadocia which is of Armenia, demanding of him that he should give the Turks free passage through the territories he governed, through these same it being the most direct and the safest road for Sultan Selim to follow. 'Alá-ad-Dawlah, however, feared

## 'ALÁ-AD-DAWLAH

that on the morrow Selim would be going back home again to Conſtantinople, and that he, 'Alá-ad-Dawlah, would then find himself left in the lurch, unprotected and declared a traitor both by Sháh Isma'íl and his friends the neighbouring princes of Armenia. He therefore made up his mind to refuse the demand of Sultan Selim, but proffering many excuses, and giving him good words in the room of good deeds. Selim was much disguſted at his refusal, and aſtonished to find that he was by far less respected and feared in these parts than he had imagined. What anger he felt, however, perforce he did not show, though he swore to himself that he would later on wreak his vengeance on the Armenian prince. Then turning off to the left hand (north-eaſt) along the Weſtern Euphrates, he marched to the Leprus mountains; but on the way thither he had to abandon much of his baggage, munitions and ſtores; also some regiments of his infantry who had remained behind loſt in the snows of that desolate country. Finally coming down to the banks of the Araxes, he crossed that great river which forms the boundary here of Armenia [at a point to the north and] near Khoy, which of old was the city called Artaxata, now finally coming in sight of the Persian camp and army.

It was here that Sultan Selim learnt how his brother,[4] Prince Murád, already become the son-in-law of the Sophi, was present with the Persians, and that he had been previously ſtirring up all Asia Minor againſt the Sultan; further that he, Murád, was much in the counsels of Sháh Isma'íl's general-in-chief, who was called Uſtád Oghlú,[5] a very valiant soldier, and that the Persian army was ſtationary, awaiting the arrival of Isma'íl before offering battle to the Turks. With much guile and many gifts to the Persian commander, the Sultan now tried to get his brother Murád delivered over to him, but this was not to be; and very shortly afterwards Sháh Isma'íl appeared with the bulk of his troops to join forces with those of the vanguard commanded by Prince Murád. Thus the opposing armies now found themselves face to face in battle array, and on the 26th of August of the year 1514, the signal to attack being given the great battle began in the plain of Chaldirán.⁶ The Persians numbered 300,000 cavalry, not counting infantry, and Sultan Selim had on his side so numerous an army, that it would appear fabulous to mention their number, were it not that, but a few years ago, there were many old men still living in Isfahán who bore witness to the fact, and would affirm, that Sultan Selim had under his command at Chaldirán 400,000 horsemen and 800,000 foot soldiers. First came the skirmishing, and then the real battle followed, lasting all day, and at nightfall the Persians had fought their way almost to the presence of Sultan Selim, and would indeed have taken him prisoner had his good fortune not well served him. The valour of Qasim Pasha, Beglerbeg of [Roumelia]⁷ the Greek Province, however, fighting with a great loss of men saved his master's life, and turned the tide of battle, for Ustád Oghlú having at this juncture been killed by a shot from an arquebus, the Persians now began to give way. Of the Turks the renegade Sinán Pasha of Epirus was indeed completely routed, for the Janissaries had failed in their duty, which had been to attack and rout the body-guard of the Sophi, but Sháh Isma'íl on this occasion had received a wound in the shoulder, and this was the prime cause that victory finally declared itself for Sultan Selim.

   The booty of which the Turks came into possession was so immense that afterwards for many a day they were rich men, but the victory proved no cheap one to Sultan Selim, for of his cavalry alone he lost 30,000 horse. Isma'íl Sophi, retiring slowly, passed through

## TABRIZ TAKEN

Tabríz, and let it be known that for the moment the townspeople must be left to submit to the Turk, as he, the Sháh, was unable to remain longer and defend the city. In company with his son-in-law, Prince Murád, he retired into the eastern provinces of Persia, and set himself to gather together reinforcements for his army. Sultan Selim felt much grief at the loss of Qasim Pasha, who died a few days after the battle of his wounds and contusions. The Sultan next distributed seven Sanjaq-banners to new commanders, thus replacing those chiefs who had been killed in the battle, and he then marched with his army back to Khoy, which city capitulated on peace terms. Peace terms also were granted to Tabríz, but hardly had the Turks come into possession of the city when they were forced hurriedly to evacuate it again, for news came to them that Sháh Isma'íl was advancing against them with double the number of his former force. The retreat of the Turkish army was precipitate, and before long they found themselves on the banks of the Euphrates with Isma'íl at their heels. Here an immense number of Turks at the passage of the river lost their lives, being drowned for lack of boats to carry them across. However, for no cause that is known, Sháh Isma'íl immediately after this had to retreat, and Sultan Selim found himself free from his pursuit. The Sultan now calling to mind the insult, or at least the lack of respect paid him, as narrated on the former occasion, by Prince 'Alá-ad-Dawlah, on this his homeward march invaded these lands, and though 'Alá-ad-Dawlah himself managed to escape to the mountains, the Turks in their passage laid waste all the unfortified townships of that district. Then Sultan Selim marched back to Trebizond, sending the troops to their homes, while he himself went on to the city of Amasiyah to await the beginning of the new year.

## CHAPTER III

*In which is continued the account of the wars between Sháh Isma'íl and Sultan Selim.*

WITH the year 1515 which now began, Sultan Selim was not unmindful of the annoyance still caused him by his brother Prince Murád, and the support to his pretensions given by Sháh Isma'íl. Further, on another distant quarter he was now threatened by a neighbouring power, for the Mamlúk Sultan of Egypt was mustering his forces [on the Syrian frontiers of Anatolia]. In the depth of the winter season, undeterred by the snow and the cold, Sultan Selim now gave the call to arms, and set out to invade the districts of Armenia. It was his intention this time, in the first place, to punish and ruin 'Alá-ad-Dawlah for his acts of opposition, but the latter having news of what Selim intended, fled, betaking himself to the strongholds of the Antitaurus mountains. Now 'Alá-ad-Dawlah had a relative whose name was Sháh-Suvár-Oghlú,[1] and 'Alá-ad-Dawlah had put this man's father to death: he therefore, taking occasion of the coming of Sultan Selim to avenge his wrongs, declared himself as of the Turk party, and offered to guide their troops through the secret defiles of that mountainous province.

No sooner had 'Alá-ad-Dawlah heard of this treachery than, descending from the mountain fastnesses with 15,000 horsemen, he sought to come on the Turkish army unawares, but his attack failed, and incontinently falling into Sultan Selim's hands, he forthwith paid the forfeit of this and last year's deeds, in that Selim caused him to be strangled. The Sultan then made Sháh Suvár governor of that region, with a very moderate tribute to pay. Immediately afterwards, for no cause

## SULTAN SELIM

that is known, Selim commanded his army hurriedly to retreat, and the Sultan returned home to Constantinople. Some indeed state that the cause of this sudden departure was a mutiny among the Janissaries, but this is hardly a reason for so precipitate a change of plan, and the true cause is unknown.

In the year 1516 Selim, finding that the princes of Christendom were all engaged in wars amongst themselves, one against the other, as is ever a matter deeply to be deplored, set out once more for Asia Minor, leaving his son Sulaymán in Adrianople, with full powers to carry on the home government. In Anatolia Selim appointed Chersi-Óghlú, the Sclavonian renegade, to be his lieutenant-governor, while as captain-general of his armies the Sultan named Ja'far, the Hungarian renegade, and then started on his campaign, more than ever desirous of abasing the power of the Sophi of Persia. News of Selim's intentions was brought to Sháh Isma'íl, and he being desirous on his side to make allies, now despatched an embassy to obtain the support and good will of Qánsúh Ghúrí[2] the Mamlúk Sultan of Egypt. Sháh Isma'íl at the same time gave support to certain home rebels against Sultan Selim, and next made an unexpected incursion at the head of a great army into [Circasia and Georgia] the countries on the borders of the Caspian Sea not far from Bákú. In Egypt at about this date, Sultan Qánsúh Ghúrí, wishing to make clear that he was now the declared enemy of Sultan Selim and the staunch friend of Isma'íl Sophi, called under arms 14,000 of his Slave-guard, and a like number of his Mamlúk cavalry, and set out from Cairo to march up into Syria. He had sent word previously to Khayr Beg, a brave warrior in his service [who was in command at Aleppo[3]], to assemble there a considerable body of [Syrian] troops, and he now effected a junction of forces with him [outside Aleppo].

# DON JUAN OF PERSIA

Here suddenly he came in view of Sinán Pasha, who had recently arrived in those parts at the head of the main body of the Turkish army, and the opponents found themselves face to face. Janberdi Ghazzálí,[4] who commanded the army of the Egyptian Sultan, began the attack, charging at the head of the Mamlúks, but Sultan Selim now coming up with the Turkish rear-guard, fell on him in flank, for the Sultan had just marched across the Amarus mountain, which is over against Aleppo—the same is the ancient Antioch. The Turks fought valiantly, making great use of their artillery, which Selim had caused to be carried over the mountain pass on the backs of his men. They completely overthrew the Egyptians, and Sultan Qánsúh did not escape, for he was trampled to death, falling off his horse under the hoofs of the cavalry as they charged, he being at that time in his seventy-seventh year. This great victory of the Turks, however, was in part due to the treachery of Khayr Beg, who abstained from the battle, and shortly afterwards came over to the side of Sultan Selim, abandoning his old master, being tempted by the promise of emoluments from the stranger, who forsooth did well afterwards to regard this treachery askance. Now all this time Isma'íl Sophi was on the alert, watching events, but noting that Sultan Selim had been so successful in overthrowing the Mamlúks and conquering the Egyptians, he abstained from interference, and left these, his allies, to their fate, though indeed it was he who had been the prime instigator of their war against the Turks.

Selim took possession of Aleppo immediately after the battle, Ghazzálí having fled to Damascus, and many towns in various parts of Syria thereupon capitulated, peaceably receiving the Turks. In Egypt Túmán Bey became Sultan, but he in vain sent to Rhodes to beg a loan of artillery [from the Knights of St. John[5]]. Sinán Pasha, meanwhile marching on with 15,000

# TÚMÁN BEY

horse, again attacked the Egyptians and captured the city of Gaza from Túmán Bey, while Ghazzálí (leaving Damascus) and escaping the Turks, reached Cairo with 6,000 Mamlúks who were of his following. Túmán Bey, still relying on the promise [given to Qánsúh, his predecessor, by Sháh Isma'íl], had sent urgently to him demanding succour, but for an unknown reason all help in his need was now refused him. Sultan Selim, having made junction with Sinán Pasha, marched south, coming to the borders of Egypt and not far from Matariyah[6] came up with the enemy, and utterly routed the new Sultan of Egypt. Túmán Bey, constrained to flight, sought shelter in Cairo, but was followed thither by Sultan Selim, who, penetrating into the city, there ensued during two days much hard fighting in all its streets. Túmán Bey in the end was again vanquished, and once more fled, going along the coast of North Africa till he came to the city of Secusa. Here the emissaries of Sultan Selim discovered him in hiding half-drowned in a lagoon of these parts, and taking him prisoner, brought him back to Cairo. Selim then gave orders that Túmán Bey should be impaled [at the city gate], and so died the last of the Mamlúk Sultans of Egypt.

Thus Grand Cairo, which had been founded in the year 979 by Jawhar [the Eunuch prime minister of the Fatimite Caliph Mu'izz], was conquered by Sultan Selim in the year 1517. Ghazzálí, with some Egyptian troops at his back, now returned from the Thebaid intending aid to Túmán Bey, but finding all to be lost, gave in his submission to the victorious Selim. There are many who say that Ghazzálí was a traitor, and that he went over to Sultan Selim before the death of Túmán Bey, his own Sultan, but what is here stated seems the more reliable account. Sultan Selim appointed Khayr Beg to be the Beglerbeg of Egypt, and Ghazzálí to be once again, but in his name, the

## DON JUAN OF PERSIA

governor of Damascus, and the Sultan sent his son-in-law, Farhád Pasha, with 40,000 cavalry to guard the Turkish frontier on the east against any possible attack from Isma'íl Sophi. Sultan Selim, finding that the frontiers of his European dominions against the Christians were still at peace, now betook himself to collecting a great armada of ships, but for what enterprise none knew,[7] but in the very midst of these great warlike preparations of a novel kind, and while the princes of Europe and Asia were kept in suspense as to his ultimate intentions, Sultan Selim suddenly died at a place called Chorlú,[8] in September of the year 1591. Then at a date some three or four years later—namely, about the year 1522, or maybe 1524[9]—Isma'íl Sophi, at the age of fifty-four, likewise passed away, and thus those two who had been rivals for sovereignty in life, came to the end of their respective careers almost at one and the same time.

Sháh Isma'íl left four sons: the eldest, who succeeded him on the throne, was Sháh Tahmásp; the second, who held the principality of Mesopotamia, was Alqás; the third, Bahrám, was the governor of the province of Azerbayján; while the fourth was Sám Mirzá, to whom Persian 'Iráq was given. We now come to the year 1520, and remark that in this same year, when the Emperor Charles V was being crowned at Aix-la-Chapelle, Sultan Sulaymán, the son of Selim, was also crowned in Constantinople. Of matters that concern our purpose, however, nothing was done by Sultan Sulaymán until we come to the year 1534. At this date, urged thereto by Ibrahím Pasha, his most powerful minister, Sultan Sulaymán, collecting a fairly large army, passed through Asia Minor, and guided by one Vlaman,[10] who was a traitor fleeing from Sháh Tahmásp, the Sultan marched on and suddenly appeared in force before the walls of Tabríz. At this juncture Sháh Tahmásp found himself unable to defend the city against the Turkish army; he therefore retired at the head of his army into the inner lands of Persia, the Sultan in vain seeking to lure him out into the open to meet him in battle. Sultan Sulaymán therefore marched on down into 'Iráq, and had himself crowned Emperor of Mesopotamia at the hands of the [Grand Mufti] of Baghdad.[11] The pomp of the coronation having been brought to its close, Sultan Sulaymán returned to the neighbourhood of Tabríz, and wrathful at not being able to come up with Sháh Tahmásp, and so match him in a pitched battle, the Sultan in revenge set the city of Tabríz on fire, and leaving it to burn, began his march back into his own country.

The lamentable state of Tabríz was a horror that affected both the eyes and the ears of Sháh Tahmásp, who in sorrow and shame was witness of the slaughter of his people, and heard of the sufferings of his friends and of some even of his relatives, following on his forced retirement. He now assembled all the troops he could command, and returning back to Tabríz in haste with his new army, was most sorrowful at the lamentable sight he there saw. He then marched on to rejoin those of his people who were awaiting his coming in the Rimak mountains, and from there, at the head of a considerable force, proceeded forward to the river Qoyún Chay. From this place he sent on one of his captains, named Deli Muhammad,[12] with orders to make a night attack on the rear-guard of the Turks. Falling on the stragglers of Sulaymán's army that same night, which was the 13th October, Deli Muhammad took them by surprise in the darkness, when an immense number of the enemy were put to the sword. In this way Tahmásp took vengeance for the insults suffered by him in the matter of Tabríz, and not a man of the enemy who fell into his hands was spared. With his own hands he decapitated a number of the Beglerbegs, and other men of count among the Turkish officers. Of the enemy's cavalry more than 40,000 had been slain in the battle, and of the infantry above 70,000.

This indeed was one of the greatest and most signal defeats that the House of Ottoman ever suffered at the hands of the Grand Sophi; so disastrous in truth was it that Sultan Sulaymán was driven to offer to make an armistice with the Persian king. Then Sháh Tahmásp, being at liberty, took the occasion to chastise some of the more rebellious of his subjects, after the fashion which we shall now relate. Matters having been settled to his satisfaction in Anatolia, Tahmásp returned home to Persia, and of our authorities some tell a strange story, which for being almost laughable I here set down. No sooner did Sháh Tahmásp find himself quit of Sultan Sulaymán at Qoyún Chay than, turning back with his army, he marched down into 'Iráq to settle matters with the rebels in Baghdad. Here he burnt down a great part of the city, and the [Grand Mufti], who, as above related, had so recently crowned Sulaymán emperor, having come to die a few days before this time, Sháh Tahmásp caused his body to be dug up, and a dog's body to be buried in its place. I do confess, however, not to understand how they were able to make peace together—namely, the Sháh and the Sultan—with doings such as these taking place between them.

Sultan Sulaymán now seeing that in Asia Minor he was no longer attacked by the Persians, turned his eyes to Europe, as against the Christian princes, and proceeded to make war in Hungary. But here, when on the point of taking by storm the fortress of Szigeth, and in fact exactly ten days before the place fell to his arms, the Sultan suddenly died: according to one account, from rage at having been frustrated in an attempt to capture the neighbouring city of Erlau.

## SELIM "THE SOT"

Sulaymán had been Sultan forty-six years, and he was succeeded by his son Selim II [surnamed "the Sot"], who during the first years of his reign was engaged in wars of very small import against the Venetians, though at one time he succeeded in inflicting on them the disaster and defeat at sea off the island of Negropont that is so famous. After this, Selim II gathered together an immense armada to invade the West, but this time his forces were overcome and put to complete rout [at the battle of Lepanto] by Don John of Austria, half brother of his Catholic Majesty the late King Don Philip II.

## CHAPTER IV

*Of the great happenings which took place in Persia between the sons of Tahmásp, and of the wars of the Persians against Sultan Murád III.*

An armistice, as already said, had been concluded between Sháh Tahmásp and Sulaymán, the first Sultan of that name and the eleventh Ottoman emperor, after Tahmásp had driven the Turkish armies out of Tabríz—which city of old time had been known under the name of Ecbatana. Tahmásp, although he had suffered horror and distress on account of the sack of Tabríz by the Turks, did not recriminate on this matter, and the negotiations for the peace treaty took their course, of which one item was that the fortress of Qars, as the Turks call it, or Qaisari, as it is otherwise named,[1] should be dismantled by the Turks of all its fortifications, and delivered up by them to the Persians, in whose hands it should remain, but unfortified. The wars between the Persian monarchs and the Turk having thus been composed, soon after this [in 1566] Sultan Sulaymán died, and likewise his son, Sultan Selim II ["the Sot," in 1574], who had succeeded him on the throne, but who had accomplished nothing of any moment. Next, on the 11th of May in the year 1576, Sháh Tahmásp from the infirmities of age also died, leaving eleven sons and daughters.

The eldest son was named Muhammad Khudá Bandah, and he at one time had resided as governor at Herat—of old called Aria—but later by his father's orders he had gone to live at a place called Iiras, which is not Shíráz, as Minadoi incorrectly states,[2] this last being in truth the ancient Persepolis. The second son, Isma'íl, was at this time kept prisoner at the castle

## PRINCE ISMA'IL

of Qahqahah, which lies between Qazvín—the ancient Arsacia—and Tabríz, being 150 leagues from the former city and 30 from the latter, but at some distance to the northward in the direction of Erivan. Now his father, Sháh Tahmásp, had for some time past kept Prince Isma'íl shut up there, having come to note in him a certain marked disquietude of disposition, and a tendency towards rebellion, attributable to the overweening ambition of the arrogant youth, and the old king being a prudent parent, kept him thus sequestrated; but the death of the Sháh now delivered the prince from this paternal guardianship. The third son was called Sultan Haydar Mirzá,[3] and of him his mother's relations had charge, among whom were reckoned 'Isá Khán[4] and the Eunuch Akhtah Husayn, with a man named Pír Muhammad. The fourth son bore the name of Sultan Mustafá, and his mother had been a Christian princess from Georgia. The next three boys were Sultan 'Ali Mirzá, the fifth son, the sixth Bahrám Mirzá, and the seventh Ibrahím Mirzá: but these four last named were all at this date under age. There were also three daughters, but two of them so young that it were needless to take these into account, and all were by different mothers. But one daughter we have need here to mention by name, Parí-Khán-Khánum, the eldest of the sisters, for she was of age, also capable and ambitious, as we shall soon see.

Prince Muhammad Khudá-Bandah had always suffered from an affection of the eyes which partially or at times totally prevented him from seeing, and this defect of sight rendered him almost incapable of dealing with the affairs of government in provinces and among a people so prone to rebellion as are the Persians; and further it was common knowledge that all matters of state and government were foreign and distasteful to him. Now, seeing this condition of things his father, the old king Sháh Tahmásp, had been urged and even forced by his Kháns and the nobles of his kingdom—though much against his will, seeing the light in which he regarded the character of his second son Isma'íl—to appoint this same Isma'íl in his will and testament to succeed to the throne, thus putting him in the place of his elder brother, Muhammad Khudá-Bandah. This, of course, was not to act in accordance with precedent and Persian custom, but Tahmásp was obliged thereto by the fact of Muhammad Khudá-Bandah's blindness, and what appeared to be his incapacity to cope with the exigencies of kingship in a country where the prince or governor has in very truth need, not only of two eyes, but indeed of as many eyes to see with as in antiquity had been attributed to Argus. In accordance with the testamentary dispositions of Sháh Tahmásp, therefore, the Kháns and nobles after the king's death despatched word to Isma'íl to repair immediately to Qazvín, the capital, but before he could arrive, his half-sister, the Princess Parí-Khán-Khánum already referred to above—and her name in Persian means[5] [the Lady of the Fairy-Khán, she being own] sister of Mustafá Mirzá—now persuaded the Kháns and nobles to revoke the testament of her father the old king, or rather to suspend it.

This she did at the instance of her uncle, Shamkhál Khán,[6] a Georgian noble, he being her mother's brother and a Christian, and the Princess persuaded the conspirators to set up her half-brother, Haydar Mirzá, to be king in the seat of his father, Sháh Tahmásp. Another account of the matter, however, asserts that the Princess was not the author of this conspiracy, and on the contrary that she laboured to bring about the accession of Isma'íl in accordance with her father's testament: but she having discovered that a conspiracy was being formed against Isma'íl and in favour of Haydar Mirzá, dissembled, hiding what was her true intent, the better to unmask the projects of the rebels. Later, seeing how impossible it was for Isma'íl to arrive in Qazvín before the lapse of several days, she had then perforce to show an appearance of approval to Haydar being crowned king. Haydar, however, no sooner thus found himself almost against his will seated on the throne, than his heart failed him, and in fear of the consequences promptly fled to hide himself in the Palace, seeking shelter in the women's apartments, which to the Turks are known as the *Saray*, while the Persians call them the *Haram*. But here Shamkhál Khán[7] with a number of those nobles who were partisans of Isma'íl followed after, and coming up with Haydar slew him with their daggers. Thus the tumults and insurrections that had already begun with the sudden novelty of Haydar's coronation as king, were as suddenly appeased.

A few days after the death of Haydar Isma'íl arrived at the royal court and city of Qazvín, and his coming was a matter of very great satisfaction, in which all parties concurred. Isma'íl indeed, for some considerable time after he had been crowned as Sháh, made a pretence of good conduct and affability of demeanour, which clearly proved the violence of perturbation that his mind suffered; but no sooner was he firmly established as master than, abandoning the good custom of the royal family of the Sophis, and of the Persian kings his forefathers, he proceeded [after the evil manner of the Ottoman Sultans] to bring to death most of his younger brothers, and further gave orders for the prompt execution of all those Kháns and nobles of whom he had knowledge that they had taken any part in the coronation of Haydar. Sháh Isma'íl in his foolhardy arrogance did not, however, content himself with these cruel acts alone, but now proclaimed it his intention to abandon the Shi'ah Sect of 'Ali, which is the Persian form of faith and the religion instituted by the Sophi monarchs, as has been clearly explained in a former chapter when speaking of the rise and origin of the Sophi dynasty. Sháh Isma'íl it appeared now would fain follow the Turkish Sect of the Sunnis, honouring Abu Bakr, Omar, Othman and the other so-called orthodox Caliphs, a proceeding which, had he shown signs of so doing before he had been recognized as king, would infallibly have caused him to be torn in pieces by the Persians. While thus making public his foolish intention of a change in religion, he further proclaimed that he also proposed to betake himself incontinently to Baghdad in 'Iráq, in order there to be crowned emperor, even as Sultan Sulaymán and the other Turkish sovereigns had been wont to do, at the hands of [the Grand Mufti.][8]

All these proceedings being public, and perfectly understood by his sister Parí-Khán-Khánum and the Persian nobles, they coming together forthwith made a conspiracy to compass his death, and certain nobles disguised in female apparel having one night entered the Haram, or women's apartment of the Palace, slew Isma'íl—just as of old the Senators slew Julius Cæsar—the date of his death being the 24th of November of the year 1577.[9] After this, by agreement among the nobles who had done this deed, Isma'íl's half-sister, the Princess Parí-Khán-Khánum, was invested with the government until such time as it should become patent which of the late king's brothers was to succeed to the throne of Persia.[10]

Of the nobles one, Amír Khán by name, at this time was about to marry a sister of Parí-Khán-Khanum, who professed herself in love with him, and this had so turned his head with vanity that he imagined ambitiously that thereby he might become the next Sháh of Persia. On the other hand, Mirzá Salmán,[11] one of the chief nobles of the Persian court, wished to raise Isma'íl's elder brother, Muhammad Khudá-

## SULTAN MURAD III

Bandah, to the throne, or, failing him, his eldest son the Prince Hamzah Mirzá, who, it was proposed, then should marry one of the daughters of Mirzá Salmán, the noble aforesaid. Men of another party in the state were in favour of bringing 'Abbás Mirzá, a younger brother of Hamzah Mirzá, back from Herat, where he was governor, in order to set him on the vacant throne; while a third candidate some put forward was Prince Tahmásp [a yet younger brother of 'Abbás Mirzá]. Thus during seven years, seven months and seven days this confusion continued to last in the government, pretenders one after the other being set up and deposed, and suffering death after occupying the throne for some short space of time.

Sultan Murád III, who had recently [namely, in 1574] succeeded to the government in the room of his father, Selim II, "the Sot," son of Sulaymán, the Magnificent, was now ambitious, after becoming possessed of Mesopotamia, to conquer in addition all Western Asia. And his intention was more especially to invade the kingdoms of Persia and of Georgia, which is there known as Gurgistán, and further to add thereto all the Asiatic provinces adjacent, which at that time obeyed the rule of the Muscovite Duke of Moscow. For all these provinces, as we shall see, now remained open and unguarded, being no longer protected by the terror which the name of the great Sháh Tahmásp had inspired in the hearts of the Turks. Sultan Murád therefore, taking occasion of the confusion rampant throughout Persia from the civil wars, and after much consultation, appointed Mustafá Pasha general-in-chief of the army that was to effect this invasion. Then forthwith he sent word to the Pashas of Ván, Erzerúm and Greater Armenia, which all lie on the borders of Cappadocia, as also to the governor of 'Iráq, that all of them together should, by continued incursions, ravage the towns and castles across their respective frontiers, which belonged to the lands of the Qizil Básh (Red Heads)—for, as we have said, so do the Turks call the Persians—and thus inaugurate the new invasion by petty conquests. An account of recent events and the changes that had taken place in Constantinople had been brought to the new king, Muhammad Khudá-Bandah, who was by now established on the Persian throne, and at the same time the news came that the Turkish army under orders from Sultan Murád was already marching on Azerbayján and Georgia.

Muhammad Sháh's surname of Khudá-Bandah was assumed by him because he knew himself to be the "Servant of God," and His true envoy, who had been preserved alive, as by a special miracle, after the death of his younger brothers, in order that he might rule the kingdom, and this name certainly was not given him because he was blind, as Thomas Minadoi[12] erroneously asserts, he, Minadoi, being ignorant of the true etymological meaning of words in the Persian language. Muhammad Khudá-Bandah, therefore, as we may now state, had peacefully entered into possession of his kingdom of Persia, having as deputy in the government his eldest son, Hamzah Mirzá, who was of such capable intelligence that, though his father was blind, this defect of eyesight was made up for by the extraordinary ability of the Prince, to whom, though an unbeliever as regards the True Faith, God had granted a very acute understanding and a ripe judgment.

Further, it was that noble already referred to, Mirzá Salmán, who had by his judicious administration brought about a state of peace throughout the kingdom, and the acknowledgment by the Persian people of Muhammad Khudá-Bandah as their rightful king. Mirzá Salmán indeed had effected all this, although he was by birth and position but a small man amongst the other nobles of Persia, yet in matters of government

## MIRZA SALMAN

he had shown the greatness of his capacity. He too had been the prime mover[13] to bring it about that the wicked Princess Parí-Khán-Khánum, who, as we have said, had lured her brother Sháh Isma'íl to his death, herself was now condemned to be beheaded. Indeed, at the gates of Qazvín they had displayed her head, all bloody and dishevelled, stuck on a lance point, thus exposed to public view, a sight very sad and horrid, for in truth she was a king's daughter, and the sister of the reigning king, though a woman most culpable. After this act of justice, Muhammad Khudá-Bandah remained for the moment in undisturbed possession of the kingdom, his son Hamzah Mirzá governing in his name, though this time of peace and rest for both was indeed but short, as almost immediately thereafter the army of the Turks approached, coming in invasion upon them.

## CHAPTER V

*In which the war between Sultan Murád III and Sháh Muhammad Khudá-Bandah is recounted, with a description of Georgia and its rulers.*

MUSTAFÁ PASHA let the winter go by, and when the season bettered he put in force the powers given him as general-in-chief of the Turkish army, ordering the troops to set out on their march from Erzerúm, where they had previously been assembled. Taking the direct road through Qars, which was still in ruins, Mustafá Pasha advanced beyond this and took up general quarters in the mountainous district of Childir, in Armenia.[1] The army under his command now numbered somewhat under 200,000 men, of whom 100,000 were well armed, but of various nationalities, men from Bithynia and Phrygia mixed up with troops from Palestine and Judea, some from Pontus and Lydia: also men from Egypt and Africa and from Hungary. The Turkish army was indeed very well munitioned and provisioned, by reason of the attendance of the fleet of transports, which the Admiral Uluch-'Ali had brought, under charge of his galleys, to the port of Trebizond, whence by land-carriage all provisions were carried over to Erzerúm. Mustafá Pasha had already got the troops well in hand, everything being organized for the march, and he had reinforced his artillery with 500 pieces of small cannon.

The new king of Persia, Muhammad Khudá-Bandah, perfectly realized the designs of Mustafá Pasha, and having assembled together a sufficient body of troops gave the command to Toqmaq Sultán Khán, the governor of Eriván and Nakhcheván, whom the king made general-in-chief of his armies in Atropatene,

## TOQMAQ KHAN

Greater Media, Georgia and Persia, with command over the cities of Hamadán, Ganjah, Tabríz, Mási, Nakhcheván, Marand, Ardebíl Sufiyán, Qara-Aghach, Turkoman-Chay and Chavat. All told, however, the Persian army only amounted in number to a bare 30,000 cavalry, with infantry to match in a sufficient force. The Persians now set out in haste, having received news that Mustafá Pasha had already left Erzerúm, had passed Qars, and advancing by daily marches had reached the plains of Childir. To Toqmaq it had been falsely reported that the Turkish army did not exceed some 40,000 men, being made up of soldiers of many nationalities, none over well armed, although indeed it was truly said that there were among them many valiant warriors and excellent commanders, as for instance, Khusraw Pasha, Bahrám Pasha, Dervísh Pasha of Qara-Amid, and Muhammad Pasha. The number of these famous captains caused no dismay to Toqmaq, but what astonished him was the apparent smallness, as by report, of the numbers composing the Turkish force. For this army, as he knew well, was brought together from many remote provinces, at the command of that powerful prince Sultan Murád, and despatched against an enemy both numerous and strong, as was the force under his, Toqmaq's, command, and the Turks came forth to conquer nothing less than the whole of Persia. All this indeed was only what the public voice proclaimed, and in the Persian camp the many youthful commanders had imposed upon Toqmaq, for they induced him now to give credit to the false reports of his spies, which a general so experienced in the practice of war as was Toqmaq should never have for a moment believed.

His light horsemen shortly after this having come up in sight of the vanguard division of the Turkish army, Toqmaq in his ignorance imagined this to be the whole body of 40,000 which had been reported to him as the sum total of the invading force. He soon, however, began to suspect the truth, seeing among them only the standards of the two Pashas Bahrám and Dervísh, and feared that Mustafá Pasha—as was the case—was in the rear with the main body of his army, and as it were hiding in ambush. Toqmaq, however, felt that his honour was at stake, and that come what might he was bound valiantly to offer battle. Hardly had the first skirmish begun when Mustafá appeared and made a sudden attack on the Persian right flank, bringing against them a division of 70,000 men. Two matters of good fortune now just saved the Persians from complete annihilation—namely, the skilful generalship shown by Toqmaq, and the opportune coming on of the night and darkness. So Toqmaq, who had quickly realized his error and the danger that menaced him, began falling back by devious routes in the mountain passes, and by making use of every possible stratagem finally managed to escape destruction; but not to save a very considerable part of his army, for his loss was 7,000 men killed, and 3,000 more who remained prisoners with the Turks. Mustafá Pasha immediately sent the joyful news of his victory to Sultan Murád, who in reply greatly praised the deed done, and the Sultan added an order, as it appears of his own motion, that every one of the 3,000 Persian prisoners of war should be beheaded, an order which was forthwith carried out, a cruel and inhuman act such as had not been reported till that time as having been perpetrated, even of any barbarian potentate. This great victory of the Turks now gave cause that many of the local princes in those parts, who had hitherto been subjects of Persia, forthwith went over and gave in their submission to Sultan Murád. Thus Mustafá Pasha's army was joined without delay by the Georgian prince Salmas, and by Levente, the

## GEORGIAN PRINCES

newly installed prince of another district of Georgia, and by Prince Manuchihr, the son of Princess Desmit,[2] the widow [of Prince Lavarza], who had recently been dispossessed of his lands by the Persians. All these princes now joined the standard of Mustafá Pasha, who, receiving them with great courtesy, despatched an account of their submission to the Sultan, as the firstfruits of the conquest of Georgia which he, Mustafá, was so successfully engaged in accomplishing.

To make matters perfectly clear, it will now be well to explain fully who were all these Georgian princes, and to describe the country they ruled, which is now known as Georgia, and which of old was called Iberia. On the west Georgia touches the lands of the people of Colchis, who are the Mingrelians; while on the east it has Media Atropatene, which at the present time is the province of Shirván. On the north the Georgian border marches with Albania, which is now called Zuiria,[3] while on the south its limit is Armenia. Georgia is a very rocky, mountainous country, of many rivers, and among these is the Cyrus, or Kur, which traverses the heart of the province, its waters ultimately joining the famous river Araxes, or Aras. The Araxes rises in the Taurus range in that part of the mountains which is called Periard, beside mount Aba [or Abus], and flowing eastward till it reaches the frontier of Shirván, it then turns to the north-west to the point where, as noted above, the Cyrus river joins it. The Araxes, next flowing by the city of Eres,[4] which is of Armenia, and passing through the Araxene Lands, which at the present time are known as the Plains of Calderan,[5] finally flows out into the Caspian Sea, which same sea is now known under the name of Qulzum.[6]

Georgia comprised many districts ruled by divers lords who were as we might say dukes, marquises and counts. Of these princes the most powerful were then the following six in number. First there was [Princess Desmit] the widow of Prince Lavarza, and her two sons, named Mirzá Manuchihr and his brother Alexander.[7] [In the second place came the two sons of Prince Labassap][8] called David and Simon. [Thirdly, the son of Levente, otherwise called] Leventoghlú, and his Christian name was Iskandar, or as we should say, Alexander, being commonly referred to by his own people as "the Great." Fourthly, there was the prince Yúsuf, the son of Gory. Fifthly, the old prince Shamkhál, the lord of many lands, which lie between the province of Shirván and the country governed by Prince Iskandar, above named. This Prince Shamkhál at a later date was put to death by Othman Pasha [subsequently the Turkish commander-in-chief in Georgia], but he left a son who succeeded to his lands, and who at the present time, when we write, rules over the mountain country called Brus by the Turks, which is a most rugged district, and where the snow lies continuously. Finally and sixthly, there was a very powerful Georgian prince named Bashachuk, whose lands marched with those of Prince Gory, being divided from these last by the Lake of Essekia,[9] while on his eastern frontiers was the country of Levente ruled by Prince Iskandar Leventoghlú.[10]

To return to our story, the prince Yúsuf and his father, Gory, both now joined the Turkish armies, and Yúsuf forthwith became a Moslem. Prince Alexander, who was the elder brother of Manuchihr, as above mentioned, at that time ruled over the lands which lay adjacent to Qars on the west, while on the east his frontiers marched with those of the princes David and Simon. This country is watered by the river Araxes, and its capital is the fortress called Altun Qal'ah, a name which signifies the Golden Castle, and it stands about halfway between Tiflis and Qars, being on every hand enclosed and defended by the passes

# GEORGIA

of the Periard mountains. Prince Labassap had at his death by will and testament left his lands to his elder son Simon, but the younger brother David, with the aid of Sháh Tahmásp, who sent 4,000 men in his support, had immediately taken possession of the principality; and at the same time had declared himself to be a vassal of the king of Persia, becoming a renegade and a Moslem under the name of David Khán. Sháh Tahmásp had forthwith made him lord of Tiflis, and Simon, his elder brother, who would not at that period by any means become a renegade, was imprisoned, being sent to the Castle of Qahqahah. The towns that then belonged to this family of princes were Tiflis, Lori, Tomanis, Qars, or Qieres, and Júrji-Qal'ah, the Georgian Castle. Tiflis is the capital, standing on the river Kur, or Cyrus, which flows to join the Araxes, as already described, and to the westward of the city lies the range of the Caucasus.

Now the Turkish armies occupying this province of Georgia, with their plundering and ravaging, had already brought these lands to naught. They had invaded the country, entering thereto from all four quarters, although the Georgians before this had imagined that it was impossible for anyone to bring troops across the mountains by the defiles. On the coast of the Black Sea, however, in the quarter of the Albanians the Turkish army had been safely landed by an armada[11] of their ships, being supported by 'Ádil-Ghiray, the Tartar Khán [of the Crimea]. At the same moment also they invaded the country from the side of Shirván; and likewise by two other passes the Turkish troops came in—namely, on the one hand by way of the Lake of Essekia, on which stands the city of Bashachuk, with many other towns subject to that Georgian prince who, as we have said, also is known by the name Bashachuk; and lastly, the Turks penetrated into Georgia by the pass on the other side, where the country is covered by juniper and a pine forest, that same being the route by which, if we are to believe Strabo's account in Book II of his *History*, Pompey and Canidius Crassus brought their armies over the border. Now the son of Levente, who, as we have said, was called Iskandar, and his brother 'Isá Khán, had lands lying between the city of Eriván and the country of Shirván, and other lands beyond this again in the direction of Armenia on the further borders of Shirván. The lords of this district resided at the city of Zaghen, and 'Isá Khán, brother of Iskandar, as aforesaid, now a renegade, having become a Moslem, by Sháh Tahmásp had been appointed to be governor of the province, being set up to rule in his brother's place, but this act on the part of the Persian king before long had failed in effect. We now conclude this description of Georgia, adding that in its most remote regions there were living many wild tribes of the Tartars, who are known as the Perikorsks, and they inhabit the foot-hills of the Caucasus in parts that look towards the valley of the Volga river, otherwise known as the Eder.

[After his victory over the Persians at Childir] Mustafá Pasha marched on, being given support and help on the part of the Georgians, which help, though small as to the numbers of his new allies, was most effective for the safe passage of the Turkish army; since it was through their own country that the Georgians were now engaged in showing the enemy the way. With his new friend Manuchihr as guide the Pasha advanced, though with great difficulty on account of the constant rains, and finally reached the lake called Kieder Gul, from which the river Euphrates has its source. Here he found the Turkish vanguard already in possession of the Castle of Arkikelek, and the army rested for a space of time, finding all requirements in the pasture grounds which lie round the lake.

## TIFLIS TAKEN

Then the Pasha passed on, going by the Lake of Pervana Gul, near to which stand the ruins of [Triala],[12] an ancient city that was founded by the Crusaders who afterwards conquered Jerusalem. There are still at the present day some priests with a number of Christian folk who live here, and who being Catholics are subject to Rome. Next, marching forth again the Turkish army reached the near side of the Tiflis mountains, and having crossed their crest, descended without halt and took possession of a castle called Jurji-Qal'ah, the Georgian Castle already mentioned, which stands on the bank of the Kur, the river of Tiflis. Some of the Turkish soldiers were disbanded here, and seeing that the land was defenceless and at peace, forthwith they took to robbing and plundering the people. On this the princes Yúsuf and David joined forces with Iskandar, being now desirous of giving aid to their old allies the Persians, while at the same time they appeared to be acting in defence of their native country and their own people. The three princes with their men, therefore, suddenly fell on these disbanded Turkish troops, and killed no small number of them.

This, however, did not prevent the Turks from soon capturing the city of Tiflis; for Prince David, who had at the first alarm hastened his return in order to defend his capital, now realizing that against him was the great superiority in numbers of the Turkish forces, proceeded anon to vacate his capital after dismantling the fortifications. It appeared also to be his better chance to join forces with his friends in the field: and leaving Tiflis, he marched forth into the open. Mustafá Pasha, having thus come into possession of the town, proceeded to repair the walls of the castle on the rock, furnishing it with a hundred pieces of cannon, setting a garrison in guard of 6,000 men, commanded by Muhammad Pasha, son of Farhád

Pasha, who he appointed to be the governor of Tiflis. Then Muṣtafá Pasha continuing his march passed down into the province of Shirván. But now those Turkish troops who were from Aleppo and other parts of Syria, being wearied out by the long marches, mutinied, and unmindful of their duty and the prayers and proteſts of the Pasha, went off, under the leadership of one of their captains named Nasr-ad-Dín Cheleby. They, however, rejoicing to be quit of the service, soon were dearly to pay for their revolt, for the Georgians fell upon them when they saw these Turks separated from their fellows, and very few of the mutineers escaped the massacre with their lives.

Muſtafá Pasha now advanced to the base of the mountains[13] near Tiflis, where ambassadors from Iskandar Leventoghlú appeared with the proposition that the prince should come to pay his respeɛts to the Pasha, and give in his allegiance to Sultan Murád. At the same time Iskandar offered the Turks to aɛt as their guide, giving them passage through his territories: such was the inconſtancy of these Georgian princes, who changed their friendships as easily as they changed their religion. Muſtafá Pasha was indeed glad to be granted a safe passage through this dangerous country, and immediately accepted the offer of Iskandar Leventoghlú, to whom he forthwith sent the Robes of Honour which it is cuſtomary for the Ottoman Sultan to beſtow on those princes who become his allies, or indeed on any general who conquers a new province for the empire; and Prince Iskandar expressed himself much gratified by the favour done him. So Muſtafá Pasha began his march forward, and for twelve days was engaged in passing through marsh lands and cane-brakes, but with so much hindrance and discomfort from the badness of the road that more than once his soldiers for a time refused to go on, cursing the ambition of Sultan Murád and the vainglory of

## KANAK RIVER

their Pasha. At last, however, the army came through, reaching the borders of Shirván.

At this moment there arrived, in more fear than joy, people from the city of Shakí, which stands on the confines of the province of Shirván, who offered their submission to the Turks, promising the obedience of all the tribes whose abode lay along the banks of the river Kanak.[14] The Turkish troops were now suffering from great fatigue, and there was a scarcity of foodstuffs, and the soldiers imperiously demanded of their general a halt for some days' rest, though the place in which they found themselves was not well suited for a camp. Under advice from the inhabitants of those parts, and in order to procure most necessary provisions, Mustafá Pasha now proceeded to despatch a body of 12,000 of his men, though not of his best armed infantry, with some squadrons of cavalry, under their several commanders; for the Pasha had been informed that beyond the marsh which lay at the junction of the Kanak river with the Araxes there were great pastures, with corn lands, where wheat, barley and rice might be come to, also many flocks and herds.

This information was believed to be reliable by the Pasha, and the foraging parties departed: but it was false and it was the occasion for an ambush so much desired by the Persian commanders—namely, Toqmaq, 'Ali Quli Khán, Imám Quli Khán and Sharaf Khán— who now longed to retrieve their defeat at Childir. The Persians therefore now very stealthily followed on the rear-guard of the foraging Turks, and came up with them as soon as these had separated from the main body of their fellows. Falling on them unexpectedly, they put them completely to rout, so that hardly a man of the foraging parties escaped with his life. In the sequel, however, the Persians gained little by their victory, for such few Turks as escaped the ambush bringing news of the disaster to Mustafá

## DON JUAN OF PERSIA

Pasha, he by a forced march suddenly came upon these victorious Persians, and next surrounded them in a peninsula lying between the rivers Araxes and Kanak. Here Bahrám Pasha and Dervísh Pasha skirmished and charged in on the Persians, while Muŝtafá Pasha later marching up with the remainder of his forces, Toqmaq and his fellow commanders were forced to give battle and defend themselves at a disadvantage. As a result, very few of the Persians managed to escape with their lives from this counterŝtroke of the Turks, though even their meaneŝt camp-followers fought valiantly as though they had been the beŝt of warriors. The carnage was terrible on both sides, and the Persian commanders, Toqmaq himself being the firŝt to give the example, managed to escape death by swimming the river, thus encouraging his soldiers to make the like attempt. Of these laŝt, however, very many were killed; while of the Turks 12,000 sutlers and 3,000 soldiers of the flower of their army perished. Imám Quli Khán after this defeat returned to Ganjah,[15] Sharaf Khán to Nakhcheván, and Toqmaq proceeded to Eriván, neither side, Persian or Turk, being in a position to diŝturb the other side, each of the parties awaiting fresh orders from his maŝter, the one from the Sháh, the other from the Sultan.

## CHAPTER VI

*In which is continued the account of the campaign of the armies of Sultan Murád against Muhammad Khudá-Bandah, king of Persia, and details are given of the death of 'Ádil-Ghiray, the prince of the Tartars, and what was the cause of the same.*

ALTHOUGH to all appearance the frontiers of the province of Shirván were closely guarded, and the whole district in the peaceable occupation of the Turkish army, yet no sooner did envoys with offers of submission appear from one quarter of the province, than from some other quarter would come news of fresh revolts in districts thought to be securely held by the Ottoman troops. Mustafá Pasha therefore now determined to overpass the Kanak river, although his army murmured loudly against any further conquests which must cost so many lives. The men, however, were forced, though much against their will, to obedience, and in the result the loss of the Turkish troops was again over 8,000 men, before Mustafá Pasha had come to the city of Eres, which is the chief town in those parts. Here the Turks found that the place had been abandoned and dismantled, as also proved to be the case with Shamákhí, for the Persian commander, Samír Khán, had betaken himself to the mountains, where, having been joined by Aras Khán, the two were now watching the further proceedings of the Turkish commanders.

Mustafá Pasha remained for twenty-two days in the town of Eres, building here a fortress which he furnished with one hundred small cannon,[1] and in command of this fortress he appointed Kaytás Pasha, with a garrison of 5,000 men. Next he despatched Othman Pasha with 10,000 to occupy the town of

## DON JUAN OF PERSIA

Shamákhí, the capital city of Shirván, which stands on the road to Derbend, otherwise called Dimúr-Qapí [the Iron Gate], and which anciently was known as Alexandria. The people of Shamákhí, as also those of Derbend, forthwith submitted themselves to Othman Pasha, although indeed they were truly the subjects of the Persian king. Mustafá Pasha, now that the affairs of Georgia were in so good a way, and that the authority of his master the Sultan had been emphatically vindicated and established throughout this province, at last therefore gave the order for the return march, an order most grateful to his weary troops. In passing through the provinces ruled by Iskandar Leventoghlú, and by Shamkhál the lord of the Brus mountain, these two princes came out to meet Mustafá Pasha, offering him their humble submission, and matters were forthwith arranged on terms of amity. The Pasha had ordered the bridge over the Kanak river to be restored, and crossing it he marched up the Araxes bank back to Tiflis, where the troops took two days' rest.

They were now about to be conducted through the passes of the mountains, in easy stages, by the people sent to be their guides by Prince Iskandar, and it was recalled that here a year before the Turks had suffered much hardship and hunger at their incoming. Thus the Turkish army was at last leaving behind them the mountain villages of the Georgian country, but even as they were thus peaceably passing out of these districts the Georgians assembled, plundering their rearguard, composed of the baggage train and the sick and wounded, of which company Hasan Pasha, son of Jambulát,[2] was in command. The Turks, however, in the end came through without a disaster, and vanquishing a thousand dangers and difficulties, all at last arrived back at Erzerúm. Hither Mustafá Pasha had brought in his train the two sons of the

# 'ÁDIL GHIRAY

widowed Princess Desmit—namely, Manuchihr and Alexander—who now were to be sent as hostages to Constantinople. Of all these matters the Pasha wrote fully to give account to Sultan Murád, and the troops were dismissed to their home quarters; but while Mustafá was thus taking his ease, the king of Persia, Sháh Muhammad Khudá-Bandah, and his son, Prince Hamzah, were working and not idle.

Now at the call of the Turks, 'Ádil Ghiray, already mentioned, a gallant youth who was prince of the Perekop Tartars of the Crimea, had recently entered into an alliance with the Sultan against the king of Persia, and in consequence was at the moment marching on Georgia at the head of a fine army of his people, coming from the lands round the Sea of Azof and the rugged shores[3] of the Black Sea. To this prince Othman Pasha, acting under orders from Mustafá Pasha and from Sultan Murád, had written enjoining that his Tartar hordes should ravage and lay waste in every possible way the lands of the province of Shirván, which 'Ádil Ghiray forthwith began to do. News of this had been brought into Qazvín, where King Muhammad Khudá-Bandah was in residence with the prince his son, the Amír Hamzah, otherwise known as Hamzah Mirzá, and many were the councils held and the counsels given, as to what it were best for the Persian government to do. At this period it was indeed plainly manifest to the Sháh and his council of nobles that, by reason of the rigour of the winter season, no aid from Constantinople could possibly be sent to the Pashas who had been left as governors in command of the various strong places throughout Georgia which Mustafá Pasha had taken into possession; and realizing this, Prince Hamzah forthwith determined to march into Shirván with a body of troops amounting to 12,000 cavalry. By so doing it was his intention to throw back the raids of the Tartars under 'Ádil Ghiray, and also at the same time to punish those cities in the Shirván province where without due cause of dire necessity the people had gone over, as of free will, to the side of the invaders: for this indeed had been the case with the inhabitants of Shaki and many other townships.

During all this campaign [Sháh Muhammad Khudá-Baudah's wife⁴] the Begum, who was the mother of Hamzah Mirzá, insisted on accompanying the prince, though having sons all grown-up men she was now a woman of a certain age, yet still beautiful beyond the ordinary of her time of life; further she was a princess of much prudent counsel. Mirzá Salmán, the prime minister, also accompanied Prince Hamzah on this campaign. Coming up through Ardebíl the Persian army reached Qara Aghách, where a short halt was made for reasons now to be explained. Aras Khán and other nobles of Shirván had been of late put greatly to shame, for they were all outcasts and wanderers in the land, the Turks being in occupation of their homesteads. They now had news of the communications established between the Tartar prince 'Ádil Ghiray and Othman Pasha, and had learnt what the Pasha had instructed him to do. Aras Khán and his friends therefore took counsel, and having collected a force deemed sufficient, had marched out into the field intent on making a diversion that should have an effect in favour of their master the Persian king. Aras Khán, however, had laid his plans badly, for the Tartar Khán knew of all his designs, and marching against the Persians he suddenly attacked Aras Khán and his men, routing them completely. Aras Khán was taken prisoner, and being sent to Othman Pasha, he forthwith had him hanged.

Prince Hamzah had news on his march of this disaster as he was approaching the city of Eres. His army had recently been augmented by a reinforcement of some 10,000 cavalry, and he now learnt that Kaytás

## ERES TAKEN

Pasha, the Turkish commander of Eres, had gone out from the fortress on an expedition for plundering and laying waste the country round. Hamzah Mirzá therefore determined to seize the occasion, if possible, to surprise the city. Making a sudden attack he slew some 7,000 Turks of the garrison, and immediately became possessed of Eres city, where, finding the 200 pieces of artillery left there, as before noted, by Mustafá Pasha, he despatched these as booty to the king, his father, in Qazvín. Much elated by his victory, and leaving his mother, the Begum, established in Eres, Hamzah Mirzá next marched on to Shamákhí, where his coming was unexpected, and before any warning had been given, suddenly he appeared in sight of the camp of the Tartar prince, 'Ádil Ghiray. The Tartars were at the moment in some disorder, and for a people making war on a potent enemy they had been strangely negligent of precautions. Their camping ground here was ill chosen, and no sentinels were posted on guard. Hamzah Mirzá resolved on prompt action, and made an immediate attack, which turned out very successfully, for in matters of war promptness is the mother of good fortune. When the Tartars, thus surprised, had regained their senses, it was found that more than half their number had been killed, and that their prince, 'Ádil Ghiray, was a prisoner. Him Hamzah Mirzá now sent under a strong guard to his father in Qazvín.

Prince Hamzah did not rest content with merely thus defeating the Tartars, but immediately after his victory marching on, proceeded to make a successful attack on Shamákhí, of which city Othman Pasha had recently been appointed governor. The Pasha indeed contrived in time to make his escape from the city, and fled in haste to Derbend, but had to abandon all his artillery, and also his Persian allies the people of Shamákhí were now left unprotected. Prince Hamzah, on entering that city, inflicted heavy chastisement on all its inhabitants, and proceeded to dismantle the town walls. Next marching back to Eres, where he had left his mother, the Begum, he, taking her in his train, now returned to Qazvín, which capital he entered in triumph laden with the spoils of his Turk and Tartar enemies: and here he remained till the winter of that year had been overpassed.

At about this period two events occurred worthy of note on account of what followed after in the region of Georgia, and they may here be profitably recorded. As we have already narrated the Tartar prince 'Ádil Ghiray was at this time a prisoner of war in Qazvín, he being the younger brother of Tartar Khán, grand prince and monarch of the Tartars of the Crimea. After a time Sháh Muhammad Khudá-Bandah did not any more treat the Tartar prince with rigour as a prisoner, but showed him kindness as a friend and neighbour, and it was indeed his intention to have married him to one of his daughters, and thus to have established a friendly relationship by this family connection between his Persian subjects and the Tartar folk. Unfortunately at this very moment it was reported that a shameful treason had been discovered—namely, that 'Ádil Ghiray had dared raise his eyes to look on the Begum, Sháh Muhammad Khudá-Bandah's queen, and the mother of Hamzah Mirzá. Further, it was put about that the Queen had returned his advances, and that illicit communications had resulted. When therefore these matters had become known to certain of the nobles, in wrath at this great shame, they conspired and one night forced their way into the palace, putting both the Queen and the Tartar prince, her lover, to instant death, and immediately spread the news abroad openly to explain and justify what they had done. All this, as here narrated, is the account of the matter which Thomas Minadoi has given in his *History*,[5] but, as we have learnt, it seems certain that

## 'ÁDIL GHIRAY

the truth was far otherwise—namely, that these nobles were merely acting under a feeling of petty jealousy against the Tartar prince, a sentiment that had been aroused in their minds at the sight of the intimacy he had gained in the affections of the Sháh Muhammad Khudá-Bandah. For these men feared lest, if the king made 'Adil Ghiray his son-in-law—as in fact he intended shortly to do—the Tartar prince would then gain a party in Persia, with power in the affairs of the government. They therefore, unwilling that a stranger should thus come in, slew him, and pretexting his shameful intimacy with the Queen put her also to death, though innocent, a victim to serve the infamous purposes of her very jealous subjects.

The other event of importance which happened at about this time was connected with the doings of Othman Pasha. He, professing great friendship for Shamkhál, the Georgian prince already mentioned, constrained Shamkhál [who was a Christian] to give him, Othman, one of his daughters in marriage. The old prince Shamkhál perforce did as he was bid, but his conscience troubling him that his new son-in-law was none other than the chief commander of the forces of the Turkish invaders, and a sworn enemy to all those of his blood—namely, to his friends and relations among the other princes of Georgia—Shamkhál, I say, began secretly to show an inclination to the Persian alliance. Through the intermediary of his new wife Othman Pasha got wind of this matter, and by giving a safe-conduct lured his poor father-in-law into his power, and then forthwith had Shamkhál beheaded. And this should serve as a warning to all those who in the future may put their trust in the word of an infidel and a barbarian Turk.

In the following year Sultan Murád, acting under the advice sent by Othman Pasha, and listening to the friends in Constantinople of Mustafá Pasha—who was still stationed in Erzerúm—now determined on more vigorous action. He was urged to the same intent by Tartar Khán, the prince of the Crimea, who was now the more at enmity with the Persians by reason of the recent murder of his brother, 'Ádil Ghiray; but who, none the less, never could accomplish what he might promise. By the Sultan's orders in the first place the road from Erzerúm into Georgia was to be fortified and made good, and in consequence he sent instructions for engineers and masons to be brought hither from Aleppo, Damascus and Amid, also from Syria, Mesopotamia and Egypt to effect this purpose. It was about this time that Manuchihr, being still detained in captivity at Constantinople, became a Moslem, changing with his religion his name to Mustafá, and he was now given the title of Pasha of Altun Qal'ah. His brother Alexander, however, refused to become a renegade, and Sultan Murád therefore delivered him as a prisoner into the hands of the Moslem Mustafá, allowing him to do as he would with Alexander. Mustafá therefore, taking Alexander under strong guard, departed from Constantinople on his way home to his lands in Georgia, where he was now to govern as the vassal of the Turkish Sultan.

The king of Persia, Muhammad Khudá-Bandah, meanwhile did not remain nothing doing, but, foreseeing what must take place, named Imám Quli Khán, the governor of Ganjah, to be commander-in-chief of his armies, sending him orders to march against Othman Pasha and drive him out of Derbend. To this end the Sháh further gave instructions that the following commanders should join forces and serve under him— namely, Amír Khán, the governor of Tabríz; Toqmaq, the governor of Eriván; and Sharaf Khán, the governor of Nakhcheván. The Sháh also ordered the son[6] of the late prince Shamkhál to join his men to theirs, but he declined and would not obey the king's command.

## DAVID AND SIMON

When matters now were at this pass, two events occurred that were entirely unexpected by the Persian monarch. The first was that David Khán, who had been greatly favoured by the Shah since he had become a Moslem and a renegade, for no apparent cause now took flight from the Persian lands and went to join the Turks, voluntarily giving in his allegiance to Sultan Murád. In the second place, this David Khán's brother, Simon, who had been thrown into prison [by the Sháh], because he would not abjure Christianity, through the corruption of evil companions in his captivity, had at last been brought to abandon his faith, abjuring Christ. He therefore, now become a Moslem, was set at liberty, and reinstated in possession of his lands, the title of Khán being restored to him. With a view of giving due and effective help to the Persian commander-in-chief, Simon Khán now joined forces with 'Ali Quli Khán, bringing with him many pieces of cannon which had been taken from the Turks, and further with 3,000 horsemen he now was busy to ravage and plunder all those lands of Turkish Georgia that lay near and about his own frontiers.

## CHAPTER VII

*Of the deeds of the Renegade Simon and of 'Ali Quli Khán as against the Turks, and what the armies of Murad III accomplished under the command of Manuchihr.*

MUSTAFÁ PASHA, carrying out the orders of Sultan Murád his master, having collected together the engineers and masons sent to join him at Qars from Memphis in Egypt, which is also known as Cairo, and from Damascus and from other parts of the empire, now began to build in Qars a fortress as had been commanded him. Further he despatched reinforcements to Tiflis under charge of Hasan Pasha, a good general, more commonly known as the Pasha of Damascus, he being a son of the Grand Vizier Muhammad [Sokolli], who at that time directed the affairs of government at the Sublime Porte. With him too went Rizván Pasha, at the head of a body of volunteers. Now Simon and 'Ali Quli Khán (the Persian commander-in-chief) had news of the coming of these reinforcements, and it being reported that the Turks only numbered 8,000 men in all—although in this misinformed, for in fact they amounted to over 20,000—Simon and 'Ali Quli Khán took post in ambush in the neighbourhood between Tiflis and Tomanis, and choosing the right moment, as it seemed to them, fell unexpectedly on the advancing Turkish force, killing of them a very great number. Among those who fell was Mustafá Bey, of Cæsarea [Mazaka] in Qarmania, a man of note, and his standard too was taken.

'Hasan Pasha felt this blow, more for the loss of honour than for the loss of men, and with a view of taking reprisal, affected to have been utterly put to rout by this unexpected Persian attack, and in so doing managed to draw his assailants from their shelter in the woods and gorges. 'Ali Quli Khán being enticed forth, in his ardour to profit by the good fortune that he had gained threw himself rashly upon the Turks, and shortly became so involved and surrounded among the enemy troops that his friend Simon, hastening to his support, failed to catch up with and follow him. Then Hasan Pasha with his superior numbers was able to put to slaughter a multitude of the Persians and Georgians; 'Ali Quli Khán himself was taken prisoner, and Simon barely by good luck escaped the same fate. Hasan Pasha was much gratified by the capture he had made, and resting for twelve days in camp, then threw his relief force into Tiflis, where the Turkish garrison indeed were in dire want of succour. Hasan Pasha now saw fit to change the command in Tiflis, taking it from Muhammad Pasha and appointing Ahmad Pasha Hajji Begoghli to be governor in his place, with 3,000 new men to reinforce the garrison. Also, as the fortress did not appear to him strong or very well secured, he removed, carrying the same away with him, the whole of the military chest of moneys, with most of the stores.

Hasan Pasha now set out on his march back to Erzerúm, and Simon, being much affected by the capture of his dear friend 'Ali Quli Khán, determined to effect his release, if the matter could by force or fraud be brought about. He therefore proceeded to block and then to fortify the pass at Tomanis in order that Hasan Pasha might in passing be forced to halt and give him battle, for there was by this route no other passage through the mountains. The Turks now discovered they could only force their way through the pass with considerable delay and loss of men; whereupon Hasan Pasha was in great straits, but sought refuge in guile and stratagem, as these barbarian commanders are ever wont to do. He sent word to Simon, promising to release to him his friend 'Ali Quli Khán if Simon would allow the Turks safe passage by any road where they might safely pass on to Erzerúm. Simon, as he should not, put trust in the promise of the Turk, and Hasan Pasha with his army was given the passage of the passes. Then the Pasha, first despatching his prisoner well in advance, dishonourably refused to fulfil his pledged word and escaped. Simon, much angered by this fraud, could only follow on rapidly after him; then later gathering all the forces at his command, Simon fell on the Turkish rear-guard, capturing part of the treasure of the military chest which the escort had in charge, and killing every man of that company. Hasan Pasha, none the less, by good fortune was still able to continue his retreat, saving himself from capture, and carrying his men of the vanguard safely into Erzerúm, where he delivered up what remained of the military chest to Mustafá Pasha, who bestowed it in safety in the castle.

Up to this point the historical account given in the present work has been compiled from the best available authorities, and by the help of my friends [the Licentiate Remón and others who have aided me in the composition of my book], but in what follows much of my information will be derived from what my father, Sultan 'Ali Beg Bayát, has told me in days gone by, he himself having acted his glorious part in all the events which are now about to be narrated.

Mustafá Pasha reported all that had taken place during the past year to Sultan Murád, who expressed his approval as to the fortifications erected at Qars: and he commended more especially the manner in which Tiflis had been relieved. To mark his appreciation the Sultan sent expressly a brocaded robe of honour for the Pasha, adding also a shield of arms for Hasan. Further orders came that 'Ali Quli Khán was to be well guarded in prison, he being a man of

## SINÁN PASHA

mark and a notable warrior. To the king of Persia it was now sadly manifest that most of the Georgian princes for the sake of peace with the Turkish Sultan had had to give in their allegiance to him, and this in spite of all the efforts of Simon in various parts of the province to prevent matters coming to this pass. Sháh Muhammad Khudá-Bandah therefore began now to fear for the future, and especially lest Tabríz should next be attacked, when all Persian 'Iráq inevitably would be threatened. On the advice and counsel of Iskandar Leventoghlú, therefore, and persuaded by him, the Sháh now determined to send an embassy with peace proposals to Constantinople; but incontinently his ambassador returned without having been able to effect anything of moment. Meanwhile, Sháh Muhammad Khudá-Bandah had ordered continuous raids to be carried on against the enemy, thus to encourage those of the Georgian princes who were of his party, and in order that in Constantinople it might be imagined that his treasure of money was great, and that he had a mind yet to fight; but these efforts were more for ostentation than for any real good that was apparent in the result. Then the Sháh went in pious visitation to the tombs of his ancestors, passing through the cities of Sultániyah, Zanján and Miyanah with other places, and returning to his capital at Qazvín he gave command for the mustering at the city of Tabríz of all troops, every squadron under its captain, in preparation for the campaign which shortly must begin.

It was at this time that Sinán Pasha arrived in Tiflis temporarily to take command, superb and in his glory, for news had been brought that at Constantinople Sultan Murád already had named him to be Grand Vizier. His captains being much encouraged by the honour bestowed on their ¹commander, determined forthwith to effect some notable deed of war against the Georgians, who at this season were ravaging the countryside; and with this end in view Tal-oghli[1], the Aga of the Damascus Janissaries, and Omar, the former governor of Safed (in Palestine), set forth to counter the Georgian raids. Prince Simon, however, had news of the intentions of these Turkish commanders, and learning that their troops had marched out in some disorder, and that they were in no great numbers, fell suddenly on them and made so great slaughter that the Aga of the Janissaries alone escaped, for he was nimble of foot. Sinán Pasha, coming to Tiflis, had brought refreshments and some troops, who in part relieved the garrison, this fortress being now put under the charge of Yúsuf Bey the Georgian renegade. While Sinán was at Tiflis Iskandar Levent-oghli sent in to offer his services to the Pasha, who received him favourably, giving him a fine present, and the like of this favour was also shown to other Georgian princes. Then Sinán Pasha started to journey to Constantinople. On the march back towards Qars a portion of the Turkish army, being the advance guard, went out under their commanders to water their horses and get forage. Suddenly they were attacked by Toqmaq, who had joined forces with Simon, and so had under him a body of 8,000 Persian troops. In this skirmish 7,000 Turks were slain, and indeed, of the foragers none would have escaped death if Sinán Pasha had not opportunely come up with the main body of the army. But following the now retreating Persian cavalry, Sinán managed to catch up with and kill fifty of them; then causing their heads to be cut off, he stuck these on the points of spears in sign of a great victory.

On arriving at Triala (which is halfway to Qars) Sinán Pasha learned from his spies that the king of Persia in person was now marching up behind him. The news threw the Turkish army into some confusion, fearing a sudden attack, but Sinán Pasha quickly re-

# TRICK ON THE PERSIANS

establishing order, sent to have the porters set down their loads, and drew up his troops in battle array, with fifty pieces of artillery in the front line. But while thus awaiting the appearance of the Sháh and the attack of the Persian army, to his surprise an envoy from the king, advancing from the Persian side, presented himself with proposals of peace. Of terms the chief point was an offer to leave the Turks in undisturbed possession of both Tiflis and Qars, and a compact of amity to result. Sinán Pasha could give no definite reply in acceptance, for he held no powers thereto from the Sultan. What he did was to entertain the envoy hospitably till they had marched in to Qars, whence he forwarded him on to Constantinople. Haydar Aga, for that was the name of this Persian envoy, returned in due course thence, bearing a preliminary acceptance of terms, and this news he carried to his master, whereupon the king of Persia named Ibrahím Khán ambassador plenipotentiary, a man of great experience, who immediately proceeded on to Constantinople.

On arrival he found that Sultan Murád was busy with the rejoicings and festivals arranged in celebration of the circumcision of his son Prince Muhammad, who afterwards came to be his successor on the throne. On the day of the great ceremony nothing definite as to the peace had yet been settled for the treaty with the Persian ambassador, though he had been received officially in audience by the Sultan. The Turks now secretly determined to play off a trick on the Persians, which same was to invite these to occupy a stand whence they could conveniently see the procession and ceremonies, and to arrange the planks of support in such wise that, at the supreme moment of the procession passing, these should give way and precipitate the Persian ambassador and his suite down into the roadway in a manner very laughable to all beholders. So it happened, and the ambassador had to swallow the affront, not being in a position to retaliate.² He, shortly after this, asked for a definite reply to his embassy, but Sultan Murád would give none, ordering that the ambassador should be sent back to Erzerúm as a prisoner, and there be kept under strict ward until further instructions came from Constantinople.

At the outset of the following year Sultan Murád issued his commands for the assembling of a new army, though contrary to the advice of Sinán Pasha the Grand Vizier. The Sultan, however, overrode all opposition, and as commander-in-chief of the new forces, appointed Muhammad Pasha, the nephew of that Mustafá Pasha who had always been the rival in power to Sinán. This Muhammad therefore now set out for Erzerúm with the style and title of Pasha of that province, and the patent of commander-in-chief, orders coming to displace Rizván Pasha, who had been up to this date in command there. To join Muhammad Pasha also were sent the Pashas of Aleppo and Ma'arrah (in Syria), these two commanders having passed the preceding winter stationed in the city of Ván. Muhammad Pasha set out on his march to Tiflis in company with Hasan the Eunuch [who was Pasha of Ámid in Mesopotamia], and the renegade Mustafá, who formerly was known as the Georgian prince Manuchihr. With these also came the various Kurdish captains and others from the districts of Erzerúm; and having thus an army under his command of 25,000 men, Muhammad Pasha began to invade and occupy the Georgian province which was the home of Prince Manuchihr. The Persians soon had news of the arrival in Georgia of Muhammad Pasha, and though they could not openly act in opposition to the Turkish army by reason of the peace treaty with the Sultan that was still being negotiated, yet in secret, by disguising themselves in the Georgian habit, and under guidance of Simon and

## MUHAMMAD PASHA

other Georgian chiefs, they were able to offer some hindrance to the march of Muhammad Pasha's troops, who, however, managed to evade their attack in the first instance. But later, at the passage of the river Kur, Cyrus, the Persians came up with the Turkish army, and slew not a few of them, taking possession of the money of the military chest and plundering much of their baggage. The Turks therefore reached Tiflis in a condition of some disorder.

Muhammad Pasha on entering the fortress of Tiflis found himself faced with a mutiny among his soldiers, who demanded that a sum of 30,000 ducats should be distributed among the troops of the incoming army, and these, on receipt of the money, forthwith proceeded to share their gains with the soldiers of the garrison. The Pasha, leaving a company of his men in charge of the fortress, now marched back from Tiflis, after substituting Omar Pasha for Yúsuf Beg, the Georgian, as governor of the city. For the return route to be taken to Erzerúm, Muhammad Pasha was at variance with the Kurdish commanders as to the safest road to follow, for they insisted that it would be best to go by the pass of Tomanis, while he gave it as his intention to pass through Altun Qal'ah. Finally, the one and the other party each followed a different way, coming together and joining forces at Qars. Here the Pasha called together a secret council—or as the Turks say, a *Divan*—and this court was to judge whether or not in the past the renegade Manuchihr had been playing traitor; for the Pasha was convinced that it was through his treachery that so many misfortunes had befallen the Turks during the late campaign. The council came to the decision that his treachery was manifest, and that he was worthy of death, and Muhammad Pasha hoped that by this stern act of justice he would appease the wrath of his master, Sultan Murád, and compound for all his previous mistakes. The matter, however, turned out as had not been expected, and what happened shall now be related. The council therefore had assembled, deliberated, and having resolved that it were well to put Manuchihr to death, Muhammad Pasha sent for him, and under the Pasha's letter of safe-conduct he appeared, but there were many who had given him warning. Secretly he carried arms, and leaving before the door of the council-chamber his guard of Georgian soldiers, who were all his servants and fully armed, he entered the hall.

Muhammad Pasha invited him to be seated, so that he might listen to a despatch just come, said he, from Sultan Murád, which commanded that he, Manuchihr, should be despatched forthwith to Constantinople under arrest. On this Manuchihr (having heard the despatch read out) answered that he would go immediately, and stood up. They told him to sit down again, but this he would not do. Muhammad Pasha's Chief Door-keeper them made a snatch at his sleeve, but seeing what was coming, Manuchihr drew his sword and cut down one of the Pasha's servants who was coming up. The Eunuch Hasan Pasha (of Ámid) now approached, but had his ear cut off and part of his cheek sliced; indeed, but for his turban, which saved him from the full force of the blow, he had been killed outright. Muhammad Pasha himself received five wounds that were thought to be mortal, though later he recovered. Then Manuchihr getting free, managed to mount his horse and fled. The Turkish army, though not understanding what was happening, had begun to get under arms; but the soldiers did nothing. Then several persons proceeded to attend to the wounded men. In a despatch sent by messenger Sultan Murád was informed of what had taken place. The Sultan expressed much anger on coming to know these details, and cast much blame on the Grand Vizier Sinán Pasha, who, he said, had kept him ill-informed throughout. He now degraded Sinán from office, calling up as Grand Vizier Siyavush Pasha, who was by birth a Hungarian, and thus ever showed favour to the Christians.

The king of Persia, when he had news of these events, was sure that the Turks during the ensuing summer would have their hands full in Georgia settling matters with Manuchihr, and be in some difficulty as to throwing any relieving force into Tiflis. Feeling, therefore, secure on this quarter, he appointed Amír Khán to take command of the western frontier, giving him orders that if the Turks attempted any aggression he should valiantly combat them. Then Sháh Muhammad Khudá-Bandah, with his Turkoman allies and other troops, marched forth from Qazvín on the way to Herat, to bring into subjection his son 'Abbás Mirzá, and the cause for doing so it were now time and place fully for us to explain.

## CHAPTER VIII

*In which is related the reason why the king of Persia marched to Herat as against his son 'Abbás Mirzá ; how Mirzá Salmán was punished ; further, how Farhád Pasha was appointed by the Sultan commander-in-chief at Erzerúm.*

MATTERS being now left on the Georgian frontier as explained in the last chapter, the king Muhammad Khudá-Bandah returned to Qazvín, where he assembled an army of 20,000 horse. Setting out on the march he had the province of Gílán on the Caspian Sea to his left hand, and to the right hand Shíráz and Káshán. Then passing by the Mazandarán province, and going through the cities of Samnán, Dámghán and Bístam, he arrived before Sabzivar, which is the first town on the western border of the province of Khurásán. Here the Sháh sent command and injunction to the governor of this city, who was holding it in the name of Prince 'Abbás Mirzá, that he should deliver up charge of the same; but he would not. On this the king ordered the town to be besieged, and using scaling ladders, his soldiers before long entered the fortress, making the governor prisoner; and on this they cut off his head. Then marching on, the army carried with them the garrisons found at Níshápúr, Meshed, Turshíz and Turbat-i-Haydari, at the same time punishing those governors of towns that were not loyal to the king; and now the army arrived at Herát, a very strong place, occupying a height, well walled and defended by ditches that were filled by water from springs, for in former days the Great Tamerlane had entirely rebuilt this city.

Now at this time 'Ali Quli Khán Shamlú in Herát was holding the young prince 'Abbás Mirzá in his

## PRINCE 'ABBÁS

power, and indeed he was the prime cause of all the troubles. As said above, Thomas Minadoi has written his account of these and other events entirely from the Turkish authorities, and in the matter of happenings at Herát he has been very ill-informed, wherefore, as I shall relate the affair it will appear very differently from what he has set down in his *History*. But the facts are as I state them, for my father was there present in person at that time, and with him many of our relations and kinsmen, who can bear witness.

'Ali Quli Khán therefore, it seemed, was holding 'Abbás Mirzá completely under his thumb, the prince being heir in the second degree to Sháh Muhammad Khudá-Bandah, and the prince being as yet incapable, by reason of his youth, of forming any judgment in politics for himself. The intention of 'Ali Quli Khán now was so to dominate the prince and his affairs that he, 'Ali Quli, should remain in fact the independent regent of the great western province of Khurásán, and to this end he had always shown himself very mutinous to the Sháh, and had not sent him succour of troops [in the Georgian campaign] when ordered so to do, which in Persia is a crime of rebellion that entails immediate punishment. Intent on signally chastising him for his misdeeds, the Sháh, in company with the prince Hamzah Mirzá, therefore had come before Herát, to which city the royal army now was laying siege, the Sháh, as has been said, having already crushed many rebels as he passed through the land. But the city of Herát being strongly built, was well defended, and the siege dragged on for three months, 'Ali Quli Khán having sufficiently provisioned the fortress. Matters turning out as they did, and so unfavourably, it began to appear that to take Herát was beyond possibility; further, news now came that Sultan Murád once more was making preparations to invade western Persia. Thus, it seemed prudent to abandon the Herát enterprise, at least for the time being. The cause, however, of this present state of affairs was well understood by all the nobles in command of the king's troops. They had seen how the campaign had been from the first misconducted, what great sums had been uselessly squandered, and they asserted this to be entirely the fault of Mirzá Salmán the Grand Vizier, who had originally urged the Sháh to undertake this unfortunate enterprise.

The nobles therefore came together taking counsel, and laid the issue on one of their number whose name was Shabdah Sultán. He, under pretext of business to transact with the Vizier, entered his presence and forthwith stabbed him to death. A mutiny among the troops was soon appeased, and the Sháh, with Prince Hamzah Mirzá, turning back from Herát marched direct to Qazvín, the capital. Now Thomas Minadoi[1] has related in his *History* that Mirzá Salmán had given one of his daughters in marriage to the prince Hamzah Mirzá, for it was his ambition that a grandson of his, and a great-grandson afterwards by this marriage, might both come to reign as Sháhs of Persia. Hence it was that he had counselled the king to undertake the Herát campaign, to the intent that he might compass the imprisonment or perchance the death of 'Abbás Mirzá. Further, Minadoi states that when the royal army reached Herát Prince 'Abbás wrote direct explaining matters to his father and to his brother, by which means the treason of Mirzá Salmán—or Salmás, as Minadoi always wrongfully calls him—was made patent. Thus a peaceable accommodation became possible between the young prince and his father and elder brother; and next the order was given to cut off the Vizier's head. But all this of Minadoi is quite contrary to what in fact happened. For Mirzá Salmán never had a daughter given in marriage to Prince Hamzah. Nor was Prince 'Abbás then of an

## FARHÁD PASHA

age to wage war.² Nor was Mirzá Salmán beheaded by order of the king: the true account being as I have written it above.

But to return: as already stated, Sultan Murád having heard how the king of Persia was fully occupied at Herát with matters in connexion with the affairs of his son Prince 'Abbás, nominated Farhád Pasha to the command of the armies on the Persian frontier, with orders to continue the war in Georgia. Also he was now to make the attempt to carry by assault the city of Eriván, where Toqmaq Khán was governor. Farhád Pasha was further commanded to hold and strongly fortify the direct road running from Qars to Eriván, and he was to throw succour of troops into Tiflis. In regard to the recent acts of Manuchihr—who was now called Mustafá—Farhád Pasha was enjoined for the time being to close his eyes to what the Georgian prince had done, lest he should come out against the Turkish army in the ensuing campaigns: for it was the Sultan's intention in the following year to make the attack on Tabríz. The Turkish army being now assembled, Farhád Pasha in command left Constantinople and reached Erzerúm, where a short rest was given and a general review held. From Erzerúm the army set out for Qars, and on the way the Pasha arranged that a certain castle which commanded an important mountain pass here, and which is known to the Turks as Akcheh-Qal'así (Silver Castle), should be strongly fortified. Here a commander was left, with sufficient artillery and a force of 400 men. Qars being come to and fresh garrisoned, the army now passed on and finally reached Eriván. This city lies near very high mountains that are covered most of the year by clouds and frozen snow, though in the valleys below there is much good pasture for beasts and excellent corn lands.³ The country round is well watered by streams which flow to join the Araxes.

# DON JUAN OF PERSIA

On the march to Eriván the cities of Nakhcheván, Marand and Sufiyán had been captured; and Farhád Pasha unopposed, with no incident worthy of note, now sat down before Eriván and proceeded to lay siege to the town, the defence having been entrusted to that valiant soldier Toqmaq Khán. The Persians, however, were unable to make any effective resistance by reason of the very unequal number of men that their general had to set against the opposing force. The Georgians, without, could give no aid, being occupied with holding and keeping guard on the country round Tiflis: nor was any succour possible that should come in time from Sháh Muhammad Khudá-Bandah and Prince Hamzah. Thus, perforce, Eriván must fall, but capitulating to terms, which Farhád Pasha readily granted, and Toqmaq then evacuated the town. Farhád Pasha on coming into possession proceeded immediately to erect a fortress on the spot where Toqmaq had built his palace and laid out his pleasure gardens, and thus their place became a great stronghold. Eriván was now put under the government of Sinán[4] Pasha, son of Cigala, with Hasan Bey, son of Janbulát Khán, as second in command; and a suitable force of artillery, with 8,000 men, was placed under the orders of Sinán, son of Cigala. Farhád Pasha after this returned from Eriván to Erzerúm.

Eriván is a great city and the capital of its province, but for some years past in our days it has remained in possession of the Turks. Formerly, indeed, it had always been counted as belonging to the Persian Empire: it is enough here to mention the fact of its having thus fallen under the Ottoman power, though it ought, of course, ever to have been retained as an integral part of the Persian kingdom. Eriván lies on the borders of Georgia, and to the north[5] of it lies the city of Tiflis and the Calderán Meadow-lands [below the junction of the Araxes and Cyrus rivers].

# MANUCHIHR'S TRICK

Towards the Tropic of Capricorn (to the westward) lies Ván city, with the Lake of Ván, which anciently was known as the Sea of Marciana.

As soon as Toqmaq Khán found himself thus turned out of Eriván with his garrison, he gathered together what troops he could muster and proceeded to raid all the neighbouring country, one day putting to the sword a hundred Turks, and the next day two hundred, mostly of those that were sent out from the Eriván fort, either to take possession of lands near by, or to forage for provisions. It was at this season that an event occurred that became almost a matter of jest, though sufficiently annoying to Sultan Murád. Commands had been given—as already said—to Farhád Pasha to overlook for the time being and to ignore all that Manuchihr had been guilty of doing in the past. With intent to show him that the Sultan further had every confidence in his loyalty, Farhád Pasha received orders to entrust 30,000 ducats to his care, which treasure he, Manuchihr, was to convoy, as one well acquainted with the mountain passes, into Tiflis, where it was to be delivered for the pay of the garrison to the Turkish commander of that fortress. Manuchihr promptly accepted the commission, and set out on the road to Tiflis in company with the guards, and porters who carried the money chests. On the way, however, he chanced to come up with the renegade Simon, and then God put it in their hearts to know how evil was the deed they had both done in having shamefully been perverted to Islam. Repentance fell on them, and their hard hearts were softened, and they determined, after taking much counsel together, to kill the guards and porters of the treasure, and thus to become possessed of those moneys. This excellent intention was forthwith carried into effect, and the two Georgians made off, the Turkish treasure being no more seen or heard of.

# DON JUAN OF PERSIA

News of these happenings was soon brought to Erzerúm, and Farhád Pasha with the least possible delay despatched Hasan Pasha to carry needful succour to the garrison of Tiflis. Taking with him a squadron of picked men who knew how to make the march from Erzerúm to Tiflis in twelve days, he departed, and meeting with no opposition on the road, carried in to Tiflis from Erzerúm moneys to the amount of 40,000 ducats. Matters being thus adjusted, Farhád Pasha next organized a considerable force that should avenge the affront that Manuchihr and Simon had put upon him. The Turkish troops raided all Manuchihr's lands, devastating the whole neighbourhood, for no resistance was offered to their proceedings.

The spring of 1584 being now come, Sháh Muhammad Khudá-Bandah and his son, Prince Hamzah, began to make their arrangements for marching to garrison Tabríz with a great body of troops. Having news of this, Farhád Pasha, on his side, immediately made plans to strengthen the fortifications of Khoy and to throw into this place a body of 8,000 men with 200 small pieces of cannon, under the command of 'Ali, the Pasha of Greece. Further, this 'Ali Pasha had orders to refortify Shaytán Qal'ah—which in their language means the Devil's Castle—and which is a stronghold lying some ten miles distant from Khoy, being a fortress of much importance. Farhád Pasha next marched at the head of his army to Tomanis, which Simon had lately dismantled of its walls, he having no cannon with which to provide for their defence. Tomanis, under Farhád Pasha's inspection, was forthwith greatly strengthened and enlarged, the mountainside at the narrows of the pass was excavated and made flat, and the foundation of an immense fortress laid, with long walls, and built round so that the place was now capable of harbouring a garrison of more than 12,000 men. In the centre of this new fort they erected a huge tower, and hereabout, and in its turrets, they set 200 pieces of artillery. This strong place now commanded the frontier pass from Armenia into the lands of Georgia, whereby all the country round Tomanis was thenceforth sufficiently protected. Further, the road was now held in force, by which convoys when needed could be sent in to Tiflis; and to prove that this was as it should be Farhád Pasha immediately despatched Rizván, the Pasha of Anatolia, in company with the Pasha of Qara Ámid [which same is Diyár Bakr of Mesopotamia] at the head of a force of 20,000 men, who in one day's march reached Tiflis from Tomanis, escorting treasure and needful supplies. At the same time the governor of Tiflis was relieved, Bagli Pasha[6] being left there in command, and the return march of the troops to Tomanis was brought off without incident.

It was at this season that David, brother of Simon, presented himself before Rizván Pasha—who had just come back from laying waste the lands of Manuchihr—giving in his allegiance to Sultan Murád, which was cause of gratification to the two Turkish Pashas, for Rizván was proud to have him as an ally and for counsel. Simon, as soon as he had news of what his brother David had done, sent spies to reconnoitre Rizván Pasha's camp, but these gave him false information, reporting that the Turks were in no great number. Simon therefore now marched out, and making his attack on the Turks in camp under Rizván Pasha, at first threw their flanks into great disorder. News of this attack was brought to the camp of Farhád Pasha, who getting under arms came up to the support of Rizván, for both Pashas imagined that the whole Persian army was upon them, with the Sháh in person in command. With this confusion and tumult of troops marching and counter-marching, Simon now seized the occasion to make his retreat, before the Turks should come to know how insignificant was the force of the enemy attacking them. Simon indeed had made this demonstration with his small force, with intent, if possible, of detaching his brother David from the Turkish alliance, or at least to spoil the new friendship between him and Rizván Pasha. Simon, however, had soon perceived that his men were too few to carry out the enterprise, and indeed the enemy were in such superiority of numbers that he ran grave risk himself of being completely overwhelmed. He therefore beat his retreat, after doing what damage he could, and not any too soon, for he, Simon, found himself at the end of the fight on the point of being taken prisoner. Later both the Turkish camps returned to quiet, and the truth of the whole incident became known.

Winter now was coming on, and Farhád Pasha, leaving Hasan Pasha with a garrison of 8,000 men in the new fortress of Tomanis, prepared to depart. He, however, determined that it was expedient on his homeward march to make a further example, and again to lay waste the lands of the rebel Manuchihr. He therefore marched the whole of the Turkish army into camp in these territories, before he should set out on his way back to Qars and Erzerúm. The Pasha's intention in thus delaying their homeward march was much to the dissatisfaction of his men, who, however, murmured to no purpose, and the Turkish army took its way forward, arriving after three days of a harassing march at Triala. Here heavy privation and famine fell on the Turks from the entire lack of foodstuffs, for all the countryside had been stripped bare, and the population everywhere had fled into the hills. The same happened beyond this at Akhalkelek, and in the neighbourhood of Altun Qal'ah and at Kliska, where the men suffered so much by reason of their hunger, that three and a half bushels[7] of corn—which is

## AMIR KHÁN

the quantity of a Venetian *staia*—was priced at 50 ducats. Two regiments of the Janissaries and some men of the Constantinople infantry[8] here mutinied, but they were brought to reason by the efforts of Veys, the Pasha of Aleppo. Farhád Pasha now attempted to storm the fortress of Altun Qal'ah, which was well provided with provisions, intending then to build for his troops a stronghold at Kliska, but his men frustrated all that he would have done, again making a mutiny, and threatening to kill him. Farhád Pasha thus was forced to march on to Ardahán; and here the Georgians made a raid, attacking the Pasha's women in the carriages guarded by their eunuchs, and their convoy was plundered. There were not wanting many who said it was not the Georgians but the mutinous Janissaries who did this deed, and in Constantinople Farhád Pasha lost all reputation for having allowed himself to be so basely plundered.

Farhád finally reached Erzerúm, where his troops were forthwith dismissed to winter quarters. Another event now happened which effected the complete discredit of the Pasha. The Persian general 'Ali Quli Khán, who, as already said, had been taken prisoner and was for safety being detained in the fortress at Tomanis, now managed to make his escape, reaching Persia in safety, and this was a piece of mismanagement that greatly angered Sultan Murád. In Persia, on the other hand, events were taking place which came near to causing the loss of Tabríz to the Sháh: as later was to be the sad case when that city was indeed taken from him: the detail of which last disastrous event will be told the reader later in its proper place. What now took place was this. Amir Khán was at this time holding the government of Tabríz, as has been mentioned above, and he was the chief Khán and Amir of the Turkoman tribesmen, and a great soldier. For some unknown cause—and the true reason of the same never was made clear—Amir Khán had betaken himself to a certain strong castle which he had caused to be built in the city of Tabríz, and now let it be known that he declined to deliver the command of this place into the hands of the Sháh [who, as already noted above, was coming up from Qazvín]. It was suspected indeed that there lay behind all this some treason plot against Sháh Muhammad Khudá-Bandah, but nothing ever could be proved. The stronghold in question, and the city quarter lying round it, where Amir Khán's men lay in camp, both were very well fortified, and as soon as the Sháh and Prince Hamzah at the head of their army had marched into Tabríz, all became aware of Amir Khán's rebellion. The king thereupon commissioned my father, Sultán 'Ali Beg, to go to Amir Khán, and if possible persuade him peacefully to give in his submission. My father succeeded in effecting this, for after some delay he managed to persuade Amir Khán to appear in the presence of the King, but the Sháh being wroth, forthwith ordered him to be arrested and conveyed as a prisoner to the castle of Qahqahah under a strong guard. On arrival there, or some say on the way thither, Amir Khán was incontinently put to death, this by the Sháh's previous command.

It was at this date that Sultan Murád appointed Othman Pasha to the chief command of his armies [in Georgia to supersede Farhád Pasha], though the Grand Vizier at the Porte, Siyavush Pasha, did his utmost to traverse the Sultan's will, for he was Othman Pasha's declared enemy. Finding that the Sultan's intent of mind in this matter was irrevocable, the Grand Vizier was forced to draw up the deed of appointment and send official intelligence thereof to Othman Pasha, who was at that time stationed in Shamákhí. Siyavush Pasha, however, when he perceived that he could not openly prevent Othman taking Farhád's place as

## OTHMAN PASHA

commander-in-chief in the coming campaign against Persia, determined forthwith to set about a plot to compass the death of Othman Pasha, and the business was to be done in the following way. Othman Pasha had for some time past again and again been sending complaints to Sultan Murád against Kuman,[9] the prince of the Tartars of the Crimea, who, he wrote, was the worst of neighbours, always favouring the Persian cause, and never mindful of the respect and allegiance due from him to the Ottoman State. These complaints of Othman Pasha, however, being written and despatched by messenger, never reached the eyes of Sultan Murád, for the Tartar prince by bribes had gained over to his interest the Grand Vizier Siyavush Pasha, who kept to himself all these despatches from Othman Pasha. Sultan Murád therefore imagined the Tartar prince still to be his good friend and ally.

'Matters thus seeming to be ripe and favourable, Siyavush Pasha wrote to the Tartar prince, who was at the city of Kaffa on the Sea of Azov, that if he wished to keep his peace with Sultan Murád, he must now compass to prevent Othman Pasha getting to Constantinople, lest he should become aware of the secret understanding that was in existence between the two, and unmask their intrigue to mislead the Sultan. Therefore, as the Grand Vizier wrote, it would now be convenient to murder Othman Pasha, and to bring about this as though by mischance, a body of Tartar horsemen should be sent under disguise to the lands about Colchis and Iberia [which is Albania], where they might fall on Othman Pasha and put him to death. He, the Vizier, would then easily persuade the Sultan that the deed had been done by some nomad tribesmen of the Mingrelians or Georgians, or it might be the Muscovite brigands. Thus the plot was laid, and Othman Pasha having received official information of his new appointment to be commander-in-chief, as was due from him, set out for Constantinople to present himself before the Sultan. He intended to travel by the way along the north coast of the Black Sea, and the Tartars on their part now set out to waylay and kill him as arranged; but they failed to carry through their plan, for Othman Pasha's escort in fact overcame them, taking many of the Tartars prisoners. Othman Pasha by torture extracted from certain of these men the true history of the matter, and subsequently reached Constantinople in safety. Here he related the adventure to Sultan Murád, explaining that he had in obedience to his master's orders left Derbend—which some call Demír Qapú—and passing along beside the heights of the Caucasus, leaving Media and Iberia and Colchis on the left hand, and on his right the rivers Volga and Tanais, he had finally come to the shores of the Euxine, where he had suddenly found himself beset by 12,000 Cossacks or bandits, but these with the 4,000 men of his escort he had easily vanquished, and from his prisoners had come to know of a plot laid for his destruction.

Sultan Murád was extremely angry on hearing all this, and straightway called up and dismissed Siyavush Pasha from his post of Grand Vizier. He further declared that the Tartar prince Kuman was the public enemy: vengeance was to be taken on him, and paying him back in his own coin, Othman Pasha received command to have him made prisoner and put to death. After which Sultan Murád set up to be prince of the Perekop Tartars in the place of Kuman, the latter's younger brother,[10] whom the Ottoman government till then had been keeping as a prisoner of state at Qonia, which same is a city of Lycaonia. Sultan Murád having thus shown his regard for Othman Pasha, and formally appointed him commander-in-chief in the coming campaign against the Persians, told him that he should for the present let it appear that

## EGYPT AND SYRIA

the main objective was Nakhcheván, though in truth it was the secret intention of the Sultan that he should push on and make the attempt to capture Tabríz. Othman Pasha, who was in haste to set off, had, however, for a time to delay beginning his march on account of recent happenings in Cairo.

Not long before this Sultan Murád had sent Hasan Pasha the Eunuch to Grand Cairo as governor of Egypt, and it was now reported that he was showing excessive tyranny in his office, and giving the people no justice, being only intent on amassing riches. The Sultan therefore despatched orders that he should forthwith appear before him in Constantinople to give answer to the complaints which had been brought against him by the natives of the land, but it had been impossible as yet to persuade him peaceably to come. The Sultan thereupon at last decided to send Ibrahím Pasha [to Cairo, who should depose him from office], but Ibrahím Pasha, instead of acting discreetly with justice, forthwith proceeded even more arbitrarily, plundering the Egyptians, acting tyrannically, and himself amassing great sums of money, after having finally forced the Eunuch Hasan to set out by sea for Constantinople. Then Ibrahím Pasha, on leaving Egypt, took the route homewards by the lands of Judea and Palestine, where on his passage he forcibly suppressed the revolt of certain amirs of those provinces who had set themselves up to be independent princes. These were men of the Druse people, who are the descendants of those Crusaders who in times past gained possession of Jerusalem and the Holy Land, but who in these present days have become Moslems and are tributary to the Ottoman State. From these people also Ibrahím Pasha squeezed great sums of money, plundering their towns, and with all this treasure he, in due time, arrived at Constantinople. Now the yearly tribute of Egypt and Cairo had been established at the sum of 600,000 gold sequins, and it was due at this time to be paid over to the Treasury, but in place of this sum Ibrahím Pasha had now brought Murád a million sequins, which so delighted the Sultan that forthwith he gave him one of his daughters in marriage.

Sultan Murád having thus satisfactorily settled the affairs of [Egypt and the Druses] with Ibrahím Pasha, now issued orders that Othman Pasha should proceed on his campaign against Tabríz, and the Pasha now set out for Erzerúm, where he made a grand review of his armies. Then on the 11th of August of the year 1585 he marched out from Erzerúm, on the Tabríz road, under the guidance of one Maqsúd Aga [a native Persian), who as was commonly reported had recently fled to the Turkish camp from Persian territory. This matter is related, as above, according to what Thomas Minadoi has set down in his book,[11] but in this instance again the details were given to him incorrectly by his Turkish authorities. I, however, know the truth of the matter, which is somewhat different from what Minadoi has written, and this I would now set down. For Maqsúd was not a Khán, a title that Minadoi gives to him, nor was he a noble of any sort, for not even did he have the title of Bey, which is, as we should say in Spain, *Don*. He was simply an Aga—that is to say, a rich husbandman who had bought, out of his money-bags, a property near Tabríz, well inhabited by some 500 peasants, the place being there known under the name of Kúzah-Kunán (the Potteries).[12] This Maqsúd had been a great friend of Amir Khán, late Chief of the Turkonian tribesmen, and when he learnt that the Sháh had ordered his friend to be put to death, and further learnt that he himself, Maqsúd, was under suspicion because he was a Sunní, which is of the sect of the Turks, very prudently taking warning by how another had lost his head, he had fled to Con-

# TABRIZ

stantinople. At this moment he had come back to Persia to act as guide to Othman Pasha's army, being a man who was perfectly acquainted with all the lands and neighbourhood of Tabríz.

As has already been said, when Othman Pasha had come out of Erzerúm he held a great review of his troops, when he found that they numbered 230,000 men, or as some report, 300,000: and it appeared to him that here were numbers out of the way in excess: so he dismissed 50,000 of those least experienced in war, and then made public proclamation that he was going to march against Nakhcheván. However, it soon became evident that Tabríz was his true objective, and the troops began to mutiny, holding that they had been deceived, but Othman Pasha was able to pacify them, and they proceeded to Khoy, which is a city above Ván, and here the army rested. Next passing through Marand, the first city across the Persian frontier, they came then to Sufiyán, a small town on a height from which, looking down, they could discover Tabríz. This was cause of much rejoicing to the troops, and they were especially glad when they reached the orchards round Tabríz, and as yet without having seen a single soldier of the enemy's forces. Prince Hamzah Mirzá had, however, by this time come up and was reconnoitring to see what the Turkish army was doing beyond Sufiyán: and he now put himself in ambush with 10,000 horsemen, noting that the enemy were, so to speak, disbanded among the orchards. Then suddenly he attacked, and put their vanguard completely to rout, killing 7,000 of them. Othman Pasha on discovering the near presence of Prince Hamzah had called up Cigala Pasha, with Muhammad the Pasha of Qara Ámid, and sent them forward with 14,000 men to give battle to the prince; but Hamzah Mirzá fought valiantly and inflicted yet more damage than he received, capturing many Turkish banners;

finally, however, he had to retreat, and leaving the battlefield, rejoined his father, the king, who had remained behind with the bulk of the Persian forces, at a place twelve miles from Tabríz.

At this time 'Ali Quli Khán was the military governor of Tabríz, having under him only 4,000 horsemen for garrisoning the great city, and he knowing the force that Othman Pasha was bringing against him—namely, 70,000 cavalry and 150,000 infantry—all he as a valiant soldier could effect was thrice over to march out and skirmish against the Turks, of whom, on these several occasions, he managed to kill some three or four thousand of their best men. With his small army, however, for garrison, he could not hope to defend so great a city, for the population, though numerous, was not used to war, and to remain, therefore, stationed in the city would be to risk his honour with small chance of gaining any advantage. He now decided to dismantle the fortifications of the town, betaking himself to the mountains, while at the same time he gave instructions to the people of Tabríz that since they could not possibly defend their city they should, after making a treaty of peace, surrender it to the Turks. The men of Tabríz, however, would not do this, being valiant folk, and they went on defending the city for a length of time. Othman Pasha had in the end to take Tabríz by force of arms, and, wroth at the long resistance that had been made him, granted free licence to his soldiers to sack the town: whereupon were seen such horrors as never before even a barbarous nation had perpetrated at the capture of any enemy city.[13]

Tabríz stands at the foot of mount Oronte,[14] which rises on its north side. It is distant eight days' journey from the Caspian Sea, and to the south stretches all the whole land of Persia. With the mountains near the Caspian on the one hand, the city stands in the forefront of Greater Media. Its inhabitants are for the most part merchants, and Tabríz is built at the spot where the East has passage to Syria, and where Europe with its numerous countries can best join commerce with the Orient. The climate is very cold, and snow lies here for a season of the year. The houses are built partly underground; most are low, few being of any height, but they are constructed of kiln-burnt brick, and thus have a fine appearance. Unfortunately, Tabríz had now a second cruel misfortune to suffer, for some of the Janissaries having been found murdered in their lodgings in one of the quarters of the town, Othman Pasha ordered his troops again to sack the city, when such and so many were the cruelties practised by the Turk soldiers against the people that at last the women and children, in terror to escape alive, fled to the hills. Othman Pasha, while he was occupying Tabríz, caused a fortress to be built, surrounding it with a ditch 30 feet across and a fathom deep. This fortress was defended by many pieces of cannon, and a strong garrison was left on guard. Thus for long years to come Tabríz remained in the power of the Ottomans.

It might seem that there was anent Tabríz a difficult question to answer, and a matter which he who may read this book would fain have explained—namely, that seeing Tabríz to be a city of such great importance both to the kingdom and to the honour of the king, how came it that the Sháh Muhammad Khudá-Bandah, who was encamped with his army only twelve miles distant from the city, made no effort to succour the garrison and allowed Tabríz, undefended, to be taken by the enemy? The real cause of all this was the putting to death of Amir Khán, which has been related above, for he was the hero and chief of the Turkoman tribesmen, and the Turkomans are the only people of Tabríz and its province who are by nature warlike and capable of fighting. His being thus done to death made them so wrathful against the Sháh of Persia, that the king could never dare face Othman Pasha in the field, realizing that he had at his back these mutinous tribesmen, for he knew not but what some great disaster might through their treachery come to pass. Thus the king had to look on helpless, and even fearing for his personal safety, while he saw Tabríz fall. But when message was brought to him of the utter ruin of the great city, and the wretched fate of its inhabitants, the king, now furious with rage and grief, marched up against the Turkish camp, and despatched 600 horsemen, challenging and defying the Turks to come out and fight. On this Muhammad Pasha of Qara Ámid and Cigala Pasha appeared at the head of 40,000 Turks, and the 600 Persian horsemen managed cleverly to lure them back to a place where Prince Hamzah was in ambush with 20,000 cavalry. These charging, fell on them with such vigour that the Pasha of Qara Ámid took to flight, and Cigala Pasha alone stood his ground. The Persians there, in hand-to-hand fight, showed clearly how superior they were to the Turks, for they at last put Cigala Pasha to flight, capturing many of his men.

Prince Hamzah was so encouraged by this victory that he sent Othman Pasha his defiance to fight, army against army, and the Pasha took up the gauge. Now the prince had his camp at a place eight miles distant from the Turkish headquarters, being fearful on account of their superiority in artillery, for their cannon had wrought him much damage in the past, and hence the Turks had to march out this distance to the attack. Their battle front was under command of the Pasha of Qara Ámid, and Cigala Pasha led the troops of 'Iráq and Mesopotamia, the Pasha of Anatolia commanded the left wing with the squadrons from Greece under his orders, while the right wing was given to Murád Pasha of Qaramán, who also led the Syrian troops. In all the Turks numbered about 70,000 fighting men, and their camp followers had remained behind in Tabríz, being engaged in the search for treasure, buried, as was supposed, in the Mosques and in private houses. The Janissaries also had remained behind on guard round Othman Pasha, who at this time was lying sick. The Turks came up to where Prince Hamzah was awaiting them at the head of 40,000 excellent Persian troops drawn from all parts—namely, from the provinces of Mazandarán, Persian 'Iráq, and Shirván, and it was at this battle that I for the first time was present, fighting at my father's side.

The opposing armies immediately formed issue, and this indeed was one of the hardest fought engagements that ever took place between these two enemy nations. A great number of notable people lost their lives in this battle, more especially of the Turks, among the rest, Muhammad Pasha of Qara' Ámid, whose head Prince Hamzah caused to be cut off and stuck on a lance point. The Pasha of Trebizond was killed, also the Commander of Brusa, with five commanders of other battalions, while Murád Pasha of Qaramán was taken prisoner, for he, while fighting, fell helpless into a ditch. Had the night not begun to come on, in truth not a Turk would have escaped alive, but the darkness forced Prince Hamzah to end the attack and retire with his army to where the blind king, his father, had remained in camp.

Meanwhile, day by day Othman Pasha was getting worse in his sickness, and he therefore determined to begin his march back to Erzerúm. He gave the command of the new fortress at Tabríz into the hands of the Eunuch Ja'far, the Pasha of Tripoli, making over to him the right to collect the tribute of Tabríz district during three coming years, also leaving with him a garrison of 12,000 men. The remainder of the Turkish army now marched out from Tabríz, and when they reached the place known as

# DON JUAN OF PERSIA

Shenb Ghazán[15] [the Dome of Ghazan]—which is an ancient Mosque lying out in the countryside, crowning a height—the same being two leagues distant from Tabríz, Prince Hamzah caught them up with a body of 28,000 horse, and falling on their rear-guard plundered the baggage train. The advance guard of the Turks hearing what had come about, now opened on the rear-guard with their cannon, killing many, and our men, who were all inextricably mixed up with their troops, were soon forced to retire, but not without having inflicted on them a shameful loss. Indeed, it was afterwards known that this amounted to 20,000 men, which with their losses on the taking of Tabríz made the sum total of the Turkish casualties amount to 70,000 killed in the Tabríz campaign.

Hardly had we Persians drawn off our forces, when news from the Turkish camp was brought that Othman Pasha had died of his sickness, and though Cigala Pasha had tried to keep the fact unknown, to do so was impossible. On this Cigala Pasha came into the chief command of the Ottoman army, and we on the Persian side followed the retreating Turks all through the night with 14,000 horse, under command of Prince Hamzah. At dawn next day we again came up with them, but Cigala Pasha now had with him as his guides and counsellors the two Georgians—namely, David and Maqsúd Aga—who thoroughly understood our prince's method of attack, and the enemy, instead of being lured forth by our feints, remained stubbornly entrenched on the defensive. The prince understanding the new state of affairs, now began to retire, and attempted to recross the stream of the Achi-Chay, over which he had just advanced to make his onslaught, but by reason of the rain-floods, he was caught at the freshet, and 3,000 men of the Persian army were drowned. Cigala Pasha thus escaped [and setting out on his homeward march reached Erzerúm in safety].

## CHAPTER IX

*As to what the king of Persia did to get back Tabríz into his power, and how he laid siege to the fortress, and what happened on the part of those who defended it; and the death of my father, Sultán 'Alí Beg Bayát.*

By the aid of Maqsúd Aga and David Khán, who from their experience knew how to forewarn Cigala Pasha against the wiles of Prince Hamzah, the Turks managed to escape the ambuscade where the prince was lying in wait for them, and further were guided to pass safely across certain streams and swamps, from which otherwise none of them could possibly have escaped with their lives. The Turks, in fact, of their good fortune escaped destruction, and further, as has been described at the close of the last chapter, they witnessed the discomfiture and death by drowning in one of these streams of more men of the Persian arms than ever they, the Turks, had slain in the five preceding battles of the campaign. Thus the Turkish army was left in peace to make its way back to Erzerúm, where the troops were disbanded, and the Viziers, Pashas, Commanders and Begs all returned to Constantinople to give their report to the Sultan of what had taken place. Sultan Murád felt much regret at the death of Othman Pasha, for he had been a man of worth and great experience in war, especially in the campaigns against the Persians and Georgians. Rejoicings to celebrate this Ottoman victory were now set on foot in Constantinople, although there were not lacking those who murmured, for it was said that though the Sultan indeed was now lord of the Fortress at Tabríz by a deed of arms that had caused terror to the Persians, and the loss was to these a grievous insult, and also that the Turks were holding Tiflis in Georgia, yet to take and hold these two strong places had cost the Sultan so many lives, that in lieu of these public rejoicings, solemn dirges had better have been ordered for the soothing of the hearts of all the widows and orphans who were now thronging the streets of Constantinople.

In Persia, the Turkish army having for the time being retired, vacating the districts round Tabríz, Sháh Muhammad Khudá-Bandah and his son Prince Hamzah, although it was at this season mid-winter, sought to profit by the occasion; for they were fain to reinstate their reputation in the public mind, so discredited by the loss under their very eyes of this famous city, now lying for the most part in ruins. The Sháh with the prince therefore marched in, with so much of the Persian army as was to hand, and reoccupied the town quarters of Tabríz, the court establishing itself here, and the citizens who had escaped death and fled to the hills now returning to their homes. [Next the siege of the Turkish fortress was undertaken.] Here without, side by side, according to the military art, two immense siege-guns were set in position, and these were of so huge a calibre as never before had been seen in Persia. The two guns night and day bombarded the Turks; bastions with cavaliers built in between having been erected over against the fortress among the ruins of the former town quarter. The Turkish garrison of 3,000 men, however, appeared in no wise dismayed by these proceedings of the Persians, for, in the first place, they were all seasoned soldiers of much experience in war; and secondly, because, by order of the late Othman Pasha, there had been provided in the fortress munitions and provisions sufficient to last for a three years' siege, and the walls of the same were, in truth, of an immense strength. Noting the tenacity and valour of the besieged Turks, Prince

## TABRIZ FORTRESS

Hamzah now determined to construct and run a mine under the fortress, which should be filled and finally exploded. This work was begun, and the Turks knew nothing of it, for the Persians contrived to dig very secretly, and pushed the mine deeply, choosing their hours for work and using their tools with much caution, while at the same time, night and day, the two great pieces of artillery continued to bombard the fortress, thus distracting the attention of the Turks from what was going on below ground.

Further, the destruction wrought by the two great guns prevented it being seen, by the besieged, what earth was being thrown up from below by the men who were digging the mine, for all the surface of the ground hereabout was now getting covered with fragments of stone from the effects of the bombardment of the walls. These two cannon were of such size that the bore of each at the mouth spanned a yard[1] across, the length of the barrel being five yards. Thus the Turks never would have suspected what was going on at the place where the mine was being dug, had it not been for the treachery that unfortunately happened at this time on the part of two Persian officers of the royal army. One of these bore the title of Qúrchí Báshí Khán,[2] he being the comptroller of the Royal Household-servants —and his title of Khán shows that he was a grandee of the kingdom—and the other traitor was Ja'far Quli Beg, his brother-in-law. Now these two nobles had learnt of certain information which spies had given them, that the king Muhammad Khudá-Bandah and the prince had issued an order for them to be both put to death, but for what crime never was justly known, and therefore, having come of a surety by the news, they took occasion one night before dawn of day to leave the royal court, and escaping through the town precincts gained entrance to the Turkish fortress, seeking safety with the enemy of their country. To the garrison they then gave news of the mine which by the king's orders was being constructed, whereupon the Turks immediately began a counter-mine. Thus the advance of the Persian mine was soon blocked by stones and earthwork, while the whole of this side of the fortress was promptly strengthened, and they rebuilt a curtain of the great wall in this part, which had latterly been giving cause of anxiety. All these works were carried through with quickness and dexterity on the part of the Turks, the Persians losing an infinity of men in ineffectual attempts to prevent the building of this curtain, and in a vain struggle to carry on the work of digging their mine.

Prince Hamzah now realizing that the two traitors who had escaped to the fortress were the cause of his secret designs having become known—and thus his reasonable hopes now being frustrated of blowing up the Turks in their entrenchments—was filled with wrath and impatience. He tried next to carry the fortress wall by storm, with scaling ladders, in face of day, and though at first the Turks were somewhat taken aback by this unlooked-for assault, they rallied, and rushing on their assailants who were fixing the scaling ladders, began shooting down on them point-blank, fighting hand to hand from the loopholes and embrasures in the wall, also from the battlements and the cross-beams of the neighbouring houses. This open attack on the fortress lasted for six whole days, but seeing the very small advantage obtained, the prince at length ordered the retreat to be sounded. In this attack more than 6,000 Persians had been killed, some falling into the ditch off the scaling ladders, others being shot down by musket fire, whilst those who finally had climbed over the wall-top were easily slaughtered by the enemy within the fortress.

My father, Sultán 'Ali Beg Bayát, who was at that time in attendance on the king Muhammad Khudá-

## SULTAN 'ALI BEG

Bandah, now received the command from Prince Hamzah to make a quite different attempt, at the head of 300 chosen men of his own clan, whom at his personal expense had been armed and brought to the royal army. It was arranged that with his companions my father should one night, in the watch before dawn, secretly approach the fortress wall with a movable mantelet [or wooden tower borne on a platform running on wheels] which 200 pioneers were to work up to the edge of the outer ditch, where it would then overtop the cavalier or bulwark.³ This wooden tower was built up and protected by bags filled with earth nailed on outside; and it had an upper work so high that from it the square inside the fortress might have been overlooked; and from this upper piece a drawbridge with ropes could, at the proper moment, be let down over the parapet of the fortress wall. The whole of this machine was planked and protected by sandbags adjusted to serve their purpose. The Persians were to make their attack on the enemy at dawn, as said above, before the Turkish sentinels who might be on guard should notice their coming. Then the 300 of our men-at-arms were to surprise and hold within the fortress a certain tower which from that side overlooked the ditch, rising above the wall. This tower was in that part which faced the Persian siege guns, which last had been established below the houses of the town-quarter now held in force by the royal troops engaged in besieging the fortress.

On the night in question my father started, being carried forward with his men in the movable wooden tower but although the axles of the wheels under the platform had been well greased, and the tyres had been cased in cotton to muffle the sound, and the lights from the matchlock fuses, and priming horns, and cannon-vents had been all carefully masked, yet the Turks heard us coming, and before we could fetch up at the border of the outer bulwark of the fortress they had beaten to arms within. Then they opened their attack on the tower and its platform with a storm of musketry and fire-balls, while at the same time 700 Turks issued from the fortress by a postern gate that was in the bulwark at this point, and from thence, too, made their attack on us. My father, perceiving that matters had gone so far that it was impossible now to beat a retreat, and realizing that whatever happened this was a matter to gain little honour and less advantage, began to fight desperately, standing within the tower, for the press of the incoming Turks was such that to issue forth was not possible. When at length, however, he had managed to kill seven men of note among his assailants, besides two commanders and three Begs, he forthwith himself fell dead, pierced by numberless wounds. What indeed brought on the end the quicker, was the crushing in of the curtain of the parapet of our platform beneath the tower; for on this side the wheels below had been burnt by the fire-balls which had struck us. The enemy were yet forcing their way in across this parapet, which, falling back, crushed under its mass more than a hundred Turks whom our men were struggling to repel. This parapet wall here referred to was the obstacle that prevented me and the soldiers under my command from coming to my father's aid, when I saw that I could not die defending him, as I gladly would. The Turks now began to desist from their attack on our tower, finding that the whole Persian army under command of the king and the prince was marching up to our support, and the day had already dawned. The Turks therefore retired within their fortress by the postern gate, which they immediately closed, but their loss had amounted to 200 men.

Protesting and against my will they carried me before the king, who praised and sought to give me comfort, but I was in that state when all reason fails:

and yet the more so when I came to see that from the wall of the fortress the Turks were exhibiting, stuck on a lance point, my poor father's head, thus further to insult and humiliate me, for his body in their brutal rage they had already burnt. The king and prince both did great honour to the memory of my father by what manner they spoke of him to me, and they made me a promise of future favour. Later Sháh Muhammad Khudá-Bandah, who had indeed loved my father, ordered a picture to be painted, representing him standing above the bodies of the seven Turkish commanders whom with his own hand he had slain, and this picture still may be seen placed above the door of one of the Mosques of Tabríz, that is dedicated to the honour of the great Amir Haydar, the father of Sháh Ismaʿíl, who is held by us Persians to have been a saint.

## CHAPTER X

*In which is recounted the arrival of the Turkomans at the king's camp, and the troubles that arose from their coming.*

As we have already explained, Turkomania, the Turkoman country, is no province of the Persian Empire, nor is it the name of any city, wherefore we have not counted it as such among the other provinces [mentioned in Chapter II of Book I]: but the Turkomans form a commune of very great importance among the other nationalities of the Persian kingdom, for they are a most valiant folk, and the number of their population is very considerable. Great importance often attaches to their views and actions, as was seen in what has been related in regard to the loss of Tabríz, where the fact that the Turkomans would grant no aid was the prime cause of the fall of that city. This was by reason of their anger at their chief, Amir Khán, having been, they said, unjustly put to death. At the moment of which we are now speaking, though the Sháh was still greatly vexed by their past defection at that critical juncture, he affected to have forgotten, hoping that they might patriotically be prompted to serve him, for their aid or support was of much import to him in the attempt on hand to turn the Turks out of the fortress of Tabríz. And it is to be remembered that the Turkomans were settled in great numbers in all the country round and about Tabríz, even as for us in Spain we see the Moors camped in all the communes that lie adjacent to Oran in Africa.

The state of affairs therefore being at the moment as has been told in the preceding chapter, the Turks in great force occupying the fortress inside Tabríz, and our hope of ejecting them therefrom being but small,

# THE TURKOMANS

unexpectedly 40,000 Turkomans assembled under arms and marched up to encamp within half a league's distance of the town walls of Tabríz. They were under the leadership of two of their principal chiefs, whose names were Muhammad Khán and Khalífah Khán,[1] and their coming at first caused the greatest hopefulness to the Sháh. To the besieged Turks, on the other hand, their arrival was a heavy blow, for they deemed them a mighty reinforcement to the royal army that was besieging them. The Turks, therefore, without delay came to the conclusion it were wise to petition for terms, and they sent an envoy to Sháh Muhammad Khudá-Bandah and Prince Hamzah promising them that they, the Turks, would now deliver up the fortress, provided they were allowed to march out with their banners and war-drums and be given free passage to Sufiyán fort. The negotiations being thus fairly set on foot and promising so well for the Persian cause, incontinently the bad faith of the Turkomans was made manifest, and what came about shall now be explained.

'Among the Turkomans, as with many of the other semi-independent nations who were in name subjects of the Persian crown, it was customary of old that a son of the Sháh should be given them to be, nominally, their governor and chief, thus to rule them independently. The Turkomans were still at that date wrathful at heart on account of the execution—as has been above narrated—of their beloved Amir Khán by the Sháh's order, and it was secretly now their intention to make an insurrection and attempt to kidnap Tahmásp Mirzá, the king's youngest son, who was with him at this time in the royal camp before Tabríz, being a lad about eleven years of age. The better to mask their intended treachery, the Turkomans had given it out publicly that it was their feeling of honourable patriotism alone that had now led them to come in and offer their aid to the king, and that all ill-will on their part had been set aside and forgotten. On the very night of their arrival in camp, however, and after the Sháh had granted all their demands in full, three hundred of the Turkoman men-at-arms, of the most lawless and irresponsible of any found among them, under the leadership of Saqalí Sultán, burst into the royal quarters at an hour when the sentinels were asleep. Also they had previously overpowered the main-guard of the army encamped within Tabríz city, for the Turkomans had managed to steal away all the lantern-lights from the guard-posts—which is in effect as though here in Spain the name of the Saint, which is the password for the night, had got to be known—and the kidnappers then made their way unopposed into the royal quarters. Here they killed most of the soldiers and door-keepers on duty, and seized in their arms Prince Tahmásp, to whom they spoke words of promise, which, though a mere child, he seemed to understand and so did not cry out. Next bringing him forth from the palace and the town, they betook themselves to their camp, accompanied by certain fellow-conspirators, who had been among the personal attendants of the young prince.

The kidnapping party had brought off their attack on the royal quarters with only a loss of some fifty of their men, and the Turkoman chiefs Muhammad Khán and Khalífah Khán[2] joyfully received the captive prince. Forthwith orders were issued for the whole force of the tribesmen to set out on their march to Qazvín in battle array, at any moment prepared to repulse every attack. Great had been the confusion and alarm in the king's quarters and in the royal camp, also in the city of Tabríz: on every side there was a calling to arms. The Turkish garrison of the fortress, also imagining in their alarm that their last hour was come, were preparing for the worst, some indeed

## QAZVÍN OCCUPIED

proposing a plan to kill their Pasha and send his head in to Sháh Muhammad Khudá-Bandah as a peace-offering. All quieted down, however, after a time, and men again took heart, and then it became known that the young prince had been carried off. The Turkoman tribesmen reached Qazvín unmolested, and immediately gained possession of the royal capital—for such Qazvín was at that date—plundering, ravishing, and violating homes on all hands, occupying the city not as fellow-subjects of the king, but as though it had been an enemy-town given over to them to sack. I myself can bear witness to their evil ways, for in my father's house there, into possession of which I had just come by inheritance, every kind of damage was done. The Turkomans next proclaimed Prince Tahmásp to be the new Sháh of Persia, but making him do their bidding in all things, and they assembled a council of state, which forthwith assumed the government. The king's nobles and loyal subjects were expelled the city, edicts being proclaimed and enforced which terrorized the citizens. The ignorant folk of the commonwealth being totally misinformed on all public matters, none ventured any opposition or resistance to their doings, and the Turkomans even dared to coin new money [which is always held to be the prerogative of royalty] and the old coins were restruck with a punch which altered the arms and titles of the face.

And all this was done at a distance of barely 130 leagues from the king's court. Never have I heard tell before of even the most rebellious of subjects having done such deeds against their lawful sovereign and natural prince as these men did. And forsooth, matters had to rest thus, for continual rains and snows now abundantly setting in, the Turkomans were able to remain for the incoming winter season unmolested at their quarters in Qazvín, where they proceeded to set up or to dismiss, turn about, all the officers of state. At last, however, when the spring came, Prince Hamzah, who all during the season of the rains and snows had been full of impatience, on the one hand seeing the Turks holding their fortress in Tabríz, and on the other hand having daily news of the insolent conduct of the Turkoman tribesmen, now at last, as soon as the month of March had set in, obtained his father's licence, and the full approval of his council to proceed against the rebels. With 14,000 horse we marched forth, the prince at our head, and his highness had done me the honour of placing me in command of one of the squadrons. The Sháh, Muhammad Khudá-Bandah, remained behind in Tabríz with 50,000 men, part infantry, part cavalry, with Toqmaq Khán Qáshlú and Imám Quli Khán Qájár as his lieutenants in command. Prince Hamzah reached Sultániyah, which is only 30 leagues from Qazvín, and there we rested and refreshed ourselves, men and horse, for it is a very rich countryside.

We were joined here by Ja'far Quli Khán, with his three brothers Nicheps Sultán, Sháh 'Ali Sultán and Bedel Sultán, who marched in at the head of 12,000 horse and foot soldiers, and they had come to give their aid and support to the prince. All these were of the Bayát clan, being of my family, which same counts as of the best and most noble blood in Persia, and their joining us was a great satisfaction to me, for these four commanders were in fact my cousins in the second degree. Now the Turkomans, as soon as they had heard of the approach of Ja'far Quli Khán and his three brothers, had despatched an envoy to them, proposing that they should take part with them in their rebellion, and that they should give in their allegiance to Prince Tahmásp as Sháh. The four Bayát Kháns being loyal subjects of their prince, answered not a word, they only issued orders that the envoy should be thrown head

# VICTORY OF PRINCE HAMZAH

foremost into a neighbouring swamp, whence he escaped half drowned, and returning to Qazvín, gave the Turkomans this answer of the Bayát nobles. It was at about that time also, but two or three days later, that Devlahar Khán also came in, joining up with 10,000 horse and infantry, in support of the prince's cause, and these were all men well practised in warfare, being of a clan held in very high esteem throughout Persia known as the Curthasi Amanzir.[3]

The prince, now finding himself at the head of some 40,000 cavalry and infantry drawn from the various provinces faithful to him, resolved forthwith to march straight on Qazvín, though he heard that the Turkomans there had been reinforced by a new contingent of 10,000 men. We thereupon started on our march, using much caution and by short stages, and on the first night out, as we were setting our camp, news was brought that 20,000 Turkomans were come out from Qazvín to surprise us with a night attack. We stood to our arms and were on the watch, every man ready to leap into the saddle should the word be given, but their patrols having discovered that we were thus ready and awaiting them, their approach perfectly known to us, they forthwith began to beat a retreat. They made the dawn following, it is true, an ineffectual attack, skirmishing, but the main body of our men coming up, the Turkomans all suddenly disappeared from view. The next day, which was Friday, the whole Turkoman army came in view at early dawn, and as is the custom with us Persians they immediately sent their heralds to the prince to challenge us. We accepted their challenge, and the signal was given to attack, in which action, at first, we did not have the better part. Fortune, however, in the end changed and the victory was ours, to the which happy result an incident that I will now relate in no little part contributed. One of the servants of Khalífah Khán, the Turkoman chief, was carrying a musket slung over his shoulder, and he was running along in front of his master when, without his hand touching the weapon, it went off, and by mischance shot Khalífah Khán dead. And but a short time before, under the eyes of all the Turkoman chiefs, our men had killed 'Ali Paghman, a most valiant captain, and one in whose leadership the enemy had founded their main hopes of success.

With these two casualties the Turkomans were now quite disheartened, and turning their backs fled from before us, the prince charging them home. The victory was complete, some 8,000 were slain, the heads of many leaders of importance were cut off, and among the rest Saqalí Sultán was decapitated, he being the brother of that chief already so many times mentioned by us, the late Amir Khán. More than 3,000 captives were taken, and the young prince Tahmásp Mirzá was delivered up to his brother, who despatched him as a prisoner to the Castle of Alamút.[4] Then, after his victory, Prince Hamzah entered and took peaceable possession of Qazvín, now his capital, lately that of the Turkomans. And I think I hear one who is reading this book asking for explanation of the reason as to how it came about that Qazvín, the most important city of Persia, was so easily taken and retaken by foe and friend in turn. Him, my reader, I would answer quoting the Spanish proverb: "The worst thief is he who is of the household."[5] The immense population of Qazvín, as is the case with the population of every capital city in all countries, is made up from peoples of all parts, and the Turkoman tribesmen always had many friends and relations among them. There were therefore as many hands to open the city gates to them, as there might have been to close these gates against them. This, too, is the reason why it is never possible to keep the secret of the court of one prince from the knowledge of those at the court of the prince his

## TABRIZ ABANDONED

neighbour, for the gate that for egress muſt be left unclosed in the city-wall of every king's capital is as the story related of the cutler who had his throat cut with the knife blade that was of his very own making. But I need not explain further these matters of ſtate, and should be speaking prolixly, for wars in Persia are waged very differently to what we have any knowledge of in Spain, and there all things are alien to the politics of our weſtern lands.

To return therefore to the matters in hand: Prince Hamzah having re-eſtablished his government in Qazvín and chaſtised those of the population who had been in rebellion, marched out after a sojourn of two months, and returned to Tabríz, where he had left the king his father. We found him well, and ſtill superintending the blockade of the Turks in the fortress, but joining him, as will be easily underſtood, we took no reſt whatever even for an hour from our recent labours of war. The spring-time was now advanced and fine weather coming with it, but we gained neither ease nor good fortune, for the Turks in Tabríz were shortly after this reinforced by the relieving army, which unopposed by us marched in, numbering, it was said, upwards of 200,000 men. The commanders were Sinán Pasha [otherwise known as Cigala] and Farhád Pasha, but Cigala was to hold the chief command. At this time it became manifeſt to Sháh Muhammad Khudá-Bandah and his son Prince Hamzah that it would in the immediate future be impossible to hold the city quarters of Tabríz againſt this immense force of the Turks, and they resolved therefore, without further delay, to dismantle the town fortifications, and carry off the whole civil population, with as much of their goods and chattels as it was possible to remove to neighbouring places of security, and all this was accordingly done. The Persian camp was next broken up, and the army marched out, taking the road north to Ganjah [in Qarabágh], the king being accompanied by the youngest of his sons, Abu Tálib Mirzá. When we reached Ganjah, the news came of how the Turkish army had now occupied Tabríz, and how they had laid the whole of the town quarters in ruin, the fortress alone being left standing, but the old city wall they had rebuilt.

While he was sojourning in Ganjah Prince Hamzah made arrangements for the guardianship of his two sons, these young princes being the children of different mothers. This action was almost as though he had foreseen the sad event that was so soon to occur. Both his sons were still of very tender years, and their names were Isma'íl Mirzá Sultán and Haydar Mirzá, and they were put under the guardianship and in ward to Esmí[6] Khán Shámlú and 'Ali Quli Khán. While in camp at Ganjah, Imám Quli Khán Qájár came in at the head of a considerable body of men, a notable reinforcement to the king's army, now under the supreme command of Prince Hamzah, though even with this augmentation it did not seem prudent to the prince to attempt any further action against the Turkish forces in occupation of Tabríz, and hence, it being now intended to return to Qazvín, the whole Persian army acting as convoy to the person of the king, with the court in attendance, all marched out of Ganjah. It was now the winter season of rain and snow, and our first day's march took us in to camp at a place only three leagues from Ganjah, where we were under canvas, in tents, this short distance being all that we could come to by reason of the bad weather. It was in this camp that the terrible event occurred, the detail of which must be related in the following chapter.

## CHAPTER XI

*Of the unhappy death of Prince Hamzah, and of many other consequent events which took place.*

THE Turkish army, as we subsequently heard, had marched out from Tabríz [leaving the fortress well garrisoned], after laying the city in ruins in such fashion that no one of its houses was left to mark that any town had ever been there; and nothing but a memory of its former greatness remained. The Turkish army now went north into Georgia, and indeed, had they marched to invade the territories of Qazvín and of Isfahán, judging the case by their present invasion of Georgia, the kingdom of Persia would have been put into a condition of the utmost stress. But fortunately fortune never continues to favour only the one side; the chance now changed over, and we in the end came by our own.

The disastrous happening [namely, the murder of Prince Hamzah] to which reference has been made at the end of the last chapter came about after this wise. No one is safe who has always to look to another for help, and princes least of all, for though their good fortune has given them riches and ease, they are by the very same obliged to depend for many services on hands not their own, and this is no small evil. Some think it is a grand matter to be always served by other hands: I say it is the greatest of misfortunes to be forced to depend, not on yourself, but on servants. Esmi Khán, of the Shámlú clan, as explained in the last chapter, now found himself promoted to be guardian and governor of the young prince Isma'íl Mirzá Sultán, who was the eldest son of Prince Hamzah, and therefore in the second degree heir-apparent in the state, and Esmi Khán was in a way overset by the greatness of his position and the honours of his post. It seemed to him that his new charge might, and indeed should, lead to a more important office. For, from being the guardian of the heir-apparent, he might become the prime minister of the future king, the two offices not being dissimilar, and if the next step up could follow swiftly on the first, already so recently taken by him, then the power of all Western Asia might be controlled by his hands. From what I have been able to learn, there were in all fourteen Kháns and great persons in this plot, all relations or connexions of Esmi Khán, he being the chief conspirator, and it was their intention to bring about the death of Prince Hamzah by the hand of a certain Khudá Verdí Dallák, and the word *Dallák* in Persian has, in the Spanish tongue,[1] the signification of "barber."

Thus Khudá Verdí was indeed by office the king's barber, being also groom of the chamber to the prince, and very intimately in his favour. The barber had in his possession an attested list with all the names of the conspirators. This had given him a sense of his own great importance in the plot, and he had undertaken to kill the prince that same night in camp, for he, the barber, slept in the ante-chamber of his tent. And so it all came about, for choosing the first watch of the night as most convenient, and after the close of a great supper party that had taken place in the royal pavilion, this murderous servant entered the prince's sleeping apartment without being perceived, very quietly, and forthwith cut his master's throat with all the skill of his barber's art. Then, on going out by the door of the tent, he was asked by the guards what was doing for him to be leaving the royal precincts at such an undue hour, and answered that his highness the prince had given him an important piece of business to despatch, and so went off to place himself for safety

## PRINCE HAMZAH MURDERED

under the protection of Esmi Khán, the chief conspirator. At this moment, and while the barber was thus escaping from the royal tent, the old king Muhammad Khudá-Bandah began to call aloud, which had the effect of turning out the main-guard. It was then immediately discovered that the prince had been murdered, and the news becoming public the whole army was soon in an uproar, everybody crying that all was lost.

And this indeed would have been the case had 'Ali Quli Khán and Esmi Khán, the two rivals, and the most powerful nobles in the state, come to a quarrel, with the army taking sides: which forsooth almost happened when 'Ali Quli Khán, learning of the prince's death, came further to know that the murderer had taken refuge with Esmi Khán, claiming his protection. The old king, however, managed to quiet the disorders, for he feared lest the Turks hearing of the matter should march in and, serving us in this case even as they had served us at Tabríz, bring ruin to the state. Since it was impossible to bring the prince back to life, all left for his father to do was to curse his evil fortune, and accept the fate that he could not elude. He immediately gave orders to have the barber found and brought before him, who forthwith would have shown the king the attested list of the conspirators which it had been his care to carry on his person, but Esmi Khán promptly struck him with his dagger in the mouth, an act indeed which was sure proof of who was the real traitor. The matter was thus hushed up, none being brought to justice, except this unlucky barber, whom the king now ordered to be burnt alive. As soon as matters had been brought to this peaceful issue, and the commotion assuaged among the troops, the army set out on its march to the city of Ardebíl, bearing the body of the dead prince, for it is in this town that all the Sophi princes are buried—namely, in the mausoleum of the first great Sophi, Sháh Ismaʻíl I, who is known as Shaykh Sophí, which is as much as to say, Sophi the Saint. His tomb is in a Mosque, which is a sanctuary to all the country round, and here daily more than a thousand poor persons are wont to be fed and alms are distributed at the expense of the king. The city of Ardebíl was distant about 100 leagues from our camp where the prince had been murdered, and having regard to the ceremony proper to this royal funeral we marched at a very slow rate that proved most wearisome to the soldiers of our army. However, at last we reached Ardebíl, and there completed the burial rites, immediately on which the army set out for Qazvín.

The old king had not been many days settled in his capital city of Qazvín, and before he had indeed recovered from the toils and troubles that had beset him, when news was brought in that ʻAli Khán,[2] son of Muhammad Khán the Turkoman, had taken possession by assault of the town of Káshán, where he was committing every sort of evil deed, his Turkoman tribesmen, whom he had brought in from all parts of the country, plundering that city and all the neighbouring hamlets. Thus, although we with the old king were still mourning for the prince, we had to march out with the Sháh at our head to combat them, and the arrangements for this expedition lacking due organization, our campaign against these Turkomans did not result in any very notable success to the royal arms. Matters were now getting into a most deplorable confusion throughout the whole land of Persia. There was no king of whom the great nobles stood in awe. Many of the provinces were in open revolt, and hardly had one been brought under subjection than another would rise in arms. No sooner had we returned from Káshán, when we had to march on Isfahán, where Farhád Beg, the Georgian

## FARHÁD BEG

renegade, was at the head of an insurrection, and little could we accomplish here, for the rebels proved to be in great force and defied all our efforts. In short, there was not a Khán or a noble in command of troops who would obey the poor blind king; whereby this is the place to cite the lines of the well-known Castilian ballad:

> For none was deemed to be good Moor,
> Save who had given his lance thrust [3]

[to wit, against his sovereign lord the king].

While we in the west were thus occupied ineffectually in putting down insurrection and trying to bring the provinces under control to the royal authority, in the east in the province of Khurásán matters were also in a state of anarchy. In Herat, as we have already explained, Prince 'Abbás, young in years, was nominal governor, but at that time entirely in the hands of 'Ali Quli Khán, who held authority throughout most of that province. In Meshed Murshíd Quli Khán was governor, and he was the declared enemy and rival on all points of 'Ali Quli Khán, and though Meshed lay 100 leagues distant from Herát, each of these two men had already sent his defiance to the other. Both now were marching out to bring their differences to the trial of battle, Murshíd Quli Khán having under his command 12,000 horse, and 'Ali Quli Khán 20,000. Both were so eager for the fray that, coming in sight of one another, forthwith they brought their men to battle array and attacked. The fight was one of the most fiercely contested engagements ever seen in those parts, and as Murshíd Quli Khán had the better disciplined troops, though in number inferior to those of his rival, fortune turned in his favour: 'Ali Quli Khán was completely vanquished, and Prince 'Abbás changed over, coming now to be under the control of Murshíd Quli Khán. As has been already explained, with the death of Prince Hamzah and with both his sons of an age, and indeed of parentage, considered not to be capable of succeeding [to the throne of their grandfather, the blind king], the heir to all the kingdoms of Persia was Prince 'Abbás, who, as we have just seen, was now under the tutelage of Murshíd Quli Khán. News of the death of Prince Hamzah and of the various rebellions in the western province had only very recently become known in Khurásán, but Murshíd Quli Khán felt that he had nothing in the immediate future to fear, having entirely got the better of 'Ali Quli Khán, and having Prince 'Abbás at his side, resident under his very eye in Meshed.

In Qazvín, the Kháns and great nobles being very weary of the confusion under which the kingdom lay, now took counsel together and resolved on despatching envoys immediately to Prince 'Abbás, beseeching him of his grace to come to them forthwith, and promising that they would publicly recognize his rights to the kingship. Further they pointed out that any delay in coming would be highly prejudicial to the state, for the king his father was now entirely incapacitated from governing, being blind and old, so that his position at the head of affairs was an obstacle to all good government, and a matter prejudicial to the settlement of the kingdom. When the envoys had come and set all these things clearly before Prince 'Abbás, he, prompt in action, immediately, with no great escort, rode in from Meshed to Qazvín, leaving his orders for Murshíd Quli Khán to follow on with a considerable army. As soon as the news became known at the palace in Qazvín that Prince 'Abbás was come—and on his arrival before the city gate all the people had flocked out to welcome him— the Kháns and Begs with scarce an exception, also the other commanders present at court, all immediately hurried to the house where the prince had taken his lodging, so that indeed hardly one remained behind in

## PRINCE 'ABBÁS

attendance on the old blind king. All gave in their allegiance to the prince, recognizing him as their lord and master, he being in the prime of his youth to hold power: and forsooth, as it is commonly said, what is novel, ever pleases. Many were now the councils called and held by the chief nobles and Kháns. It was agreed that all men should combine and help the government, forgetting their former enmities, and their rivalries must be laid aside, lest civil war should continue bringing ruin to the state: for many indeed were the heads that had fallen already, and numberless had been the victims of the party feuds.

Thus it was agreed that weapons of war were to be laid aside, all were to join, enemies were to become friends. Then the nobles in a body presented themselves before the old blind king at the palace, and with many protestations of their respect and obedience brought him out, together with some twenty-eight of his Kháns and commanders, who were found there in attendance on him. They forced both the king and these men to come and wait upon the prince, whereupon the old king embraced his son the prince, and delivered over to him the sceptre and crown of the empire. Then all present acknowledged the prince for their king and lord, paying him their homage by kissing his hand, and 'Abbás Mirzá immediately assumed the style and title of Sháh 'Abbás—for Sháh in Persian has the signification of king. The new monarch now took into his service to form his bodyguard 12,000 Georgians, renegades [who had become Moslems], and proceeded with his reforms in the military government and civil administration: although indeed at this date he was yet but a youth, being little more than fifteen years of age.[4] Then at length there was peace throughout the land, for such was his prudence and the favour accorded him, that all the provinces gave in their obedience and the neighbouring potentates paid him their respect.

# DON JUAN OF PERSIA

Now on the first day when, as described above, the ceremonies of swearing allegiance to the new monarch had been completed, Sháh 'Abbás gave command that on the following day all the Kháns and commanders should attend him at his palace in the garb of peace and unarmed, since he wished to consult them and arrange for the establishment of a Divan, or Grand Council of State, to ensure the pacification and due administration of the kingdom. The next morning therefore the nobles all assembled as commanded, but Sháh 'Abbás had secretly instructed his bodyguard of Georgians to hold securely all the issues of the streets that opened on the square round the palace. When the Kháns and the commanders now entered the royal presence they found Sháh 'Abbás seated on his throne, and on his right hand sat his father, the old blind king Muhammad Khudá-Bandah. Then Sháh 'Abbás forthwith put a question to the assembled nobles—namely, what was the punishment due to him who had killed his prince? To this question those who felt themselves to be most guilty gave as little possible any reply, while those who felt at ease in their consciences loudly proclaimed their judgment, some opining for one form of punishment, others declaring for another and a sterner penalty. In the end, however, all agreed unanimously that the servant who had compassed to slay his prince was worthy of death. No sooner had this sentence been pronounced than, Sháh 'Abbás making a sign to his bodyguard, the Georgians fell upon those present in the palace hall, slaying among them all the conspirators without exception, after which twenty-two of their heads stuck on the points of lances were exhibited from the palace windows to the populace below, a sight of terror that struck awe into the hearts of the boldest and most arrogant.

The king's anger did not even halt here, for sending

## SHÁH 'ABBÁS

for his two younger brothers, Tahmásp Mirzá and Abu Tálib Mirzá, he commanded them forthwith both to be blinded, and then consigned them as prisoners to the strong castle of Alamút. It was at about this same time that 'Ali Khán the Turkoman and Farhád Beg, who, as has been related above, were the two commanders who had rebelled [against Sháh Muhammad Khudá-Bandah] in Káshán and Isfahán, came in to pay their allegiance and kiss the hand of Sháh 'Abbás. The king accepted very graciously their submission, but immediately afterwards ordered that they should both be beheaded. Sháh 'Abbás, to remove all doubt as to who was now the master of the kingdom, persuaded his father, the old king, formally to abdicate in his favour,[5] and thus, though his accession and his assumption of command throughout the kingdom of Persia had caused some searchings of heart among the older nobles of the court, matters now were settling themselves in the capital and none there dared to think even of rebellion or opposition to his will and command.

## CHAPTER XII

*In the same is narrated the campaigns which the king Sháh 'Abbás undertook against the rebels.—Also of the death of Sultan Murád III, with the accession of his son, Sultan Muhammad III, to the Ottoman Empire.—How Sháh 'Abbás changed the seat of government and the Court from Qazvín to Isfahán.*

ALTHOUGH, as we have just remarked, at his court and in the immediate vicinity of the king all feared him for his exemplary punishments meted out to all those who opposed his commands, yet there were many whose abode was not near at hand, especially some among the relatives of the men the king had put to death, and some among the viceroys and governors of far-off provinces, who began now to rebel, for they declared that this new king, Sháh 'Abbás, was to them naught but the public enemy of the realm. This defiance Sháh 'Abbás, in all the glory of his youth and pride of empire, could not stomach; but first taking counsel of Murshíd Quli Khán, who was at that time his confidential adviser, the king determined [in order to free his hands in one quarter] to send his ambassador to Constantinople, seeking to arrange a treaty of peace with Sultan Murád, although to many so to do appeared a derogatory act implying his submission to the Turk.

The Persian ambassador chosen, who was Qara Hasan Khán,[1] a noble to whom one of the king's nieces had been given in marriage, found on arrival at Constantinople that the Ottoman Government would only consent to make peace with Persia on certain most harsh terms—namely, that the Sultan should remain peacefully possessed of all those lands, formerly included in the Persian kingdom, that his armies had overrun and conquered during the late campaigns,

## THE PEACE TREATY

and that in future the river Araxes should be considered the boundary dividing the Ottoman Empire from the kingdom of the Sháh. Further, it was only merchants and traders or ambassadors who might cross this boundary river, and under pain of death no armed soldier, Turk or Persian, should overpass it. To this treaty finally the Sháh and the Sultan put their hands, pledging their word of honour, and each protesting himself ready to forfeit his reputation should he fail to carry out the treaty in all its terms, and that he should of right then be considered none otherwise than as a perjured traitor incapable of nobility of act or deed. Thus was the treaty sworn to, and of it two formal copies were made public, one in Constantinople signed in the presence of all the viceroys of the Porte, the other in Qazvín before all the Persian Kháns and commanders. Thereto also was this stipulation annexed among the rest, that Sháh ʿAbbás should send to Sultan Murád, as a hostage in pledge to reside at Constantinople, his nephew, Sultán Haydar Mirzá, the second son of his dead brother Prince Hamzah, and the young man was forthwith despatched thither under charge of Khán Muhammad Quli Khalífah.[2]

The treaty with the Turks being therefore finally concluded [and his north-western frontier safeguarded], Sháh ʿAbbás brought together a force of some 30,000 infantry and marched forth out of Qazvín, the cause for this his first campaign being as follows. Among the Kháns and nobles present in the palace of Qazvín on the day following the king's accession, when, as has been related in the preceding chapter, twenty-two traitors of their number had been summarily executed, some of the remaining disaffected nobles had managed to escape death, and among these were the three following: Muhammad Sharíf Khán, Sultán Mahmúd and Aʿzam Beg Colgachi. These three Kháns had since fled, taking refuge with Khán

Ahmad, prince of Gílán, Baſt and Guesher, which are provinces and districts lying on the southern shore of the Caspian Sea. This prince, Khán Ahmad, had been married to a siſter of the late king Sháh Muhammad Khudá-Bandah, and the province being tributary to the Persian crown was assessed to pay yearly about a million gold pieces to the royal treasury. Sháh 'Abbás had immediately sent demanding of the prince of Gílán that the three rebel Kháns who had fled to him should be delivered up, but Khán Ahmad had refused; further, he at the same time had declined to pay the tribute now due from him, and Sháh 'Abbás was filled with wrath by this insult and act of rebellion. The province of Gílán is a very mountainous and impassable land, where horses are of little use for transport, wherefore it was infantry only that the king could take with him, and their number on this campaign was as has been ſtated above. All, from the greateſt noble to the meaneſt camp-follower, muſt go on foot, and for their convenience of wear an immense supply of foot-gear had been provided—namely, shoes made of cow-hide of the sort there known as " Charuk." The king himself wore these to set the example, marching thus at the head of his troops, we all following in his foot-ſteps.

Thus we proceeded, and in twelve days covered the 50 leagues that separate Qazvín from Gílán. Khán Ahmad and his nobles meanwhile had not been reſting unconcerned, for they were well informed of our march: by orders given great trees had been cut down and laid so as to block the roads and passes, where further many an ambush had been set with arquebus-men in wait to oppose us. All opposition, however, was unavailing, and our troops marched in to Gílán, with, it is true, a loss of some of our men, though not as many as might have been expected. The rebels were indeed in no case effectively to oppose

## GÍLÁN

us, for Sháh 'Abbás had sent on as the vanguard, preceding the main body of our troops, a regiment under orders of Shaykh Ahmad, who was the chief magistrate of his court, being his superintendent of police, and all these men were dressed in scarlet, from the shoes on their feet to the plume in their caps, this being with us Persians the uniform of the executioners of the king's justice. These men, therefore, having come to a town called Nohum, put 10,000 of its inhabitants to the sword, of whom more than half were women and children, and seizing on the wife of the governor of the town, who had fled, they burnt her alive, she being a most beautiful woman.

We of the main army had meanwhile arrived in Gílán, coming in by roads and passes for the most part unfrequented or forgotten, and no sooner was Khán Ahmad, the prince of Gílán, informed of our coming than he decamped with all his court, abandoning his capital, which same is the great city of Láhiján, as we have stated in Book I, Chapter II of this work. He left the city fortifications completely dismantled, and had carried off with him his treasure, also a very beautiful Georgian slave-girl of whom he was deeply enamoured, she having been recently bought by him at the price of 10,000 crowns. The prince of Gílán and his suite proceeded to embark at a port on the Caspian Sea that was in his dominions [and landing on the coast beyond to the westward travelled across Georgia to the Euxine, where] he took ship for Constantinople. After his flight all the cities of the province of Gílán submitted to Sháh 'Abbás, who now returned back to Qazvín joyful and victorious, having left a garrison of 12,000 Persians in Gílán under the command of Mahdi Quli Khán Shámlú, who had been named governor. Sháh 'Abbás in his train brought home the princess his aunt, whom her husband, the prince of Gílán, had abandoned in his flight. We thus re-entered Qazvín, but had little time for repose, before two months were past news coming in that the prince of Luristán, called Sháh Verdí Khán, was now in revolt.

This prince, who had married a niece of Sháh 'Abbás, she being a daughter of Prince Isma'íl,[3] yearly, as regards the province of Luristán, had been assessed for tribute to the amount of 50,000 ducats. Now the cause of his rebelling was that Sháh 'Abbás at the time of his accession as king of Persia had sent him no invitation to be present, although he, Sháh Verdí, was so nearly connected by marriage with Sháh 'Abbás. Further, at this moment the Turkomans and the Tartars [his near neighbours, who were already in insurrection] had sent urging him boldly to refuse all payment of tribute, which thus advised he did, though the princess his wife sought most urgently to dissuade him therefrom. He, however, was no longer to be restrained from his folly, and in place of taking the counsel she offered, gave her a great buffet on the face, an insult so vile that to avenge it the princess secretly informed her uncle, Sháh 'Abbás, of all the plans of the rebels. The Sháh now called out 30,000 horse, and, without telling us of our destination, in eight days led us the 150 leagues towards the southwest, which is the distance between Qazvín and Khurramábád, the capital city of the princes of Luristán. Of our approach Sháh Verdí Khán had thus no warning until we were at his gates. We had reached a mountain pass on his frontier where he kept stationed a guard of a hundred men to hold the same, to whom the coming of our army was a great surprise, and one of the guard immediately went off to tell the prince of Luristán of his danger. Sháh Verdí's only guerdon for the warning brought him was then and there to cut off the messenger's head.

Next taking his wife and his treasure, he fled from

# LURISTÁN

his capital, seeking asylum with the Turks at a place they held in garrison some twelve leagues this side from Baghdad. We on arrival, therefore, at Khurramábád found that Sháh Verdí had escaped us, and all the people of the city had also fled, seeking shelter in the hills round and about. Sháh 'Abbás now therefore despatched one of his commanders named Allah Verdí Khán in pursuit of the prince, at the head of a body of 12,000 Georgian troops, all of them renegades for they had embraced Islam, abandoning Christ, and these carried out their orders so discreetly that coming to that town, garrisoned by the Turks, they craftily burnt down its gates, but this without doing the Sultan's troops any other harm—and thus technically avoided a breach of the peace treaty still in force between Persia and the Ottoman Empire. This done they entered, seized on the person of Sháh Verdí and brought him back with the princess his wife to Sháh 'Abbás in Khurramábád, who immediately ordered his execution. The princess, however, being the king's niece was honourably treated, a pension for her maintenance was granted her, and Husayn Beg, who throughout had been a faithful servant to Sháh 'Abbás, was appointed governor of the Luristán country, he also having formerly been one of the servants of the late prince Sháh Verdí. On this we all returned again to Qazvín, but as we entered the city by one gate, by another gate came news of further rebellion—namely, now in the province of Mázandarán, which lies on the borders of Tartary, while on the one part its frontier extends along the shore of the Caspian Sea.

'Here the reigning prince went by the name of Bengi Melik [but this was his nickname, for] it signifies the mad, drunken king,[4] and the title had been given him because he was of disreputable life and morals. Resolved no longer to pay the usual tribute, he had now rebelled, and though, as we have said, he was a man of evil living, he was none the less a skilful soldier in the battle-field. The king Sháh 'Abbás did not intend in this case to march against him in person—for what reason I do not well know—and therefore sent as his deputy in command the Chief Comptroller of the Royal Household, who is known with us Persians as the Qúrchí Báshí, and who was a noble of the Qájár clan.[5] He therefore marched out of Qazvín, at the head of an army of 50,000, and passed the whole of the following winter in Mázandarán occupied with the siege of a certain fortress there, in which Bengi Melik had safely ensconced himself. This, however, was by means of a most cunning fraud, such as only a crafty man might plot to use, and the plan of which is worthy of being fully explained.

The prince Bengi Melik had caused to be built on the summit of a high mountain in those parts a castle very marvellous for strength, in outward appearance, with many bastions and towers, but entirely constructed of woodwork, mere thin planks being used, and these were then coated over with gypsum. This was done with such art and skill that the whole castle appeared to be actually built of solid stone, and anyone would have had to touch the walls with his hand to discover the fraud. Now the Qúrchí Báshí who was besieging the castle had no cannon with him, for in the armies of the king of Persia little or no field artillery was then commonly in use. The castle to all appearance therefore was inexpugnable, except by assault, and this the Persian commanders did not care to attempt, being threatened and kept off by the arquebus-men on the castle walls, and by certain small pieces of ordnance which Bengi Melik had got together and placed in position. Thus he held the Qúrchí Báshí in check for the whole of that winter season with this fraud, the Persians blockading the castle, and hoping in the end to starve out the garrison. And so matters might or

## BENGI MELIK

might not have come to the issue, but that, as it happened, one of Bengi Melik's men managed for private reasons to get away from the castle, and from him the Qúrchí Báshí learnt of the trick that had been played him. Making his way very secretly one dark night up to the castle walls he convinced himself of what material they really were made, and then took his time to set these planks on fire, when Bengi Melik rushing out was taken prisoner. He was forthwith beheaded by the Qúrchí Báshí, who had been thus put to shame, and was very wroth at the trick that had been played upon him. On his return to Qazvín he was indeed much laughed at, songs being sung about the Qúrchí Báshí's siege of the impregnable castle—so that for a long time he did not dare appear at court.

This jesting, however, was but of short duration, for 'Ali Beg, the prince of Astarábád [which is a district that lies near the south-eastern corner of the Caspian Sea] and who till then had been tributary subject to Sháh 'Abbás, now declared himself independent, declining to pay his subsidy. Sháh 'Abbás in this case marched immediately against him in person with 30,000 horse, but unfortunately I, being at the time sick, could not take my part in the campaign. According to the one account that I heard, 'Ali Beg was taken prisoner at the first attack; other reports give it that he came in of his own accord pleading for pardon. Whichever of the two be the fact of the case, what happened in the result was that Sháh 'Abbás ordered him forthwith to be blinded, and then after appointing one of his commanders to be governor of the Astarábád district, which on the one side marches with the Tartar border-land, the Sháh with his victorious army came back to Qazvín.

In previous chapters we have more than once spoken of the great power and state of the Tartar nation [who are now commonly known as the Uzbeks], and whose princes are the descendants of the great Tamerlane or Timur Beg, whose race went back to Chingiz Khán: and his name is said to mean the All-Highest, or the Highest above All. Now at the time when in Persia Sháh 'Abbás came to the throne, the monarch of the Uzbek Tartars was 'Abd-Allah Khán, and his custom was to make, ever and anon, raids over all the frontiers that bounded his lands. He now noting that Sháh 'Abbás for the most part was taken up with many campaigns against his rebellious subjects—as we have described in the foregoing pages—forthwith proceeded to plunder the neighbouring provinces of the kingdom of Persia on his border. The Tartar hordes overran the whole of Khurásán, taking possession of thirty-two of its towns, including the capital city, which is Herát. Here they killed 'Ali Quli Khán Shámlú, the governor, who was holding the place with a garrison of 6,000 Persians, but these men sold their lives dearly. From Herát to Meshed is a distance of 100 leagues, and thither the Uzbeks passed on. Here it is that he whom the Shi'ah Moslems especially honour as a Saint lies buried, a descendant of the Caliph 'Ali, called the Imám Rizá, and to his shrine, as we have said elsewhere, the Persians from many leagues round are wont to come barefoot in pilgrimage. It may also be mentioned that there is here a small turret, the same being of about the height of a pike-staff and its half, or something over, which is built entirely of massive gold. On its summit are arches constructed of precious stones, which in turn support at their summit a diamond of the size of a large chestnut, and this by night shines so as to be seen at a league distance all round illumining the darkness. I would not mention this marvel but that I, with my very own eyes, have seen it.

At Meshed 'Abd-Allah Khán the Uzbek found Ismet Khán of the Ustájlú clan, he being the Persian

## MESHED SACKED

governor and viceroy of Khurásán, and for three months he most valiantly defended the city. The Tartars, however, in the end effected an entry, though it is reported that they had lost 200,000 men during the siege. Thus at last taking possession, 'Abd-Allah the Uzbek was guilty of great cruelty, for by his command all the chief Persians were assembled together and shut up in the Great Mosque and its courts, and, said he, for the sake of the holy Imám Rizá he would grant them their lives. When, however, all had been assembled, and their number amounted to over 40,000, they being thus shut in, by the orders of the Uzbek chief every man of them was put to death. News of these events was brought to Sháh 'Abbás, who was at the time in Qazvín making arrangements for transferring his capital from Qazvín to Isfahán. But the matter in hand the Sháh forthwith abandoned, being resolved immediately to march out and take vengeance of the Uzbeks for this great cruelty and affront that they had put upon him. Now the king at this instant found himself in straits for funds and he knew not where to turn for money to pay the troops. Verily gold is the nerve and the true motive power of war: he who has money will always find soldiers. In this matter I speak as one having experience, and shall mention the wise saying which I myself once heard quoted by our king Sháh 'Abbás, and indeed it was on this very occasion. Now at the moment, as mentioned above, finding that there were no funds in the treasury for the said campaign, he had given command that forthwith all his service of plate should be melted down, for indeed, of the whole world his store of silver and gold vessels was the richest of that of any prince. Three times the order was given, and thrice over his chamberlains delayed to carry it out: whereupon the Sháh asked why, and was answered that 900,000 ducats had been the cost of its making, and all this would be wasted. None the less, said the king, it must all go to the melting-pot and be used to pay the soldiers, thus to content them, for said he: "My father the blind king Muhammad Khudá-Bandah was heard often to repeat the saying that good pay had brought about as many or more victories as ever good fortune had alone accomplished." After this all his vessels of plate were melted down and coined into money, whereby 80,000 horse were got together and equipped. Then we marched on Meshed.

The Tartars, however, no sooner had news of our coming than they took their departure, and we returned bootless to Qazvín without having accomplished anything against them. But when we were back safe in the capital once more, the Uzbek Khán made another raid at the head of 200,000 of his Tartars, this time laying siege to Turbat-i-Haydarí [a town lying some distance to the south of Meshed], where Muhammad Khán Bayát was governor. For a month or more he valiantly kept back the Tartar hordes, and indeed in his sallies from the fort killed over 30,000 of them, but every day more Uzbeks coming to join in the siege, it appeared a prudent act to come to terms with the enemy. Muhammad Khán agreed to give up the town, and the Persians were allowed by the capitulations to march out with banners flying and beating their kettle-drums. None the less, Sháh 'Abbás on hearing of the event was far from being satisfied, and but that Muhammad Khán Bayát had good friends at his back in Qazvín to plead his cause, he would have lost his head. In the end, however, the king pardoned him for what indeed he had been forced by circumstance to do.

For a period of nearly eight years that followed there was constant war waged by Sháh 'Abbás against 'Abd-Allah Khán and the Uzbek Tartars. Time after time we recovered most of the province of Khurásán

## SULTAN MUHAMMAD III

from them, but they in turn would overrun it again and occupy some of its outlying districts. Nor was Sháh 'Abbás to be prevented more than once sending his personal defiance to 'Abd-Allah Khán, calling on him to come out at the head of his men and let there be a pitched battle, or else let the two monarchs alone combat as champions, man against man. Either way it would be a fight worthy of kings, said Sháh 'Abbás, whereas these raids and retreats were but robber skirmishings. The Tartar prince, however, always gave answer that his forbears had ever fought after this fashion, and he did not propose to change the immemorial custom of his people. Thus, therefore, for the time mentioned this border warfare continued, until at last death brought 'Abd-Allah Khán's vain-glories and boastings to a close. Then by good fortune his son ['Abd-al-Múmin, who succeeded him] followed him also to the tomb a few months later. On one head I can as a witness testify, that during the seven and a half years, or thereabout, during which these wars continually went on, more than fifty important campaigns were undertaken by Sháh 'Abbás, and I myself was present in twenty-two or twenty-three of them: and I shall not be wrong in my estimate that counting both sides, Persians and Tartars, more than a million men must have perished on the battle-field during these years.

After the death of the Uzbek 'Abd-Allah Khán many notable events succeeded. Sháh 'Abbás being now rid of his chief enemy was at leisure to establish order in the affairs of his government and kingdom, the more so that at about this same date Sultan Murád III died in Constantinople, his son Muhammad III succeeding him, who at the moment of our writing these pages is still the reigning Sultan of the Ottoman Empire. Thus on either frontier north-west and north-east of Persia the domestic affairs of the Turks and the

Tartars gave promise of rest from attack, for Sultan Muhammad III showed every sign of wishing that the capitulations of the peace treaty should hold good, to which many years before his father, Sultan Murád III, had put his hand in concert with Sháh 'Abbás. Sháh 'Abbás now found himself at liberty to attend to the building of many edifices that he was planning, and at this period he went on a visit of filial respect to the tombs of his ancestors at Ardebíl. At this same time new laws and institutions were promulgated, and then came the changing of the capital from Qazvín to Isfahán. Isfahán was the chief city, as we have said, of the province of Persian 'Iráq, which of old had been Parthia; and the same possessed a more convenient situation than was the case with Qazvín, for a great capital with a growing population such as now was gathering into the central metropolis of Persia; and the districts round Isfahán, so broad and fertile, were fully capable of victualling all the inhabitants of the new capital.

While, however, we were thus resting from our labours in war and establishing ourselves in our new quarters, Tálim Khán[6] had become chief of the Uzbek Tartars, having lately succeeded to the supreme power on the death of his uncle, 'Abd-Allah Khán aforesaid. This Tálim Khán was a youth very desirous of making a name for himself, and he set forth to war having no wise counsellors to put a check on his ambitious ardour. Having therefore assembled a force of 300,000 Tartars, he proceeded to invade Khurásán, where no sufficient body of Persian troops to resist such an onslaught of raiders was stationed. Tálim Khán was soon in occupation of the whole province, establishing his residence in the city of Herát. Sháh 'Abbás by this time was becoming weary of peace, and on learning of these events in the Khurásán province immediately despatched Farhád Khán, the general then most in

# TÁLIM KHÁN

his favour, at the head of 12,000 cavalry to oppose the Tartar inroad. Farhád Khán tried by every means in his power at first to avoid making his attack on the enemy, but finding himself at last face to face with the Tartar force, he turned his back on them and fled. Sháh 'Abbás on learning of this cowardice was secretly angered, but as was proper, showed no dismay or outward displeasure. He now assembled a force of 100,000 cavalry in order to march in person against Tálim Khán: and in this campaign I myself took part, together with my friend 'Ali Quli Beg—who, as will be told later, afterwards accompanied me to Spain, where, subsequently at his baptism, he received the name of Don Philip of Persia—and both of us now by Sháh 'Abbás were given positions of high trust in the army.

The Persian forces having reached the neighbourhood of Herát, Sháh 'Abbás, who had till then remained behind in Isfahán, came riding post and joined his troops to stand at the head of the army. Tálim Khán, in youthful ardour, it now appeared was desirous of fighting a pitched battle: he immediately attacked us, whereupon the Sháh accepted his challenge, although we Persians had, in fact, only a force of 100,000 as against 160,000 of the Tartars. On that day, however, fortune declared in our favour, for the Uzbeks beginning a great skirmish against us, discovered to their cost how differently our nobles and our men would fight when it was their king in person who was present in command. The Tartars were quite unable to resist our onslaught, and turning their backs fled, forfeiting all the honour they had gained and at the same time losing possession of the province of Khurásán. In their rout they abandoned their king, Tálim Khán, who, falling a prisoner into our hands, was immediately put to death by order of Sháh 'Abbás. We then reoccupied Herát, having taken prisoners more than 6,000 of the Tartar soldiers, and in addition a like number of their women. The order was now issued by the Sháh for the army to return to the capital, Isfahán, seeing that all his enemies had been overcome. Further, he had forgiven Farhád Khán for his cowardice and even was proceeding to name him as governor of Herát; but Farhád had no stomach to take up the appointment, he being more at ease in the intrigues and scandals of a court than of capacity in the conduct of government and the bearing of arms. Farhád Khán therefore would have excused himself, but the Sháh, in anger coupling this refusal to serve with his late disgraceful conduct, incontinently ordered that he should be beheaded. The governorship of Herát was then conferred upon Husayn Khán Shámlú, with a force of 40,000 Persian troops to be quartered there in garrison; and everything being satisfactorily settled, and happy with our rich booty, we all set out on our return, carrying with us 24,000 cut-off Tartar heads, besides the many captives.

On our return journey, however, we did not pass to Isfahán, for those of us who were in attendance and servants of the royal household kept with the king, who went direct to Qazvín. Here some of the nobles were given charge to wait on Prince Safí Mirzá, eldest son and heir-apparent of Sháh 'Abbás, he being the child of a Georgian lady, and at that time a boy about ten years old. It was ordered next that the young prince should be conducted to Isfáhan, and thither we now accompanied him, establishing him in a suitable palace, with service in accordance with his rank. Then in Isfahán two years went by, no events happening that need record, at the end of which time news came in that troubles were beginning again from the repeated inroads of the Turks on our north-western frontiers. This matter, however, Sháh 'Abbás treated as of little moment, for he was not averse to breaking the peace

## THE SHERLEYS

with Sultan Muhammad III, and to this end, namely, war with the Ottoman power, the timely arrival of certain Englishmen gave him much encouragement.

These men had come from Scotland, and passing through Venice had travelled by way of Aleppo and Baghdad, being disguised as Turks. In accordance with the terms of the existing peace treaty [between Persia and Turkey they with their armed escort] had been stopped at the frontier on the Chisir river,[7] where they had pretended to be travelling Turkish merchants —for they were perfectly acquainted with that tongue and their Turkish guard had there left them. Next some Persian merchants passing had carried them across the stream and thence brought them on to Qazvín, where they had made known the truth as to who they really were. On our arrival, as aforesaid from Khurásán, we had found these men already waiting in Qazvín, where, however, Sháh 'Abbás did not see them. Subsequently they were allowed to come on to Isfahán and were there introduced at court, when the king received them in audience, his Majesty, as already said, not having hitherto had sight of them. From all of which it came about in due time that we of the embassy went on our journey to Spain, as will be explained fully in the Third Book of our Account.

THIRD Book of the Account of Don Juan of Persia, in which is related the cause of his coming into Spain, and the notable things which he saw during his journey, together with the manner of his conversion to the Christian Faith, and the conversion later of two other Persian gentlemen.

# CHAPTER I

*Wherein is recounted the arrival at the Court of the King of Persia of two Portuguese Friars, and of two Englishmen, brothers, and how the King determined to despatch an embassy to eight Christian Princes.*

THE king Sháh 'Abbás now living in quiet and content, reposing in his estates, being at peace after the victories gained over his enemies, and by the subjugation of the outlying provinces, there arrived at the Persian Court Muhammad Aga, Grand Chaush [Pursuivant] of the Sultan Muhammad III of Turkey, accompanied by 300 gentlemen and noblemen of his suite, on an embassy. The demand of the Sultan was that Sháh 'Abbás should send his son Safí Mirzá to the Court of Constantinople—he being at that time a youth twelve years of age, and the heir-apparent—to rejoice and entertain the Sultan. To the ambassador the king answered, being well experienced in the cruel ways of the Ottoman Court, after this fashion: that he, the Sháh, was indeed only the servant of his son, for in Persia when the prince heir-apparent is born he nominally is king of the land, wherefore he, the Sháh, would himself rather, in case of need, go to pay his respects to his Majesty the Sultan and do honour to his court; but as to his son being sent, even though he might wish to send him, the grandees of his kingdom would indeed never consent to let the prince depart, nor would he himself, for the present, think of going.

The Ottoman ambassador was not a little vexed at this reply; and even more angry was the Sháh at the impudent demand of the Sultan, and at the artfulness and craft with which it had been set forth: seeing that all this was done presumably with a view of putting the heir of Persia to death—as indeed the Ottoman Sultans are wont to do in their own family. The Sháh thus having perfectly understood the intention of Sultan Muhammad, now gave command that they should shave off the beard of his ambassador, and send the same as a gift to the Sultan. This mode of insult was one very common at the time between these princes, and Sháh 'Abbás was indeed within his right to use it, in order that Sultan Muhammad should recall to mind the trick played by order of his father, Murád III, on a former Persian ambassador, who, it will be remembered, during certain solemn ceremonies at the Court of Constantinople, was put to stand upon a flooring, traitorously set, thus ignominiously to be thrown down beneath the same at the most important moment of that ceremony.[1]

At about this same time there arrived at the court of the Sháh, also, that Englishman [already spoken of in the last chapter of Book II], called Sir Anthony Sherley, with his suite of thirty-two attendants, and they halted at Qazvín. He gave himself out as cousin of the Scottish king James, saying that all the kings of Christendom had recognized him as such, and had now empowered him as their ambassador to treat with the king of Persia, who should make a confederacy with them in order to wage war against the Turk, who was indeed the common enemy of all of them. Now this Christian gentleman had by chance arrived in the very nick of time, for the king of Persia was then himself preparing to send an ambassador with many gifts to the king of Spain, by way of the Portuguese Indies. Sir Anthony, however, brought it to the knowledge of the Sháh that there were, besides his Catholic Majesty of Spain, many other Christian kings in Europe and the West, who being most powerful monarchs would willingly join him against

## SIR ANTHONY SHERLEY

the Turk: hence it would now be proper to send also with his ambassador letters and presents to each of these other kings. Sir Anthony succeeded so well in setting forth this matter as urgent, that the Sháh was satisfied to do as he advised, and gave orders forthwith that arrangements for these embassies should be set on foot, proposing that Sir Anthony should accompany his envoy the Persian ambassador. To all this Sir Anthony readily agreed, thanking his Majesty for the honour he was doing him, and he proceeded to name the Christian Powers, to the number of eight, to whom he and the Persian ambassador were to be accredited; and these were: the Roman Pontiff, the Emperor of Germany, the King of Spain, the King of France, the King of Poland, the Signiory of Venice, the Queen of England and the King of Scotland.

All matters were thus set in order, and Sir Anthony agreed to leave his younger[2] brother Robert behind him in Persia, together with fifteen other Englishmen, for whom the Sháh then appointed a house with a sufficient upkeep in accordance with the rank that these were said to bear. At this same moment there arrived by the Indian route, and journeying up from Ormuz, two Portuguese Friars, natives of Lisbon. One was a Dominican, the other a Franciscan, and the former called himself Fray Nicolão de Molo.[3] These men also heartened the Sháh in the idea of sending his ambassadors to the Christian Powers, and his Majesty now gave them gifts, calling the Friars by the name of "Padre" and showing them every courtesy: on the which they besought the king to grant them a separate letter of recommendation for his Holiness, and yet another letter for his Catholic Majesty the King of Spain. The Sháh forthwith acceding, commanded such letters to be written and given to them, separately and apart from all the other credentials. Now in coming to Persia Sir Anthony had made his voyage through Greece [and the Ottoman Empire] in the dress of a Turk, being a man cognizant of the Turkish language, but it was not possible or advisable for him to seek to return home by that route. On the other hand, the way by India would demand too long a sea journey, and it was in consequence determined that the voyage of the present embassy should be taken through Tartary and Muscovy.

All needful preparations having thus been made, his Majesty granted his patents and orders for free provisions throughout all his lands and territories where the embassy should pass; further, the needful credits with orders for cash to pay our travelling expenses, and the same was done for the Englishmen—all to be thus defrayed at the charge of the king of Persia. The Persian gentlemen who were as secretaries to accompany the ambassador being also now duly appointed, we took leave in audience of Sháh 'Abbás in Isfahán, where the Court was then in residence, and started on our journey, it being Thursday evening, the 9th day of July, in the year of the Incarnation 1599. Now those who thus went out from the royal palace travelling at the king's command and expense, were all grandees of his court, of high rank, and they were habited and accoutred suitably for their voyage. The Persian ambassador was called Husayn 'Ali Beg,[4] and with him were four gentlemen the secretaries of embassy and fifteen servants. Next came the two Friars and then Sir Anthony with five interpreters, and fifteen other Englishmen. There were withal thirty-two camels carrying the presents, besides the needful number of riding horses for those who went the journey, and the usual sumpter-beasts required for carrying the baggage of the various persons already mentioned. Diverse were the feelings in the hearts of those who were thus departing, and different their expression: for some set forth most joyfully, but others very dolefully. To all the king had graciously given his royal word to bestow on us at our return many favours, but such were the tears of our relatives, the sad faces shown by our friends, the sorrow and despair expressed differently but grievously by wives, fathers and children, that we had perforce at last hurriedly to conclude and depart, and that evening leaving the capital, we forthwith took the road to the city of Káshán, our first stage.

The journey from Isfahán to Káshán occupied us four days; we rested there two, and then went on to the town of Qum; and the next morning we reached the city of Sávah. From Sávah we travelled during three days, coming to the city of Qazvín, formerly the capital city of Persia, as we have already stated in the chapter of our book describing the provinces of Persia. Here we remained eight days, for the Sháh had ordered us to procure from here certain articles for gifts that we were to present to the kings of the Christians, these in addition to those with which from Isfahán we were already in charge; this matter therefore we now attended to. After leaving Qazvín, we came in five days to Gílán, a territory and province where a different language to Persian is spoken, although, as already explained in a former chapter, it is indeed an integral part of the kingdom of Persia. This province lies along the coast of the Sea of Bákú, also called[5] Qulzum, which is the Caspian Sea of the ancients, and as here we had to embark aboard ship, we were delayed ten days while the necessary arrangements were being completed. Now many of our friends and relations had come out accompanying us hither on the road from Isfahán, and when we had at last embarked in our ship very sorrowfully we bade them good-bye, we standing on board, and finally set sail.[6]

The Caspian Sea was not very well known to the ancients, who till after the times of Cæsar Augustus believed it to be a bay of the Ocean; but the Arabs knew it to be otherwise and called it the "Closed Sea." It is 800 miles in length, and 600 in breadth; it receives into its waters many copious rivers, and although there is no lack of those who have stated that for this cause the water of the same is neither bitter nor salt, I who sailed over it, and once or twice tried to essay its taste, can affirm that it is gross, bitter, and salt, being indeed anything but palatable. The chief rivers that flow into this Sea are the Chessel, the Geicon, the Teuso, the Coro and the Volga. This last is in those parts known as the Eder, and on this river, as will later be described, we were destined to take our journey inland to Russia. Now, having, as already said, got on board our ship, we put out to sea, and in a day and a night reached a little island far from the land, where a number of fisher-folk are wont to live, for the fish here are abundant and of many kinds. More especially they catch hereabout great quantities[7] of dog-fish, and the same provide the fish-skins which being first dried are afterwards used as bags for holding olive-oil, and these skins are sold for a great price. Here we stayed a day and the night, waiting for fine weather, and the following day, as the sea appeared calm, we set sail. Very soon, however, it was manifest how little the seamen knew of the weather, for, after sailing three or four miles, a tempest arose, and the violence of the wind split our sails, whereby more than once one might have thought that we should all drown. But in truth we Persians are so entirely unused to sea-faring, that most of us were now unapprehensive of either danger or death; and we laughed heartily at the Portuguese Friars, who had fallen to weeping, being apparently prepared to die. The storm lasted the whole of that night, and in the morning we found ourselves back once again at that port and town, in Gílán, where we had embarked some days before.

## MANQISHLÁGH

It appeared to some who were faint-hearted that we should best now disembark and return to Isfahán, for it seemed to them as though it were not the will of Heaven that we should undertake this long journey. But in sooth we all feared too much the wrath of Sháh 'Abbás, and as fine weather had set in we again put to sea, in two days retraced the way already gone, and in another day, proceeding forward, reached a port where there were indeed no houses, but a settlement of folk of divers tribes. These men were all living, as is the fashion we see among the nomad Moors of Morocco, in the midst of their flocks and camels; they are of the Tartar nation, and the country goes by the name of the Land of the Great Tamerlane of Tartary; though, in fact, it is subject to the king of Persia. The manner of life of these people is quite barbarous, and they talk little that is matter of sense; they go almost naked, wearing only[8] fisher-breeches, or a very short shirt. They are poor and very humble folk in their ways, and welcome anybody who comes to their country. They treated us well, giving us of their flocks a liberal and sufficient entertainment during the fortnight that we were delayed here, for by reason of the dead calm which lay upon the sea, it was impossible for the ship to set sail all this time. In this country, which otherwise is called Manqishlágh [and lies on the east coast of the Caspian] there is a native Persian Idol very greatly venerated by the folk of the land, also by strangers, and to this Idol we, offering many gifts, forthwith made sacrifice that the Idol might grant to us a favourable wind. We met here with a Persian, who begged to join us, and having at last a favourable wind we again made sail. None the less, during the next two months we were constantly set back by foul weather; so we coasted the shore, and had we but had a favourable wind, in twelve days we should easily have accomplished this our journey across the Caspian.

## DON JUAN OF PERSIA

At the end of these two months we came into what is an arm of the Caspian, where the water is clearer and less salt than out at sea, and indeed Giovanni Botero[9] has already remarked this matter in his book, but this gulf is a separate arm of the Caspian and it is no part of the main sea. And here it is proper to point out that the water is thus less salt here by reason of the rivers which flow into this bay or estuary; but, as proving clearly that the water of the Caspian is by nature truly salt, when a storm wind drives the waters back through this estuary, of which we are speaking, into the river mouths, their waters then become as bitter as gall, and of this fact I satisfied myself by experiment. The people of the country call this river, which is the Volga, by the name of Idel.[10] Thirty leagues up this bay or estuary, sailing north we began to enter the territories which the Muscovites occupy in Asia, and the first inhabited place we came to was a town of the Christians, which is called Astrakhan. One of our Persians and an Englishman, with some of the sailors to row, now got into a small boat and went to wait upon the captain-general of the town, which lay thirty leagues above where the ship had come to anchor, for the water above here is so shallow that she could not have passed the bar without running aground. Now as we lay here, by a change of wind our vessel was in great risks, for though of considerable size, when a squall fell on us, she was all but overset, and we already accounted ourselves as doomed men. Immediately we began to throw overboard first a thousand bushels of wheat and flour, next many provisions with which we had been supplied, many boxes of clothes, lastly some chests of valuable gifts; whereby finally, and by the loss thereof, the tempest came to be appeased, and the ship saved.

This danger being overpassed, those who had gone up to the city returned, and with them the captain-

## ASTRAKHAN

general had sent down to us many gentlemen, aboard four galleys, with provisions and refreshments. We now trans-shipped and were taken on board their galleys, and our ship weighing anchor,[11] sailed away, leaving us. On arriving at the city we disembarked from the galleys, when they gave us a very great and solemn reception, for there was a mighty assembly of folk present. Here we found another ambassador from the king of Persia, especially accredited to Muscovy, who was on his way thither, and in his suite 300 persons. In Astrakhan we sojourned for sixteen days, for they gave us excellent entertainment, and it being the autumn season, there was in that country an abundance of melons and apples of very good quality. Also not only was the land pleasant, but the people likewise, for the captain-general, whom the Grand Duke of Muscovy has appointed here as governor, had caused it to be proclaimed that no one should presume to demand money for anything that we might need or desire, and this under pain of 200 lashes for disobedience. The city of Astrakhan—more properly Astarkhan—has a population of 5,000 householders[12] [or 22,500 souls]; all its houses are of wood, the fortress alone excepted, a strong place where the captain-general resides. This is high built, and constructed of very thick stone walls; it is well guarded and garrisoned by many soldiers, and no one is allowed to enter, unless by special permission. The churches here are numerous, but none very large; they are full of images of saints which are painted in varnish, but of a small size; and each image has all day before it a lighted candle burning; further, the natives do not allow any stranger to their country to enter the churches.

According to the account given by Giovanni Botero, we learn that Astrakhan is one of the towns where, by government order, the Tartars are permanently settled, as also, numbered by their tribes, the Jews; but, indeed, the Tartars all now live out in the open countryside, after the fashion we see the Moors do [who are our neighbours in Morocco], and the Muscovite Christians alone inhabit the city. Astrakhan stands on the bank of the Volga, or Eder, and is much frequented by merchants coming from Muscovy, Armenia, Persia and Turkey, and its chief commerce is in salt. Botero states that the township lies one day's sail by boat from the Caspian, but I, who have been there, say that with a very good wind you may only reach it thence with difficulty in two days. This city was in times past completely destroyed by the great Tamerlane; and during more recent times it has again suffered in the wars that have been recently waged between Persians and Turks.

## CHAPTER II

*In which, travelling through Muscovy, the land and what we saw most notable therein is described.*

HAVING sojourned sixteen days in Astrakhan, and the five galleys being now ready which had been prepared for our accommodation and for that of that other Persian ambassador whom we had joined company with in Astrakhan, we all now came together and embarked—namely, we Persians, and the Englishmen and the Friars. Along with us were sent a hundred soldiers of the Duke of Muscovy, who were to serve us as guard and escort, by order of the captain-general at Astrakhan. The galleys were very well built, and each had a crew of a hundred rowers. We got on board down at the strand of that river, which, as already said, is called the Eder, otherwise the Volga, the stream here having a width across of half a Spanish league. The land is well inhabited on either bank by the Tartar folk, who are divided up into Hordes[1] or tribes, and who for the most part live out in the countryside among their flocks, which supply them with their chief sustenance and livelihood. The river is much frequented by fishermen, and they catch here a great fish —namely, the sturgeon, not unlike the salmon of Spain, but of greater length and much finer in appearance. The smallest weigh as much as twenty or thirty pounds, and the wonder is that no one dare eat of the flesh of these fishes, and that they are caught solely for the roe [or caviare] which they bear within them. This may amount in weight to six or seven pounds in each fish, and it is black, like a ripe fig. It is very good to eat, and being dried they can keep it for one or two years without its going bad, even as here in Spain we keep quinces and pomegranates. Indeed, it is one of the greatest delicacies of that country.

Along the bank of the Volga, on the right hand as you travel up towards Muscovy, there are seen some of the Tartar folk, who herd camels and horses and flocks of sheep. They live as do the nomad Moors of Morocco, changing their habitations with the four seasons, even as those men are wont to do. They go by the name of the Nogay,[2] and when the pasturage fails on the one side, and is to be found only on the other bank of the river, since there are no bridges by which to carry over their flocks, it is their custom to make the passage over the river breadth during the month of August, when the water is at its lowest. To accomplish this fording of the river, they have contrived a method as follows. The horses and camels are tied together by their tails one to another, thirty by thirty, or fifty by fifty, and then being driven into the water their number enables them to struggle against the force of the current, and thus they get over. For the sheep to cross they lay over the surface of the water great pieces of coarse frieze[3] which have been tarred, as is done to the sides of ships, and these being strongly linked together, they push these across one after the other with poles, like the pans in a turning-table,[4] and thus the rams and ewes, having been set on them, may be got over. But as the distance across the stream is very great, it is not uncommon for half the flock to get drowned, for indeed, in the narrowest places the river here is a league from bank to bank. These Tartar people are subject some to one lord, some to another, and the flocks which they own are so numerous, that a sheep is here worth less than a *real*.[5] These Nogays are heathens in matters of religion, but they are most hospitable to guests, for when any stranger comes he immediately is invited to a feast, and a horse having been killed, the tenderest

# KAZAN

parts of the flesh are cut out and cooked, and set before the guest in proof how much he is esteemed and honoured.

During the two months following we now travelled in our galleys up the Volga, but every ten days we disembarked and went ashore to some village, for all along the river bank there are small settlements with houses that are built of wood. At each stopping place we changed some of our rowers, taking on fresh men to row the galleys. All this was done under command from the soldiers who accompanied us by an order sent from the Duke of Muscovy. The hills which the Volga has on either side its banks are very high, and are populated with settlements. We saw on these hills numerous bears, lions and tigers, also martens of many species. Every hundred leagues or so along the river there stand cities of the Duke of Muscovy, and the first that we came to was called Cherny Yar, the next Tzaritzyn, the third Samara, and so on with the rest we do not name. When there was a contrary wind blowing down the river, the boatmen would land the horses on one or other bank, and these towed the galleys with great ropes. Every night we were wont to land to sleep comfortably ashore in the fields, and our escort of a hundred soldiers then kept watch and ward for us. At the end of two months' journeying by river we came to a very great city of the Duke of Muscovy called Kazan, and its population, numbering over 50,000 householders [or 225,000 souls], are all Christians. This town is extremely full of churches, each having many great bells, and on the vesper of feast days no one can sleep or indeed stay in the city for the noise. On the day when we arrived at this city so great a concourse of people came out to meet us and wonder at the sight, that we scarcely could pass through the squares and streets. We stayed in Kazan eight days, and they provided us with such abundant supplies, that the food we could not eat had to be thrown out of the windows and wasted.

In this country none are poor, for the victuals are so cheap, that any that are hungry go out to find it in the highways. What they lack is good wine, and they have only one kind of drink, which is made from wheat or barley, and this is so strong that those who drink it are often drunk. For this reason there is a law and ordinance that no officer may carry any kind of weapon, otherwise they would be killing each other every other moment. The climate here is extremely cold, hence all go clothed in marten skins, which are to be had in abundance. They have no succulent fruits, only crab-apples, and no plenty even of these, and they are not sweet, being indeed quite sour. The people of Kazan are a fine race: the men are fair, tall and stout, and the women, as a rule, good-looking. They appear very well dressed in the marten furs of which the robes and hoods that they wear are made. They have great use for stoves, and in each house is a dog, as big as a lion, for they fear robbery by night from him who might be an enemy. In the daytime the dogs are chained up, but at the first hour of the evening the bells ring to warn people that the dogs are about to be let loose in the streets, and thus the passengers abroad must take care. For they now set their dogs free, and no one then dare go out of his house, lest he should be torn to pieces by them.

All the houses of Kazan are made of wood, but there is a great fort, very strongly built with stone walls; it is garrisoned by soldiers, and they keep watch here at night in their quarters, as is done with us in Spain, Italy and Flanders. This guard was first established because it was the evil custom formerly of the Turks and Tartars to come in by night and, having set fire to the houses, plunder the people.

From Kazan we set forth in seven galleys with which

the captain of the city supplied us, together with a guard of a hundred soldiers ordered to conduct us safely to the Court of the Duke of Muscovy. We continued to travel up the same stream, and advancing northward, began the more to feel the rigour of the climate of that region; and six days after leaving Kazan we came to a town on the same river bank, which is called Cheboksary. That same night the Volga, or Eder river, was frozen so thick all along where we were about to go that perforce we had to change our way of travelling. The people here now carried on shore all our luggage and goods that we were taking in the galleys, and next provided us with horse-sleighs and sleds for the transport of baggage, thus enabling us to proceed on to the court without delay.

Giovanni Botero has stated[6] that the mouths of the Volga are seventy-eight in number, and that this river, like the Boristhenes [the Bug] and the Dvina, takes its rise in Lake Volappo.[7] In this matter he seems to be rightly informed, for its stream appears to come down from the further parts of Lithuania. The reason why all these mouths, estuaries, and branches of the Volga are frozen up in winter, is because the land hereabout can but little profit from the sun's heat, this being always diverted away, for the noonday here has its aspect to the eastward, and the rigour of the winter lasts for nine entire months. Further, the woods along the river bank make the land here impenetrable to the sun's rays, these woods being the outlying tracts of the great Hercynian forest, which stretches up thence into the north. Thus the sun is never able thoroughly to warm the earth through during the three months of summer-time. However, although the winter here is so cold, and the surface of the earth everywhere covered with ice and snow, this season is in truth the more suitable for going about and the transport of goods and for making journeys, than is the summer-time; for in the short time of great warmth that then occurs, the frost and snow having gone, the ground is everywhere covered with lakes and swamps; and these are almost impassable, until, again being frozen hard, the waters and the surface of the ground can be safely traversed.

The horse-sleighs with which they provided us in this town on the Volga called Cheboksary were a fashion of portable chairs, like small litters, or little coaches, set on runners made of smoothed wooden beams. These sleds are, in appearance, just like the sleighs which the Flemings make use of in the Low Countries or in Flanders on the Meuse and Scheldt when the waters freeze, and in Italy also by the people who live round the sources of the river Po, except that those which the Muscovites make use of on the Volga are much larger, and run smoothly without cutting into the frozen surface, as those of Germany are wont to do. The form of sled here used is after this wise. There is a square box like a little turret, and inside of it two seats; the roof ends above in a pyramidal form, being covered over by skins with the fur left on. In front there is a stool, or half seat, where the man can sit who drives the horse which draws the sledge, while inside are safely accommodated the two travellers who are making the journey. At the back, as it were on the shoulder of the square box, is a kind of shelf, where some of the luggage may be carried. The horse is driven swiftly, and they go twelve or fifteen leagues in a day; but as each sled can accommodate but two passengers, to transport all our people and goods more than five hundred of these sleighs were required. After this fashion, therefore, we travelled beyond Kazan till we came to a city called Nizhni Novgorod,[8] which holds a population of about 8,000 householders [or 36,000 souls]. The houses, as elsewhere on the Volga, are of wood, but the city has a stone wall round it, which on one side overhangs the river bank. As

# NIZHNI NOVGOROD

soon as we had arrived here, an order came from the Duke of Muscovy—to whom news had been sent of our approach—that we should delay a month, remaining stationary here, and so for that time we postponed further travelling.

The people of Nizhni are Christians, and subjects of the Duke of Muscovy; but they are of a lascivious habit, and the fame of the place lies in its bath-houses, where the men and the women are wont to bathe in company, promiscuously, with no clothes to cover their nakedness; hence their commerce is exceedingly free, more so indeed than in any other country would be tolerated or possible. Provisions in Nizhni are very cheap, as indeed elsewhere in Tartary and Muscovy—but we have noted this already. Clothes-stuffs, however, are dear, though we by a special order of the Duke had all we required freely given to us, and forsooth we had an abundance of garments. At the end of the month we have spoken of, and which we passed quietly in Nizhni, orders came for us to proceed, and we set out for the court. We travelled in the manner arranged by one of the major-domos of the Duke, who had come to Nizhni for us, in sleighs with covered chairs similar to those we had already used; and were now accompanied by the captain-general of the fortress at Nizhni. This fort is held by a garrison of 6,000 soldiers, who night and day keep ward here against the Turks and Tartars. Now I do not exactly know whether these Tartars we are now speaking of be indeed of the Perekop Horde,[9] but it seems to me that these [living on the Volga], though they occupy lands situated so much to the north [of the Crimea, which is] the true Perekop country, are yet true Tartars, who live as do the nomad Moors of Morocco, their ways being those of men of the uncivilized outlands.

During six days we now travelled on, keeping always the banks of the river Eder in sight, and then came to a town which is called Murom. This is a large place and very populous, but as we were travelling post-haste, we were unable to enjoy much of the curious amenities of that city. One matter, however, they showed us and explained to us, which for being most peculiar, though certainly a very gross superstition, I cannot pass over in silence. It appears that the chief commerce and occupation of this township consists in the tanning of the hides of cattle, and these are in such abundance that there are one thousand and one tanning-houses here, entirely occupied in this business. Further, the town possesses a certain well, into which each man who is a tanner throws one thousand and one hides, which the waters do promptly tan. But when in due time they take up the hides from this well, they always find that the thousand and one skins of a certain particular one of the thousand and one tanners are entirely perished and spoiled. Then his friends among the other tanners having gathered together each his thousand and one well-tanned hides, will forthwith present to him whose skins have all been spoiled—and which are known by certain marks and signs to be verily his—exactly one thousand and one other hides well-tanned of theirs, in compensation. I opine that all this must be a wile of the Demon, and we would have said it was a lie and a story, such as could not be credible, had we not ourselves seen the fact. But on this point we comment further, that since for this purpose of tanning there is but one well of water, and since all the skins are of one kind and quality which they throw into it to be cured and tanned, it seems almost impossible to believe that the hides belonging to one person should suffer perishment more than those of any other person. For indeed, how can it be upheld that one party may profit more than another party in the quality of the water, and the peculiar property of the well—tanning in the one case, and spoiling in the other? Further we say, how does it come that the number of skins be so exactly held to, that always only just one thousand and one are perished? Whereby forsooth, indeed, it is very manifest that this is no natural effect of the water, but truly the diabolical work of Satan.

We passed by the city of Murom, therefore, and in three days reached Vladimir,[10] travelling as formerly up towards the source of the Volga, in other sleighs, but like those already described. This town is of larger size than Murom, being of 12,000 householders [or some 54,000 inhabitants], and it has the appearance of a well-organized community and one that is well governed. The women here are extremely beautiful, but their mode of dress is so ugly and eccentric, and they display so little taste for a suitable combination of colours, that their clothes do not favour them. The men are very tall and stout. The natural character of the place is much the same as that of other towns we passed through since leaving the borders of the Caspian Sea; and as we stayed no longer in Vladimir than one day, we were unable to profit by its amenities. From this place onwards we began to lose sight of the river Eder, leaving it to the right hand. Travelling still after the fashion above described, under the escort of the captain-general and the major-domo of the Duke, who had with them a guard of two hundred soldiers, after three more days we finally arrived at the Court of the Grand Duke, who is the Sovereign of Muscovy.

His capital city is called Moscow, and it is very populous. From its name comes that of the dukedom, Muscovy, and the name itself is derived from the river Moscova, which runs by and waters Moscow. This river rises ninety miles above the city, and its navigation is very difficult, by reason of the tortuousness of its course, more particularly between the capital and the town of Kolomna. This matter is mentioned by

## DON JUAN OF PERSIA

Giovanni Botero, who has taken it from the work of Antonio Possevino.[11] He further states that Moscow, after it had been burnt down and ruined at the hands of the Crim Tartars and Turks in the year 1570, had come to be of no greater size than to measure two leagues in circuit. But I with particular regard walked all round it, examining the matter very carefully. Its population I reckon to number 80,000 householders [or 360,000 souls] and more. These, too, live in detached dwellings, with store-houses and sheds, and hence the space of ground occupied by the people is more than otherwise would be needful. Indeed, the area of occupation appeared to me fully to occupy a circumference and circuit of at least three leagues, and perhaps more. The city, however, is not walled, and stands in an open country, and its defences are the marshes, streams and lagoons which intersect and surround it. The great palace [of the Kremlin] alone is walled, and this is so extensive that it is itself in truth a fair-sized city. The palace is all built of stone, and beautifully constructed, more especially the royal quarters, which are planned in the Italian fashion. [The Kremlin] is so large that all the nobles who personally serve the Duke live within its circuit. I do not indeed know the sum total of those who inhabit the precincts, but the houses seen within the wall are counted to be over six thousand in number. Our reception here was after the mode which will be detailed in the next chapter.

## CHAPTER III

*Of the reception given us at the Court of the Duke of Muscovy, of what we saw in Moscow, and of what passed between us and the Duke, up to the time when we took our departure.*

ON a certain Friday, at about 10 o'clock in the morning, in the month of November, we entered the capital, and there came out, very courteously, to meet us an infinity of people, for the Muscovites are folk much given to ceremony. Thus on the day when any prince or foreign ambassador comes to the Court of their Duke, or, indeed, should one such enter any city of his that is a seat of government, holiday is proclaimed by public edict, and none shall that day do any work. Further, everybody must then appear, dressed each in his best and finest clothes, in order to go out to the place of reception at the entry of the city. It is indeed a good thing that they do no work of any kind on those particular days, none daring to set his hand to labour even for an instant, for on the other sacred festivals of the year they do not scruple to work the whole day long. In most other points, however, they exactly observe the precepts inculcated by the Greek Church, which is the sect to which they belong.

The number of noblemen who thus came out to meet us, in accordance with the command and ordinance of the Duke—all of them grandees and men of title, lords of many vassals, and gentlemen of position—their number, I say, appeared to me to exceed six thousand. And to bring us in, the Duke had sent two hundred little carriages or litters, each drawn by a well-favoured horse, every carriage being covered in for warmth, the coachman well dressed and the horse furnished out in lion and tiger skins; all this, on the

## DON JUAN OF PERSIA

one hand for the due pomp of the occasion, and on the other to keep horse and man from the cold, which is very severe in those parts at this season. Half a league before we reached the city gate we found the men of the Duke's bodyguard drawn up to receive us, and next by his order they lined the roadway to right and left along which we passed. The bodyguard are all infantry and matchlockmen, and not counting other soldiers armed with bows and arrows, those who carried matchlocks must have numbered 10,000. Through their line we made our way, and every soldier of the bodyguard stood to attention holding his match lighted. That you may understand how great a prince is he who resides in this capital city, I should mention that the Grand Duke of Muscovy[1] is doubly a king, for he is lord of fifteen dukedoms, of sixteen principalities, and of two kingdoms. His lands extend on the north to the Arctic Ocean, from the Bay of Granwick to the river Ob; on the south the frontier marches with the river Eder or Volga, where it reaches the Caspian Sea; on the west the limit of his state is closed by Livonia, where the river Boristhenes or Bug is found; while on the eastern border we again find the Volga. In length Muscovy covers 3,000 miles, and in breadth extends to 1,500 miles.

The Grand Duke is extremely rich, for he is lord of both the lives and goods of all his subjects, to do therewith at his will; and they all serve and worship him. He allows no schools or universities in his kingdom, in order—as he says—that no one may come to know all that he himself knows; and hence no one of his presidents, governors, or secretaries of state can know more than what the Grand Duke wishes him to know of his affairs. No one is allowed to call in any physician, who is a foreigner, to cure him; and no one, under pain of death, may leave Muscovy to go into any foreign country, lest he should get into com-

## MUSCOVY

munication with other folk and learn better. There are neither paupers nor thieves in Muscovy; to the first abundant food will always be given at any time, and to the last imprisonment for life is adjudged. And no one is put to death for any crime, for he who would elsewhere be capitally condemned here is given life-imprisonment. Thus the man who has committed a crime has no chance of committing a second, for he is, so to speak, buried alive in his cell. In matters of religion, these Muscovites are very attentive to their Church. There are no books other than the Gospels and Lives of the Saints, and all the people go hung about with crosses. When a man enters a church he will first kiss the ground, and in his right hand he will carry an image of our Lord and Saviour Jesus Christ. In the palace, over the throne or chair of the Grand Duke, placed so as to appear above his head, there is always set the image of Our Lady, mitred and with a staff, and wearing vestments like those of a bishop, and on Her fingers are many rings.

Now when finally we had been brought thus into Moscow, they lodged us all in very magnificent houses, that were like fortresses: in one they lodged the Persian special ambassador, who had been accredited to the Duke; another house they appointed to us with our ambassador; and in a third lodgement they accommodated all the Englishmen, and for our guard they appointed three hundred men-at-arms. The Duke then provided us with nine interpreters who spoke perfectly our Persian language, three interpreters to each of the houses our embassies occupied; further he sent us many provisions. Then, we having rested for eight days, on a certain Sunday the Duke commanded his major-domo to bring us to him, and we set out in the order observed when we entered the city. As on the day of our entry the bodyguard of infantry lined the road, which was more than a quarter of a league in length, that we had to pass through going from our lodging to the fortress, in which was the palace. This place, where the Duke lives, is the citadel [Kremlin] of which we have already spoken, as containing some 6,000 houses, all built of wood, saving only the royal abode and the outer wall, both of which are constructed of stone, as already noted, adorned everywhere and fortified after the Italian fashion. There are a great number of churches within the citadel circuit, and in the biggest church is an immense bell, which they struck, that we might hear its wondrous sound.[2] Thirty men could barely move it, and it is never rung except for the birth of a duke, or for his coronation.

When we had come to the palace, we found outside waiting for us the major-domo or chamberlain of the Duke, a man of gigantic stature, who held chained up at his side a most ferocious dog, which at night-time is let loose; and this chamberlain conducted us as far as the second palace door. Here was standing a second chamberlain, who led us as far as another door, where again was a third chamberlain, who brought us to the inner door which opened into the Duke's hall. Here were five hundred gentlemen of the court, all dressed in robes of brocade lined with marten fur, wearing caps set with many precious stones, and their garments were all sewn over with jewels of incredible value. These gentlemen received us very courteously and conducted us up to the further end of the hall, where the Duke was seated. This hall is so spacious that from the entrance door it is scarcely possible to distinguish what may be going on at the other end. The style of its building is that of a nave or aisle of a church, but much longer, as has been already said. The domes and cupolas forming the ceiling were supported on forty wooden columns, all gilded over, and these were sculptured with a leaf ornament, and each column was so thick that two

## THE KREMLIN

men could scarce have compassed it about with outstretched arms. When we reached the upper end of the hall, we found here the Grand Duke, and he was seated on a chair raised up on many steps, and this chair was made of massive gold, encrusted with precious stones. The Grand Duke was dressed in a robe of cloth of gold, lined with marten fur, clasped by many diamond buttons, and he wore a hat that was shaped like a mitre. In his hand was a sceptre, like a pastoral staff, and behind the Duke stood forty noblemen each holding a silver staff in his hand; which is the insignia of their office. Further, the Grand Duke carries this sceptre with him when he goes to battle.

When now we had come before him, we all prostrated ourselves, and the special ambassador from Persia, who was, as before said, accredited to Muscovy, came forward. His name was Pír Quli Beg, and he was a Persian nobleman of high rank. Then before presentation he kissed the Letter which he bore, and next put it into the hands of his Highness. On this the Grand Duke rose from his seat, and receiving the Letter kissed it likewise, and then handed it to the interpreter, who forthwith read and translated it into the language of the Russian country. Next our ambassador, who was accredited to Spain, advanced and presented his Letter, in the which the Grand Duke was besought to give us his favour with fair passage and licence: and this he forthwith promised to do in our behalf. His Highness now commanded us all to be seated, and we took our places on long benches, or on stools covered with velvet and stuffed with feathers. After an interval the Grand Duke rose and retired within the palace precincts, with his nobles, but returned shortly again to the hall, when he, and the nobles accompanying him, appeared all dressed in white robes lined with white marten fur, like what in Spain we call ermine.

During the time that his Highness had been absent

the tables had been laid, and the Grand Duke now sat down to dinner, everyone being placed according to his rank. The fare was in great abundance and very magnificently served, for each guest had more than forty dishes set before him, and in each was an entire portion, whether it might be of veal, or venison, mutton, or duck, tame or wild. The loaves of bread they gave us were so huge that two men with difficulty could carry the load in; and there was also to every guest a silver dish as big as a brazier, with its handles on either side. The Grand Duke favoured each of us by sending portions of food from his own plate, according to the rank of the recipient. Then more particularly he took wine with us, wine of grapes, which is the most precious of all that they have in their country, it being imported thither from a distance of many leagues for the sole use of the Grand Duke, and for the bishops who distribute portions to the churches where it is used for the Sacrament. In a chamber, adjacent to the hall in which we were dining, music was being played at this time on a great variety of instruments, and they also sang. The feast lasted from two o'clock in the afternoon till eight at night, and then we were conducted back to our rooms in the palaces where we lodged with more than a hundred torches, and the same attendance and guard as we took when we left in the morning. Further, all our Persian servants during this time had had a great abundance of victuals supplied to them for their regalement at a feast.

On any occasion when we might wish to go forth to view the city of Moscow, it was due from us to send to the Captain of the Citadel for his licence, and he would then give us four soldiers to walk with us as a guard. After a second week had passed following on our arrival in Moscow, we were all taken out in this fashion to view the wonders of the city, and more especially the treasury of the Grand Duke. Here, before the gate,

## MOSCOW CITY

were two statues of lions: one appeared to be of silver, the other of gold, but they were of clumsy make. Of what we now saw inside the treasury the richness was incredible, hard to describe, and so impossible to tell of it all that I must be silent. The wardrobes of the Grand Duke, too, were of inestimable richness; and the armoury so well furnished and complete that 20,000 men could have been fully equipped therefrom with weapons. They also showed us here a great den that was full of wild beasts; among the rest a lion, as big as a horse, whose mane came down on either side of his neck, and he had been lately in such a rage that he had broken in two the great wooden beam of his cage. And after this we walked through the city, and saw the wonderful variety of shops there, and the chief square where are parked many great pieces of artillery. These cannon are of so huge a size that two men may crawl down into the bore when it becomes necessary to clean out the same. Every one of these pieces of cannon is seven yards in length, and to charge it they put in 50 pounds of gunpowder.

After we had been for five months staying in this, the capital city of Muscovy, being detained here on our journey by reason of the rains and the snow, the Grand Duke at last gave us licence to depart. So we went to him to take our leave, and on returning to our lodgings, he sent to the ambassador three most rich robes of cloth of gold, each lined with marten fur, a cup of gold big enough to hold half a gallon[3] of wine, further, 3,000 ducats[4] for journey expenses. And for each of us secretaries, his attendants, the Grand Duke sent three robes, one rich and two of more common stuff, with eight yards of cloth to each person to make us travelling clothes. Further, a silver-gilt cup to each, of the same size as the gold one sent to the ambassador, and 200 ducats each as a free gift. After this we took leave affectionately of our countryman the special

Persian ambassador, who was remaining on in Moscow; and he accompanying us for more than two leagues when we finally set forth from the capital, we said good-bye to him very sorrowfully.

Four of our servants had now with permission left us, who were to return home to Persia; and we further here lost sight and all knowledge of the Dominican Friar, for he suddenly had disappeared and we could get no news of him, though we diligently sought to find him. It was our suspicion that Sir Anthony Sherley had made away with him, for at the time when we were voyaging up the river Eder in the galleys, he had often threatened to kill the Friar, and for a time had kept him prisoner down below decks in a cabin of the galley. But we Persians had then managed to rescue him, for the Friar had explained to us that he had lent Sir Anthony a thousand crowns, and further entrusted him with ninety small diamonds to keep safe for him, and that it was because he had wanted these and the money back from Sir Anthony that he was so treating him to compass his destruction.[5] But after this time we saw him no more, and so we departed from the capital of Muscovy at Eastertide,[6] being accompanied by a Captain of the Guard with a hundred soldiers. Every day we now journeyed about ten leagues, and in three days' time came to a great city which is called Pereyaslav, holding a population of more than 30,000 householders [or 135,000 souls]. All are Muscovites and Christians, and they have many churches beautifully adorned after the fashion of the country. The city wall, which is built of stone, is encircled by the waters of a great river, which we later crossed, for it barred our passage. As far as I could judge it ran down towards the country from which we had just come—namely, to the neighbourhood of the capital.[7] Its current was very strong, and we crossed it on a raft of timber, serving as a ferry-boat,

# YAROSLAV

which was drawn over by strong ropes. This raft was so great that they could carry over, at one time, as many as a hundred sumpter-beasts. I do not know the name of this river, but it appeared to me to be an affluent of the Moscova.

From this place we journeyed on for three days, coming to a city called Yaroslav, and our way went towards the north-west. This town has a larger population than Pereyaslav, for it holds 40,000 households [180,000 souls]. They are all Muscovites and Christians, and it is well built, having many churches and monasteries after their Russian fashion. Further, there is here one of the strongest fortresses that we ever saw in all Muscovy, which is made the stronger and more gallant by the river Barem[8] [here, to wit, the Volga], which runs by it, enclosing a part of the outer wall. Now it was our intention to have travelled forward from here through the countries of Lorraine, Saxony and Germany, but they informed us that from Yaroslav thither our quickest, surest, and most direct way would be to embark on the river [Volga] in galleys, and go by its stream to the sea, which in fact is the Arctic Ocean, a distance of about a hundred leagues. Some of our informants, however, said that this river ran out to the Baltic Sea, into which I believe a portion of the Western Dvina does flow, or it is the Boristhenes [the Bug] of which they were speaking. This, too, is what the most reliable cosmographers have asserted. Be it as it may, we now embarked and voyaged for a hundred leagues along the river [Volga towards the White Sea], travelling some fifteen or sixteen leagues each day, and they had now provided our party with two galleys, one for us Persians and the other for the Englishmen.

The river [Volga] on both its banks has many towns, and two days after embarking at Yaroslav we came to a city called Rybinsk, which, as I judge, may have a population of 10,000 householders [or 45,000 souls], and more rather than less. At this place we changed the men who had charge of the galleys, others being given us in their stead, and they supplied us also very plentifully with provisions. After two days' further travelling [and a portage to the head waters of the Dvina] we came to another town on the bank of this stream, which was named Totma, which to my mind must have had a population of about 3,000 householders [or 13,500 souls]; and there was here a fortress, one of the best that we had yet seen. Again we changed the crews who rowed in the galleys, other men being supplied; and then after the next day's journey we reached Brusensk, whence going on one day further we came to the town of Ustyug, and here again abundant supplies were forthcoming. Another day's journey brought us to the town of Turavets. From this place in our voyage onward the darkness of night ceased, and all the time it was daylight, for in this part of the country during the months of March, April and May there is no night: but conversely, in the corresponding months of the winter season the day is all night, and no light appears. This continuous daylight was because we had now come to a very high degree of latitude, and the reason is as we have said, but our manner of life became very strange to us, there never being any proper night-time for sleep.

Travelling on we came now to a very great city, which lies near the shore of the Arctic Sea, and it is named Kholmagory. It holds a great population numbering over 30,000 householders [or 135,000 souls], and it stands ten leagues from the place where the river Barem [or Dvina] flows out to the ocean. In Kholmagory we sojourned for twelve days, resting, and waiting for news of some English or German ship. Then we went forward, and finally reached the settlement called Archangel City,[9] five leagues further down

## ARCHANGEL

the river, and at the mouth of its estuary. The population of Archangel, to my judgment, is about 12,000 householders [or 54,000 souls]; it is a very famous port, where the French, English and German ships having commerce with the northern regions of Asia discharge their cargoes. There is here a great breakwater, which covers the entrance to the port; and this last faces south, being very spacious and safe where vessels may anchor. Very often there are as many as 400 ships lying in this harbour, and the customs levied here bring in a good revenue to the Duke of Muscovy. We stayed twenty days in Archangel, getting through our business, and finally made arrangements to embark in a Flemish ship of a thousand tons burden, chartered to sail from this port and well armed, having twenty pieces of cannon.

And here it will be well not to pass over in silence a business matter which we settled with Sir Anthony Sherley, and the sequel to which will be told later. Sir Anthony was a man of great parts, although short of stature, and he was much given to ostentation, in spite of the fact that fortune had not dowered him with wealth. As became evident later, he had always had a mind to get the better of us, and thereto he was helped by the order given us by Sháh 'Abbás that we should always attend to what Sir Anthony advised, he being more experienced with foreigners in business matters than we. When, therefore, we were now about to embark on our sea voyage, Sir Anthony told us that it would be much safer not to carry the great cases containing our presents for the various Christian sovereigns with us in the Flemish ship, seeing that she was an old vessel and not of burden to bear such heavy goods. And further, that if we should encounter bad weather, and that they should have to lighten the ship by throwing cargo overboard, the cases with our presents would infallibly be the first to go. Then he told us that he

## DON JUAN OF PERSIA

had a great friend in Archangel, an Englishman, who was master of a very fine stout ship, and that he would take charge of our cases, and deliver them to us again safely when we got to Rome. All this, therefore, appearing to us trustworthy and reasonable, we consigned our great chests to this Englishman, as Sir Anthony had advised us, but what happened with them afterwards will appear in a subsequent chapter.

## CHAPTER IV

*As to what followed in our navigation of the Arctic Sea, and of the notable things that we saw.*

It is proper that we should now describe the manner of folk who inhabit this sea coast. The men and the women are both of one appearance in the face, the men having neither beards nor eyebrows; further, they are of very short stature, so that if any people may be named in truth the Pygmies, they are the [Lapps]. They are smaller even than any of the dwarfs that we have in Spain. These people mount and ride on stags and hinds [called reindeer]. The eyes of these men are so small that scarcely can they see out of them. All are very superstitious, and their wizards promise by their witchcraft to grant fine weather to those about to navigate their seas, and they pretend to sell good fortune. They came to us offering, if we could pay handsomely, that they would ensure us fair weather, but our ambassador questioned how forsooth could they promise what was in the hands of God, and so dismissed them.

We now set sail, and during forty days we never saw night, for the sun was always up; but at the end of that time we had darkness again, with the moon and the stars. In these seas we came on many ships of English corsairs, and two of these would fain have attacked and robbed us. We, however, made ready to fight, and the cannon were manned; but when they got near the Englishmen of our crew hailed the others, saying who we were, so they offered us no hurt. Then coming aboard the corsair Englishmen saw the Franciscan Friar a passenger in our ship, and wanted to know why we did not throw that devil into the sea—on which we told them that the king of Persia had expressly commanded us to carry him along with us; and they paid no more heed to him. These questions and answers now being given and received, the corsairs took their leave of us, but warning us to beware of twelve other Christian ships that were cruising in those parts. Very soon after we had parted company with them, so great a tempest arose that we all repented us of having embarked on board ship. The force of the storm was such that not a rope of our rigging was left standing uninjured. At last we had to furl all sail, and let the ship run before the wind, steering by rudder as best we might and trusting to God's mercy. More than once we thought we were lost by reason of the great seas that poured down our hatchways in the upper deck, and all hands were constantly at work on the pumps. At the end of five days the weather abated, the squalls ceased to burst on us, and a favourable wind springing up behind we sailed on and came finally to anchor.

But another ship that we during the gale had seen near us did not have this good fortune, and though our seamen set out in our skiff to help, they came too late. Some of the cargo indeed was salved, but not one of the crew could be picked up, all being drowned, so that we never knew from whence that ship had come. During the time that we were navigating this sea we saw wondrous varieties of fishes: some so great that we had held them to be ships that were driving over the surface of the deep. We saw, too, great numbers of those fish called sea-horses;[1] these go in squadrons of thirty together, and they came up close to the ship's side, putting us in some fear; whereupon and seeing them so near we discharged one of our cannon, on which they avoided us. From this great northern ocean we had now come forth, but suffering so from sea-sickness that our faces no longer were of good colour; all that we did

## STADE

eat we did cast up again. Then after navigating for two whole months in these northern seas, we began again to have sight of land—for the which we had greatly longed—and we came to the mouth of a great river, up which the ship sailed to [Stade] a harbour standing at the head of its estuary.[2] And now, in the sight of us all, our Franciscan Friar dressed himself in Persian clothes, for this place is wholly inhabited by Lutherans, and Sir Anthony had assured him that should it become known as how he was by religion a Papist, infallibly they would tear him to pieces.

The harbour [of Stade] is but a small place, and it is entirely inhabited by fisher-folk. Our ship having sailed up the [Elbe] estuary we now disembarked, but later came down again to the river mouth aboard two galleys into which we had trans-shipped. The [Elbe] estuary is here so broad that great ships can pass along it, and the banks of the river above are studded with towns, numbering, it is said, in all more than a thousand. From the place where we were now lying might be discovered somewhat of the lands pertaining to Suabia and to the Duchy of Würtemberg, also to Nuremberg, Franconia, Bavaria, Hesse and Bucavia.[3] These, indeed, are lands lying far from where we had been sailing, but nearer at hand might be perceived the country of Minden, also Brunswick and Luneberg. We had now turned round in the galleys, and following out from the estuary [of the Elbe], after three days more journeying came to a city which is called Embden, which has a population of over 30,000 householders [or 135,000 souls]. It has many fine buildings, and one of the strongest fortresses of all that countryside. The roofs of all the houses here are covered with lead, a matter which at a distance gives them a very pleasing appearance, for in the daytime when the sun is shining they all seem as though roofed with silver. From this city there came out to receive us a captain on behalf of the Prince[4] of this district; but we shall not be able to give any very particular account of his lands, because we brought no Letter of Credence from the king of Persia for him, and we were further much embarrassed by our Friar, who trembled from terror, knowing that all the people were Lutheran.[5]

The city of Embden stands between two famous rivers [the Weser and the Elbe], having them on either hand, and it lies two days' journey from the sea. The port here has much trade, and its merchants are always abundantly supplied with goods, which for the most part are English. Having next disembarked, they lodged us in a house, that was a sort of hostel, very clean, however, and curiously furnished, for it contained more than a hundred beds, each with its feather mattress and holland sheets. Here they entertained us suitably; and the following day that same captain came, conducting us to the palace of the Prince, to whom we made a presentation of Persian head-dresses and some pieces of stuff and cloths. These he was pleased to receive very graciously, and invited us to dine with him the following day. The great feast he gave us lasted during six hours, and, it being the custom and habit of this country, they made us drink so much, that many of us were overcome with the slumbers of drunkenness. What we found most notable in this country was the head-dress of the women. It resembles a round shield, which just above the face juts out, as one might say, as do the tiled gables of the roofs in Spain, and the same is to shelter the face from the continued rains and snows of their climate. And it appeared to me that in no other country did I ever see so many beautiful women collected all together as here might be seen. The day afterwards we were engaged in seeing the Prince's treasury and armoury, in which were many precious objects. These truly were well worth the sight, though indeed not more than the common. But they showed us, among other matters, a storage-house for wheat, so huge, with so many separate granaries, and these so full of corn, that we were assured there was a supply here to last ninety years. This we could scarce credit, but they insisted so much on it, that we ended by believing them. But this wheat of theirs has in it no heart, and is all husk, and the grain is longer than it is in Spanish wheat; on the other hand, in substance it is no heavier than the grain of our oats, being less even than the weight of rye. This sort of wheat we too have in Persia, and the Persians know it by the name *Chaudar*.

From the city of Embden we set forth, travelling in eight coaches after a week's sojourn, and came to another town called Aurich, well walled and with a population of 10,000 householders [45,000 souls]. It has a fortress that seems very strong, and we stayed here one day, but the ways of the people presented nothing to remark, and I shall say no more about them. From here in two days we came on to a place of no great size, but very strongly fortified, which was called Freudenberg. Travelling further we reached a town of the name of Nienburg, whose population is considerable, and as far as we could judge it is strongly defended by fortifications. The next day we went on again to another city which is called Oldenburg, well walled, and with a fortress; and all these places and forts are, for the most part, very carefully guarded and defended, their gates being shut at nightfall, and on no account opened again until eight of the clock next morning. This is because each belongs to a different lordship, each prince being the enemy of his neighbour, who is the chief of another government, and some of these are Catholics. We now came to Thuringia, which is under the Landgrave of Hesse-Kassel and is one of the most fertile regions of Germany. Thuringia is the country that lies between the rivers Saale and Werra, and it is the place which Georgius Agricola[6] says is the very Heart of Germany. The province is not very broad or long, but it is the most densely populated of any district in the whole world; for within a limit of about twelve German miles square it comprises twelve countships or regions, in which are massed 140 walled cities, and a like number of open townships, also 2,000 hamlets, 150 fortresses and 12 abbeys.

The first town that we now came to was called Weimar,[7] the next was Alsfeld, and the third is the great city of Kassel, a very large place, strongly fortified and very populous, the town wall being so broadly built that three coaches can drive abreast along it. Kassel further has a fortress with an earthen rampart that protects it perfectly against any artillery that they may bring against it. As soon as the Landgrave[8] heard of our approach he sent his chamberlain to meet us with three coaches, each lined in black velvet, and in these we were brought to the palace. The Prince now received our ambassador and Sir Anthony and the rest of us very amiably, showing such courtesy as was due to the rank of each one. They then lodged us in certain rooms of the palace, very sumptuously furnished and with beds in richly embroidered hangings. The Prince bestowed our servants at various hostels, bearing himself the cost, and all were well provided for during the ten days that we remained here. Every day they showed us some new sight. One day it was a room with walls of white stone, as might be alabaster, and each stone was set with such art that no joint or pointing was to be seen round door or window, and it was as though Nature herself had made it all of one piece. We judged this indeed to be one of the rarest sights that we saw in the court of any prince. The Landgrave also showed us the cabinet of his jewelhouse, full of an inestimable quantity of precious stones, more particularly diamonds. But the most

# KASSEL

wondrous sight of richness that we noticed was, that instead of tapestry, the walls of this cabinet from ceiling to floor were entirely sheathed in slabs of unworked coral, a matter most wondrous to look upon.

We must not either pass over in silence the Prince's armoury and stables, for both are extensive and very curious to visit, being so well furnished that it appeared to me ten thousand horsemen could be provided therefrom with all necessary equipment. There was not a night, while we remained in Kassel, that they did not give some particular entertainment in our honour. And more especially on one occasion when the Prince's son, the heir-apparent, a boy of twelve, with other youths of a like age, the flower of their nobility, all most sumptuously apparelled, jousted in a tourney, by the light of torches. Then after ten days' sojourn we finally departed from Kassel with many presents of sweetmeats bestowed upon us. Indeed, in all my life I never saw more things made of sugar than here. On the very first day, when we dined with the Prince, the loaves of bread, the napkins, knives and salt-cellars that stood on the table, all were made of sugar, as also the various kinds of fruit. And in every case each item exactly resembled and imitated the form and texture of the object it simulated. Great was the laughter when we tried to cut some fruit with these knives, which, of course, crumbled and went to pieces in our hands. For our journey onwards all our necessities were well provided for. Before going the Landgrave had presented to our ambassador two goblets of gold, and to each member of his suite one goblet apiece likewise. On the last day before we left they had brought us out to see two galleys that were in the river which here runs by the palace walls, and on shipboard we saw a new fashion of artillery of most ingenious make, for each piece every half-hour could be made to discharge forty rounds in succession.

# DON JUAN OF PERSIA

The Landgrave appointed a captain of his Guards to go with us through his territories, and a sufficient escort, till we should come to the frontier of the Empire. Further, he had commissioned this captain as a special ambassador with us to the Emperor, for he had been much pleased at the receipt of the Letter which we brought him from the king of Persia, which same Sir Anthony had presented: and, in consequence, he now proposed to join the Emperor with 12,000 troops, when these princes together should march against the Turkish Sultan. We therefore set out joyfully, travelling through the various cities of the Landgrave, which are many in number and magnificent in their richness. Of those that we more particularly noted are the following: Leipzig, Roberg, Quimendec, Jub, Quimidac, Labinc, Aslaben,[9] Xipric, Wilfuesen and Perbyn, which is the last town in the State of Hesse-Kassel. Then we entered the territories of the Duke of Saxony, through which we passed travelling more expeditiously. The Duchy of Saxony has within it the territories of Mansfeld, Magdeburg, and Misnia,[10] though many count this last as lying outside the duchy. Saxony is divided into Upper and Lower. Of Upper Saxony the chief town is Wittenberg, one of the finest and strongest fortresses of these parts. Of Lower Saxony the capital is the famous city of Halle, standing on the river Saale, and to the west of it lies the great city of Mansfeld, the chief town of a district that supplies the whole of Europe with minerals, worked in the mines round and about. To the westward, and standing on the banks of the river Elbe, is the very strong city of Magdeburg, which is divided into three quarters; and it is held to be useless to besiege and impossible to take this place, by reason of the strength of its walls and the depth of the ditches that surround it.

We entered the Saxon Duchy, passing by the town of Beltcy,[11] where there are many silver-mines. All the

## SAXONY

people hereabout that we met were unhealthy and of bad colour, more particularly those whose business it was to work down in the mines: and this is a manifest proof how harmful is the quicksilver, which they come across in the workings. This mineral, indeed, is generally found mixed up with other substances in the veins of metal which underlie the ground throughout these districts. All along the roads as we passed through the Duchy of Saxony we noticed a very great number of windmills, and seeing that the rivers in this region are powerful streams, and that the Germans are men of much ingenuity, I wondered—seeing the number of saw-mills established everywhere, and set to work by water, for cutting the wood used in the mines—that they should solely depend for the grinding of the flour for their bread on the uncertainty of the wind. The second city of Saxony that we came to was Ilmenau, and the third Leipzig.[12]

This last is a very large town, with a considerable population, and its buildings seemed to me to be of the best of any that we had seen since we had come to travel through Europe. Here the Duke of Saxony has his palace, where he resides. The present Duke[13] is indeed a youth of fourteen or fifteen, and the day that we passed in his capital he had gone out hunting, so that we did not see him, and in fact he took no notice whatever of our ambassador's coming. We therefore only stayed that one day at his court, and we shall give no further account of him. From this city we and the captain who was the ambassador of the Landgrave of Hesse to the Emperor passed on entering the Empire and came to the first Imperial city which lies beyond the Saxon border, and which is called Aussig.[14]

## CHAPTER V

*As to how we arrived at the Court of the Emperor of Germany, and of what happened to us there, till the time when we left.*

Now when we had come to Aussig we forthwith made arrangements to proceed on to the Court of the Emperor, and journeying forward passed through the following places: Neutri, Estratassenc, Berexen, Klussen, Kling, Pouscin,[1] and so to Trinka, which last is but three leagues[2] from the Imperial capital.

The cosmographers are wont to divide Germany into High and Low, but indeed I do not know why they should call the Low Countries Germany, for not Germans but Flemings are the people who inhabit these parts. Giovanni Botero[3] gives the name of Germany to all those lands where the language is German or Teutonic, and he includes under this name all the country extending from the Meuse to the Vistula, and from the Alps to the German Ocean. What, however, we now have to deal with is High Germany, which is a most noble country, having very many fine populous cities, for the Teutons excel all other nations in the neatness and beauty of their houses and streets, the buildings being constructed either of stone or of timber, or of both together. Besides the country ruled directly by his Imperial Majesty, Germany includes within its boundaries many lesser Potentates and Powers, such as the rulers of Austria, Denmark, Saxony and Thuringia; further, there are the Ecclesiastical States, to wit, Mainz, Treves and Cologne; next the Palatinate of Cleves on the Rhine, and Magdeburg, besides which there are many other cities. The land is throughout most fertile and easy to work, so that with a single horse enough can be

# GERMANY

ploughed to keep a family for a whole year. We find here many kinds of wild animals and birds, and very particularly horses are bred here abundantly. Wine is made in most parts, especially in Alsace, and on the banks of the Neckar and the Rhine, also in Austria. Germany is famous for its fine rivers, as for instance the Danube, which is the greatest river of all Europe; next come the Rhine, the Elbe, the Oder, the Meuse, the Moselle, the Neckar, the Main, the Inn, the Moldau, the Ems and the Weser, with some others.

There are many broad lakes, but those of greatest size are found in Switzerland: such are the Lakes of Leman, and Neuchatel, with those of Lucerne, Zürich and Constance. There are also in Germany many great forests, indeed the greatest in all the world, and more particularly three, which are: that known as the Black Forest, which lies round the sources of the Danube; secondly, the Vronica Forest, which is in Franconia; and the Hercynian Forest, which covers Bohemia and extends as far as Muscovy. Throughout most of Germany all kinds of minerals are found very abundantly, such as iron, lead, copper, tin and steel; there are, too, some gold mines, and these mines taken one with another are estimated to produce a revenue of at least a million crowns yearly. Much sulphur, saltpetre and alum-stone comes to hand, also there are salt mines. As to the costumes and accoutrements of the Germans both are well known in Spain, and no exact specification will be needed here of their various nationalities, customs, assemblies and diets. What, however, may be deemed most interesting and worthy to be noted among such matters, concern the customs observed in connection with the election of his Imperial Majesty the Emperor, but this, indeed, has been described fully by many grave authors, and he who would know how the Cæsar must be chosen, let him consult the Bull of the sainted Pope Gregory V

# DON JUAN OF PERSIA

[A.D. 996], and the Constitutions [called the Golden Bull] of the Emperor Charles IV, in the year 1356, and he will then know all that is needful as regards this matter.

There are many most noble cities in Germany, as Cleves in the duchy of that name, with Crefeld and Duisburg;. others are of the Duchy of Jülich, to wit, Duren, and many more might be mentioned. Thus on the banks of the famous river Rhine lie Cologne and Neuss in the Duchy of Westphalia. Cities with a great population are Paderborn and Osnabruck, also Münster on the Moselle, with Treves in Alsace. Between Austria and Bâle lies Strasbourg, one of the strongest and richest cities in all Germany; and lastly, in Switzerland, which is the highest land of all Europe, there are the famous Thirteen Cantons. I have given this short description of Germany [taking it from the work of Giovanni Botero], for I myself indeed did not see more of the country than what I could note from the direct road as I passed through the land travelling to the Imperial Court, and thence on to Italy. It is certainly one of the most celebrated districts of Europe, being the seat and state of his Imperial Majesty, and I informed myself with particular care of all details from persons worthy of credit. From the first moment when I set out from Isfahán on my journey, I diligently carried out the intention I had made to write down carefully all I saw, in order to give an account thereof later to the king of Persia: and now through the merciful grace of God I hope, in the first place, to be granted to lay the same at the feet of his Catholic Majesty King Philip III, our lord and sovereign.

Returning now to the subject of our journey, finding ourselves in the town of Trinka, which lies five leagues distant from Prague, where [Rudolf II] was holding his Imperial Court, we sent forward to his Majesty craving of him his permission to proceed with our embassy. It took five days to send and get back the answer; but at the end of this time his Imperial Majesty despatched one of his chamberlains to us and six coaches to bring us in to the capital.[4] Before we reached the city, however, nay, at a considerable distance outside the walls, his Grand Chamberlain, with six other splendid coaches came out to meet us, and as far as I could judge there were more than ten thousand persons along with him, who followed out from Prague to see us enter, and all these persons were either in coaches or on horseback. Among the rest there appeared all the ambassadors of the various kings and princes of Christendom who were in residence and accredited to the Imperial Court, and these accompanied us in, with much rejoicing and pomp, until they finally left us at our lodgings. These were given us in a great palace which had been apportioned to us Persians, while a like lodgement had been set apart for the Englishmen. Later his Majesty did send us guards for our palace, and many of his servants came to wait on us; further, he appointed for the expenses of our table, daily, the sum of 150 crowns.[5]

At the end of a week, when we had rested, his Majesty sent his secretary to us with his commands, and on the following day they came and took us up in five coaches, when we were brought to the great Imperial Palace [of the Hradschin], the most sumptuous and beautiful building that we had ever yet seen. From the outer gate to the first staircase there were ranged on either hand four different regiments of the Imperial Guards, each company armed differently, and we passed up between them. On reaching the top of the stairs the chamberlains of his Majesty came out to meet us, and they with the grandees there present and the nobles accompanied us thence as far as the Imperial antechamber. On entering the door of this great hall, where his Majesty was awaiting us, these chamberlains and nobles stood back, and we went in alone. We found his Majesty[6] standing on a most beautiful carpet at the upper end of the hall; against the wall here was a chair, on the back of which his hand was resting, and beyond the carpet there was stationed in attendance his Chief Secretary, who is the interpreter, greatly skilled in many languages in which he can converse, and who is a personage very high in favour with the Emperor. Our ambassador advancing made his obeisance, then kneeling on the ground he presented the Letter of the king of Persia, and this the Emperor, reaching forward, took.

Then through the interpreter he enquired if the ambassador were well, and how he had come, and if he from the fatigue of his journey were now well rested. The ambassador answered to all this, through the interpreter, with due respect and courtesy, and then severally named to his Majesty each of us Persian gentlemen who were of his company and suite, we being sent hither, he said, with him by the king of Persia. On this his Majesty ordered every one of us separately to be brought forward and presented to him, and through his interpreter enquired of each of us how we had fared, showing thus his favour to us, and all with an affable condescension that was more remarkable even than the imperial majesty of his demeanour, and with that incomparable nobility of bearing characteristic of the House of Austria, and which is the distinction of his Imperial race. The Emperor afterwards dismissed the ambassador very graciously to his lodgings, giving answer to his message saying that he, the Emperor, would, after being well informed, consider carefully what the king of Persia had requested of him in his Letter, and that if the matter were possible he would have pleasure in complying with it. Then one

# PRAGUE

of his Majesty's chamberlains in attendance brought us back to the palace where we were lodged, and left us.

In the days following we often rode out in coaches to view the city, which is of a very considerable population, with fine houses, exceedingly well built.[7] A great river [called the Moldau] flows through the city, making it the more beautiful and pleasant, across which river stretches a magnificent bridge which connects together the two chief quarters of the city, and linking these up with the third quarter, which is called Old Prague. This bridge, as I myself measured it, is 400 paces in length. The climate here [in the month of November] is so cold that this great river was at that time completely frozen over; and there is not a house throughout Prague, be it of the poorest, that has not a great stove in it for warmth. His Majesty next ordered us to be shown his armoury, the jewel-house, the imperial wardrobe, and the stables; in all of which establishments we noticed many notable objects. Further they showed us cages containing many extraordinary animals, and more particularly we saw four lions and four tigers of the largest size that ever we could have imagined.

For the next three months we took our ease resting at the Imperial Court, during all which time they entertained us sumptuously, and then [in the spring of 1601] the Emperor sent granting us permission to depart on our further journey. To the ambassador he now gave fifty pieces of silver-gilt plate—namely, dishes, lavers, plates, flagons and candlesticks; also 4,000 ducats for the expenses of the way. To each of us gentlemen of the suite he sent a very large tankard in silver-gilt, and to accompany it, 200 crowns[8] for road money. Two coaches being now provided, we set forth from Prague accompanied by an Imperial Chamberlain, and came the first day to a town called

Beraun, where we slept. The next morning the chamberlain took his leave of us, returning to the capital, and we passed on to our journey down into Italy, travelling at first through many and various cities of the Empire, as will be detailed in the following chapter more particularly.

## CHAPTER VI

*Of the journey we made through Germany and Italy, coming to Rome, and of the reception that his Holiness granted to us there, and how we came on thence and finally reached Spain.*

THE chamberlain of his Imperial Majesty having taken his leave of us in the town of Beraun, we next day continued our journey, passing through the following places: Rokitsan, Pilsen, Kladrau, Pfraumberg, Waidhausen, Fuderitz, Wernberg, Hirschau, Hahnbach and Sulzbach.[1] This last is a very populous town, with most beautiful houses, and though we passed in haste through it, the prince and lord of the same, whose name is Otto Heinrich, received and entertained us nobly, ordering us to be supplied with all that we needed during the day of our sojourn with him. Thence we came on to the town of Hersbruck, and next to a place called Lauf, well built and of a considerable population, and indeed Hersbruck also had seemed to us very fine in its situation and its houses very admirably built.

Travelling on we now came to Nüremberg, where we stayed for three days. This is a very populous city, and its streets and squares are well kept; the number of its population is so great that it has the appearance of a capital city. The governor of all the district round and about Nüremberg, who is a prince appointed over the city by the Emperor, gave us a fine reception. He sent us many presents, and among the rest some flagons and cups of silver-gilt, and these of no mean value; indeed, to each of us of the suite he did also give some present. For our journey onwards from Nüremberg to Augsburg, in place of travelling by coaches we went in haste, riding post, passing through the following towns, namely: Kornberg, Roth, Windsfeld, Ellingen,

Weissenburg, Münchem,[2] Kaisheim, Donauwört, and thence to Augsburg. This last is a city with a large population, and the sumptuousness of all its houses is good to see, these being as they should be, seeing that this city was founded by the Imperial [Cæsar Augustus]. It is indeed a great republic and the chief city of many districts, to judge by the concourse of the nobility here and its immense trade. In Augsburg we stayed six days, and the governor, who is a very noble and powerful prince, treated us with special hospitality, every day providing us with a different entertainment. From here we took carriages again, and travelled in them to the city of Munich.

Munich is the capital of a separate duchy, and the duke and lord of this country is known as the Pious Duke.[3] He treated us most generously, lodging us in rooms of his own palace. He showed us his jewel-house therein, which is most rich in precious stones, and more especially in well-wrought pieces of plate, both silver and gold. Among the rest that they showed us, that seemed very curious, was a garden, and in its midst was a dining-saloon after a strange fashion. There was a fountain cut in stone, and of the same material all round it were the figures of every species of animal, bird and fish of which description is made, and each one of these figures throws out water from its mouth. A whole month would not be sufficient for anyone completely to examine all these objects. Having stayed three days in Munich, the Duke gave us coaches, and one of his chamberlains to go with us, adding all that was necessary for the journey, and then, most grateful for his hospitable reception, we took our leave of this noble prince. We now entered Italy, having left the lands of the Empire behind us, and because our destination was first to the Signory of Venice, before going on to Rome, we went straight to Mantua, which was the first notable city of Italy that

## MANTUA

we visited. This place would indeed be worthy of description, were it but for the strangeness of its site, for Mantua stands on the border of a great lake of clear water, deep enough to float an ordinary galley. The city itself is large and populous, and its palaces are magnificent. It is built after the Italian fashion of architecture, being divided up in quarters, and the streets are laid out in such a manner that each street gives a vista down before it. There is a well-built and huge city wall, which the lake encircles, and at the four corners of the city are four strong forts, which make Mantua impregnable.

The Duke and Prince, who is of the illustrious house of Gonzaga,[4] sent coaches and his chamberlain to meet us, and in these we entered Mantua. The Duke very graciously came to the antechamber of his palace to receive us, ordering that we should be lodged within the palace itself, which is most richly furnished, for the Duke is much given to hospitality. Here we stayed for two days. We were shown his rich jewels, and more particularly his pictures, which are very fine, being by great painters; also his wardrobe, full of the national dresses of divers foreign countries. Having then received us at a banquet and given us many entertainments, he ordered that a galley should be provided for us, in which we now embarked, and he sent his servants to accompany us as far as Florence. We, however, had first to turn back towards Venice, to present the Letter of the king of Persia to the Doge and Signory, before we should proceed on to Rome. We therefore travelled in the galley for a day's journey from the mouth of the lake down the river [Mincio] and landing came to a town called Otranto.[5] From here we went on to Verona, which is a city in the Venetian territory, and one of the most beautiful towns of Europe. We delayed here during three days, awaiting the return of a gentleman[6] who had been despatched by our ambassador to Venice to beg permission of the Doge and Signory for us to wait on them. The Venetians, however, now sent for answer that as a Turkish ambassador was at that very time with them treating of important matters of state, it would not be convenient for them to receive us: since it did not seem suitable, in the presence of the Turkish envoy, to pass to the entertainment of an ambassador of the king of Persia—these two Powers being notoriously contrary one to the other—lest some mischance prejudicial to the Christian state should result. All that we might require, however, should be forthwith sent us. To the which message our ambassador, being affronted, gave answer, that he cared not a jot for the Turkish ambassador, nor would pass comment on this discourtesy of the Signory of Venice; and the visit being thus put off, we proceeded on our journey and came to Ferrara.

From here we sent forward a gentleman to the Grand Duke of Florence[7] to inform him of our coming, and forthwith he despatched to us his chief chamberlain, who arranged for our lodgings on the way thither. When we had come to Florence, the Duke, who was not in residence, being abroad on a hunting expedition, sent orders for them to give us rooms in his own palace, and many of his nobles came half a league outside the city gate to receive us, they bringing us in riding in three magnificent coaches. Thus we came to the palace surrounded by a multitude of persons, where the Grand Duke's own servants waited on us. Then when we had been in Florence a fortnight, well entertained and seeing all the sights of this most famous city, which is notable for the richness of its many magnificent buildings, the Duke sent for us to come to him in Pisa, where he was residing with the Grand Duchess. On arrival we were received by his brother the prince Giovanni de' Medici, who next brought us to the palace, where the Duke and Duchess gave us a

# LEGHORN

very affable reception. Here they kept us ten days, with princely entertainment, showing us the rich and curious treasures that are the property of the Duke. Afterwards they took us to Leghorn to see a new city that was being built there, and which will be a very magnificent place. There is also a fortress in the building, and a safe entrance to be made to the harbour, which will then become one of the finest ports in all the Mediterranean Sea. To do these works they have here more than five thousand slaves at work. The Grand Duke now presented our ambassador with a fine gold chain to go round his neck sixteen times, supporting a medallion with his portrait, set in precious stones; and he gave another of like value to Sir Anthony Sherley. The gentlemen of the suite he honoured and gave presents to likewise. Then appointing one of his chamberlains to accompany us, he instructed him to pay all our travelling expenses as far as Rome, and so dismissed us.

Thus we took our leave of him, and proceeded on to Siena, where we remained while a gentleman was sent forward to Rome, riding post, to inform the Pope[8] that we were stopping in Siena awaiting permission to come and kiss the foot of his Holiness. After three days that we were waiting in Siena his Holiness sent a Cardinal to us, who welcomed us in his name, and gave orders in all matters that were necessary for our entertainment. Now here in the city of Siena our ambassador had a quarrel with Sir Anthony Sherley, and matters would have come to a bad pass, had not the Cardinal, whom his Holiness had sent to us, been present to compose the dispute, though indeed he could not prevail on our ambassador to allow Sir Anthony to enter Rome in his company, as originally it had been intended. The cause of this quarrel of our ambassador with Sir Anthony was in the matter of the thirty-two chests of presents, which, as already explained, had been given in charge of the English shipmaster [at Archangel] to be brought direct to Rome. The ambassador was now demanding of Sir Anthony the due delivery of these chests, in order that he might make his Holiness a suitable present from what was in them, which, indeed, would have been a gift of much magnificence. It now appeared that the whole affair had been a cheat, for no chests had ever been brought to Rome, Sir Anthony having sold or bartered away their contents, namely those seven gifts of price [for the Pope and the Princes], to that English merchant captain, while we were travelling by sea in the Baltic Gulf or Northern Ocean. This in truth was the fact of what had happened, for afterwards we had notice how our pieces of brocade and cloths had afterwards all been publicly sold by the English merchants in Muscovy.[9]

At length, however, this quarrel between us was accommodated by the kind offices of the Cardinal, and we went on to Rome, where a nephew of the Pope came out to receive us a league beyond the city gate in company with a following of Roman gentlemen. Many coaches too had been sent out for our convenience and honour, but it was thought to be more seemly that we should ride, and so we entered Rome, each of us Persians, on horseback, accompanied by two Roman gentlemen riding on either hand, while the nephew of his Holiness had the ambassador on the one hand, with another great nobleman on the further side. The whole country outside the gate appeared on this occasion so thronged with coaches that I reckon there were more than one thousand of them, and more than four thousand gentlemen on horseback or riding mules, while the number of those on foot who had come out to meet us was quite incalculable. As we entered the city more than a hundred pieces of artillery were fired in a salute from the Castle of Saint Angelo and from neighbouring towers, also a volley from the Papal matchlockmen, who thus were charged to do us honour at our coming. On entering the city they conducted us to a house, or palace, not very far from the Vatican Palace, where the Pope was in residence, and thither to us came a chamberlain of his Holiness, who offered to all of us much hospitality, and he lodged with us afterwards, providing till we departed whatever we required, and ordering everything for our convenience. Then, after we had been taking our rest for three days in Rome, his Holiness sent ordering us to come to him. And it was then again that our ambassador had trouble on account of the doings of Sir Anthony, for he had to send to the Pope saying how impossible it was for him to go that day to kiss the foot of his Holiness, because he lacked the needful present, which Sir Anthony had cheated him of, and prevented his bringing—as already has been explained. But the Pope sent answer that the matter of presents was of no importance, that he himself would see to the affair later and make some arrangement to remedy the evil.'

Our ambassador thereupon consented to present himself, and accompanied by many gentlemen we set out for the Sacred Palace, and as we entered all the Cardinals came out to meet us, conducting us to the hall, where we found his Holiness seated on the Pontifical Throne. At his feet, before it, was spread a carpet, on which were cushions, on one of which the ambassador took his seat, after having duly kissed the Pope's foot. His Holiness then gave us his blessing, saying, " May God make you Christians "; and on this the ambassador, with due respect, gave him the Letter from the king of Persia. This the Pope received honourably, and then conversed, through the interpreter, for some time with our ambassador, who among other matters acquainted him with the fraud and craft of Sir Anthony in the matter of the presents. To which his Holiness replied: "I do not chastise those who come to me, and still less those who are sent to me by the king of Persia. Let them carry him to the king of Spain, and let his Majesty chastise him." Soon after this the ambassador asked leave to retire, when his Holiness, on rising, again gave us his blessing and then went out. The Cardinals afterwards conducted us as far as the palace gate, whence the Papal chamberlain had charge of us to our lodging. Each day after this his Holiness would send to enquire how we fared, and then would give command that we should go out and see the sights of Rome. And daily the Cardinals or Princes would come to call on the ambassador, and then we all would go out to see those great churches and holy relics; and on the banks of the Tiber we would visit the various gardens and many orchards thereabout.

After we had passed two months thus in Rome, his Holiness sent our ambassador a gold chain and 2,000 ducats;[10] and to each of us, Secretaries of the Embassy, the Pope gave a chain and also his portrait. On this we went to take our leave of his Holiness, and to crave his benediction, asking permission to depart into Spain. The Pope granted us this most graciously, and appointed further a Canon of Barcelona, called Francisco Guasque, who should accompany us thither, the Canon being given charge of the funds of money necessary for our journey expenses as far as Spain. Now when we were just ready to leave Rome, and looked to see Sir Anthony to go with us, he did not appear, nor indeed could we come by news of any of the other Englishmen, for all of them had taken their departure, whither none knew.[11] Thus we left Rome without the Englishmen, and next, when we had gone forth we perceived that three of our fellow Persians too were wanting.[12] We therefore went back to find them, and discovered that already God had begun

## CONVERSIONS

the work of His divine Grace. For these three Persians who had now left us we found in the palace of his Holiness in Rome, and they were studying to become Christian converts. The ambassador was thereby much perturbed, and seeking audience of the Pope, his Holiness answered him that the Divine Law was indeed one of kindness, that none by force was brought to believe, that all were free to act as they would, and that what he, the Pope, was doing was done in accordance with God's will. On this the ambassador spoke to the three men apart, and finding them steadfast and firm of purpose to become Christians, left them. He with the rest of us then departed from Rome.

Fifteen days after this date we reached Genoa, where we spent a week, the Doge and Signory giving us entertainment at the public cost with all consideration; further, many of the nobles of Genoa, who are most hospitable, treated us after a magnificent fashion. For leaving Genoa we chartered two galleys, and embarking aboard, in two days' time came to the town of Savona, and there landing, we proceeded to travel through France on horseback. We first went to Avignon, where the Vice-Legate of the Pope resides, who received us and entertained us during the two days that we rested here. Then changing our horses and sumpter-beasts, we went round by Nîmes, coming to Montpellier. Thence we went on to Narbonne, and passing through Salses, reached Perpignan, where the Governor and Captain-general treated us as only a great prince could have done. From Perpignan we set out with an escort of thirty soldiers, on account of the highwaymen hereabout, and were brought in safety to Barcelona after traversing the difficult and dangerous defiles of the Pyrenees. Half a league outside Barcelona the Duke of Feria, the Viceroy, sent out horses and coaches to meet us and bring us in, and many of the Catalan nobles also came forth to welcome us. Thus we entered that spacious city, of which the splendid buildings and the broad clean streets were a delight to our eyes. The Duke with all goodwill and kindness entertained us here during ten days at his private charge, showing us every attention.

They then gave us horses and sumpter-beasts, and we came on to Zaragoza, where the Duke of Alburquerque, who is Viceroy here, learning of our approach sent six coaches half a league out of the city, with a number of horses, to bring us in. Many of the nobles of Aragon also, who were in residence, came to the city gate to meet us, and we entered surrounded by an infinity of folk, and so reached the lodging appointed for us. In Zaragoza we remained three days, being entertained as guests by the Viceroy as it became a great prince; and he caused us to be shown all the curious sights of that city, which are many, more particularly the cathedral with the Chapel of Our Lady of the Pillar. This, with the Sanctuary of Montserrat, which we had visited on leaving Barcelona, proved a great and holy joy to us, although at that time we were still infidels. On quitting Zaragoza they provided us with the necessary horses, and we set out for Valladolid, the capital, and came to a place called Olivares, where we stayed, sending on our interpreter to Valladolid, informing his Majesty our Lord the King of our arrival; and by slow stages we then came on to Tudela on the river Duero. Here we halted, awaiting instructions from the Court, and these came, ordering that we should delay for a week and remain in Tudela.

## CHAPTER VII

*How we entered Valladolid, and how we kissed the hand of his Majesty, and how a nephew of the ambassador came to be baptized a Christian.*

As soon as we had arrived at Tudela, I took the company of that Canon who had come with us from Rome, and by injunction of the ambassador, we set out together for the Court to have speech with the Duke of Lerma,[1] the first minister of his Majesty, and with the Marquis of Velada, who holds the office of Grand Chamberlain. On entering Valladolid, the novelty of my Persian dress caused such astonishment, that quite a multitude followed after me through the streets. I arrived finally at the Royal Palace, where several gentlemen who were in attendance received me courteously, and very kindly accompanied me to the presence of the Marquis of Velada, to whom I ventured to introduce myself, stating the reason of my coming before him, which was, as from the Persian ambassador, to detail what was most needful on this occasion to be set forth, as regarded the coming of our embassy from Persia. His Excellency from the first gave me command to be seated, and listened with all courtesy, and in reply told me that his Majesty had received the news of the arrival of the ambassador with much pleasure, and that the house in Valladolid where he was to be lodged was being forthwith furnished and prepared. He added that my Master should remain on for yet two or three more days in Tudela, and that then instructions would be sent for him to make his official entry into Valladolid. With this reply, and bearing an account of the favourable reception granted me by his Excellency, I straightway returned to Tudela with the Canon.

And now I described to the ambassador the magnificent appearance of the Spanish Court, and the throng of nobles gathered together there, all of which greatly pleased my Master, and in patience we awaited the call for us to proceed thither. Then a week after I had returned to Tudela we set out, for his Majesty had issued his orders to Don Luis Enrique, who is one of his four chamberlains, to proceed out of Valladolid half a league on the Tudela road to meet us. This Don Luis did, attended by many gentlemen of his household and family, which is one of the noblest in Spain, and they brought out five coaches, in which we in his company were carried into the city on that day. Here many nobles and courtiers welcomed us, and they led us to a fine house that had been prepared for us, well furnished and provided with rich bedding and tapestry hangings, in cloth and velvet of divers colours. We now were waited upon by his Majesty's servants, and soldiers of the Spanish and German Guard were posted at our door. Then our ambassador received visits from all the other foreign ambassadors who were at that time accredited to the Court of Spain, and the house was all day long thronged by guests, more particularly at the hours of dinner and supper. After we had been four days come to Valladolid, the Duke of Lerma having during this time made his public official visit to our ambassador, his Majesty gave command that we should attend at the palace. Thither therefore they brought us, sending well-caparisoned horses for us to ride, and we were accompanied on the road by all the gentlemen of the court in attendance, to where we found the Royal Guard stationed, drawn up on either hand before the palace gate. Here we dismounted, and next proceeding up the stairs, at the outer door of the ante-room the gentlemen

## KING PHILIP III

immediately in waiting on his Majesty courteously received us.

They now conducted us on to the presence chamber where the King was standing. The ambassador came forward bearing the Letter, and this, after the Persian fashion, was written in letters of gold and coloured ink on a sheet of paper more than a yard in length and curiously folded, for the length in Persian style was doubled up, as for example is done in Spain with a folio sheet, and the paper was three finger-lengths in breadth. The ambassador had brought the Letter enclosed in a bag of cloth of gold, and he carried this in his turban close upon his head, from whence he had now taken it, and first kissing it, then presented it to the King. His Majesty raising his bonnet, received the Letter, and through the interpreter informed himself of what the king of Persia had written, and now learnt what was the object of our embassy. This becoming known to him, he replied that he greatly esteemed the friendship which the king of Persia was offering him, that most gladly would he do all that the Sháh had written desiring to be done, and that he would later send a reply to this Letter. Meanwhile we were to divert ourselves and take our ease. After all this had been said and done, on either side, the ambassador begged permission to take leave of his Majesty, and we thereupon withdrew and returned to our lodgings accompanied by the escort, as we had come. We remained for the following two months nobly complimented at Court, being taken out in his Majesty's coaches, or on horseback, going to see the most notable sights of the city, and further were entertained by dancing at balls, and more particularly we saw bull-fights and tilting in the ring. Now all these public festivals seemed to us to be better done in Spain than in any of the kingdoms and countries that we had previously visited, for the Spaniards, even in matter of sport, possess a grandeur and composure which is lacking to all other nations.

In the midst of these festivities a matter was happening which was to cause much disquietude to our ambassador. Among his Secretaries of Embassy who had accompanied him from Persia, being of his suite, was his nephew, whose name was 'Ali Quli Beg, and he, because the subject pleased and interested him, was now wont to attend the rites and services of the Christian Church. He had further come to appreciate the Spanish mode of life, and for convenience was accustomed now to wear the Spanish dress. This at first apparently was done as matter of mere curiosity and amusement, but in truth it was soon patent that, as we may opine and believe, the hour had struck in which God Almighty—who in past times had opened a path, with His right hand, through the waters of the Red Sea, whereby dry-shod the Children of Israel had gone over, and with His other hand had closed again the waters to cover and drown the satraps and all the Princes of Egypt—was now intent that in Spain He should be proclaimed again as God Almighty. For from the remotest parts of Asia He would bring, to the opposite limit of Europe, men with hard rebellious hearts, these to become softened anon, and like wax to melt in the enjoyment of the warm glow of Evangelical doctrine. Blessed, therefore, be His loving-kindness, and happy eternally this Persian gentleman to have accepted and profited by the mercies which God had vouchsafed to him in causing him to become a Christian. I therefore return to my narrative and say that 'Ali Quli Beg, having now resolved to become a Christian and be baptized, forthwith acquainted us with his intention, and next retiring from among us, put himself in the hands of certain Fathers of the Society of Jesus, that they might instruct him in the Faith and proceed to become a catechumen.

It appears to me also a matter of conscience that I should declare my belief, here in this place, that the true faith has been revealed by God, for His greater glory, solely and wholly to the Church [Apostolic of Rome], this indeed for the greater good and advantage of all true Christians, who thereby may through her teaching learn to walk in the way of truth and orthodoxy.

The ambassador and the rest of us Persians, being misbelievers, were forsooth much troubled by all this, but we were at this season occupied diverting ourselves with sights and festivals [and could do nothing to prevent what was going forward]. Then at the end of these two months of our pleasant sojourn in Valladolid his Majesty ordered a gold chain to be presented to our ambassador, of the weight of 500 crowns, and to each of us three Secretaries of Embassy who still remained with him a chain of the value of 3,000 *reals*.[2] Other chains of lesser value were given to our Persian servants. A letter for the king of Persia also was delivered to us, and a sum of 10,000 ducats [in respect of the sea voyage] was added, with 1,000 ducats besides for defraying our journey into Portugal. Further a grant in aid was allowed to the Canon who still accompanied us, and an order on Lisbon was sent for our embarkation at his Majesty's charge, with freight for our baggage, and free maintenance on board, so that no cost would be at our expense until we should be landed in the port of Ormuz, reaching Persian territory again. This was indeed munificence worthy of the august bounty of his Catholic Majesty Philip III, who is the glory of Spain and of the House of Austria, the true support of the Faith, and the protector of Christianity throughout all Western lands. When all these matters had been adjusted, we went to take leave of his Majesty, expressing our gratitude for all the benefits that he had showered on us.

# DON JUAN OF PERSIA

We had with us for our journey across Spain an interpreter whom the king had appointed to attend us, he being one of his Majesty's body-servants, and a person cognizant of many languages, whose name was Diego de Urrea. Forthwith we set out for Segovia, at which place the civil-governor, with some gentlemen from the town, came out to receive us, paying us much honour. In accordance with an intention that I had set to myself ever since I started from Persia on my travels—namely, to see everything I could, and to set down in writing all I saw on the journey, in order later to publish the same in Persia—I now earnestly begged the civil-governor that we might be shown the four sights for which Segovia is so famous.

The first of these is the Hermitage, with a beautiful statue of Our Lady, known as the Fuenzisla,[3] and this stands protected under a rock on a neighbouring height which faces south. The Face of this image is of a divine beauty, such as I never saw the like of elsewhere, and before it burn several great silver lamps, of a size so great that none would believe the same to have been of silver who had not actually seen them. I enquired who were the sovereign princes who had given these, and I was told that they were the gift offered to Our Lady by the men of this commune of the province, who worked to make the woollen cloth, the manufacture of which is so famous. The second notable sight to be seen in this city is the Alcázar,[4] the palace which the kings of Spain have here; indeed it is one of the finest and most famous buildings of any that we had yet visited. It is built on a rock which has been scarped artificially on either hand to form the wall of the very deep ditch, in which the streams of the Eresma [and Clamores] running below make the fortress-palace the more impregnable. The third notable sight of this town is the [Roman] Aqueduct[5] built of stone blocks, all chiselled and worked square, and set without mortar. Along the top runs the channel which brings in the water used throughout Segovia, and the length of this Aqueduct is such that it has more than two hundred arches to carry the conduit. Within the city in some parts it runs as high as may be counted at two full casts of a pike. The fourth wonder to be seen is the Mint,[6] where many million coins are struck in gold, silver and copper. This work is not done by hand, but by a machine which is worked by a mill on the river [Eresma] which flows below the Alcázar. While at Segovia we went out from the town two leagues [to the south-east] to see a winter-palace belonging to the Spanish kings, which is named Balsaim, and so called [to wit, Balsam], though it is no palace in a garden, but only a building standing down in the deep valley [of an affluent of the Eresma] enclosed by great mountains, that are covered by pine forests: yet so situated in that wilderness it is indeed a perfect Earthly Paradise.

Leaving Segovia we went on to the Escoreal, the most wonderful work of man the world holds, and only to look on it one should come from the most distant parts. This is a palace built for himself to live in by the late king, Philip II, who rests now in Glory. It stands in the folds of the mountain range which is known as the Guadarrama, on the bank of a stream coming down from the same. The site is thus protected from the north and faces south; the building forming a huge quadrangle, and displaying a great variety of styles, Doric, Ionic and Corinthian, all wrought in dressed stone based on hewn foundations. There are so many courts, towers, columns, separate palaces, galleries and halls, and within these so many rich ornaments and so many fine pictures, that with reason the Escoreal is known as the Eighth Wonder of the World. I myself opine assuredly that no one of the other Seven of ancient days could have come near to it as a marvel. They relate that King Philip built it in accordance with a vow he made when he was encamped at the town of St Quintin in France, where there was a church dedicated to Saint Lawrence which by reason of the war it was necessary to demolish, and hence it is likewise to Saint Lawrence that the church at the Escoreal is dedicated. Its altar-pictures are the most wonderful work of painting in all the world. It is a monastery of the Jeronimite Friars, and these have here their colleges and schools. The Escoreal further is the burying place of the kings of Spain, their bones having been collected and brought hither from wheresoever they were to be found in the divers provinces.

We went on from here to a winter-palace of the Emperor Charles V of glorious memory, which stands five leagues distant from the Escoreal and two leagues from Madrid. This too is a fine building, very curious to visit. It is surrounded by many plantations, full of all kinds of game, both great and small; indeed the game is so abundant here that the deer and wild boars are seen in droves together on every hand. Next we visited the palace known as the Casa del Campo of Madrid, where the fountains, gardens and tanks would need a special volume for their description, and then we entered Madrid, which is one of the greatest and most beautiful cities in all Spain. But its grandeur and many curious sights are so well known that it were better to be silent and not attempt to describe what others have already sufficiently portrayed. Leaving Madrid we journeyed on to Aranjuez, which is the summer-palace of the kings of Spain, built likewise by his late Majesty King Philip II on the banks of the mighty river Tagus. The gardens of Aranjuez with their adjacent shrubberies, tanks, lakes, pleasure grounds, with thickets for game, great and small, are so extensive and of so many different kinds, with such fine trees and fruit orchards, also divers beasts and birds

## ARANJUEZ

brought from remotest India, that it were impossible to describe them all even in many volumes, and thus when we state that Aranjuez has been given the name of the Ninth Wonder of the World we have said all that here is needful. We visited also, as our journey lay through it, the Imperial city of Toledo, the capital of the Gothic Kings. There is here the Alcázar, and we saw too the Machine[7] by which water is brought up from the depth of the gorge of the Tagus to the level of the city which lies high above its bed; also we were brought to the Cathedral, which is the metropolitan church of Spain, whereby the city of Toledo is known as the Spanish Rome.

From this city we made our way travelling through the province of Estremadura to the town of Truxillo, where so many noble families have their origin, and next came to the city of Mérida, which in ancient days was a second Rome, as to-day may be seen from the great extent of its ruins. The ambassador wished to rest for a day in Mérida, and here an immense number of people had collected in a vast crowd to gaze at us.

Now there was in our company, as ever had been since leaving home, our Alfaquí, he being, as one might say, the ambassador's travelling Chaplain, and the [Arabic] name by which he was known was Amyr, for though he was a Persian by birth, in point of fact he was a lineal descendant of the family of the prophet Mahomed. Now he on this occasion was standing at the door of our lodgings and there came to be much pushing in the doorway, when suddenly some man of an insolent temper in the crowd, and lacking bowels of compassion, for there was no apparent provocation, struck out at the Alfaquí Amyr with a dagger, and killed him on the spot. As it was almost night-time when this happened it proved impossible to ascertain who had done the deed, although the magistrate used every means in his power, putting in prison an immense number of persons to satisfy the loud demand of the ambassador, who seemed at first of opinion that he himself must return immediately to Valladolid to lay his complaint before the King. We learnt, however, on enquiry that his Majesty was at this moment no longer resident in the capital, being away on a hunting excursion, and it was therefore agreed that we should proceed on straight to Lisbon, and while preparations there went forward for our embarkation, that I should travel back to Valladolid and give an account to his Majesty of how our poor Alfaquí had for no just cause been killed, and make demand that the assailant should be punished. We therefore proceeded to bury our Alfaquí Amyr according to Persian rites, with the ceremonies usual in our creed, in some ground outside Mérida, and all the city came out to see the sight, which caused them much entertainment. From Mérida then we went on to Badajoz, which is a city standing on the frontier between Spain and Portugal, and the civil-governor here, who is a gentleman of noble birth, and named Don Juan de Avalos, lodged us in his own house, giving us all we required, and paying every attention to our comfort. From Badajoz we finally set out for Lisbon, the great city celebrated throughout Spain for its noble situation, the name recalling that of him who was its founder, Ulysses [for the ancients had named Lisbon Olisippo]. It is the capital and the largest town in Portugal, and has a population of more than 80,000 householders [or 360,000 souls]. Further, here is the great harbour, at the mouth of the Tagus, where the river comes out to the Ocean, which same is the chief port whence all ships start that sail for India the Greater, and the New World.

Now as soon as we, after leaving Badajoz, had come to Aldea Gallega[8] we sent across to let the Viceroy of Portugal, Don Cristóbal de Mora, know that we were there, and he forthwith despatched to us four galleys with many gentlemen in attendance, who now brought us into Lisbon. Here they gave us a grand reception, making festival, and hospitably lodged us in a magnificent palace. After we had taken our repose during some days, being sumptuously entertained by the Viceroy, and further by many of the Portuguese noblemen and private persons of Lisbon, for certainly they are the most hospitable of hosts, our ambassador ordered me to return with the Canon to Valladolid, to give his Majesty a true account of the death of our Alfaquí. I forthwith proceeded to carry out his command, and herein is made evident the truth of that which King David the man of God hath spoken—namely, that the hand of God doth guide the hearts of men in accordance with His divine will. For as soon as I had got to Valladolid I went to see 'Ali Quli Beg at the Jesuit House, and no sooner had I begun to talk with him, and to hold converse with the Fathers of the Society of Jesus—religious men as discrete as they are learned—when it became manifest how God Almighty willed that a miracle should be worked in me. For I began immediately to feel an inordinate longing in my heart to seek and find His Divine Grace—blessed a thousand times be His holy name—and while I was yet a prey to this confusion of mind, and unable to declare clearly my desire, the Divine Will loosed my slow tongue—even as with Moses of old—and just as I was returned to my lodging house I urgently called upon the Fathers to grant me baptism, though no master had yet given me any sufficient instruction in religion.

In the Persian script and language, even as before had been the case with my Diary, I now constrained my hand to write down the prayers, the articles of belief, the Commandments, and other Christian ordinances that were necessary for instructing one like me, an infidel, who was about to become a catechumen.

# DON JUAN OF PERSIA

That due praise may be paid to the Divine Grace, I have here given this very particular account of my experiences and conversion, for it is His marvellous providence which thus works in those whom He calls to His Church, and to union with the faithful. I next came to be instructed very fully in all the necessary Catholic doctrines, for Don Alvaro de Caravajal, who was chief chaplain and almoner-in-chief to his Royal Majesty, undertook to confer with me many times, explaining all difficulties to me, and encouraging me with the whole heart of a true Christian gentleman, thus favouring my conversion. Then later I ventured to solicit an audience of the Duke of Lerma, chief minister of his Majesty, on whose shoulders rests the whole weight of government of these kingdoms, and his Excellency was pleased to receive me very favourably. He was rejoiced, he said, to hear of my good intentions, and this encouraging me I was bold to lay before his Excellency my plan, which was that after having received baptism I should return to Persia and bring out thence, back to Spain, my wife and a son of mine there now living. To all this the Duke replied that after having been baptized, if I remained on living in Spain, his Majesty would doubtless give me his favour, and advance me to a place of honour. Further, he would indeed grieve with me, his Excellency said, in the loss of wife and child [should I stay in Spain, not returning to Persia], but that for the sake of God's commands trials far greater than this had to be undergone and supported with patience. Indeed, he continued, the love of a son, or of father, of mother, of wife even, was not to be held comparable with the love which God would of a certainty ultimately bestow on me—as His faithful servant.

His Excellency added many other efficacious reasonings, and I was thus completely comforted and reassured, for verily God has vouchsafed to the Duke

# CONVERSION OF DON JUAN

of Lerma a most piercing intelligence with a very charitable heart. Our Persian ambassador indeed had been of a mind to appreciate this, after he had taken his final audience with his Excellency, for whom he afterwards professed the highest esteem. But to conclude: by this time God graciously had taken possession to Himself of my whole heart—though not indeed by any merit of mine—and I was resolved to receive baptism without delay, and then to go back to Persia in search of my wife and my son. I had of a surety no intention of letting it be known there in Persia that I had become a Christian, intending later to seek some convenient pretext and opportunity for returning to Spain by way of Ormuz, which the Portuguese now hold in the name of his Catholic Majesty. With this prospect therefore in view, arrangements now went forward promptly for my immediate baptism.

## CHAPTER VIII

*As to how we were both baptized, the nephew of the ambassador and myself; and how I returned to Lisbon and of what happened to me with the ambassador; and how yet another Persian gentleman determined to become a Christian, whose name was Buniyad Beg.*

ON my return from this audience with the Duke of Lerma all the necessary arrangements for my baptism and that of the ambassador's nephew were forthwith carried through under the special direction of Don Alvaro de Caravajal, chief chaplain and almoner-in-chief to his Majesty (as already said), we Persians both having been now thoroughly instructed in all the doctrines of the Christian Faith. They brought us each a suit of white satin to wear, and riding in a coach Don Alvaro de Caravajal, the chief almoner, took us to the Palace, and we were conducted up to where their Majesties, habited likewise in white, were awaiting us. Then with a great company in attendance all went down to the Royal Chapel, and here Don Alvaro de Caravajal baptized us, the King and Queen[1] respectively acting as our sponsors. 'Ali Quli Beg, the ambassador's nephew, now received the name of Don Philip of Persia, while I, who formerly was known as Uruch Beg, became Don Juan of Persia, and thereupon their Majesties severally embraced us, honouring us greatly. Then the King handed me a letter for our ambassador and ordered his interpreter to travel with me, adding an aid for the expenses of the journey, and so forthwith I returned to Lisbon, but wearing once more my Persian clothes as aforetime.

It was my intention, as I have already said, to go back home to Persia, where I should conceal the fact that I had become a Christian, in order that I might bring away with me my wife and son. This matter of concealment, however, was to be on the understanding that, when come to Persia, no occasion arose in which I ought publicly to testify my faith in Christ Jesus and die for my belief, for I had been clearly instructed and taught the obligation that was laid upon me so to testify from the moment of my baptism, when I became a Christian. All this being made clear to me, I therefore set out for Lisbon, arriving back there without any event worthy of note. I had in my company, by order of his Excellency the Duke of Lerma, a gentleman (already mentioned) of his Majesty's servants, named Francisco de San Juan, who was the Turkish interpreter, and I soon discovered that, being now a Christian, the conversation of my Persian fellow countryman, with whom I had heretofore been on terms of inseparable comradeship, was now no longer in any sense to my taste —and blessed be Thy name, my God, for Thou hadst changed my heart. The ambassador appeared to be much pleased at my return, and forthwith proceeded to hasten the arrangements for our embarkation.

I then went to present myself, and kiss the hand of the Viceroy, giving him an account of how I had been baptized, at which news he rejoiced greatly. Going on to tell him how it was my intention to return to Persia in order to bring away my wife and son, he began to urge on me the danger, advising that I should for the present remain quietly in Spain. My ambassador, he said, knew perfectly well that I had become a convert to Christianity, and that I had been baptized at Valladolid, as also his nephew. His Excellency added that if I went back home it were at the risk of my life, for either the ambassador would have me done to death during the sea voyage, or else, not having been able to carry this through, he would inform against me on our arrival in Persia, where I should of course be burnt alive. I answered his Excellency that I was greatly obliged by the kindness shown and the advice given to me, but that for sure the ambassador was still ignorant of the fact that I was become a Christian, seeing that he continued to show me all friendship, and that I certainly intended to carry out the plan I had in mind. The Viceroy responded that I had best see to it carefully, while there was yet time, and on this I took my leave, returning to our lodgings, but somewhat perturbed in mind. It was now with Buniyad Beg, the Persian gentleman, my own particular friend [who was the third among us secretaries], that I began earnestly to talk over the matter in hand. A few days later, when after dinner the ambassador had retired to his private room, taking with him Hasan 'Ali Beg [who was the fourth in rank of us Persian secretaries], I having my suspicions aroused, continued walking up and down in the outer hall, and I put my ear to the door to listen to what the ambassador might be talking about. I heard him now saying to Hasan 'Ali Beg that he and the rest must be very careful not to let me get to know that he, the ambassador, had learnt how I had been baptized by the name of Don Juan, adding that he intended to keep the matter secret until we were both back once more in Persia. There, being safely come, he would have me seized, delivering me up to the Sháh, who would order my proper punishment.

I, of course, did not let it be known that I had overheard all this, but forthwith despatched my interpreter to the Viceroy, who arranged that I should quietly be provided with another lodging, together with all that was necessary for my maintenance and comfort. The ambassador naturally now understood what had taken place, and sought to put a quarrel on me, matters quickly coming to such a pass that each of us laid his hand on his sword, and had not the interpreter been present, who parted us, some mischance would certainly have befallen me, seeing that all the servants of the ambassador were leagued against me to do me a

## THE GALLEY-SLAVE

mischief. The ambassador indeed had no just reason on the face of it at that time to fall out with me, for I had not confessed either publicly or privately that I was a Christian. But I had said at our first meeting that I should like now to return home to Persia by land, not taking the sea route by way of India, whither he was bound. This, I said, was because the long navigation was distasteful to me, and that I proposed now going back to Venice, whence I could travel home through Turkey, in Turkish disguise, and thus in three or four months be back again in Persia. The ambassador publicly talking of my affairs, now wrangled so openly with me that all the world came to know that I had been baptized, whereupon finally I admitted that this was the truth of the case, and forthwith, then and there, separated myself from the company of the other Persians, going to live in the house which the Viceroy had assigned me, where I had the company of the Turkish interpreter.

The ambassador, thus having got me to declare myself a Christian, now realized that I was going to escape him and remain behind in Spain. Since he could not carry me along with him, for say what he might I would not consent to go, he resolved, in order to avenge himself of what he deemed the insult, to get me killed. To that end he now sought to find some rascally Spanish soldier to do the deed, but discovering no such one to his hand, he came to terms with a certain Turkish slave, whom he had recently got set free from the oar, in the galleys of the Marquis of Santa Cruz, who at that time was at Lisbon in command of the Spanish fleet. This Turk was at the moment acting as the body-servant to the ambassador, and as his interpreter, for he well knew [both Spanish and] Turkish. This galley-slave therefore was to kill me, and for the purpose carried a dagger, going about seeking a suitable occasion, but of the plot I was duly advised in time. I on my part therefore betook myself to the Viceroy, who agreed to communicate with the Marquis of Santa Cruz, who would, he said, doubtless see to the matter. The Marquis immediately took his information, ordered twenty soldiers ashore from the galleys, and choosing a moment when the Turk happened to be ſtanding outside the ambassador's lodgings, seized him. They carried him back prisoner to the galleys, where the Marquis ordered that he should be well beaten, and he was once more chained to the oar.

After this episode I had no more dealings either with our ambassador or with his servants, and the only one of the Persians I now spoke to was Buniyad Beg. On him I urged that he should save his soul, and seek to obtain baptism. He, however, was ſtill in a ſtate of doubt; sometimes he would answer me " yes " and at other times " no," and being much his junior I despaired of myself and betook me to prayer, that God would vouchsafe to bring the matter about, being the more intent on his conversion, in order that he might become my fellow-comrade in religion. We were wont both of us to meet in the house of a certain Venetian merchant, who spoke the Turkish language perfectly, and who was then living in Lisbon, his name being Nicolas Clavel. He was conſtantly trying to persuade Buniyad Beg to do what I implored of him—namely, to be baptized—using every argument and inducement that he could come by, for, said he, his salvation depended upon it. Now it chanced one day when Nicolas Clavel was arguing with him in Turkish, for Buniyad Beg underſtood this language quite well, and setting forth the myſtery of how of old the Holy Ghoſt had descended upon the Apoſtles, suddenly, no one knew from whence nor what it really might be, a White Dove flew into our room and settled upon the writing-table that ſtood in between us three, and round which we were seated talking. There having reſted awhile and being nowise disturbed, it flew away again and was seen no more. This was to the no small wonder of those of us who were there present, and indeed we deemed it to be a very great miracle. No clearer sign than this did Buniyad Beg need, for God had already changed the hardness of his heart, and he immediately made up his mind to seek baptism. I therefore brought him to the Viceroy, to whom I related all that had happened, which indeed greatly edified and rejoiced him.

Without letting our ambassador have any notice, and with the least delay possible—the Viceroy ordering what was necessary for our journey to be given to us—we set off in the company of the interpreter, making our way straight to Valladolid. As soon as we had arrived at Court, I craved an audience of his Majesty and through our interpreter gave the King an account of all that had taken place, and I added that I myself was now resolved to remain in Spain, and that not having my son to bring to his Majesty I had brought my friend, who, following my example, wished to become a Christian. His Majesty showed every sign of satisfaction and arranged that Buniyad Beg should go to Don Alvaro de Caravajal, who would prepare him to become a catechumen. Soon after this the King left Valladolid for the Escoreal, and Don Alvaro de Caravajal, being there in attendance, next sent his chaplain, ordering us to bring Buniyad Beg thither, when on examination it was manifest that he was well and perfectly instructed in the doctrines of the Christian Faith. Forthwith, therefore, he was robed in white satin and taken to the Palace, where in the Royal Chapel, and with the King and the Duchess of Lerma standing his sponsors, Don Alvaro de Caravajal baptized him. His Majesty indeed showed him much honour, and at his baptism Buniyad Beg took the name of Don Diego of Persia. The King, that most Christian prince, seeing now that we both were Christians, but strangers in a foreign land many hundred leagues distant from our own country, of his royal and Christian generosity gave command that we should each receive yearly a pension of 1,200 crowns,[2] and further a sum in ready money with which to set up house: granting thereto lodgings at his Court. Many other kindnesses also were now shown to us, and daily we received favours increasingly, coming as a free gift from his royal hand.

Blessed be the infinite charity of Almighty God for His loving-kindness and grace, in all that has been thus vouchsafed to us. First in granting to us the Light of the True Faith, and bringing us to sojourn in a Christian land, where the Sacraments are abundantly celebrated, and where, knowing now how to profit by the occasion, we find teachers who can show us the true way of Christ Jesus. Next and in the second place, we give thanks that we Persians now are enrolled under the banner of our Sovereign Lord the King of Spain, who of his charity daily showers favours and great honours upon us. To God, the King of kings, I do give thanks for granting me a zealous intention, which from the day when my mind was fixed to become a Christian, has brought me straight to the way of salvation. I have now written this Book of mine more with the intent of giving praise to God for His marvellous loving-kindness daily shown to me, than indeed for any merely mundane cause. Let me therefore confess before the Divine Majesty of God, how content I am to be a Christian, and I have at last lost all memory of the natural pain I once felt at finding myself cut off for ever from my wife, my son, my country and all I there possessed. To God let all thanks be given, for as Job hath said: To Him belong all things, and from Him come all things that are in the world. World without end. Amen, and to God be the praise given.

# NOTES

## INTRODUCTION

[1] *Page* 1. It has been plausibly suggested that this unusual name Uruch is merely a Spanish mispronunciation for Ulugh, very common at that date.

[2] *Page* 2. Sherley's own account of his journey from England to Persia will be found in Purchas *Pilgrims*, Vol. VIII, p. 375 (Glasgow, 1905). The subsequent travels through Russia, and the sea voyage to Stode, are given by William Parry in the same volume, p. 442. See also *The Sherley Brothers*, by one of the same House (namely, E. P. Shirley), Roxburgh Club Press, 1848.

[3] *Page* 3. The *Fugger News-Letters*, 1568 to 1605, translated from the German of V. von Klarwill by P. de Chary, 1924, p. 231.

[4] *Page* 5. As regards Stode it must be noted that E. P. Shirley in his interesting book on *The Sherley Brothers* has made a curious mistake which, unfortunately, has been repeated in the Sherley article of the *Dictionary of National Biography* and elsewhere. On p. 27 of *The Sherley Brothers* it is stated that "after a dangerous passage of six weeks [from St. Nicholas—otherwise Archangel] they sailed to Stettin, then called Stoade." Stettin on the Baltic is about 300 miles in a straight line north from Prague: Stode, a well-known town at the mouth of the Elbe, is about the same distance, but due north-west of Prague. E. P. Shirley's mistake is the more remarkable because on p. 31 of his work he quotes a letter, dated 17th October 1600, from Sir Robert Cecil to Mr. Lello, the English envoy at Constantinople, in which Cecil acquaints him of the recent arrival from Muscovy of Sir Anthony Sherley "with a Persian Embassador joined with him . . . and he came by sea to Embden." Then in the *D.N.B.*, Vol. LII, p. 122, we are told that Sir Anthony Sherley "took ship at St. Archangel for Stettin," and the name of Stode is omitted altogether. In Botero (I, p. 74), who wrote in 1591, and is describing Pomerania, mention is made of "Stetino" at the mouth of the Oder. C. Schéfer, in his *Introduction* (p. vii) to the work of Father Du Mans, has fallen into the same error (probably relying on E. P. Shirley), for he writes of Sir Anthony as going to Archangel, where he embarked "pour Stettin." Cf. *Estat de la Perse en* 1660 *par le Père Raphaël du Mans*, edited by C. Schéfer, Paris, 1890; and G. Botero, *Delle Relationi Universali* (in two parts): I, Rome, 1591, and II, Rome, 1602, both in 4to.

# DON JUAN OF PERSIA

[5] *Page* 6. For the visit of the Persians to the Emperor Rudolf we have two other contemporary accounts: one from the despatches of the Venetian Ambassador at Prague, Pietro Duodo, for which see Schéfer, p. 277; the other from the *Fugger News-Letters*, p. 230.

[6] *Page* 7. The entry of the Persian Embassy into Rome is the subject of a contemporary Italian pamphlet published in Rome, and translated into French under the title of *L'entrée solennelle faicte à Rome aux ambassadeurs du roy de Perse, le cinquiesme avril* 1601. Paris, 1601. The *Fugger Letters* (p. 243) also give some curious details as to the conversion to the Catholic faith of the Persian servants.

[7] *Page* 9. An account of the treatment awarded to a subsequent home-coming ambassador is given in *Persian Literature in Modern Times*, IV, p. 6, by Professor E. G. Browne, derived from a contemporary Persian historian. This ambassador was Dengiz Beg Shámlu, who was not *our* Ambassador (as Professor Browne mistakenly supposed), for he was in Spain in 1611 when Margaret, Queen-consort of Philip III, died, and returned to Persia in 1613. He must have been joint-ambassador with Sir Robert Sherley, the two (as the like had been the case with Sir Anthony and our present ambassador ten years before) having been dispatched by Sháh 'Abbás (about 1608) to the Western Powers. This Embassy travelled by Cracow, Prague, Florence and Rome, whence going on through Spain Sir Robert finally reached England. His Persian colleague, taking leave of him in Spain, went back home in company with a Spanish counter-ambassador to Sháh 'Abbás; but poor Dengiz Beg was, on arrival in Persia, incontinently put to death by the irate Sháh. This was on various counts, one of which was the indiscretion of having worn mourning at Madrid at the time of Queen Margaret's funeral. His chief crime in his master's eyes, however, was, as reported against him, his having behaved so arbitrarily and cruelly to the other members of his suite that some of them, to avoid returning home with him, had adopted the Christian faith and remained behind in Europe. It is evident that the Sháh was determined once and for all to hold heads of missions responsible for the perversion of their secretaries, and doubtless he had not been pleased with the failure of Secretary Uruch Beg and his colleagues to return with the ambassador in 1602.

[8] *Page* 10. *Obras de Salas Barbadillo*, Madrid, 1907 (in *Colección de Escritores Castellanos*), by E. Cotarelo y Mori, Vol. I, Prólogo, p. xxxii; the account of the death of Don Juan being taken from a contemporary Portuguese work called *Fastiginia*, written by Thomé Pinheiro da Veiga, which has recently been translated into Spanish by N. Alonso Cortés, Valladolid, 1916, for which see p. 33 of the translation. A full account of the law-suit, *Don Diego de Persia versus Salas Barbadillo*, will be found in Volume XXXI of the publications of the *Sociedad de Bibliófilos Españoles*, Madrid, 1894, where the documents

# NOTES

are cited from the Simancas Archives by Señor Uhagón in his preface to an edition of two of the plays of Salas Barbadillo.

⁹ *Page* 12. Numerous examples occur of these purely oral mistakes throughout the work, and the following are typical. Remón (or Don Juan) was speaking of Láhiján, the capital of the Gílán province : the scribe writes " La Ciudad de la Hichan." He refers on two successive lines to the Caliph Walíd₁ : the scribe writes this name first as " Ulit " and then (as though it were another person) as " Halid." The barber who killed Prince Hamzah was called Khudá (Verdi) Dallák, " Dallák " in Persian meaning " a barber " : the scribe wrote the name as " Cudy de Lac." The name of the town of Vladimir, near Moscow, appears as " Valla de Amor." Lastly, of William, Duke of Bavaria, surnamed " the Pius," it is written that he " se llama Du-Capi " : *i.e.*, for Duca Pi[o], but this may be merely a typographical blunder.

¹⁰ *Page* 12. See above, note 4. Giovanni Botero Benese (a native of Bene in Piedmont), 1540 to 1617, at one time acted as secretary to St. Charles Borromeo. His work is very readable and gives an exact account of what was known in the year 1600 of all the countries and cities of Europe, Asia and the Americas, North and South. This work evidently had an immense vogue. It was reprinted forthwith in Italian at Brescia and Venice ; it was translated into English by Robert Johnson in 1608, and versions in Latin, Spanish and German quickly followed. The first volume gives a description of the Old and the New World as matters stood at the beginning of the 17th century. The second volume gives the political history of each state. Don Juan (or Remón), as will be seen, quotes frequently from Botero, and more frequently takes over information without acknowledgment from his pages, but with many careless misprints. Further, his knowledge of the Italian is often not quite adequate.

¹¹ *Page* 12. Remón had a good library at his command in Valladolid. Thus, after quoting *passim* from Strabo, Suidas, Procopius, Ctesias, Berosus and Megasthenes, he refers to the Byzantine histories of Nicephorus Callistus and Nicephorus Bryennius, Agathias and Zonaras, with St Antoninus, Archbishop of Florence. Further, he consulted Christianus Massæus, Matthæus Palmerius, Georgius Agricola, Paulo Giovio, Apianus (that is Bienewitz), Abdias, Josaphat Barbaro, Juvencus, Genebrardus, Cuspianus, Laurentius Surius, Amandus of Zieriksee, Tornamira, Georgievitz, Breydenbach, Juan de Pineda, Joseph Scaliger, and for the Turkish campaign in Georgia Minadoi, Botero and Boissard. Lastly, there are two works more than once quoted, but which it has proved difficult to identify with any known published books—namely, the *Bibliotheca Susiana*, and the *Oriental Annals* of Belochus.

¹² *Page* 12. Giovanni Tommaso Minadoi (1540 to 1615), *Guerra fra Turchi et Persiani*, Venice, 1588.

[13] *Page* 16. R. Knolles, *Historie*, first edition *in folio*, London, 1603; the edition later quoted from is the fourth *folio*, London, 1631.
[14] *Page* 16. *Travels of Venetians in Persia*: Publications of the Hakluyt Society, 1872.
[15] *Page* 19. See on this point E. G. Browne, *Persian Literature*, IV, p. 20.
[16] *Page* 19. See above, note 12, for G. T. Minadoi. The *Historia della guerra fra Turchi et Persiani* was published at Venice in 1588, and in this same year a Spanish translation by A. de Herrera was printed in Madrid, while an English translation by A. Hartwell was published in London in 1595. Minadoi, also called Minadous (1540 to 1615), was born at Rovigo. After taking his degree in medicine he spent seven years travelling in the Ottoman dominions, and appears to have become well acquainted with Turkish. His *History* describes the wars of the Ottoman Sultans against the Sháhs of Persia down to the year 1587, the date of the accession of Sháh 'Abbás. On his return home Minadoi became physician to the Duke of Mantua, and also held the chair of medicine at the University of Padua.
[17] *Page* 19. *Vitæ et Icones Sultanorum Turcicorum*, by J. J. Boissard: Frankfort, 1596. Boissard (1528 to 1602) was a Frenchman and a native of Franche Comté. His book is embellished by forty-seven portraits of Sultans, engraved by T. de Bry.
[18] *Page* 19. Dates of the Turkish Sultans and contemporary Sháhs of Persia are as follows:

    Sultan Bayazíd II, 1481.
        Sháh Isma'íl I, 1502.
    Sultan Selím I, 1512.
    Sultan Sulaymán I, 1520.
        Sháh Tahmásp I, 1524.
    Sultan Selím II, 1566
    Sultan Murád III, 1574.
        Sháh Isma'íl II, 1576.
        Sháh Muhammad Khudá-Bandah, 1578.
        Sháh 'Abbás, 1587 to 1629.
    Sultan Muhammad III, 1595 to 1603.

## BOOK I

### CHAPTER I

[1] *Page* 34. See 1 Timothy i. 12 and following verses in the Vulgate and Douay Version, but much glossed.
[2] *Page* 37. The *Victoria* (of 85 tons burden) was the one ship of Magellan's fleet which, after the death of the great navigator in the island of Cebu, one of the Philippines, sailed home to Lisbon in 1522, having made the first complete circumnavigation of the globe.

# NOTES
## CHAPTER II

¹ *Page* 38. Petrus Apianus (Bienewitz) of Ingoldstadt (1495 to 1551), *Cosmographia*, 4to, Antwerp, 1574, folio 29 *verso*. For the mediæval geography of Persia see *Lands of the Eastern Caliphate*, or in the Gibb Series the Translation of the *Nuzhat-al-Qulúb*, by Hamd-Allah Mustawfi.

² *Page* 38. Botero, I, pp. 119, 120, and II, pp. 173, 174.

³ *Page* 38. In text Gerban, later Ierban, probably for Eriván. There is a confusion here between Media Major and Media Atropatene.

⁴ *Page* 38. In point of fact Shíráz stands on no river: the Kur, (Cyrus river) of Fárs, on which Istakhr (Persepolis) lies, is a day's march to the north of Shíráz.

⁵ *Page* 38. Here and elsewhere the word Don Juan uses is *vecinos*, literally "neighbours," but in the common usage standing for "householders," and each household may be reckoned as containing 4·5 souls. It is evident in some cases, however, that the number given would be nearer the mark if we took *vecino* to mean "inhabitant"; but naturally the figures must in no case be taken very seriously. See *Venetians in Persia*, Barbaro, p. 74. This work, besides the account given by Barbaro, contains five other narratives—namely, those of Contarini, Zeno, Angiolello, Alessandri; and lastly, the account of the Anonymous Merchant.

⁶ *Page* 40. Sháh Tahmásp (1524 to 1576) was the grandfather of Sháh 'Abbás.

⁷ *Page* 40. In the text given as "Ciudad de la Hichan"; on a later page written correctly as "Lahychan."

⁸ *Page* 41. There is some confusion here between the province of Shírván (which Don Juan generally gives under the form "Gerban") and the city of Eriván (which he writes "Ierban" or "Yravan"), of which city its province formerly was called Arrán. Eriván city was founded at the beginning of the 16th century to be the frontier fortress of Persia against the Georgians. The earlier Arab Geographers divide the country immediately to the south of the Caucasus into four provinces: Shírván, lying to the north of the lower Kur (Cyrus) and extending north-east to the Caucasus at Derbend; to the west of Shírván came Georgia; south of the Kur was Arrán, lying east of the Gokchah Lake; and Armenia, to the west of this, lay round the Van Lake.

⁹ *Page* 41. Probably the city of Ámul.

¹⁰ *Page* 41. Kkurásán at this date included the western provinces of modern Afghanistán.

¹¹ *Page* 42. Ganjah is the capital of the Qarabágh (Black Garden) province, so called from the dark foliage of its forest-clad hills. For lack of a few words of explanation the text reads as though the Ganjah district lay on the southern border of Sístán.

# DON JUAN OF PERSIA

[12] *Page* 42. In the present Persian usage the title Khán never precedes the personal name. But this apparently was not the invariable usage, as shown by the present case, which (in Turkish) stands for "Khán, son of the Sayyid." Other examples of this usage will be found later: thus (on p. 214) we find the king of Gílán named Khán Ahmad, and again a certain Khán Muhammad Qulí Khalífah is spoken of (on p. 213).

[13] *Page* 44. Text: "el lago Gioco"; this is taken from Botero, II, p. 172.

[14] *Page* 44. Presumably for Ab-i-Amú. See Botero, II, p. 172, from whom much of the foregoing description of Persia has been taken.

## CHAPTER III

[1] *Page* 46. It is from this Turkish clan that the late royal family of Persia was descended.

[2] *Page* 46. Qárá Qoyunlú: these are the clan of the Black-Sheep Turkomans, who will be spoken of later.

[3] *Page* 47. "Ishik-agásí-báshí"; in Turkish, Chief Aga or Master of the (Royal) Threshold. In spite of the bitter and persistent enmity, which from the time of Sháh Isma'íl onwards separated Turks and Persians, the ruling families in Persia always appear to have spoken Turkish (whether Ottoman or Azerbayjání) as well as Persian, while on the other hand the Turks of Constantinople always kept up with and read Persian literature. Further as regards the officials of the royal household in Persia, their offices, then as now, usually and for the most part bore Turkish names. See E. G. Browne, *Persian Literature*, IV, p. 13.

## CHAPTER IV

[1] *Page* 50. "Celemin," of which twelve go to the bushel.

[2] *Page* 50. "Conejos," but probably the hare is the animal alluded to, for at the present day, too, the Persians do not eat hares, deeming their flesh unclean.

[3] *Page* 50. "A la gineta," and this is the early 17th century meaning of the term, which at the present time is implied by the phrase "cabalgar a la jineta" (while "andar a la jineta" means to go at a short trot). The "Gineta" originally were men of the Berber tribe of the Zeneta who had come over from Tangiers to take service with the king of Granada, and who, like all Moorish horsemen, rode with a very short stirrup. See Dozy and Engelmann, *Glossaire*, p. 276, s.v. "Ginete." The effect is well shown in the (posthumous) equestrian portrait of Philip III by Velazquez, now in the Prado museum.

[4] *Page* 50. Text: "Celadas de pasta de azero." What the term "pasta" implies is uncertain.

# NOTES

[5] *Page* 53. This may refer to Shaykh Safí-ad-Dín (1252–1334) from whom the Safavi Dynasty took its name. His tomb at Ardabíl was a much-venerated shrine. He was the ancestor in the 6th degree of Sháh Ismaʻíl the Grand Sophi.

[6] *Page* 53. Text in error, " cintas de colgados."

[7] *Page* 54. This, it may be noted, is strangely contrary to fact, for the Turks strenuously cultivate literature. See above, ch. iii, note 3.

## CHAPTER V

[1] *Page* 58. *La Libreria Susiana* and *Los Anales de Oriente de Beloco*, both often quoted below, but to what published works these names refer it has been impossible to discover.

[2] *Page* 58. The proper names in this chapter and the four following (where the Spanish text is full of misprints) have been corrected from the lists given in I. P. Cory's *Ancient Fragments*, pp. 70–75: London, 1832; and from G. Rawlinson's *Seventh Oriental Monarchy*. This without comment, and without the misprints being included in the Index.

[3] *Page* 59. Syris, son of Abraham, is not mentioned in Genesis.

[4] *Page* 61. The Iliad makes no mention of Teuthanes, Menon or Titon : this account is doubtless derived from either Daries Phrygius or Dictys Cretenses.

## CHAPTER VII

[1] *Page* 67. Juvencus, *De historiæ evangelicæ libri quatuor* : Venice, 1502.

## CHAPTER VIII

[1] *Page* 70. Abdias having been baptized by St Simon and St Jude is said to have been ordained by them as the first Bishop of Babylon. He is credited with the authorship of the apocryphal *Historiæ Apostolicæ*, which was first printed at Cologne in 1576 : and to which as a second part Joachim Perionus, O.S.B., added his *Lives of the Apostles*.

[2] *Page* 70. Probably Artabanus III, king of Parthia, is the person here meant.

[3] *Page* 71. The *Ecclesiasticæ Historiæ libri xviii* of Nicephorus Callistus, a Latin translation of which was published at Bâle in 1535 by Beatus Rhenanus. Whereto was added the *Historia Tripartita* consisting of the *Abbreviation* of the works of Socrates, Sozomen and Theodoret by Cassiodorus. These two books go to form the appendix to Eusebius, as translated by Rufinus, and the whole appeared under the title of *Autores Historiæ Ecclesiasticæ*.

[4] *Page* 71. Text reads in error: " Esayas hijo de Adamo."

[5] *Page* 72. Otherwise Brichjesus and Elias.

# DON JUAN OF PERSIA

[6] *Page* 72. Laurentius Surius, the martyrologist, who wrote *De probatis sanctorum historia*, Cologne, 1576.
[7] *Page* 72. Agathias (in *Historiarum libri quinque*: Niebuhr, Bonn, 1828, p. 123, Book II, cap. 27) calls him a σκυτοτόμος, which the dictionaries translate by *Cortarius*, a cobbler, or worker in leather.
[8] *Page* 74. Text "Seganesna": Agathias (Niebuhr edition, p. 260, ch. iv, 24) gives Σεγανσαά with variants.
[9] *Page* 74. Text in error: "Misdates."
[10] *Page* 76. His brother Hormisdas III preceded him from 457, reigning a year or more. See G. Rawlinson, *Seventh Oriental Monarchy*, p. 311.
[11] *Page* 76. Text: "Valente y Cavades."
[12] *Page* 76. Text: "Blases o Zamblases."

## CHAPTER IX

[1] *Page* 78. Text: "hermano" in error.
[2] *Page* 79. All this is from Agathias (Niebuhr, p. 272, iv, 29), the proper names throughout being very incorrectly given.
[3] *Page* 81. Juan de Pineda, a well-known contemporary writer. The work referred to is probably his *Monarchia Ecclesiastica*, Burgos, 1588.

## CHAPTER X

[1] *Page* 83. Massæus, *Chronicorum multiplicis historiæ libri viginti*, Antwerp, 1540.
[2] *Page* 83. Text: "Dagano Rey de los Arabes." Who he was is uncertain.
[3] *Page* 84. Which is Dastagird.
[4] *Page* 84. Otherwise Qobád II.
[5] *Page* 85. Apparently here put for Queen Purándokht, of more authentic history.
[6] *Page* 85. Should be Yazdagird III.
[7] *Page* 86. The Arabic name of the Persian slave who killed Omar is Abu-Lúlúah, "He of the Pearl." In classical Arabic *Marján*, which now is the name commonly given to Coral, meant Pearl (see Dozy and Lane). The word is of Aramaic origin, from which source, too, came μαργαρίτης, said to be of Persian origin in Liddell and Scott; and pearls indeed come from the Persian Gulf, not being found in Ionian waters. The name Margancia, here given, is evidently Marján.

## CHAPTER XI

[1] *Page* 88. 'Alí was killed by the Kharijite fanatic Ibn Muljam. The statement that Mu'áwiyah was responsible is taken from Botero, II, 171, where his name is written *Mavia*, which our author misprints

# NOTES

*Manua*, and a few lines later more exactly spells the name *Moabia*, but apparently without recognizing that the two spellings indicate one and the same person.

² *Page* 88. More correctly, Damascus in Syria.

³ *Page* 88. The scattered chapters of the Coran were first gathered into a volume by the Caliph Omar, and under Othman a revision was ordered to be made for a standard text. The revisers are given as Zayd ibn Thábit, ʻAbd-Allah ibn Zubayr, Saʻid ibn ʻÁs and ʻAbd-ar-Rahmán ibn Hárith. The list of six given in the text appears to be apocryphal.

⁴ *Page* 88. Read Damascus, for Baghdad was only founded later.

⁵ *Page* 89. Text: "Aly Ozen, y otros dizen que Aly Huscein." The history of Husayn and the claims of the Alids will be more fully treated of later by our author.

⁶ *Page* 89. Mukhtar, the celebrated partisan of the House of ʻAli who avenged Husayn's death, never sought to be proclaimed Caliph.

⁷ *Page* 90. The names in the text are in great confusion here. This name, which recurs several times, is variously misprinted, as Amyr Suleyman and Luleimin, and then as Amyrmo Selemin or Amurmoselemin: to wit Amir Sulaymán, and (as though added thereto) Amir of the Moslems, a title Abu-Muslim never affected. In point of fact Abu-Muslim's first name was not Sulaymán, but ʻAbd-ar-Rahmán, or some say Ibrahim.

⁸ *Page* 91. Zelma, son of Abu-Muslim, is unknown to Moslem history. Marwan II was killed (according fo Tabari) by a man of Basrah called Al-Maghúd.

⁹ *Page* 91. Abu-Muslim was not his ancestor, nor was Mukhtar.

¹⁰ *Page* 91. Text in error: "Mahamet o Hamet Moahedin hijo menor de Ali." The mistake is from Botero, II, p. 171.

¹¹ *Page* 91. In error: he never claimed to be Caliph. See above, note 6.

¹² *Page* 91. Text, "Abu Bakr" in error.

¹³ *Page* 92. In point of fact Baghdad had been founded by his great-grandfather the Caliph Mansúr.

## CHAPTER XII

¹ *Page* 93. The text asserts in error that he succeeded "Mahamet," but Muhammad and ʻAbd-Allah, mentioned at the close of the last chapter, are respectively the Caliphs Amín and Mámún, who in turn succeeded Hárún-ar-Rashíd. Our author gets the astonishing name Imbrael (perhaps a misreading for Amín-billah) from Zonaras (Bonn edition, Vol. III, p. 369), who says that he was *Archegos* (prince) of the Saracens, which might mean Caliph. Zonaras continues that during the reign of the Emperor Theophilus (who succeeded his father, Michael II the Stammerer, in 820 and reigned till 842) this Imbrael's

# DON JUAN OF PERSIA

Saracen commanders gained a notable victory over the Greek troops of the Emperor. The date 846 is impossible if it be the Caliph Amín, for he reigned from 809 to 813, and Mámún, his brother, during the next twenty years till 833, while Michael III the Sot, " Born in the Purple " (mentioned below), succeeded his father Theophilus in 842, being murdered in 867. In point of fact the Caliph in the year 846 was Wáthiq, Mámún's grandson, among us better known as the *Vathek* of Beckford's romance.

² *Page* 93. *Ignaro* means " unlearned," but who this Muhammad was is difficult to make out, and he certainly was not a Caliph. Our author takes his information from the Byzantine historian Cedrenus (Niebuhr : Bonn, 1839, Vol. II, p. 567) who calls him Muhammad, son of Imbrael; so possibly *Ignaro* is merely a mistake for *Imbrael*, which, as we have seen, is also the form given to the name of the Caliph Amín (see above, note 1). Probably one of the later Buyid princes who was governor of the Isfahán district is the personage who is here referred to as Muhammad. As to Pysasyri, no Abbasid Caliph is known under any name that is at all like this. Nicephorus Bryennius (Bonn, 1838, p. 30) names Pysasyri as a prince only, and doubtless Basasírí is the personage meant, no Caliph, but a Daylamite Captain of the Guards, an ardent Shí'ah who made a conspiracy to dethrone the Abbasid Caliph Qáim, and bring in the Fatimite Caliph of Cairo. Basasírí was captured and put to death by Tughril Beg the Seljuq. For this, his unsuccessful attempt to promote the Shí'ah faith and doctrine, Basasírí was held in much honour more than five centuries later by Sháh Isma'íl. See E. G. Browne, *Persian Literature*, IV, p. 54.

³ *Page* 94. Otherwise Tagrolipix Mucalet, which is nearer the original (Zonaras, Vol. III, Bonn, 1897, p. 634); for his father's name was Mikhail.

⁴ *Page* 94. Sulaymán I (1077–1086), the Seljuq Sultan of Rúm, is probably the personage indicated. As to his previous name of Alphagalo, and his uncle's name Belcepho, it is impossible to suggest any satisfactory identification. The first of the two names might, of course, stand for Alp Arslán, misplaced. Neither of these two personages appear to be mentioned by any of the Byzantine historians in the Niebuhr (Bonn) edition.

⁵ *Page* 95. This probably refers to the rule of the Íl-Kháns Húlágú and Abaqa in Persia, descendants of Chingíz Khán the Mongol.

⁶ *Page* 95. Gilbertus Genebrardus, Archbishop of Aix, *Chronographiæ libri quatuor:* Paris, 1567.

⁷ *Page* 95. Johannes Cuspinianus, *De Turcarum origine:* Antwerp, 1541. Bartholomæus Georgievits, *De origine imperii Turcorum:* Witebergæ, 1560.

⁸ *Page* 95. Commonly written Amurath: in point of fact, Sultan Sulayman precedes Murád I.

⁹ *Page* 96. *Embassy to the Court of Timour*, translated by Sir

# NOTES

Clements Markham: Hakluyt Society, 1860. The Spaniards left Samarqand on the 21st of November 1404, and Timur died at Otrar on the Jaxartes, whither Clavijo had not accompanied him, on the 17th February 1405. It was after this that Clavijo visited Timur's grandson, Omar Mirza, son of Mirán Sháh, whom he found encamped on the plain to the west of Tabríz, on the 28th March 1405, as stated later. The best edition of the Spanish text is that edited by Isreznevski, with a Russian translation and a French index, published in the *Proceedings of the Imperial Academy*, St. Petersburg, 1881.

[10] *Page* 96. It was Bayazid II who was surnamed Ilderim, not Timur.

## CHAPTER XIII

[1] *Page* 97. Text in error: "Bayaceto el primero."

[2] *Page* 97. "Tall" Hasan (1466–1478), of the Clan of the Áq Quyunli (White Sheep), but who later succeeded also to the rule of the Qara Quyunli (Black Sheep) Turcomans in N.W. Persia. See *Life of King Ussun Cassano* by Giovanni Maria Angiolello; *Venetians in Persia*, pp. 73–138.

[3] *Page* 97. Afterwards Doge, 1474–1476.

[4] *Page* 97. Rhodes since 1311 was in the occupation of the Knights of St John of Jerusalem.

[5] *Page* 98. Text apparently in error prints "Pedro Immola." The Mocenigo family seem to have had no connection with Imola.

[6] *Page* 98. See *Venetians in Persia*: Zeno, p. 15, and Angiolello p. 78.

[7] *Page* 99. See *Venetians in Persia*: Barbaro.

[8] *Page* 99. Angiolello, p. 75, speaks here of *Abrain* (Ibráhím), another brother, whom Don Juan mentions later on (see p. 103).

[9] *Page* 99. B. Breydenbach, *De oppugnatis a Turca Constantinopoli*, etc.: Bâle, 1556.

[10] *Page* 99. This was the battle fought at Terján in 1473 (see Angiolello, p. 89).

[11] *Page* 100. Text in error: "antecessores." In what follows some words must have fallen out in printing, for as the text stands it makes no sense.

## BOOK II

## CHAPTER I

[1] *Page* 103. See above, note 8 to previous chapter.

[2] *Page* 104. Amandus of Zieriksee, *Chronica compendiosisima ab exordio mundi*: Antwerp, 1534.

[3] *Page* 104. Paolo Giovio, *Commentarii delle cose de' Turchi, di Paolo Giovio*: Venice, 1541.

[4] *Page* 106. See above, Bk. I, ch. xi, note 1.

# DON JUAN OF PERSIA

⁵ *Page* 107. The text gives in error, "su sobrino" (nephew), but Botero, from whom the information comes, has rightly "suo nipote."

⁶ *Page* 107. "Black John," otherwise known as John IV, of the Comneni family. He reigned from 1446 to 1461, when Trebizond was taken by the Turks under Sultan Muhammad II. The following genealogical table will be found useful for the remainder of this and the following chapters.

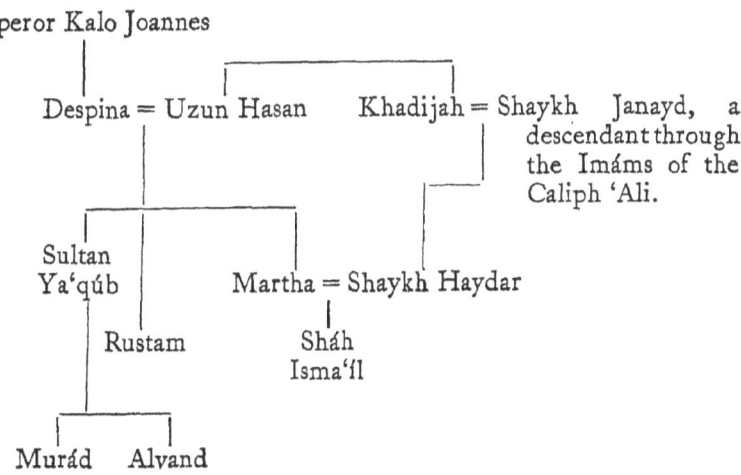

⁷ *Page* 108. Botero, II, p. 171.

⁸ *Page* 108. Italian text gives "Azembec," misprinted in the Spanish text as "Azembre." In the Hakluyt Society's volume of *Venetian Travellers* Uzun Hasan is referred to, variously, as "Ussun Cassano" by Zeno and by Contavini, but he is "Assambei" in Barbaro and in the narrative of the Anonymous Merchant.

⁹ *Page* 109. For an account of the early years of Shâh Isma'íl see E. G. Browne, *Persian Literature*, IV, pp. 47–52.

¹⁰ *Page* 110. In the text given as "Ysmael Syach Arduelino Cuseluas Nazarij." The words, a mixture of Arabic and Persian, taken literally mean: "Isma'íl, Shaykh of Ardebíl, him of the Red Bonnet of Twelve (points)."

¹¹ *Page* 110. Called "lazos" in the text. Shâh Isma'íl claimed descent from Hamzah, younger brother of the Imâm 'Ali Rizá, the two being the sons of Músá Kázim the Seventh Imám. The full number of the Imáms was twelve, the last being Muhammad the Mahdí, who had disappeared, but in the fulness of time was to return to reign in glory and justice over Persia and the rest of the Moslem world.

# NOTES

## CHAPTER II

[1] *Page* 113. Tekelli was the instigator of the Shi'ah insurrection in Asia Minor which led to some 40,000 of their sect being massacred at the hands of the Turks. The Persians called Tekelli "Sháh Quli," "the King's Servant," but the Turks knew him as "Shaytán Quli," "the Devil's Servant." It will be observed that our author makes no reference to the terrible massacre which Richard Knolles, Sir Paul Rycaut and others all speak of as having taken place in the reign of Bayazid II, though some transfer its horrors to the year 1514 after the accession of Sultan Selím the Grim (E. G. Browne, *Persian Literature*, IV, pp. 70-73). For contemporary Sultans and Sháhs see the table given above, p. 312.

[2] *Page* 113. For the convenience of his Spanish readers Don Juan, or rather the Licentiate Remón, keeps here, and generally in what comes later, to the old names of the provinces of Asia Minor, though, of course, in the 15th century all this country had long passed to a Turkish nomenclature. Cilicia (with Lycaonia and Phrygia) had become Qaramán, Bithynia was Qizil-Ahmadlú, the two Armenias (Major and Minor) occupied the ancient provinces of Cappadocia and Galatia, and Asia Minor in general was known as Anatolia, with Iconium, Qoniah, for capital.

[3] *Page* 116. 'Alá-ad-Dawlah, of the Dhú-l-Qadar family, was ruler of Kamakh, lying west of Arzinján on the left bank of the Western Euphrates. His little kingdom appears to have extended down into Lesser Armenia between the Taurus and Antitaurus ranges of Cilicia. By Don Juan he is called Aladulo; Angiolello gives his name as Alidolat; the Anonymous Merchant as Aliduli; and Knolles as Aladeules.

[4] *Page* 117. Text in error prints "su sobrino Sultan Amurath." See above, p. 115, and *cf*. Hammer-Purgstall, *Geschichte des osmanischen Reiches* (Pest, 1827), II, 395.

[5] *Page* 117. Text: "Vstaolago," and frequently mentioned in the *Venetian Travellers*: he was Sháh Isma'íl's brother-in-law, the King having given him one of his sisters in marriage; and was by birth a Turk from Anatolia. Zeno (p. 60) refers to him as Stacalu Amarbei, and Angiolello (p. 120) as Stugiali Mamet Bei, while the Anonymous Merchant has (p. 195) Ustagialu Maumut Bec, and in added error (p. 152) prints Custagialu Mahmutbec.

[6] *Page* 118. The battle-field of Chaldirán lay in the plain some distance to the west of Tabríz, and about half-way between that city and Khoy. Our author refers to the place as the "Campos Calderanos," and this same name he afterwards gives to the plains at the junction of the Cyrus and Araxes rivers in Shirván: these two different places, therefore, must be distinguished apart.

[7] *Page* 118. European Turkey was known as Roumelia, Asiatic Turkey as Anatolia, and the two comprised all the Ottoman Empire, previous to conquests in Egypt and Syria.

# DON JUAN OF PERSIA

## CHAPTER III

[1] *Page* 120. Text: " Sasso Varoglo." Knolles (p. 520) gives his name as Alis Beg. See Hammer-Purgſtall, II, p. 421.

[2] *Page* 121. Ashraf Qánsúh Ghúrí, the penultimate Burjí Mamlúk Sultan of Egypt, 1500 to 1516.

[3] *Page* 121. See Angiolello, p. 126.

[4] *Page* 122. For Janberdi Ghazzálí see Hammer-Purgſtall, II, p. 495. In the text this name is misprinted " Lamburdo Gazelle," but Knolles (p. 527) writes : " Iamburd, surnamed Gazelles, he having been a servant of the Great Kait Bey." This is " Iamburdus Gazellus " as found in Boissard (p. 148), who is doubtless his authority. There is conflict of authority as to the spelling of the name Ghazzálí, which thus written would be a nickname meaning " the Spinner," but some would write Gazálí, as though from a place called Ghazál.

[5] *Page* 122. Rhodes only fell to the Turkish arms at the end of 1522 in the reign of Sultan Sulaymán the Magnificent after the famous siege which had laſted five months.

[6] *Page* 123. Text, " Matera " : Angiolello (p. 131) has Maharra. The village lies six miles from Cairo.

[7] *Page* 124. All this was for the conqueſt of Rhodes and the expulsion of the Knights of St. John ; but this was only brought off by his son Sultan Sulaymán.

[8] *Page* 124. Chorlú, half-way between Conſtantinople and Adrianople, where in his youth Selím had fought againſt his father, the aged Sultan Bayazid II, leading to his capture and death. See above, p. 115.

[9] *Page* 124. Sultan Selím died in September 1520; Sháh Isma'íl in May 1524.

[10] *Page* 124. For Vlaman see Hammer-Purgſtall, III, p. 142, and Boissard (p. 307), who devotes a chapter to this Vlamas Begus, and writes, " qui et Zilamas et Vlammanus ab aliis dicetur," but what name Vlaman or Ulaman ſtands for in Persian it is hard to say. Boissard (p. 184) ſtates that he had beguiled a siſter of Sháh Tahmásp to marry him, and hence had been obliged to flee the country. Knolles (p. 649) speaks of him as " Vlemas, the fugitive Persian prince."

[11] *Page* 125. In the text, " por mano del Calyfa della " (*i.e.*, Babylonia), this being a translation from Boissard (p. 185), who writes of the " Calipha religionis Musulmannicæ summus Pontifex." There was, of course, no Caliph at this date in Baghdad : hence the Grand Mufti is the person indicated. If anyone was Caliph at this period it was Sultan Sulaymán himself, who had inherited the Caliphate from his father Selim the Grim, who is said to have forced the laſt puppet Caliph of the Abbasids to make over his rights to the Turkish Sultan, after Cairo (where the puppet Caliphs had resided since the fall of Baghdad in 1258) had now become the capital of a Turkish province. Boissard and other writers of the 16th century, however, frequently

# NOTES

give the title of Caliph to the Mufti or chief Mulla of a Moslem city. Thus Boissard (p. 11) refers to the "Califfe di Casbin" in the time of Sháh Ismaʻíl.

¹² *Page* 125. A conjectural emendation; the text has "Deliment." Boissard (p. 186), who refers these events to the year 1536, writes Delimannus. In Turkish *Deli* is "mad," an epithet often added to proper names, but the Oriental authorities quoted by Hammer-Purgstall do not mention him. This glorious Persian victory appears to be a patriotic invention on the part of our author. The authorities quoted in E. G. Browne (*Persian Literature*, IV, p. 87) indeed refer to a great snowstorm which overcame the Turks when invading Azerbayján at this time, but no mention is made in Boissard or elsewhere as to any great defeat of the Turkish arms.

## CHAPTER IV

¹ *Page* 128. Minadoi (p. 4) writes: "il castello Cheiseri, da Turchi nominato Chars."

² *Page* 128. This is a mistake on the part of our author. Minadoi calls Herát *Heri* and Shíráz *Siras*, and Don Juan's *Iiras* is merely a misreading for *Heri*. Muhammad Khudá-Bandah during Sháh Tahmásp's lifetime was transferred from Herát—where he left his young son ʻAbbás Mirzá, afterwards Sháh ʻAbbás, as nominal governor —going as ordered to take up his post as governor of Shíráz. See Browne, *Persian Literature*, IV, p. 100.

³ *Page* 129. It should be remembered that *Mirzá* coming after the personal name, as in this case, is equivalent to Prince; but Mirzá Salmán, with the personal name following, becomes a title for any educated person. Mirzá is the shortened form of *Amír Zádah*, "Son of the Amir."

⁴ *Page* 129. Here, for our author's Yzacau we should read, with Minadoi (p. 4), Zalchan or Zál Khán.

⁵ *Page* 130. Some words must have dropped out here in printing, for as the text stands it makes no sense; but our author is translating from Minadoi (p. 6), who writes: "Periaconcona, donna d'età maggiore di tutti questi suoi fratelli," among whom was "il fanciullo Mustaffa, uno delli otto figli sudetti"—namely, of Sháh Tahmásp. This Mustáfa is the fourth son out of the eleven children of Sháh Tahmásp, but Don Juan has not yet named him.

⁶ *Page* 130. The name misprinted here in the text is Kamal, and later the same personage is called Xamhac; see E. G. Browne, *Persian Literature*, IV, p. 101.

⁷ *Page* 131. Text: "Xamhac" (see previous note). This is the Spanish mispronunciation for the Italian Sahamal, which is Persian Shamkhál. Minadoi (p. 9), from whom our author is translating, writes of him as "Sahamal adunque Georgiano del medesimo giovane

zio," though in fact Shamkhál was only half-uncle, and goes on to relate how Zalcan or Zál Khán, his real uncle, tried unsuccessfully to save Haydar's life.

⁸ *Page* 132. Text: "el gran Calyfa." See above, ch. iii, note 11.

⁹ *Page* 132. The generally received account of the death of Isma'íl II is otherwise. According to this account, during the sacred month of the Ramazan (from dawn to dark) fast, one night the Sháh had gone out (after the hours of fasting) with a boon-companion, a pastry-cook; he had got drunk, and at dawn had returned to sleep off his potations at the pastry-cook's house. Here later in the day he was found dead, but whether death was from an overdose of opium, or by strangulation, or from poison purposely given, was a question not too closely investigated by his relations. See E. G. Browne, *Persian Literature*, IV, p. 99.

¹⁰ *Page* 132. The accompanying genealogical table will make details clear of what follows:

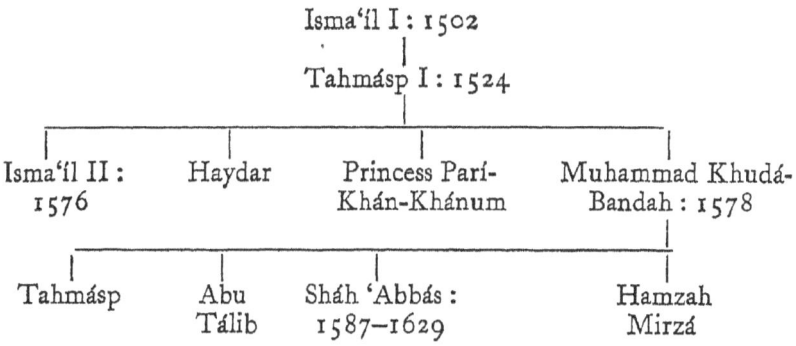

¹¹ *Page* 132. Text here and later, "Mirize Salmas," copied from Minadoi, p. 16; but see below, ch. viii, p. 168.

¹² *Page* 134. Khudá-Bandah in Persian is the equivalent of the name 'Abd-Allah in Arabic, and means "the Slave or Servant of God." Minadoi (p. 5), in mentioning that Prince Muhammad in his father's lifetime had showed no ambition for government by reason of his infirmity of sight, adds: "per la malatia de gli occhi, onde per sopra nome era detto Codabanda," as though the two Persian words had the meaning of "blind."

¹³ *Page* 135. E. G. Browne (*Persian Literature*, IV, p. 101) states that it was Khalíl Khán Afshár who put the Princess to death.

## CHAPTER V

¹ *Page* 136. In this and the following chapters the proper names of places and persons which are taken, but miscopied, from Minadoi, are rectified from Hammer-Purgstall, whose work is based

# NOTES

on Turkish sources. Thus our author's spellings "Zuyeldei" and "Quieldier" are both from Minadoi's "Chielder" or "Childir." Again, Don Juan's "Vstref Baxa" is the Turkish "Khusrev" (or "Husref") for the Persian "Khusraw": the Turks commonly pronouncing the hard *Kh* almost as an *H*, which letter the Italians and Spaniards do not pronounce at all; while the *t* has been inserted apparently for euphony. When Hammer-Purgstall fails us the name is given as in Minadoi: *e.g.*, "Bagli" for "Bally" in the Spanish text. At the end of Volume IV of Hammer-Purgstall a useful map of Georgia is given, and here made use of.

² *Page* 139. See below; the text in error has "la viuda de Desmit," as though Desmit had been the name of her husband. Minadoi (p. 34) spells the name Dedesmit. Hammer-Purgstall (IV, p. 67) has Dede Semid; and he calls the prince, her late husband, by his Persian name of Kay Khusraw. Lavarza is his name as given by Don Juan on a later page.

³ *Page* 139. Albania was then the name of the north-western part of Georgia.

⁴ *Page* 139. Here, in the text, printed as Arax, but later on always given as Eres. (The river Araxes, Remón writes of as the Aras.) Eres was a great city standing near the left bank of the lower Araxes, below the junction of the Cyrus (Kur), and close to where, below again, the river Kanak, a left bank affluent of the Araxes, flowed in. No trace of the city of Eres now appears on the map, nor is the Kanak river marked. Its ruins must lie in the neighbourhood of the marshes. See Minadoi, pp. 52 and 61; Hammer-Purgstall, IV, 70 (who refers to it as Aresh). Botero (I, p. 121) mentions Eres as one of the "keys" whereby the Turks hold Shirván; it was famous for its manufacture of stuffs in white silk, "che i mercadanti chiamano Mamodec"; for which see *Hobson Jobson* (Yule, 1903, p. 707), where *Mamoodec* is given as a corruption of *Mahmúdí*. No mention of Eres is to be found in the works of the Arab Geographers, or in Hamd-Allah Musfawfí. Sharaf-ad-Dín Yazdí describes in much detail the campaign of Timur in Georgia in 1403 and 1413, but no name like Eres occurs in his pages.

⁵ *Page* 139. See above, ch. ii, note 6.

⁶ *Page* 139. Qulzum, the Arabic form of the Greek Clysma (the name for the Red Sea), was wrongfully transferred by the Persians to the Caspian. The error arose from a confusion between "Qulzum" and "Qurzum," the name for the beaver, whose skins were so largely exported from these countries.

⁷ *Page* 140. Hammer-Purgstall (IV, p. 67) speaks of him as Gregory.

⁸ *Page* 140. See below. The name *Labassap* has been omitted here in the text: *cf.* Minadoi, p. 53.

⁹ *Page* 140. The Essekia Lake must be the present Gokchah Tengíz.

[10] *Page* 140. Tabulated thus:

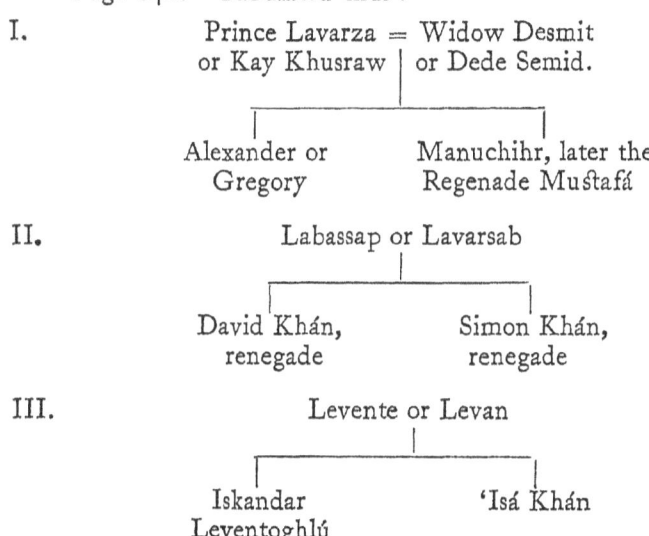

I. Prince Lavarza = Widow Desmit
or Kay Khusraw | or Dede Semid.
— Alexander or Gregory
— Manuchihr, later the Regenade Muṣtafá

II. Labassap or Lavarsab
— David Khán, renegade
— Simon Khán, renegade

III. Levente or Levan
— Iskandar Leventoghlú
— 'Isá Khán

IV. Yúsuf, son of Gori, lord of the Gori Country.
V. Prince Shamkhál and his son Imám Quli Khán.
VI. Bashachuk, lord of the city of Bashachuk on Lake Essekia.

The termination to proper names *oghlú* or *oghlí* is Turkish, and means " son of."

[11] *Page* 141. Our author makes the miṣtake of taking Minadoi's Italian word " armata " (an armada of ships) as though it were the name of a town, which he prints as Armidia. Minadoi (p. 59) writes " per la via di Colco mandando nel mar maggiore armata alla foce del fiume Facis." In our text this is given as " enbiando a Armidia al mar mayor por el lado de los Albanos." This, as noted in the Introduction (p. 12), looks as though the Licentiate diċtated his translation of Minadoi to one who wrote it down, misunderṣtanding the meaning. Further, it is evident that Remón had before him the Italian text, and not the Spanish translation by Herrera (Madrid, 1588), for he (Herrera, p. 32 *recto*) has not been guilty of this absurd miṣtranslation. But he in his turn has a small miṣtake a few lines above, where for Strabo, Book II, as given by Minadoi and correċtly reproduced by Remón, Herrera has " libro xi."

[12] *Page* 143. See Minadoi (p. 81), who has miṣtranslated the name as " Lago dei Schiavi," whereas the Turkish words " Pervana Gul " mean " Moth Lake."

[13] *Page* 144. Minadoi (p. 85), from whom the account is translated, has " hora Muṣtaffa varcato il scosceso e l'erto dei monti di

# NOTES

Tiflis," which our author gives as " passo Mustafa el rio Escoceso," taking the word " scosceso " in the Italian, which means the scarp, or foot-hill of a mountain, as though indicating the name of a stream called the Scotch River. The same mistake is repeated later on p. 149.

¹⁴ *Page* 145. See above, note 4.
¹⁵ *Page* 146. Text has " Emangulichan Aguencie."

## CHAPTER VI

¹ *Page* 147. Called "Esmeriles."
² *Page* 148. Minadoi (p. 101) has " Hossain Bey figlio del Giambulat secondo," because seven sons were born to him by his wives in a single night.
³ *Page* 149. Text: " las riberas Escocesas del mar negro." See above, ch. v, note 13.
⁴ *Page* 150. See E. G. Browne, *Persian Literature*, IV, p. 102. She was a princess of the Marʻashí Sayyids of Mazandarán and the mother of the four sons of the Sháh—namely, Hamzah, ʻAbbás (afterwards Sháh ʻAbbás) Abu Tálib and Tahmásp.
⁵ *Page* 152. Minadoi, p. 116.
⁶ *Page* 154. Hammer-Purgstall (IV, p. 77) gives his name as Imám Quli Khán (not to be confounded with the Persian commander-in-chief of the same name).

## CHAPTER VII

¹ *Page* 160. Hammer-Purgstall (IV, p. 81) describes this raid of the year 1580, but does not mention the names of the Turkish commanders. These are given from Minadoi, p. 169. What Turkish name Tal-oghli stands for is uncertain.
² *Page* 162. The ceremonies of the circumcision of Sultan Murád's eldest son, Muhammad, were celebrated for their magnificence and are fully described by Hammer-Purgstall (IV, p. 118). They took place in June and July 1582, but though Ibrahím Khán, the Persian Ambassador, is mentioned by name (IV, p. 117) nothing is said of this trick played upon him, and which, as will be duly recorded on a later page, Sháh ʻAbbás, son of Muhammad Khudá-Bandah, took occasion to avenge (see below, p. 232).

## CHAPTER VIII

¹ *Page* 168. Minadoi, pp. 209–216.
² *Page* 169. Farhád Pasha was appointed to his command in 1583 (Hammer-Purgstall, IV, p. 85), and at this time Prince ʻAbbás was only in his twelfth year.
³ *Page* 169. Ereván lies in the plain a few miles to the north of Mount Ararat. The town was founded in the reign of Sháh Ismaʻíl I

by Riván Khán, otherwise Eriván, who gave it his name, and it was then the frontier fortress of Persia against Georgia (Hammer-Purgstall, IV, p. 86). See also above, Bk. I, ch. ii, note 8.

⁴ *Page* 170. Thus Minadoi (p. 221), but Hammer-Purgstall (IV, p. 86) calls him Yúsuf Pasha. On a later page (IV, 669), however, he speaks of him as Sinán Pasha, and states that Cicala or Cigala, his father, had been a Spanish nobleman who, travelling by sea with his son, had fallen into the hands of the Turks and subsequently died in prison. His son, a boy of twelve, was afterwards brought up in Constantinople, where he embraced Islam, when doubtless he received the Moslem name Yúsuf (or Sinán). He had soon risen to high command in the Turkish service, being known by them as Chighala-zádeh (Cicala-son) Sinán Pasha. Later Don Juan generally refers to him simply as Cicala, using his father's family name.

⁵ *Page* 170. Text in error: " al Austro"; but see Minadoi, p. 219, and *ante*, Bk. II, ch. ii, note 6.

⁶ *Page* 173. See Minadoi, p. 232.

⁷ *Page* 174. Text: " fanega "; and see Minadoi, p. 236.

⁸ *Page* 175. Text: " Espaollanes."

⁹ *Page* 177. " Cumano " in Minadoi, p. 251. Hammer-Purgstall (IV, p. 94) calls him Muhammad Ghiray, surnamed Semiz " the fat."

¹⁰ *Page* 178. Hammer-Purgstall (IV, p. 95) gives his name as Islám Ghiray.

¹¹ *Page* 180. Minadoi, p. 300.

¹² *Page* 180. In the Arúnaq district; see the Translation of the *Nuzhat-al-Qulúb*, p. 82.

¹³ *Page* 182. The fall of Tabríz took place at the end of September 1585 (Hammer-Purgstall, IV, p. 171).

¹⁴ *Page* 182. Mount Valiyán.

¹⁵ *Page* 186. The tomb of Ghazán Khán, the Mongol ruler of Persia, who died in 1304. Minadoi (p. 321) gives the queer spelling " Sancazan," which our author, who must have known the place well, turns into Castilian pronunciation as " Xam Cassam."

## CHAPTER IX

¹ *Page* 189. Text: " bara."
² *Page* 189. The head keeper of the wardrobe, " Qúrchi."
³ *Page* 191. For the movable-tower (called Beffroi, or Cat-castle) see Sir C. Oman, *History of the Art of War* (1924), I, p. 134; II, p. 49.

## CHAPTER X

¹ *Page* 195. The second name as given in the text is printed " Valy Cantacaly," and on a later page " Baly," or " Bely Can." What this stands for is uncertain. Hammer-Purgstall (IV, p. 176) and Minadoi

# NOTES

(p. 336) agree that the second Turkoman chief commonly bore the name of Khalífah Khán. As will be seen below (see note 2 to ch. xi) *Baly* or *Valy* or *Galy* stands with our author for 'Alí and Khalí(fah).

² *Page* 196. Text here and later: Baly or Bely Can.

³ *Page* 199. What this name stands for is uncertain.

⁴ *Page* 200. Alamút, formerly the headquarters of the Assassins lying to the N.W. of Qazvín. Minadoi (p. 341), writing from Turkish sources, states that the young prince was sent to " la Rocca di Cahaca," which is Qahqahah, a neighbouring stronghold.

⁵ *Page* 200. " No hay peor ladrón que él de casa."

⁶ *Page* 202. Hammer-Purgstall (IV, p. 177) spells this name " Esma " (writing from Turkish authorities), and possibly this may be a corruption of the common name " Ismet." Esma Khán was also a woman's name, having been borne by the sister of Sultán Murád, who married her to Sokolli Pasha the Grand Vizier (Hammer-Purgstall, III, p. 392).

## CHAPTER XI

¹ *Page* 204. Text: " Cudy de Lac, que es como si dixeramos en Español Cudi el barbero." See E. G. Browne, *Persian Literature*, IV, p. 101. Minadoi (p. 364) calls him " un suo custode Eunucho." In Hammer-Purgstall (IV, p. 177), writing from Turkish sources, his name is given as Júdí, which Sir John Malcolm (*History of Persia*, II, p. 521, 4to, 1815) has misread as Hoodee.

² *Page* 206. The text prints " Gali Can," and later " Valichan Can," a name which tentatively may be given as 'Alí Khán. See above, ch. x, note 1.

³ *Page* 207.
" No se tiene por buen moro,
Quien no le daba lanzada."

In the text only the first line is cited and with " tenia " for " tiene."

⁴ *Page* 209. Prince 'Abbás was somewhat older than this in 1588, having been born in January 1571 or perhaps 1572. See E. G. Browne, *Literary History*, IV, p. 103.

⁵ *Page* 211. The abdication took place in 1587, and afterwards the old king lived peacefully in retirement till his death in 1596. (E. G. Browne, *Literary History*, IV, p. 102.)

## CHAPTER XII

¹ *Page* 212. Hammer-Purgstall (IV, p. 181) says the chief of the mission was named Mahdí Qulí Khán Chaushlí.

² *Page* 213. As to the title Khán preceding the personal name in this case, and again (p. 214) in the name of the King of Gílán (Khán Ahmad), see Bk. I, ch. ii, note 12. Of this well-timed treaty (March 1590), which enabled Sháh 'Abbás to settle the internal affairs of his

kingdom, details are given by Hammer-Purgstall (IV, p. 183). Don Juan discreetly omits one clause of the treaty which must have harassed Shi'ah religious susceptibilities. Sháh Isma'íl I, in establishing the new form of Shi'ah faith, had made it obligatory that every Persian in Mosque and market-place should publicly curse the first three Caliphs of the Sunnis (Abu Bakr, Omar and Othman), who, the Shi'ahs held, had unlawfully after the Prophet's death kept 'Ali from becoming Caliph. In deference now to Sunni susceptibilities Sháh 'Abbás promised that this cursing of the Orthodox (Sunni) Caliphs should cease: and publicly this must have been the case, till some twelve years later, in 1602, when the treaty was practically abrogated by the retaking of Tabríz from the Ottomans, when doubtless the cursing began afresh.

³ *Page* 216. It is not very clear who this Prince Isma'íl was. Perhaps for "niece" we should read "grand-niece," in which case her father was Isma'íl Mirzá Sultán (see above, p. 202), eldest son of the late Prince Hamzah. Sir John Malcolm, however (I, pp. 521 and 522), makes mention of a brother of Hamzah Mirzá, of the name of Isma'íl.

⁴ *Page* 217. "Beng" is Indian hemp (*Cannabis Indica*), an intoxicant, the use of which pious Moslems regard as unlawful. *Bengi* is the adjective therefrom, implying one under its evil effects.

⁵ *Page* 218. The same Turk tribe from which the late royal house of Persia is descended.

⁶ *Page* 224. See Malcolm, *History*, I, p. 528.

⁷ *Page* 227. What this river, marking the frontier, is, it is difficult to determine.

## BOOK III
### CHAPTER I

¹ *Page* 232. See above, p. 161. It is noteworthy that Hammer-Purgstall makes no mention of the Turkish ambassador Muhammad Aga the Grand Chaush, but he, of course, wrote from Turkish authorities, who discreetly might well prefer to pass the matter over in silence.

² *Page* 233. Robert, commonly known as Count Sherley (1581–1628). He remained in Persia till 1608, fairly well treated by Sháh 'Abbás, who then despatched him as his ambassador to Europe, once more eager to try and stir up the Princes of Christendom against the Turk. Count Sherley travelled by Cracow to Prague (1609), and thence through Florence to Rome, where the Pope Paul V received him. Then going from Genoa by sea to Barcelona he reached Madrid in 1610, and in August 1611 finally got back to England and was duly received in audience by James I. After eighteen months at home Sir Robert once more set out for Persia, but this time by the long sea route round the Cape of Good Hope, leaving Dover in January 1612. Being unable to land in the Persian Gulf, he proceeded to India, and

# NOTES

only left Surat in September 1614. He reached Isfahán in June 1615, and in October of the same year was again sent back by Sháh 'Abbás as his ambassador to the Christian Powers. On reaching Goa, he found that he had missed the annual sailing and was not able to set out for Lisbon till the following year. He at last reached Spain in 1617, and remained there for the next five years. In 1622 he left Spain and via Rome came to England, where he remained from January 1623 to March 1627, when for the third and last time he went out to Persia. Again he went round the Cape, reaching the Persian Gulf in November, and arrived at Isfahán in April 1628, where he saw the Sháh, but was none too favourably received. Three months later at Qazvín he died very suddenly, at the age of 47, after a life that reads like a romance. See *The Sherley Brothers*.

[3] *Page 233.* Purchas, *Pilgrims*, VIII, pp. 438 and 443, where the name of the Franciscan is given as Alfonso Cordero, and the Dominican as Nicolão Di-Meto.

[4] *Page 234.* Text reads " Uzen Ali Bech " : which name Antonio de Gouvea (*Relation des guerres de Cha Abbas*, 1646, p. 105) writes Ussem Alibeg. Pietro Duodo, however (Schéfer, pp. vi and 277), spells the name Hassan Halevech; and Purchas (VIII, p. 439) has Assan Chan. His name none the less was certainly Husayn, not Hasan, for Don Juan always spells the first with O or U in the first vowel, while Hasan has *A*.

[5] *Page 235.* See above, Bk. II, ch. v, note 6.

[6] *Page 235.* Pietro Duodo (Schéfer, p. 277) names the port of embarkation in Gílán Ruisar. The following description of the Caspian Sea is taken from Botero, I, p. 121. It was evidently all new travelling to Don Juan.

[7] *Page 236.* Text: " perros marinos."

[8] *Page 237.* Text: " pañetes."

[9] *Page 238.* Botero, I, p. 121.

[10] *Page 238.* The Arabian geographers call the Volga Itil. Later our author writes Eder as a rule.

[11] *Page 239.* Text: " El navío ajorcó," tentative translation, for the verb " ajorcar " does not appear in the Academy Dictionary.

[12] *Page 239.* Text: " Vezino," which the Dictionary of the Academy explains as a person " que tiene casa y hogar en un pueblo." See above, Bk I, ch. ii, note 5. Don Juan's views as to the population of Russian towns are, of course, founded on what he thought a likely computation, and the figures need not be taken seriously.

## CHAPTER II

[1] *Page 241.* Text: " Ordes." See Botero, II, p. 117.

[2] *Page 242.* The Nogay Tartars were one of the Five Hordes (Botero, II, p. 117).

# DON JUAN OF PERSIA

[3] *Page* 242. Text: "piexas de gerga breadas."
[4] *Page* 242. Text: "al modo de tornos."
[5] *Page* 242. The *Real* in 1600 was worth about sevenpence.
[6] *Page* 245. Botero, I, p. 97.
[7] *Page* 245. The Volga and the Western Dvina (flowing to the Baltic) take their rise in the Valdai hills, and not in any lake. Botero, who apparently is the first to give the name Voluppo, probably made this confusion, having misread the name from some map he had before him.
[8] *Page* 246. Text: "Nechena" or "Nochena." Purchas (*Pilgrims*, VIII, p. 442) writes Negson. Pietro Duodo (Schéfer, p. 277) gives Nisnogorod. Novgorod has the meaning of "New Town."
[9] *Page* 247. Text: "los Precopenses"—that is, the Perekop Tartars of the Crimea, who, Botero asserts (II, pp. 81 and 117), took their name from the title of their Prince. This, however, is a mistake: *Perekop* in Russian means "a cross-ditch," and is properly both the name of the isthmus joining the Crimea to the mainland, and the name of the little town at this place which stood on the *vallum* defending the isthmus.
[10] *Page* 249. In text given under the strange form of "Valla de Amor."
[11] *Page* 250. Antonius Possevinus, surnamed the Elder: *Moscovia, et alia opera de statu hujus seculi* : Cologne, 1587.

## CHAPTER III

[1] *Page* 252. Tsar Boris Godunof (1598–1605). He had murdered Tsar Feodor I and usurped his throne.
[2] *Page* 254. W. Parry, who acted as secretary to Sir Anthony Sherley, and wrote an account of their journey through Russia (Purchas, *Pilgrims*, VIII, p. 446), describing Moscow, says that he saw the Great Bell carried in procession from the Kremlin to a shrine some thirty miles outside the town. It weighed, he states, 20 tons, and was drawn along the whole way on a sledge, to which 3,500 men were harnessed, hauling on six great cables "after the manner of our Westerne Bargemen." So heavy was the weight that the friction of the moving sleigh set fire to the baulks of timber which there paved the streets of Moscow. Subsequently the Bell was hung in the Tower of Ivan the Great in the Kremlin, where Adam Olearius (*Relation du Voyage*, 4to, Paris, 1666, I, p. 107), the Secretary of the Dutch Embassy, saw it in 1636. He writes that he heard it had been cast in the reign of Tsar Boris Godunof, and it weighed 336 quintals according to his reckoning. In 1654, this bell having fallen and broken, the metal was recast; and the same disaster happening in 1733, again the bell was recast. This third and last bell—the Tsar Kolokol or "King Bell"—late in the 18th century became cracked, and it now

# NOTES

stands dumb at the bottom of the Ivan Tower, with a great piece fallen out of its rim. But some of its metal undoubtedly is that of the Great Bell seen by Don Juan in 1599.

³ *Page* 257. Text: " dos arrobas."

⁴ *Page* 257. Text: " una azumbre de vino." In the early 17th century the Ducat and the Escudo (Crown), almost its equivalent, were worth rather more than six shillings; we may perhaps count three to the £ sterling. Hence about £1,000 of that time, but ten times as much in modern value.

⁵ *Page* 258. W. Parry (Purchas, *Pilgrims*, VIII, pp. 443 and 449) has a different story to tell of the Dominican Friar and his fate. According to Parry, the Franciscan and the Dominican fell out while voyaging up the Volga in the galleys, and before reaching Nizhni Novgorod the Franciscan complained to Sherley of his colleague, saying " that Friar Nicolão had spent his life most lewdly in the Indies," and further had embezzled to his own use the money of his superiors which had been confided to him. On which charge Sherley imprisoned the Dominican on board his galley, and kept him in durance the whole time the party stayed awaiting orders at Nizhni. On arriving at Moscow Sherley and his colleague the Persian ambassador quarrelled, and on the representation of the latter Tsar Boris refused to allow the Englishman the rank of Envoy Plenipotentiary of the Sháh travelling to Europe. Further he ordered the Friar to be set at liberty, who finding Sherley was out of favour at court told lies, in his disfavour, to the Tsar's Lord Chancellor. At a public enquiry into the case Sir Anthony, " being inflamed with choler," knocked the Friar down, a vindication of his character and a line of conduct which evidently pleased the Tsar, for afterwards Sherley was " used the better " and ultimately dismissed from Moscow with honour. According to Parry's account the Dominican was simply left behind in Moscow when the others departed. Later, as they were on the point of taking ship at Archangel, news came in that the Lord Chancellor had finally recognized the Friar to be a swindler, had ordered him to be stripped of his ill-gotten moneys, " leaving him not so much as his Friar's Weede, and whether hee caused his throat to bee cut, it was uncertaine, but not unlike."

⁶ *Page* 258. Easter 1600. O.S., March 23.

⁷ *Page* 258. The river on which Pereyaslav stands is the Nerl, which flows directly into the Volga.

⁸ *Page* 259. Text: " Barem"; elsewhere " Batem." Don Juan is apparently unaware that this stream up which he travelled from Yaroslav to Rybinsk is the Volga. From Rybinsk they must have taken a Volga affluent, and then by a short portage have reached the head waters of the Northern Dvina, down which (also spoken of as the Barem or Batem) he proceeded to Totma. Brusensk, the next stage, is on an affluent of the Dvina, called the Sukhona. Ambassador

# DON JUAN OF PERSIA

Duodo, by report, says that they went from Moscow "a Suchno, dove di novo imbarcati nella Dvina per Colmogvo (Kholmagory) pervennero a S. Nicolas" (Schéfer, p. 277).

⁹ *Page* 260. Text: " Corer Arcancher." The first word is a mistake for "Gorod," meaning "town." Botero (I, p. 99) calls Archangel San Nicolò, as also Duodo, by report (Schéfer, p. 277).

## CHAPTER IV

¹ *Page* 264. Text: "Caballos marinos," doubtless dolphins.

² *Page* 265. This must be the estuary of the Elbe and the town mentioned below, Stode or Stade lying on its left bank some 25 miles to the west of Hamburg. Here W. Parry disembarked; see Purchas, *Pilgrims*, VIII, p. 449; and above, Introduction, note 4.

³ *Page* 265. This bird's-eye view of Germany is derived from Botero (I, pp. 69–71). Bucavia was the eastern part of Hesse, of which the chief town was Fulda.

⁴ *Page* 266. John XIII, Duke of Oldenburg, 1577–1609, or his deputy.

⁵ *Page* 266. This is the last time Don Juan mentions the Friar, but he apparently accompanied the Embassy at least as far as Bohemia, for Pietro Duodo (Schéfer, p. 278) writes of "un certo frate scalzo Portuguese" who visited the Papal Nuncio in Prague.

⁶ *Page* 268. Text: "el riñon de Alemania"; Botero, I, p. 71: "il grasso di Germanis." Georgius Agricola, a writer on scientific subjects, died in 1555.

⁷ *Page* 268. These places are given out of order, coming from Embden. Alsfeld is south of Kassel, and Weimar a considerable distance to the west, and south of Halle. Both must have been visited after leaving Kassel, not before. What follows is taken from Botero.

⁸ *Page* 268. Lewis II, Landgrave of Hesse-Kassel, 1596–1626.

⁹ *Page* 270. This may be either Eisleben, 20 miles west, or Aschersleben, 30 miles to the north-west, of Halle; and it is the only name on the list which can be recognized: the others seem beyond identification in the forms printed, and none of these names are mentioned by Botero.

¹⁰ *Page* 270. Misnia is the district round Leipzig. See Botero, I, p. 72, from whom the details are derived of towns enumerated in Saxony.

¹¹ *Page* 270. Possibly Belzig, 45 miles S.W. of Berlin, but not lying on the direct route from Kassel to Leipzig.

¹² *Page* 271. The readings of both names are tentative, being uncertain. The first name as printed in the text is "Menil Warat," of which the prior half seems probably to be a misprint for Ilmenau, in Saxe-Weimar. Warat (or Warta in O.H.G.) is common in place-names, meaning a Watch-tower, or Out-look. It is best known

# NOTES

as occurring in the name of the celebrated Wartburg at Eisenach. As regards the name of the second city, Leipzig, it is true, has already been mentioned, but in quotation from Botero. In the text the name of the town is given as "Syplilit," which can hardly be taken as a misprint for the name Dresden, then, as now, the capital of Saxony. At Leipzig (a name which was spelt variously in the 16th and 17th centuries) the Elector of Saxony had a palace called the Pleissenburg (now the Rathaus), where at times he was in residence. It seems probable that Don Juan, who was only there for a single night, mistook this minor palace in Leipzig for the chief electoral palace of the capital city of Dresden.

[13] *Page* 271. Christian II, 1591–1611 Elector of Saxony, born 1583.

[14] *Page* 271. It seems probable that in the text, where we find the name given as "Anyz Vverc" or "Anyzvverch," the second letter (n) is misprinted for u, and that this curious mis-spelling is meant for Aussig on the Upper Elbe, where the river breaks through the mountain of Bohemia.

## CHAPTER V

[1] *Page* 272. Neither in the recently compiled Ordnance Map of Bohemia, nor in Blaeu's great Atlas (Amsterdam, 1662), are any places with names like these to be found between Aussig and Trinka. They must have been copied here from Don Juan's Persian diary, and represent the names of the villages passed through by the travellers, and written down as our author heard them.

[2] *Page* 272. Trinka is here given as 3, but later as 5 leagues from Prague; and in fact, Trinka lies about 9 leagues north of Prague on the Moldau river.

[3] *Page* 272. What follows describing Germany is from Botero, I, pp. 60–65, and II, p. 93.

[4] *Page* 275. Duodo reports that the ambassador halted, for his official entry, "alla Stella, discosto da due miglia Italiani di quà (Praga)," and the *Fugger Letters* mention "the royal pavilion on the Stern," otherwise called the Sternschloss. Our ambassador's entry into Prague took place on the 11th of October according to the *Fugger Letter* of next day's date. There were, says the writer, some thirty members in the Persian Embassy. They were given lodging in "the Wild Man Inn" on the Klein-Seite in Prague. The *Fugger Letters* here make the mistake of reporting that the Embassy had travelled from Persia to Prague via India and the Cape. Sir Anthony Sherley at the head of the Embassy is described as "an Englishman, and he is short and dressed in English fashion." Husayn 'Ali Beg, his Persian colleague, was "an elderly grey-haired man, a princely official of the King of Persia, attired in Turkish dress, as are likewise his servants." See the *Fugger News-Letters*, p. 230, and for Pietro Duodo, Schéfer, p. 277.

[5] *Page* 275. The *escudo*, as already said, was at the rate of about three to the £ sterling. The reception took place on the 7th of November, says Duodo.
[6] *Page* 276. Rudolf II (1576–1612), grandson of Ferdinand I, Charles V's brother. His sister was the mother of Philip III of Spain.
[7] *Page* 277. For a description of Prague at this time see Botero, I, p. 76.
[8] *Page* 277. £1,333 and £66 respectively.

## CHAPTER VI

[1] *Page* 279. All the places in the above list (the names are wondrously mis-spelt in the Spanish text) may be identified on the map, as also those that follow later as far as Augsburg. Otto Henry, the Pfalzgraf of Sulzbach, reigned from 1569 to 1604. The little city is celebrated for its printing-press.
[2] *Page* 280. This Münchem (Munich) here must be in error: probably a gloss got in from the margin, having been added lower down to explain Minicem, as Don Juan writes the name München for Münich.
[3] *Page* 280. Duke William II, surnamed Der Fromme, reigned from 1579 to 1598, when he abdicated in favour of his son Maximilian, the first Elector of Bavaria. William II survived till 1626. The text runs: " Esta ciudad es Ducado de por si, y el Duque y señor della se llama Du-Capi ": evidently meant for " Duca Pio."
[4] *Page* 281. Vincenzo I, Duke of Mantua, 1587 to 1612.
[5] *Page* 281. What town is intended it is difficult to say. The place where, before passing up the river Adige to Verona, they were most likely to have rested for the night, presumably was Ostiglia.
[6] *Page* 281. Called Michael Angelo Cerray of Aleppo, according to C. Schéfer, *Introduction*, p. viii.
[7] *Page* 282. Ferdinand I, Grand Duke of Tuscany, 1587–1609: his wife was Christina, daughter of Charles II, Duke of Lorraine, and through her mother a grand-daughter of Queen Catherine de Medici.
[8] *Page* 283. Hippolito Aldobrandini, Pope Clement VIII, 1592–1604.
[9] *Page* 284. See *The Three Sherley Brothers*, p. 32, where a letter is given, dated the 30th April 1601, from the celebrated Jesuit, Robert Parsons, who had escaped from England after the execution of Campion, and was now Rector of the English College in Rome. The letter is addressed to a friend in England, and according to Parsons Sherley asserted that the boxes on investigation by him were found to be charged with articles for presentation of very little value; indeed, instead of being worth 300,000 crowns as invoiced, 3,000 was their limit. He had therefore sent them all back to Persia as being entirely unsuitable for presentation to the European potentates by an ambassador, a personage of his degree.

# NOTES

¹⁰ *Page* 286. About £666.

¹¹ *Page* 286. Sir Anthony Sherley here disappears from Don Juan's narrative. He and the Persian ambassador had never agreed, and in the matter of the presents there clearly had been fraud on Sir Anthony's part. After leaving Rome in June, Sherley, taking no thought of his Embassy, passed back, travelling very slowly, to Venice, which he only reached in March of the following year (1602), from which place he memorialized Philip III of Spain. According to Father Parsons, since his sojourn in Prague Sir Anthony had become a member of the Church of Rome; this naturally was no recommendation in the eyes of Queen Elizabeth, and his letters to Sir Robert Cecil were now ignored. In the spring of 1605 he appeared once more in Prague and Rudolf II was persuaded to despatch him on a mission to Morocco. This proved a complete failure, and he shipped thence to Lisbon. In 1607 we find him in Naples, becoming a member of the Council of State; in 1610 he was back in Madrid, where his brother Robert found him (see above, Book III, chap. i., note 2) and supplied his wants with assistance of money. From this time onwards for nearly a quarter of a century what little is known of his movements is unimportant; he was a pensioner of Spain, and almost a beggar. He lived for the most part in Madrid, sinking into complete obscurity, and died there apparently in 1635. See *The Sherley Brothers*.

¹² *Page* 286. The Ambassador had left Rome, according to the *Fugger Letter* written on the 9th June, on the preceding Wednesday, after the Pope had presented him with 3,000 crowns (say £1,000: a third more than what Don Juan reports). The three converts were the barber, the cook and a certain private secretary; not, however, one of the four official Secretaries of Embassy (see Introduction, p. 3), three of whom later joined the Roman Communion in Spain. Of the converts we learn: "the Pope is to give them ten crowns monthly, and he is in hopes that the King of Persia may likewise abandon the Mussulman Faith." See the *Fugger News-Letters*, p. 243.

## CHAPTER VII

¹ *Page* 289. Philip III had succeeded his father in 1598 at the age of twenty. He was completely dominated by the Duke of Lerma, who in 1600 persuaded the king to leave Madrid and establish his court at Valladolid.

² *Page* 293. About £30; and the sums mentioned in the following paragraph may be taken as equivalent to £3,333 and £333 respectively.

³ *Page* 294. That is *Fons Stillans* (see R. Ford, *Spain*, 3rd Edition, 1855, p. 770). The Image was supposed to date from the times of the Gothic kings, and to have been miraculously hidden away during the Moslem dominion. The present church, called Santa Maria del Salto, built to commemorate the miraculous escape from death of a

Jewish maiden who had embraced Christianity, and who died in 1237, only dates from 1613.

⁴ *Page* 294. The Alcázar, famous through *Gil Blas*, Book IX, chap. iv., was almost completely burnt down in 1862, and now has been rebuilt.

⁵ *Page* 294. The Aqueduct dating from the reign of Augustus and restored under Trajan.

⁶ *Page* 295. The Mint remained here, and coined for all Spain till the year 1730, when the works were transferred to Madrid.

⁷ *Page* 297. This Machine, "el artificio" as Don Juan calls it, was constructed by Juanelo Turriano, a native of Cremona, in 1565 for Charles V. It could force up 600,000 buckets of water daily from the river-bed to the city on the height above, but before long fell into disrepair. See Ford, *Spain* (1855), p. 784.

⁸ *Page* 298. Aldea Gallega was due east of Lisbon, on the further side of the Tagus estuary.

## CHAPTER VIII

¹ *Page* 302. Queen Margaret, King Philip III's second cousin, was the daughter of Charles, Duke of Styria, younger son of the Emperor Ferdinand I, Charles V's brother.

² *Page* 308. About £400.

# INDEX

AB-I-AMU (Oxus), 314
Aba or Abu, mountain, 139
Abaqa Khan, 318
'Abbas, Prince, afterwards Shah (Xa Bas), 2, 22-26, 133, 166-168, 207-227, 231-234, 310-329
'Abd-Allah, son of Mu'aviyah, 89
'Abd-Allah Khan the Uzbek (Abdalacan), 220-223
'Abd-al-Malik, Caliph (Abduc Melic), 89
'Abd-al-Mumin the Uzbek, 223
'Abd-ar-Rahman, Ibn Marjan (Ebene Marchen), 106, 306
Abdias, Bishop, 70, 315
Abiano (Oxus), 44
Abu Bakr, Caliph (Abubaxic, Bubac), 105
Abu Luluah, 316
Abu Muslim, Sulayman (Abu Moslum, Amyr Sulayman, Luleimin, Amirmo Selemin, Amurmoselemin), 90, 317
Abu Talib, Prince (Abutolef Mirza, Butaleph), 202, 211
Achi-chay river, 186
Acraganes, 60
Adaliyah, 98
Adarman (Aden Manes), 79
'Adil-Ghiray, Prince (Abdilguiray), 141, 149, 151-153
Afshar Clan (Afxar), 45
Aga, meaning a rich husbandman, 180
Agathias, 14, 72, 316
Agazago, 84
Agricola, Georgius (Icorgio Agricola), 268, 334

Ahmad Pasha, Hajji Begogli (Amet Baxa Agy Beolly), 157
Ahmad, Prince, son of Sultan Bayazid II (Acomath, Sultan a Comet), 113
Aix-la-Chapelle (Aquisgrano), 124
Akcheh Qal'asi (Agiacalasi), 169
Akhalkelek (Arguelec), 174
*Akhtah*, 48
Akhtah Husayn (Acta Osein), 129
'Ala-ad-Dawlah (Aladulo), 116, 119, 120, 321
Alamut, Castle (Halamud, Alamud Calassi), 25, 200, 329
Albania of Georgia, 139, 325
Alburquerque, Duke of, 288
Alcazar of Segovia, 294
Alcazar of Toledo, 297
Aldea Gallega, 298, 338
'Alem, Prince (Sultan Alen), 115
Aleppo, battle, 122
Alessandri, 313
Alexander the Great of Macedon, 66
Alexander the Great of Georgia. *See* Iskandar
Alexander, or Gregory of Georgia, 149, 154, 325
Alfaqui or Priest, 52
Alfaqui Amyr, 8, 297, 298
'Ali Beg, Prince of Astarabad, 219
'Ali, Caliph, 88, 105, 316
'Ali, House of, 91
'Ali Khan the Turkoman, son of Muhammad Khan (Gali Can, Vali Chan Can), 206, 211, 329
'Ali Paghman the Turkoman, 200
'Ali Pasha, Khadim: Vizier, 114

339

# DON JUAN OF PERSIA

'Ali Pasha of Greece, 172
'Ali Quli Beg, or Don Philip of Persia (Ali Guly Bech), 3, 9, 226, 292, 299, 302, 336, 337
'Ali Quli Khan, Shamlu (Aliculichan Xamlu), 155-159, 166, 167, 175, 202, 205, 207, 220
Allah Verdi Khan (Alahuerdi Can), 217
Alp Arslan, or Alphagalo, 94, 318
Alqas Mirza (Elias), 124
Alsace (Alsacia), 273
Alsfeld (Alfel) 268, 334
Altun Qal'ah, 140, 154, 175
Alvand (Levente), Prince, 110-112
Amandus of Zieriksee, 104, 319
Amid, or Qara Amid, or Diyar Bakr, 44, 137
Amin, Caliph, 92, 93, 317
Amir Khan (Emircan), 132, 165, 175, 176, 183, 194
Amul, 313
Amurath, or Murad, 318. *See* Murad
Amyr the Alfaqui, 8, 297, 298
Anacyndaxaris, 60
Anatolia, 321
Angiolello, 313
Angora (Ancyra), 114
Anonymous Merchant, 313
Antoninus, Archbishop of Florence, 81
Anyz-Werc, 335
Apianus (Bienewitz), 38, 313
Aq Qoyunlu, 319
Aqueduct of Segovia, 294, 338
Aranjuez, 296
Aras Khan (Areschan), 147, 150
Araxene Lands (Campos Calderanos), 139, 170
Araxes, Aras river, 139
Arbaces, 63
Arcadius, Emperor, 76
Archangel (Corer Arcancher), 260, 334

Ardahan (Ardachan), 175
Ardashir I, Babegan (Artaxerxes), 72
Ardashir II, 75
Ardebil Mosque and Sanctuary (Ardevil, Arduel), 206, 315
Ardistan (Argistam), 40
Arfaxat, 70
Arkikelek (Arquiquelich), 142
*Arroba*, 333
Arses, 66
Artabanus, the Parthian, 73, 315
Artabanus III (Xerxes), 70, 315
Artaxerxes I, II, and III, 66; *and see* Ardashir, 68
Artillery, Hessian, 269
Artillery, Persian, 98
Artillery, Turkish, 23
Arunaq, 328
Ascatades, 59
Aschalius, 59
Aschersleben, 334
Asia Minor, provinces of, 321
Aslaben, 270
Assayshlu clan, 46
Astarabad (Estarabat), 41, 219
Astrakhan (Hastarcan), 238, 239
Augsburg (Agusta), 279, 280
Augustus, Emperor, 67, 280
Aurich (Haucec), 267
Aussig (Anyz Werch), 271, 272, 335
Authorities used by Remon, 311
Avalos, Don Juan de, 298
Avignon, 287
Ayishah (Aysa), 105
A'zam Beg Colgachi (Azem Bec), 213
Azerbayjan (Haderbaichan, Media Grande), 42
Azumbre, 333

Baario, 88
Babek (Paveco), 72
Badajoz, 298

# INDEX

Baghdad (Baldac, Bagdat, Baldat), 43, 92, 125, 126
Baglī Pasha (Bally Baxa), 173
Bahram Chubin, or Varahran, 80
Bahram, Prince, son of Shah Ismaʿil (Brechamo Mirza), 124
Bahram Mirza, son of Shah Tahmasp (Bahiram), 129
Bahram Pasha (Beyran Baxa), 138, 146
Balas, or Palash, 76
Balaus, 58
Bâle (Basilea), 274
Balsaim, 295
Band-i-Amir (Bendeamir), 38
Barachlu clan, 46
Barardach, 70
Barasichus, 71
Barbadillo, Salas, 10, 310
Barbaro, Josaphat, 38, 98, 313
Barcelona, 287
Barem, or Batem (Volga and Dvina), 4, 259, 260, 333
Barnares, 85
Basasiri, 318
Bashachuk, Prince (Bassa Quiuch), 140
Bashachuk, town, 141
*Bashi*, 47
Bayat clan, 45, 198
Bayazid I, Sultan (Bayazeto), 95, 96
Bayazid II, 19, 103-113, 115, 319
Bayburtlu clan, 46
Baysunghur (Bayzangures), 96
Bedel Sultan, Bayat, 198
Beffroi, or movable tower, 328
Begum, wife of Shah Muḥammad Khuda Bandah, 150-153, 327
Belcepho, 94, 318
Belesys (Beloco), 63
Bell, great, at Moscow, 254, 332
Belochus II (Beloco), 60
Belochus, *Annals*, 58, 311, 315
Belus, or Beleus (Belo), 58

Belzig (Beltcy), 270, 334
Beng, or Indian hemp, 330
Bengi Melik (Bengui Melic), 217-219
Beraun (Viron), 278
Berexen, 272
Biṣtam (Vaṣtan), 166
Black Foreſt, 273
Boissard, J. J., 19, 312
Boris Godunof, Tsar of Moscow, 3, 252-257, 332, 333
Boriſthenes, or Bug river, 252, 259
Boschalu clan, 46
Botero, Giovanni, 12, 36, 309, 311
Brasier, sacred Persian, 78
Breydenbach, 99, 319
Brichjesus (Barasichius), 315
Browne, E. G., *Persian Literature*, 310
Brus, mountain, 140
Brusa (Bursa), 114
Brusensk (Brusinisca), 260
Bucavia, 265, 334
Bunyad Beg (Boniat, Benyat), later Don Diego of Persia, 10, 304, 306, 307
Buora, 88

Cairo, 123, 179
Calderan plains or meadows (Campos Calderanos), 20, 118, 139, 170, 321
Caliph for Grand Mufti, 322
Cambaya, 44
Cambyses, 66
Candelor, 95
Cannon, great Persian, 188-189
Cannon, great Russian, 257
Cap or Turban of twelve colours, 18, 49, 110
Caraman, 95
Caravajal, Don Alvaro de, Court Chaplain, 10, 300, 302, 307
Casa del Campo, 296
Caspian Sea (Mar de Bacu), 235

# DON JUAN OF PERSIA

Cat-Castle, 328
Caviare, 241
Cedrenus, 14
*Celemin*, or peck, 314
Cerray, Michael Angelo, of Aleppo, 336
Chaldiran battle, 20, 118
Chamish Qazaqlu clan (Chamizcazaclu), 46
Chares of Lindus, 87
Charles IV, Emperor, 274
Charles V, Emperor, 103, 296, 338
*Charuk*, a kind of sandal, 214
*Chaudar*, Persian wheat, 267
Chauslu clan, 46
Chavat (Gravat, Grauat), 137
Cheboksary (Chapuazar), 245
Cherny-Yar (Iamar), 243
Chersi-Oghlu (Chersiogoli), 121
Chessel (Quesez), 236
Childir (Zuyeldei, Quieldier), 136
Chingiz-Khan (Chinguis), 220
Chisir river, 227
Chorlu, 124, 322
Chosroes I, Anushirvan, 78
Chosroes II, Parviz, 82-84
Christian II of Saxony, 5, 335
Christina, Duchess of Tuscany, 336
Cidi Daud, 88
Cidi Noccio, 88
Cidi Tenuin, 88
Cigala Pasha (Ciqala, Chighala-Zadah), 170, 181-186, 201, 328
Clavel, Nicolas, 306
Clavijo, Embassy of, 96, 318
Clement VIII, Pope, 7, 284-287, 336
Cleves (Clevia), 274
Clysma, 325
Colchis (Colquides), 177
Cologne (Colonia), 272
Colossus of Rhodes, 87
*Conejos*, rabbits or hares, 50, 314
Constance, Lake, 273

Constantine V, Emperor, 90
Constantinople, 115
Contarini, 313
Conversions to Christianity, 7, 9, 287, 299, 337
Coran, 88, 317
Cordero, Alfonso, Franciscan Friar, 331. *See* Friar
Coro (Car), 236
Corsairs, English, 263
Cortes, N. Alonso, 310
Cory, I. P., 315
Cossi Boyezlu clan, 46
Cotarelo, Señor Emilio, 10, 310
Crassus, 142
Crefeld (Calcaria), 274
Crimea, Tartars of the, 332
Cross, True, taken by Persians, 83
Cross, sign adopted by Turks, 81
Crusaders, afterwards Druses, 179
Crusaders in Armenia, 143
Cudy de Lac, 329
Cuiniorilu clan, 46
Curthasi Amanzir, 199
Cuspinianus, J., 318
Cyrus, 66
Cyrus, river of Georgia, 139, 313
Cyrus, river of Fars, 313

Dagan, king of the Arabs, 83, 316
*Dallak*, barber, 204
Damascus, 124
Damghan (Tangan), 166
Danube, 273
Daras, 78
Darius I, II, and III, 66
*Daroghah*, 46
Dastagird, 316
David Khan (Daudchan), 140, 155, 173, 174
*Dawlat Khanah*, 47
Deli Muhammad (Deliment), 125
Dengiz Beg, 310
Derbend, or Dimir Qapi (Derbent, Demycarpi, Demyrcarpi), 22, 148

# INDEX

Dercylus, 60
Dervish Pasha (Druis Baxa), 138, 146
Desmit, Princess (Dedesmit, Dedesemid), 139-140, 149, 325
Despina, Princess (Espina), 17, 107
Devlahar Khan, 199
Dhu-l-Qadar, 321
Dhu-l-Qadarlu clan (Dulgadarlu), 46
Diamond at Meshed, 220
Diego of Persia, Don, 10, 304, 306, 307
Di-Meto, Nicolão, Dominican Friar (De Molo), 258, 331, 333
Diyar Bakr, or Qara Amid (Diarbech), 44, 137
Dog-fish, 236
Dolphins, 334
Dominican Friar, 331, 333
Donauwört (Donauwireth), 280
Dresden, 335
Druses of Palestine, 179
Ducat, or Escudo (Crown-piece), 333
Duisburg, 274
Du Mans, Father, 309
Duodo, Pietro, 310
Duren (Dura), 274
Dvina, northern, 259, 260, 333
Dvina, western, 332

Edel, Eder (Itil), 236, 331; *and see* Volga
Egypt, 123
Eisleben (Aslaben), 334
Elbe (Albis), 265, 273, 334
Elias, Martyr, 315
Ellingen (Alencen), 279
Elmacin, 14
Embden (Emdem), 265, 266
Emperor, election of, 274
Ems (Ens), 273
Enrique, Don Luis, 290
Ephthalites, 76

Eres (Arax), 139, 147, 151, 325
Erivan (Yruan, Yrauan, Yrban, Ierban, Gerban), 23, 41, 169, 170, 313, 327
Erlau (Iula or Iulia), 126
Erpenius, 14
Ertoghrul (Orthogoules), 95
Erzerum (Erzirun), 136
Esaias, son of Adabas, 71
*Escoceso*, not meaning Scotch, 327
Escoreal, 295, 307
Escudo (Crown-piece), 333
Esma, or Esmi Khan Shamlu (Esmican Xamblu), 202-205, 329
*Esmariles*, 327
*Espaollanes*, 328
Essekia Lake, 140, 325
Estratassenc, 272
Eudocia, Empress, 82
Eunuchs, Palace, 13, 47
Eupacmes, 60

Fabia, Empress, 82
*Fanega*, bushel, 328
Faqih (Fachines, Facohines), 106
Farhad Beg (Faraat Bech, Farhat), 206-211
Farhad Khan (Farat Can), 224-226
Farhad Pasha (Ferat Baxa), 124, 169-175, 201, 327
Fars, Farsistan (Farsi), 38
*Fastiginia*, 310
Ferdinand I, Grand Duke of Tuscany, 6, 336
Feria, Duke of, 287
Ferrara, 282
Florence, 282
Fons Stillans, 337
Freezing of the Volga, 245
Freudenberg (Fritberc), 267
Friars, the two Portuguese, 233, 236; Dominican, 258, 331, 333; Franciscan, 263, 265, 266, 331, 334
Fuenzisla, 294, 337

# DON JUAN OF PERSIA

Fuderitz, 279
*Fugger Letters*, 309
Fulda, 334
Funerals, 53

Gag (Gago), 58
Ganges, 58
Ganjah (Genche, Guienche), 42, 146, 202, 313
Gaza, 123
Geicon, 236
Genebrardus, Gilbertus, 318
Genoa, 287
Georgia (Gurgiſtan, Gurgia), 21, 139-142
Georgian Guard (Chriſtian renegades), 209
Georgian Princes, 326
Georgievits, B., 318
Gerban, 313
Germany, High and Low, 272
Ghazan Khan, tomb of, 328
Ghazzali, 122, 123, 322
*Gil Blas*, 338
Gilan (Guylan), 40, 214
*Gineta*, 314
Giovio, Paolo, 104, 319
Gokchah Lake (Lago di Gioco), 44, 314, 325
Golden Bull of the Empire, 274
Gonzaga, Duke, 6, 281, 336
Gory, Prince, 140
Gouvea, Antonio de, 331
Granwick Bay (Gradusco), 252
Gregory V, Pope, 273
Gregory (Alexander), 149, 154, 325
Griclu clan, 46
Guasque, Francisco, 11, 286, 289
Guesher, 214
Gypsies, 57

Hahnbach (Quienpu), 279
Haji-Faqihlu clan (Achifaquilu), 46
*Hakim*, 46

Halle (Alla), 270
Hamadan (Amadan, Gerban), 38, 40
Hamd-Allah Muſtawfi, 14, 17
Hamete ford, 94
Hammer-Purgſtall, J., 321
Hamzah, Prince (Amjamirza, Emir Amze, Emir Hamze Mirza, Amzam Amsan), 21, 26, 133, 134, 149, 181, 184-186, 198, 203-206
Hamzahlu clan (Ambzalu), 46
*Haram*, 13, 47
Haram-Ishik-aqasi, 48
Hares or rabbits, 50, 314
Harmandalu clan, 46
Harnares, 85
Harun-ar-Rashid, Caliph (Haron Rekid), 92
Hasan (Azan, Azen Assum, Hazen Cassam, Asayn Hassain)
Hasan. *See* Uzun Hasan
Hasan 'Ali Beg, Secretary (Azen Ali Bec), 304
Hasan Beg, Turkish Chief (Assum Beyo), 95
Hasan Beg of Qaraman, 99
Hasan Khalifah, 113
Hasan Pasha, the Eunuch (Azan Baxa), 162, 164, 179
Hasan Pasha, son of Muhammad Sokolli, 156-158
Hasan Pasha, or Bey, son of Janbulat (Asayn Bech, Hassain Baxa Granbulat), 148, 170
Hashimites, 90
Haydar Aga, Ambassador, 161
Haydar Mirza, son of Shah Tahmasp, 129-131
Haydar Mirza, son of Prince Hamzah, 202
Haydar, Shaykh, of Ardebil (Aydar, Heydar), 16, 104, 107, 108; his Mosque at Tabriz, 193
Heads, decapitated, 28
Hecatompylos, 39

# INDEX

Helmets, 50
Henry, Prince, the Navigator, 37
Heraclius, Emperor, 82-84
Herat (Herjia, Hieri, Heri, Iiras), 22, 41, 128, 166-168, 220, 225
Hercynian Forest (Erzinia, Ercinia), 245, 273
Hersbruck (Yzpruch), 279
Hesse (Asia), 267, 280, 334. *See* Kassel
Hirschau (Hirjo), 279
Hisham, Caliph (Hexen Aben Alas, Hachum Ebue Alas), 90
Hoodee, 329
Hormisdas or Yazdagird III, 316
Hradschin, 275
Hulagu Khan, 92, 318
Husayn (Huscein, Hossain Huzen, Ozen, Osein, Uzen)
Husayn, Caliph, 89, 106
Husayn Akhtah (Eunuch), 129
Husayn (or Hasan) 'Ali Beg, Ambassador, 3, 234, 303-306, 331, 335
Husayn Beg (Uzen Beg), 217
Husayn Khan Shamlu (Huzen Can Xamblu), 206

Ibn Marjan, 106, 306
Ibn Muljam, 306
Ibn Sayyar, Nasr (Iblinio), 91
Ibrahim Khan (Ebrain Chan), 99, 103, 319
Ibrahim Khan, Ambassador, 161, 327
Ibrahim Mirza, son of Shah Tahmasp, 129
Ibrahim Pasha (Hebraim Baxa), Governor of Egypt, 179, 180
Idel, 238. *See* Volga
Idol at Manqishlagh, 237
Ierban, 313
Iesdri (Lyedro), 38
Ignaro, 318

Iiras (Shiraz), 128, 323
Ilderim (Eldrim Turbellino), 96, 319
Il-Khans, 318
Ilmenau, 271, 334
Images in Russian churches, 239
Imam Quli Khan Qajar (Mangulican Cacher), 145, 146, 154, 198, 202
Imam Quli Khan, son of Shamkhal, 140, 326
Imam Quli Khan, 327
Imam Riza Shrine, at Meshed (Eman Reza), 220
Imams of the Shi'ahs, 320
Imbrael, 16, 93, 317
Imola, 319
Inazlu clan, 46
Indus, 58
Inn river (Eno, Eyno), 273
Iraq, Arabian, 43
Iraq, Persian (Herac), 39
'Isa Khan (Yzacan, Ysacham), 129-142
Isfahan (Espahan), 39, 206, 224
*Ishik-aqasi-bashi*, 47, 314
Iskandar, Prince, Leventoghlu (Eskender), 138-140, 142, 144, 148, 160
Islam Ghiray, 328
Isma'il I, Prince, then Shah, 2, 15-17, 19, 104, 110, 124, 206, 315, 320, 329
Isma'il II, 21, 128-132, 324
Isma'il Mirza Sultan, son of Prince Hamzah, 202, 203, 330
Isma'il, brother of Shah 'Abbas, 216
'Ismet Khan Ustajlu (Ymet Can Extexelu), 220, 329
Ispihrlu clan (Ispyrrhlu), 46
Itil, 331; *and see* Volga

Ja'far, Imam (Imamchafer), 90
Ja'far Pasha the Hungarian renegade (Zafero), 121

## DON JUAN OF PERSIA

Ja'far Pasha the Eunuch (Ajafer), 185
Ja'far Quli Beg (Cha Bargulibec), 189
Ja'far Quli Khan (Chabarguli Can), 198
James, Bishop of Nisibis, 75
Janberdi Ghazzali (Lanburdo Gazelle), 122, 123
Janbulat (Gran Bulat Chan), 148, 170
Jawhar the Eunuch (Ioar), 123
Jem, Prince, Jamshid (Zezimo), 103
Jenkinson, Anthony, 8
Jews in Russia, 240
John of Austria, Don, 127
John IV, Emperor of Trebizond, 17, 107, 320
John XIII, Duke of Oldenburg, 334
Jonas, Martyr, 72
Juan, Don, of Persia (Uruch Beg), 10, 11, 24, 185, 192, 198, 223, 225, 299-308
Juanelo Torriano, 338
Jub, 270
Judas Thaddæus, 70
Judi or Hudi, 329
Julian, Count, 90
Julich, 274
Jurji Qal'ah (Gurgicalassi, Quiurquiur, or Guarchingala), 141, 143
Justin, 78
Justinian, Emperor, 78
Justinian, son of Germanus, 80
Juvencus, 67, 315

Kaffa, 177
Kaisheim (Cazerchen), 280
Kalo Joannes, Emperor (Juan), 17, 107, 320
Kamakh, 321
Kanak river (Chanac, Canac), 145, 325
Kashan (Cassan, Caxan), 40, 206
Kassel, 268-270. *See* Hesse
Kay Khusraw, Prince, 325
Kaytas Pasha (Caytas Baxa), 147
Kazan (Cazzan), 243
Keysite Arabs of Modar (Caysmoros Amonitas), 90
Khadijah, sister of Uzun Hasan, 320
Khalifah Khan (Baly Can), 195, 199, 329
Khalil Khan Afshar, 324
Khan, title preceding name, 314, 329
Khan, implies a noble, 46
Khan Ahmad, Prince of Gilan (Can Hamet), 214, 215
Khan Muhammad Quli Khalifah (Can Mahamet Culicalefa), 213
Khan Sayyid Oghlu, 42
Khayr Beg (Cayerbeyo), 121-123
Khayr-ad-Din Pasha (Cherydemo Baxa), 116
Kholmagory (Cormacury), 260
Khoy (Coy), 43, 117
Khuda Bandah, Shah, meaning of name, 134; *and see* Muhammad
Khuda Verdi the Barber (Cudy de Lac), 204, 205
Khurasan (Coraçan), 41, 220, 313
Khurramabad (Cormaba, Cormava), 42, 216, 217
Khusraw Pasha (Ustref Baxa), 137
Kieder Gul Lake (Quierdergul) 142
Kirman (Quierman), 38
Kladrau (Cludra), 279
Kling, 272
Kliska (Cliska), 174
Klussen, 272
Knights of St. John, 122
Knolles, R., 16, 312
Kolomna (Colona), 249
Kornberg (Curinberc), 279

# INDEX

Kremlin, 250
Kuh-Giluyah-lu clan (Cohequilu), 46
Kuman the Crim Tartar, 177, 178
Kur river (Cyrus) of Fars, 313
Kur (Cyrus) of Georgia, 139, 313
Kurdistan, (Curdistan), 43
Kurs, the Scythian (Cuyso Scytha), 78
Kutahiyah (Cuteya), 113
Kuzah-Kunan village (Cuzacunan), 180

Labassap, Prince, 140, 141, 325
Labnic, 270
Lahijan (Lahychan, Ciudad de la Hichan), 40, 215, 313
Lampraes, 60
Laosthenes, 60
Laplanders, 263
Lauf (Luf), 279
Lavarsab, 325, 326
Lavarza, Prince, 325
Leghorn (Levorno), 283
Leipzig, 270, 271, 335
Leman, Lake of, 298
Lepanto, battle, 127
Leprus mountain (Lepro), 117
Lerma, Duke of, 289, 290, 300
Lerma, Duchess of, 307
Levente, or Leventoghlu. *See* Iskandar, Prince
Lewis II, Landgrave of Hesse, 334
*Libreria Susiana*, 315
Lisbon, 298
Lory (Cory), 141
Lovers, in Persia, 54
Lucerne Lake, 273
Lur, Luristan (Lar), 39, 216

Machchalatheus, 59
" Machine " at Toledo, 297, 338
Madrid, 296
Magdeburg (Madeburg, Mademburg), 270

Magellan, 312
Maghud, 317
Magi, the Three Kings, 67
Mahdi, Caliph (Mahamet Mehedi), 92
Mahdi, the Twelfth Imam (Mahamet Mahedin), 91
Mahdi Quli Khan Chaushli, 215, 329
Mahdi Quli Khan Shamlu (Mediguly Can Xamblu), 215
Mahmudlu clan, 46
Mahomed the Prophet, 104
Main, river (Meno, Meyno), 273
Mainz (Maguncia), 272
Makran, 44
Malcolm, Sir John, 329
Mamodee Mahmudi, 325
Mamun, Caliph (Menon), 92, 93, 317
Mamuthos, 59
Manqishlagh (Minquezlac), 237
Mansfeld, 270
Mansur, Caliph, 91
Mansur, Captain of the Guard (Amansar, Amanzar), 109
Mantua, 280
Manuchihr, or Mustafa, Prince (Manichor, Manicha-Munyquier), 139, 149, 154, 162-165, 169-171, 174
Maqsud Aga (Mahud Aga), 180
Maraghah (Malaga), 43
Marand (Moran), 181
Marciana (or Van) Lake, 171
Marco Polo, 36
Margancia the Slave, or Marjan, 86, 316
Margaret, Queen of Spain, 10, 302, 338
Marjan, 316
Marriage customs, 55
Martha, mother of Shah Isma'il, 107
Martyropolis, 80

Marwan II, Caliph (Maruia), 90-91
Masi, 137
Massæus, Chriſtianus, 316
Matariyah (Matera), 123, 322
Matthæus Palmerius, 82
Maurice, Emperor, 79, 80
Mazandaran (Hyrcania), 41, 217
Medicis, Giovanni de, Prince, 282
Melitene, 79
Menil Warat, 334
Menon, 61, 315
Merida, 279
Meshed (Maxet, Mexet, Massahat), 220
Meshed 'Ali (Massadal), 106
Meto, or Molo, Dominican Friar, 258, 331, 333
Meuse river (Musa, Mosa), 273
Michael, Emperor, 93
Minadoi, G. T., 12, 19, 36, 311, 312
Mingrelia, 139
Mint at Segovia, 295, 338
Mirza before or after a name, 323
Misnia, 270, 334
Miſtakes in spelling proper names, 15, 311, 326
Mocenigo, Pietro, 97, 319
Moldau (Molta), 273, 277
Molo, Nicolão de, Friar, 258, 331, 333
Montpellier, 287
Montserrat, 288
Mora, Don Criſtobal de, 298, 303-307
Moscova river (Mosco), 249
Moscow (Mosca, Moscao), 249-258
Moselle (Mosella), 273
Mu'awiyah, Caliph (Manoa, Manua, Mabia), 88, 106
Mufti, Grand, of Baghdad, 125, 322

Muhammad, Governor of Qara Amid, 181, 184, 185
Muhammad, Governor of Tiflis, 157
Muhammad, son of Ignaro, or Imbrael, 93
Muhammad the Prophet. *See* Mahomed, 104
Muhammad I, Sultan, 96
Muhammad II, Sultan, 16, 97-100
Muhammad III, Sultan, 27, 161, 223, 231, 327
Muhammad Aga, Grand Chaush, 231, 330
Muhammad Ghiray, 328
Muhammad Khan the Turkoman (Mahamet Can), 195
Muhammad Khan Bayat, 222
Muhammad Khuda Bandah, Shah, 21, 128, 134, 209-211, 222, 324, 329
Muhammad Pasha, nephew of Muſtafa Pasha, 162-164
Muhammad Pasha, son of Farhad Pasha, 137, 143
Muhammad Sharif Khan (Mahamet Xerif Can), 213
Mu'izz, Fatimite Caliph, 123
Mukhtar (Mucthar), 89, 317
Mulciano, 88
Munich (Minicen, Munchem), 280, 336
Munſter (Monaſterio), 274
Murad I, Sultan (Amurathes), 95
Murad II, Sultan, 96
Murad III, Sultan, 21, 133, 161, 162, 169, 178, 223
Murad Khan, son of Sultan Ya'qub (Morat Cham), 110, 112
Murad Pasha of Qaraman, 184, 185
Murad, Prince, son of Sultan Bayazid II, 82, 115, 117, 119
Murom (Morlo), 248

# INDEX

Murshid Quli Khan (Murjud or Marxud Guli Can), 207, 208
Musa Kazim the Seventh Imam (Musacacazem, Muzaicazen, Mussa Cassun), 17, 91
Mus'ab ibn Zubayr (Mohezen, Mahazan), 89
Mustafa. *See* Manuchihr, 154
Mustafa (or Sultan Mustafa), son of Shah Tahmasp, 129, 323
Mustafa Bey, 156
Mustafa Pasha, 21, 133, 136, 148, 156
Mu'tasim, Caliph, 93

Nakhchevan (Nasiban, Naciuan, Nacchiuan, Nachuan), 170
Narbonne, 287
Narses, 74
Nasr-ad-Din Chelebi (Nasserdin), 144
Nasr ibn Sayyar, 91
Nauplia, or Napoli di Romania, 98
Neckar (Neccaro), 273
Negropont battle, 127
Nerl river, 333
Neuchatel (Neoborges), 273
Neuss (Nuyz), 274
Neutri, 272
Nicephorus Bryennius, 71, 315
Nicephorus Callistus, 71, 315
Nicheps Sultan Bayat, 198
Nienburg (Nimbrec), 267
Nimes, 287
Nimrod (Nembroth), 58
Nisf-i-Jahan or Isfahan (Nispechahan), 39
Nishapur (Nichahur), 166
Nisibis, 75
Nissat mountains (Montes Nissatos), 112
Nizhni-Novgorod (Nechena, Nochena), 246, 332
Nogay Tartars (Nocay), 242, 331
Nohum, 215
Nuremberg (Norimberga), 279

Ob river, 252
Ochus, 66
Odenathus of Palmyra, 74
Oder (Odera), 273
*Oghlu*, 326
Oldenburg (Holdreberc), 267, 334
Olearius, Adam, 332
Oliga, Mount, 114
Olivares, 288
Oman, Sir C., 328
Omar, Governor of Safed, 160
Omar I, Caliph (Homar, Hozmaz), 85, 105
Omar II, Caliph (Omarebene Moar), 90
Omar Mirza, grandson of Tamerlane, 96, 319
Omar Pasha, 163
Ophrataeus, 60
Oriath clan, 46
Orkhan (Orcanes, Oranes), 95
Ormuz, 8
Oronte, Mount, 182
Osnabruck, 274
Ostiglia, 336
Othman, Caliph (Odman, Osman, Oromaz, Ottomar), 87, 105
Othman (Ottomano), the Turk, 95
Othman Pasha, 24, 147, 153, 154, 174-186
Otranto, 100, 281, 336
Otto Heinrich, Pfalzgraf of Sulzbach (Ottuhynzic), 279, 336
Ottoman Turks, rise of, 95
Oxus (Osso, Abiano), 44, 314

Paderborn, 274
Palash, 76
Pannas, 60
Pari-Khan-Khanum, Princess (Pericancanon), 21, 129-135
Parry, W., 309, 332-334
Parsons, Robert, the Jesuit, 336, 337

Pausoutes, 66
Peck, measure, 50
Pedigree of Shah Isma'il's ancestors, 320; of his descendants, 324; of Georgian Princes, 326
Perbyn, 270
Perekop Tartars, or Precopenses, Turks, 149, 247, 332
Pereyaslav (Parasvalt, Paraslap), 258
Periard Mountains, 139
Perikorsk Tartars (Perecroseos), 142, 240
Perionius, 70
Perozes, 76
Perpignan, 287
Persepolis, 38, 313
Pertiades, 60
Pervana Gul, Lake (Vanachul), 143, 326
Peyclu clan, 46
Pfraumberg, 279
Philip II of Spain, 295, 296
Philip III, 7, 291, 307, 308
Philip of Persia, Don, 3, 9, 226, 292, 299, 302, 336, 337
Phocas, Emperor, 82
Pilsen, 279
Pineda, Juan de, 81, 98, 316
Pious Duke of Bavaria, 280
Pir Ahmad (Pyramet), 99
Pir 'Ali (Pirehaeli), 108
Pir Muhammad (Piramahamet), 129
Pir Quli Beg (Pergoly Beg), 255
Pisa, 282
Pisasiri, 93
Pleissenburg Palace, 335
Polo, Marco, 36
Pompey, 142
Possevinus, A., 250, 332
Pousein, 272
Prague, 277
Presents given to the Embassy, 8
Prester John, 42
Priam, 61

Ptolemy, 66
Purandokht, 316
Purchas, *Pilgrims*, 309

Qahqahah Castle (Gagaha, Cahaca), 129, 329
Qaim, Caliph (Cain Adam), 93
Qaisari (Queisen, Cheuseri), 128
Qajar clan (Cacher), 46, 314, 330
*Qali*, 48
Qandahar (Candahar), 42
Qansuh Ghuri Ashraf, Sultan (Chanpsou Zyauro), 20, 121, 122
*Qapuchi-bashi*, 47
Qara Aghach (Caragach, Caracach), 150
Qara Amid (Carahemit), 44, 137
Qarabachiqlu clan (Carabachaclu), 46
Qarabagh, 313
Qara-Chumaqlu clan (Carachomaclu), 46
Qara Hasan Khan (Gara Hazen Can), 212
Qarakush (Caracux, Caracuh), 113
Qaramanlu clan (Garamanlu), 46
Qara-Qoyunlu clan (Garacoinlu), 46, 314
Qars (Cars), 128, 141, 156
Qasim Pasha (Cassin), 118
Qastamuniyah (Castlemoth), 114
Qazvin (Casbin), 24, 40, 197-200
Qizil Bash, Cap. (Cuseluas), 18, 110
Qobad I, 76
Qobad II, 316
Qonia, Iconium, 113, 178
Qoyun-Chay battle (Coinchay), 125
Quieres (Qars), 141
Quimendec, Quimidac, 270
Qulzum, the Caspian (Curzum, Colzun), 139, 325
Qum (Gom), 40
Quran (Coran), 88, 317

# INDEX

Qurchi Bashi Khan (Gorchi Bassi, Gorgivassi Can), 189, 218
Qurqud, Governor of Qastamuniyah, 114
Qurqud, Prince (Corcut), 20, 103, 113

Rabbits or hares, 50, 314
Rawlinson, Canon G., 315
Real, coin, 332
Red Cap of the Shi'ahs, 18, 49, 110
" Red Head," 110
Reindeer, 263
*Relaciones*, writing of the, 11
Remon the Licentiate, 10; his authorities, 311
Rhine, 273
Rhodes, 97, 122, 319, 322
Rhodes, Colossus of, 87
Rimak mountains (Rimac), 125
Rivan Khan, 328
Riza, Imam, Shrine, 220
Rizvan Pasha (Resuan Baxa), 156, 162, 173
Roberg, 270
Rokitsan (Roquencan), 279
Rome, 284-287, 310
Roth (Brot), 279
Roumelia, 118, 321
Rudolf II, Emperor, 6, 274-277, 310, 336
Ruisar, 331
Rustam, Prince, 100
Rybinsk (Xibisca), 259

Saale river (Salas), 267, 270
Sabzivar (Sapzoar), 166
Safavi Dynasty, 18
Saffah, Caliph, 91
Safi, Prince (Sophi Mirza), 226, 231
Safi-ad-Din, Shaykh, 18, 315
Sahamal (Shamkhal), 323
Salamansa, 94
Salamenus, 64

Salman, or Salmas, Mirza, 132-134, 150, 168, 169
Salmas, Prince, 138
Salmas, town (Salma), 43
Salsas, 287
Sam Mirza, Prince (Samirza), 124
Samara on Volga, 243
Samir-Khan (Sanmyrchan), 147
San Juan, Francisco de, 303
San Nicolo, Archangel, 260, 334
Santa Cruz, Marquis de, 305, 306
Sapor I, 74
Sapor II, 68, 71, 74, 75
Sapor III, 75
Saqali Sultan, the Turkoman (Sacholi, Sacoli), 196, 200
Sardanapalus, 60, 63
Sarozolachlu clan, 46
Sasan, 72
Savah (Saba), 40
Savona, 287
Saxony, 270, 271
Saymarah (Zeymara), 39
Sayyid Oghlu, Khan (Can Ciadogli), 42
Sayyids (Zeythes), 106
Scaliger, Joseph, 86
Schefer, C., 309
Schiavi, or Slaves' Lake, 326
Scotch River, 327
Scylitzes, 14
Secusa, 123
Segestani, 74, 316
Segovia, 294, 295, 337
Selim I, Sultan, the Grim, 20, 115, 120, 124
Selim II, Sultan, the Sot, 21, 127
Shabdah Sultan (Chabda), 168
Shah 'Ali Sultan Bayat (Sahaly), 198
Shah Rukh, 96
Shah Suvar Oghlu (Sasso Var), 120
Shah Verdi Khan (Xavardi Can), 216, 217

# DON JUAN OF PERSIA

Shahr Banu, Princess, 17
Shahr Barz (Sarbard, Sarbaras), 83-85
Shaki (Sequi), 145
Shamakhi (Symiach, Sumachi, Sumachia), 109, 147, 148, 151
Shamkhal, Prince (Sahamal), 140
Shamkhal, Prince of Brus, 148, 153, 323
Shamkhal Khan (Kamal, Xamhac), 130, 131
Shamlu clan (Xamblu), 45
Sharaf Khan (Serapychan, Seraphchan), 145, 146
*Shari'ah*, 87
Shaykh Ahmad (Xic Hamet), 215
Shaykh Sophi (Xiek Sofi, Xiche Sophi), 19, 53, 206
Shaytan Qal'ah (Assaythan Calassi), 172
Sheba (Sabo), 58
Sheep, big Persian, 43
Sheep, black and white, Turkomans, 319
Shenb Ghazan (Xan Cassan), 186
*Sherley Brothers, the Three*, 309
Sherley, Sir Anthony, 1, 4, 7, 227, 232-234, 258, 261, 283-286, 333, 335-337
Sherley, Sir Robert, 1, 233, 337
Shi'ah Cap, 18, 49, 110
Shi'ah cursings, 330
Shi'ah Doctrine, 17
Shi'ahs, massacre of, 321
Shiraz (Syras, Siras, Xiras), 38, 128, 313
Shirvan (Iervan, Geruan), 22, 41, 139, 313
Shuster (Suster), 39
Siena, 283
Simon, Saint, 70
Simon, Prince (Simaorz), 140, 155-158, 171, 173, 174
Sinan Pasha (Synan Baxa), 118, 122, 159-162, 165, 328
Sinan, son of Cigala. *See* Cigala

Siroes, 84
Sirto (Syrtho), 38
Sisebuth the Visigoth, 82
Sistan (Cistan), 42, 74
Sittas, 80
Sixtus IV, Pope, 100
Siyavush Pasha (Chaus or Xaus Baxa), 165, 176-178
Skulls of deer in a tower, 40
Skulls of Turks in a tower, 42
Sledges, horse, and sleds, 246
Smerdis, 66
Sogdianus, 66
Sokolli, Grand Vizier, 156, 329
Solachlu clan, 46
Sophi, Grand, 18, 111
Sophi Kings of Persia from Imam Musa Kazim, 91
Sosares, 60
Sosarmus, 60
Spain, Moslem conquest of, 89
Sphærus, 59
Stade, or Stode, 265, 309, 334
St. John, Knights of, at Rhodes, 122
Sternschloss, 335
Stettin not Stode, 309, 334
Stirrups, short, 50
Strasburg, 274
Sturgeon, 241
Suanyr, 71
Suf and Sufi, 18, 111
Sufiyan (Sophian), 181
Sugurghatmish (Sagruco), 96
Sugut (Soguta), 95
Sukhona river, 333
Sulayman, Caliph (Sulayman Hastian), 90
Sulayman, Prince, 109
Sulayman, Sultan, the Magnificent, 20, 121, 124
Sulayman the Seljuk (Salamansa), 318
Sultan Ali Beg Bayat, 3, 23, 24, 158, 176, 190-193
Sultan Ali Mirza, 129

# INDEX

Sultan Haydar, Prince, 213
Sultan Mahmud, 213
Sultan Muṡtafa, 129
Sultaniyah, 198
Sulzbach, Pfalzgraf of (Sultzbahac), 279, 336
Surius, Laurentius, 72, 316
Susiana (Sosian), 39
Susianian Library, 58, 315
Swiss Cantons and Switzerland (Helvecia, Elvezia), 273, 274
Syplilit, or Leipzig, 5, 335
Syris, son of Abraham, 59, 315
Szigeth (Liquet), 126

Tabriz (Tauris), 24, 40, 42, 110, 119, 124, 176, 181-184, 188-193
Tahmasp, Prince, 24, 133, 195, 200, 211
Tahmasp I, Shah (Tahamas), 2, 21, 40, 45, 124-130, 141
*Taj*, cap, 49
Takkeh-lu clan (Thacalu), 46
Talim Khan the Uzbek (Telin Can), 224, 225
Taloghli, Aga of the Janissaries (Tailloli), 160, 327
Tamchosro (Thamar Cosdroes), 79
Tamerlane (Tambur, Tamur Bec, Tanburlan), 95, 96, 166, 220, 237, 240
Tangrolipix, 16, 94, 318
Tanning Wells, 248
Tartar Khan, of the Crimea, 152-154
Tartars in Russia: Perekop Tartars, 149, 247, 332; Perikorsk Tartars, 142, 240; *and see* Uzbeks
Tassia, 114
Tekelli Qizil Bash (Techelle Cuselvas), 19, 113, 321
Terjan battle, 100, 319

Teuso, 236
Teutamus, Teutaus, 60
Teuthanes, 61, 315
Theodosius II, Emperor, 76
Theophanes, 15
Theophilus, Emperor, 93
Thonus Concolerus, 60
Thuringia, 267
Tiberius I, Emperor, 69
Tiberius II, Emperor, 79
Tiflis, 141, 143, 156, 157, 158, 163, 171
Timeus, 60
Timur Beg. *See* Tamerlane
Titon, 61, 315
Toledo, 279, 297
Tomanis (Thomanis), 141
Toqmaq Khan Qashlu (Tocomac Can Caxelu), 136, 145, 146, 160, 170, 198
Tornamira, Juan de, 76
Totma (Turmen), 260
Tower of deer skulls, 40
Tower of Turkish skulls, 42
Treves (Reucri misprint for Treveri), 272
Triala, 143
Trinka (Trinc), 272, 274, 335
*Tripartite Hiſtory*, 71, 315
Truxillo, 279
Tudela del Duero, 288
*Tufangchi*, 52
Tughril Beg (Trangolypico Moncaleto), 94
Tuman Bey, Mamluk Sultan, 122, 123
Turavets (Turavichis), 260
Turbat-i-Haydari (Turbeth, Turbhat), 166, 222
Turkish Ambassador at Venice, 282
Turkish Amirs, Seven, 95
Turkish Artillery, 23
Turkish Sultans, Ottoman, 95
Turkoman Chay, 137
Turkoman clan, 45

Turkoman tribesmen of Tabriz, 24, 184, 194-200
Turkomans of the Black Sheep, 46, 314
Turks in Persia, 93, 94
Turshiz (Turcis), 166
*Tzar Kolokol*, 332
Tzaritzyn (Zarecen), 243

Uhagon, Señor, 311
Uluch Ali, Admiral (Alyucheli), 136
Urrea, Diego de, 294
Uruch or Ulugh Beg, 1, 309; *and see* Don Juan of Persia
Ustad Oghlu (Ustaolago, Ustaoslago, Ustadoalu), 117, 118, 123, 321
Ustajlu clan (Ustaxelu, Estexelu), 45
Ustyug (Restuc), 260
Uzbek Tartars, 26, 219-226
Uzun Hasan (Ussan, Ussam Cassano, Cassun, Cassen, Cassem Bech, Azem Bec, Azembre), 16, 97-100, 107, 319, 320

Vahan, 76
*Vakil*, 46
Valdai hills, 332
Valerian, Emperor, 74
Valiyan Mountain, 328
*Valla de Amor*, 332
Valladolid, 289-293
Van Lake (Vuan), 171
Varahran I, II, and III, 74
Varahran IV, 75
Varahran V, 76; *and see* Bahram
*Vecinos*, or householders, 313, 331
Veiga, Thome da, 310
Velada, Marquis de, 289
Venetians and Turks, 97
*Venetians, Travels of, in Persia*, 16, 312, 313
Venice, 281
Verona, 281

Veys Pasha, 175
*Victoria*, Magellan's ship, 37, 312
Vincenzo I, Duke of Mantua, 6, 281, 336
Vladimir, town (Valla de Amor), 249, 332
Vlaman, 124, 322
Volga (Eder, Itil), 44, 236, 238, 241-245, 259, 332, 333
Voluppo Lake, 245, 332
Vronica Forest (Euronica), 273

Waidhausen (Wilithaucen), 279
Walid I, Caliph (Ulit, Halid), 89
*Warat*, 334
Wartburg, 335
Wathiq, Caliph, 318
Weimar (Brymer), 268
Weissenburg (Bicembrec), 280
Wernberg (Ginthaoth), 279
Werra river, 268
Weser river (Wisurgo), 273
Wilfuesen, 270
William II, Duke of Bavaria, 6, 336
Windmills in Saxony, 271
Windsfeld (Bilifilith), 279
Wittenberg (Witinberg), 270
Wives, plurality of, 49

Xerxes I and II, 66
Xerxes, or Artabanus III, 70, 315
Xipric, 270

Ya'qub, Sultan (Iacopo, Iacob Bech), 100, 107-110
Yaroslav (Iaraslap), 259
Yazdagird I, 76; III, 316
Yazid I, Caliph (Iezido), 88, 106
Yazid II, Caliph (Iezid Calid or Gelid), 90
Yezd (Est), 40
Yunus Pasha (Iunnu Baxa), 115
Yusuf, Prince (Usuf, Guisuf), 140

# INDEX

Yusuf Bey (Guusufay, Guzesuf), 160
Yusuf Pasha, or Cigcala Pasha, 328

Zaghen (Zagam), 142
*Zahr Mar*, poison snake (Zahar que mar, Zachari mar), 106
Zal Khan (Zalchan), 323
Zalga Fortress, 109
Zandarud river (Senderu), 39

Zaragoza, 288
Zaroes, 70
Zayn-al-'Abidin, Fourth Imam 17
Zelma, 91, 317
Zeneta Berbers, 314
Zeno, 313
Zezian city, 108
Zonaras, 14
Zuiria, 139
Zürich (Zurioz), 273

www.ingramcontent.com/pod-product-compliance
Lightning Source LLC
Chambersburg PA
CBHW021753230426
43669CB00006B/67